i_E	total emitter current	r_L	a-c load resistance
I_E	d-c emitter current	R_R	reverse resistance
$I_{E(sat)}$	emitter saturation current	r_p	plate resistance
I_F	forward current	r_s	source resistance
i_L	load current	r_z	zener resistance
$I_{leakage}$	collector leakage current	R_K	cathode resistance
I_R	diode reverse current	R_L	d-c load resistance
IV	current-voltage	$R_L \| R$	R_L in parallel with R
K	beta sensitivity	v_C	total collector-ground voltage
kHz	kilohertz (kc)		
MHz	megahertz (mc)	v_{CB}	total collector-base voltage
n	turns ratio, or number of stages	v_{CE}	total collector-emitter voltage
Q	figure of merit	v_F	feedback voltage
$R_1 \| R_2$	R_1 in parallel with R_2	v_p	peak a-c voltage
r_{ac}	a-c resistance	v_s	a-c source voltage
r_b'	base spreading resistance	V_{BE}	d-c base-emitter voltage
r_B	bulk resistance	V_C	d-c collector-ground voltage
R_B	external base resistance	V_{CC}	collector supply voltage
r_e'	emitter a-c resistance	V_{CE}	d-c collector-emitter voltage
r_E	unbypassed emitter resistance	V_E	d-c emitter-ground voltage
R_E	external emitter resistance	V_{EE}	emitter supply voltage
r_F	forward resistance	V_K	knee voltage
r_j	a-c junction resistance	V_R	reverse voltage
		V_Z	zener voltage

TRANSISTOR CIRCUIT APPROXIMATIONS

Albert Paul Malvino

Foothill College
Los Altos Hills, California
Vice President
Time Systems Corporation
Mountain View, California

McGraw-Hill Book Company

New York • St. Louis • San Francisco
London • Toronto • Sydney • Mexico • Panama

TRANSISTOR CIRCUIT APPROXIMATIONS

Library of Congress Catalog Card Number: 68-13521

39846

5 6 7 8 9 10 (MPMM) 7 4 3 2 1 0

To my wild Irish rose

It is the mark of an instructed mind
to rest satisfied
with that degree of precision
which the nature of the subject admits,
and not to seek exactness
where only an approximation
of the truth is possible

ARISTOTLE

Preface

When using a transistor, we must realize that we are dealing with a device that is inexact and unreliable as far as its characteristics are concerned. For instance, one important transistor quantity is its current gain β (also designated h_{fe}). Typically, the β can vary over at least a $2:1$ range when we change from one transistor to another of the same type. Because of this variation, it is impossible to predict exactly how a transistor will operate in a specific circuit arrangement. Also, when the surrounding temperature changes, the β changes, thereby adding another degree of uncertainty to transistor circuit operation.

There is a way out of this predicament. To eliminate the wide variations in transistor circuit performance, we can use negative feedback or some similar technique for trading off some of the gain in exchange for more stable operation. However, when we do this, we are making the operation of the circuit almost independent of the transistor characteristics. In other words, after using enough negative feedback to stabilize the circuit operation, knowing the exact value of β and other transistor characteristics is no longer important.

The point is simply this: exact formulas for transistor circuit analysis are of limited value to most of us because the exact characteristics of a transistor are seldom known. Considering the tolerances of transistor parameters, it is appropriate to use approximations in analyzing various transistor circuits. Most of this book stresses the *ideal-transistor* approach, that is, an approximation that retains only the most significant features of transistor action. With this approach, the novice can quickly obtain a feeling for how transistor circuits work; oddly enough, this highly simplified approach is adequate for much of the transistor work that we encounter.

In the later chapters of the book we discuss some of the second-order effects that are discarded in the ideal-transistor approach. To round out the presentation, the last chapter deals with the h-parameter approach, because this technique, at least in theory, gives exact answers.

This book was written for an electronics technician in a junior college or technical institute; many others in the electronics field will find the book useful, especially if they need a practical introduction to transistors. The length of the book makes it suitable for an introductory three-unit course. The prerequisite is a sound knowledge of algebra and basic electricity.

I would like to express my thanks to Daniel J. Mindheim of Time Systems Corp. for his advice throughout the writing of this book and to Clifford Burrous of Ames Research Center for his careful review of the final manuscript and for his many excellent suggestions.

A. P. MALVINO

Contents

1

Semiconductor Physics

Throughout most of this book we will be interested in how the transistor is used in typical circuits. We will develop a number of simple approximations to allow a rapid and easy analysis of such circuits. At the outset of our discussion, however, it is important to consider some aspects of atomic theory. In this chapter we discuss semiconductors, free electrons, holes, and doping. This material will make it easier for us to understand how the transistor actually works.

1-1 Germanium and Silicon Atoms

In this section we examine the atomic structure of germanium (Ge) and silicon (Si) because these materials are widely used in the fabrication of transistors.

Most of us already know that all matter is composed of atoms and that atoms contain a nucleus surrounded by revolving electrons. If we examine an isolated atom of germanium, we find that the nucleus contains 32 protons. When this atom is in a normal state, there are 32 electrons revolving around the nucleus. Further, these revolving electrons distribute themselves in a definite pattern and occupy what are commonly called *shells*.

Figure 1-1*a* *symbolically* illustrates a germanium atom. In the center there is a nucleus with 32 protons. The revolving electrons distribute themselves in different shells, following the pattern of

$$2, 8, 18, \ldots , 2n^2$$

where n is the number of the shell. In other words, there are 2 electrons in the first shell, 8 in the second shell, and 18 in the third shell. The last 4 electrons are in the fourth, or outer, shell.

In a similar way we find that an isolated atom of silicon has a nucleus with 14 protons. When this atom is in a normal state, there are 14 revolving electrons. As shown in Fig. 1-1*b*, the first shell contains 2 electrons, and the second shell contains 8. The 4 remaining electrons are in the third, or outer, shell of the silicon atom.

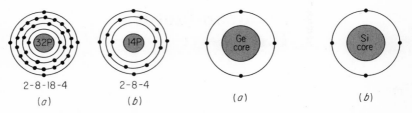

2-8-18-4   2-8-4

(*a*)   (*b*)   (*a*)   (*b*)

Fig. 1-1   (*a*) Germanium; (*b*) silicon.   **Fig. 1-2**   Outer shell of (*a*) germanium and (*b*) silicon.

We are primarily interested in the outer shells of germanium and silicon atoms; as a result, we will simplify the diagrams of these atoms. In Fig. 1-2*a* we have shown only the outer shell of the germanium atom. The inner part of this figure is called the germanium *core*, and it contains the nucleus plus the inner shells. In similar way, Fig. 1-2*b* shows a silicon core surrounded by an outer shell with four electrons.

1-2   Germanium and Silicon Crystals

In the previous section we were discussing *isolated* atoms of germanium and silicon. Now we discuss how a number of germanium or silicon atoms combine to form a solid piece of germanium or silicon.

Let us consider germanium first. The outer shell of an isolated germanium atom contains four electrons. This shell is incomplete in the sense that more electrons can be added to it. It is an experimental fact that germanium atoms combine with each other in such a way as to have *a total of eight electrons* in the outer shell of each atom. In order to accomplish this, the atoms align themselves in a structure known as a *crystal*. When we examine a crystal of pure germanium, we find that each atom is surrounded by four neighboring atoms that actually share electrons with the central atom.

Figure 1-3 brings this concept out more clearly. The central atom has *a total of eight electrons* in its outer shell. Four of these electrons belong to the central atom; an additional four electrons have been added by the neighboring atoms because each of these neighbors actually shares one of its outer-shell electrons with the central atom. In turn, each of the neighboring atoms will have four neighbors; in this way, every atom within the crystal has an outer shell with eight electrons.

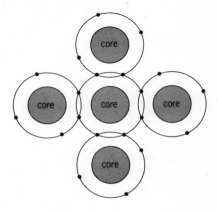

Fig. 1-3   An atom within a crystal.

In a completely analogous way a large number of silicon atoms will join to form a crystal in which each atom has four neighbors that share electrons. Once again, each silicon atom will have a total of eight electrons in its outer shell.

For our purposes, we will accept as experimental fact that the outer shell of a germanium or silicon atom is incomplete until it contains eight electrons. When there are fewer than eight electrons, an atomic force of attraction exists until enough electrons are added to produce a total of eight electrons in the outer shell. Once there are eight electrons in this outer shell, these electrons are tightly held or bound to the atom and cannot escape from the atom unless some outside force is applied.

1-3   Conduction in Pure Germanium and Silicon

How well does a crystal of germanium or silicon conduct an electric current? To answer this question, consider Fig. 1-4a, in which we have shown a crystal of pure germanium connected to a battery. When the temperature is at absolute zero, we find that there is no current in the circuit. The reason for this is that there are no free electrons within the crystal. All electrons are tightly held within the atoms of the crystal; the electrons in the inner shells are buried well within the individual atoms and cannot contribute to current flow; the electrons in the outer shells are also tightly bound to the atoms and cannot participate in current flow. Therefore, at absolute zero temperature the germanium crystal is an insulator.

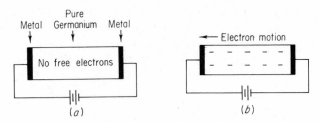

Fig. 1-4   Conduction at (*a*) absolute zero temperature and (*b*) higher temperatures.

As the temperature increases, however, thermal energy is added to the germanium crystal. This energy can actually dislodge some of the outer-shell electrons, thereby making them available for current flow. An electron that has been knocked out of an outer shell is called a *free* electron. In Fig. 1-4*b* we have indicated the free electrons by minus signs. These electrons are now free to move, and under the influence of the battery they move to the left, setting up a current flow. The size of this current is usually small because only a few free electrons are produced by thermal energy.

Of course, if the temperature is increased further, more electrons will be liberated from outer shells, and a larger current will result. At room temperature (around 25°C) we find that the amount of current is too small to consider the germanium a conductor and yet too large to continue calling it an insulator. Therefore, we refer to the germanium crystal as a *semiconductor*.

A silicon crystal behaves much the same as a germanium crystal as far as electric current is concerned. At absolute zero temperature all electrons are tightly bound to their atoms, and the silicon crystal acts like an insulator. As the temperature increases, some electrons are knocked out of outer shells and become available for current flow. However, in silicon the outer-shell electrons are more tightly held than in germanium; as a result, more thermal energy is needed to dislodge an outer-shell electron from a silicon atom than from a germanium atom. Therefore, we note one important difference between silicon and germanium: at the same temperature there are *fewer free electrons in a silicon crystal* than in a germanium crystal.

1-4   The Hole Concept

An interesting concept in discussing semiconductors is that of a *hole*. To bring this idea out clearly, consider Fig. 1-5. A typical atom of germanium (or silicon) is shown with four neighboring atoms. As already indicated, thermal energy can dislodge an electron from the outer shell of an atom.

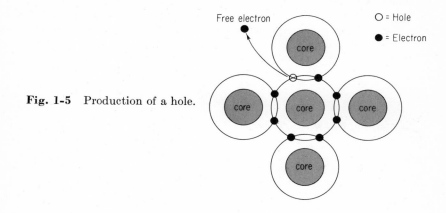

Fig. 1-5   Production of a hole.

When this happens, the released electron becomes a free electron and is capable of moving to another part of the crystal structure. The departure of this electron produces a vacancy in the outer shell that is called a *hole*. The hole behaves like a positive charge in the sense that it will attract and capture any electron in the immediate vicinity.

In a crystal of pure germanium or silicon, an equal number of holes and free electrons are created by thermal energy. The free electrons drift randomly throughout the crystal structure. Occasionally, a free electron approaches a hole closely enough to be attracted and captured by the hole. When this happens, the hole disappears, and the free electron becomes a bound electron. The action of a free electron moving into a hole is called *recombination*.

At any one instant in time the following takes place within the crystal:

1. Some free electrons and holes are being generated by means of thermal energy.
2. Other free electrons and holes are recombining.

3. Some free electrons and holes exist in an in-between stage; that is, they were previously generated and have not yet recombined. The average amount of time that these free electrons and holes exist before recombining is called the *lifetime*.

There are actually two components of current possible in a semiconductor: the movement of *free electrons* is one component, and the movement of *holes* is another component. The movement of free electrons was briefly discussed in Sec. 1-3 and is illustrated in Fig. 1-4.

The holes also move. To understand how this takes place, consider Fig. 1-6. At the extreme right a single hole is shown. Adjacent to this hole is a *bound* electron at position A. This bound electron is attracted by the hole and can move into the hole. When this happens, the original hole disappears, and a new hole appears at position A. The new hole at position A

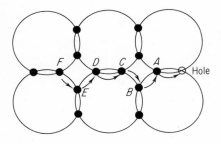

Fig. 1-6 Hole movement.

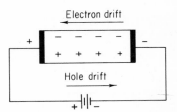

Fig. 1-7 Components of current.

can now attract and capture the bound electron at position B. When this happens, the hole at position A disappears, and a new hole appears at position B. This process can continue with a bound electron moving along the arbitrary path shown by the arrows. In this way, a hole can move from one atom to another. Note that the hole moves *opposite* to the direction of the bound electrons.

In the absence of an electric field the hole movement is a random process; that is, holes move in all directions, so that there is no net current in any one direction. If, however, an electric field is present within the crystal, a net current takes place in the direction of the field. For instance, in Fig. 1-7 a battery is connected to a pure semiconductor. Thermally produced holes and free electrons are represented by plus and minus signs. Because of the battery polarity, the free electrons move to the left, and the holes move to the right. Of course, there will be some recombination of free electrons and holes. However, free electrons and holes are being continuously produced by thermal energy, so that at any one instant in time there are some free electrons and holes that can participate in a current flow.

Note the two distinct components of current in Fig. 1-7. The drift of free electrons to the left is one component of this current. When the electrons reach the left end of the semiconductor, they are collected by the metal plate and enter the positive terminal of the battery. In the meantime, the negative terminal of the battery injects *free* electrons into the right end of the semiconductor, thereby maintaining a continuous flow of free electrons. The movement of holes to the right is the second component of current. When the holes reach the right end of the semiconductor, electrons from the battery combine with these holes and become *bound* electrons. In the meantime, new holes are generated within the crystal by means of thermal energy. In this way, a continuous flow of holes is maintained.

There is one more point. Strictly speaking, a hole is not a positive charge; it is simply a vacancy in the outer shell of an atom. Yet, a number of experiments (such as those involving the Hall effect) indicate that holes move and act as though they were positive charges. For this reason we will use a plus sign to represent a hole and will think of it as a positive charge.

1-5 Extrinsic Semiconductors

The number of free electrons and holes produced by thermal energy in a pure semiconductor is generally too small to be of any practical use. It is possible, however, to increase the number of free electrons and holes by a process called *doping*. This simply means that we can add impurity atoms to the germanium or silicon crystal. A semiconductor that has been doped is called an *extrinsic* semiconductor; a semiconductor that is still pure, or undoped, is called an *intrinsic* semiconductor.

One way of doping pure germanium (or silicon) is to first break down the crystal structure by melting it. A small amount of an impurity element with *five* electrons in its outer shell can then be added to the molten germanium. (Examples of elements with five outer-shell electrons are phosphorus, arsenic, antimony.) Assume that we add a small amount of arsenic. The arsenic atoms will diffuse throughout the molten germanium. When the germanium is cooled, a solid crystal will form. Once again, we find that each atom within the crystal has four neighboring atoms which share their outer-shell electrons. Examining the crystal on the atomic level, we find that most of the atoms are germanium; occasionally we find an arsenic atom. This arsenic atom has taken the place of a germanium atom in the crystalline structure, and, as a result, it has four neighboring atoms. In Fig. 1-8 we see that the central arsenic atom has eight electrons in its outer shell. This atom originally had five electrons in its outer shell. Each neighboring atom is sharing one of its outer-shell electrons with the arsenic atom. Therefore, there is an extra electron which becomes a free electron. It is clear that each arsenic atom in the doped semiconductor produces one free electron. Obviously, by controlling the amount of arsenic that is added, we can control the number of free electrons in the doped crystal.

Note that the production of free electrons by doping is quite different from the thermal production of free electrons and holes. Only free electrons have been produced by doping the semiconductor with arsenic. As

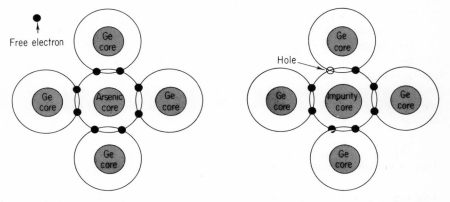

Fig. 1-8   An *n*-type semiconductor.   **Fig. 1-9**   A *p*-type semiconductor.

a result, there are more free electrons in the doped germanium than there are holes. The only holes present are those produced by thermal energy.

A pure semiconductor that has been doped by an element with five electrons in its outer shell is called an *n-type* semiconductor. The *n* stands for negative, referring to the excess of free electrons in the doped germanium. Since a piece of *n*-type semiconductor has more free electrons than holes, we commonly speak of the electrons as the *majority* carriers and the holes as the *minority* carriers.

We can also dope a semiconductor to obtain an excess of holes. In this case, we must use an impurity element with three outer-shell electrons (elements like boron, aluminum, gallium, etc.). If a small amount of this kind of impurity element is added to the molten germanium, then after cooling to obtain a crystal we find that each impurity atom has displaced one of the germanium atoms. Again, we note that most of the atoms in the crystal are germanium. Occasionally, we find an impurity atom. In Fig. 1-9 we have shown an impurity atom with the usual four neighbors.

As shown, there are only seven electrons in the outer shell (three originally in the impurity atom, and four from the neighboring atoms). Thus,
there is a hole in the outer shell of the impurity atom. Clearly, by varying
the amount of impurity we can control the number of holes in the crystal.

A semiconductor doped by impurity atoms having three outer-shell
electrons is called a *p-type* semiconductor. The *p* stands for positive,
referring to the excess of holes in the crystal. Since the *p*-type semiconductor has more holes than free electrons, the holes are the majority
carriers, and the free electrons are the minority carriers.

Figure 1-10 summarizes the two types of semiconductors.

Fig. 1-10 Majority and minority carriers.

Doping makes it possible to obtain usable levels of current in semiconductors. Of course, a single piece of *n*-type or *p*-type semiconductor
is not much better than a carbon resistor. It is when *p*-type and *n*-type
materials are brought together that something new and useful results. This
is discussed in later chapters.

SUMMARY

The two most widely used semiconductor materials are germanium and
silicon. Isolated atoms of these materials have four electrons in the outer
shells.

A crystal refers to the geometric structure that results when a large
number of germanium or silicon atoms combine to form a solid piece of
material. Each atom in the crystal has four neighboring atoms which
share electrons to produce a total of eight electrons in the outer shell of
each atom.

At absolute zero temperature, pure germanium or silicon acts like an
insulator because there are no free electrons available for current flow.
All eight electrons are tightly held in the outer shell of each atom. As the
temperature increases, however, thermal energy dislodges some electrons
from outer shells. This results in free electrons and holes, which can drift
under the influence of an electric field to produce a current. The size of
this current is usually too small to be of any practical use. Generally

speaking, pure silicon has fewer free electrons and holes than pure germanium at the same temperature.

A hole refers to a vacancy in the outer shell of a germanium or silicon atom and occurs when there are fewer than eight electrons in this shell. A hole will exert a force of attraction on any nearby electron. Movement of a free electron into the hole is called recombination. In this case, the hole disappears. On the other hand, when a bound electron moves into the hole, the hole simply moves to a new position.

A pure semiconductor is called an intrinsic semiconductor. Adding impurities to a pure semiconductor is called doping, and we call the doped semiconductor an extrinsic semiconductor. Whereas the n-type semiconductor has an excess of free electrons, the p-type semiconductor has an excess of holes.

GLOSSARY

crystal   The internal structure of a solid piece of germanium or silicon. In this structure each atom has four neighboring atoms that share outer-shell electrons.

doping   Adding impurity atoms to pure germanium or silicon in order to increase the number of free electrons or holes.

extrinsic semiconductor   Doped germanium or silicon.

hole   A vacancy in the outer shell of an atom. It can be produced either by thermal energy or by doping.

intrinsic semiconductor   Pure germanium or silicon. The only current carriers are the free electrons and holes produced·by thermal energy.

lifetime   The average amount of time that a free electron or hole exists after being generated but before recombining.

n-type semiconductor   A semiconductor that has been doped to produce an excess of free electrons.

p-type semiconductor   A semiconductor that has been doped to produce an excess of holes.

recombination   The merging of a free electron and a hole.

semiconductor   Material like germanium or silicon whose electrical properties lie between those of an insulator and a conductor.

REVIEW QUESTIONS

1. What does a silicon core refer to?
2. How many electrons are found in the outer shell of an isolated germanium atom under normal conditions?

3. What is a crystal?
4. In a crystal of germanium or silicon how many outer-shell electrons are there in each atom?
5. Why does a pure semiconductor behave like an insulator at absolute zero temperature?
6. Why do we use the word *semiconductor* to describe a crystal of pure germanium or silicon?
7. At the same temperature which conducts better, a crystal of pure silicon or a crystal of pure germanium? What is the reason for this?
8. What is a hole? Name two ways in which a hole is produced.
9. What word describes the merging of a free electron and a hole?
10. Define an intrinsic semiconductor and an extrinsic semiconductor.
11. To produce an *n*-type semiconductor we add an impurity element with how many electrons in its outer shell?
12. What are the majority carriers in a *p*-type semiconductor?

2 | The *p-n* Junction Diode

To understand how transistors work in different circuits it is first necessary to understand how a typical semiconductor diode works. We begin this chapter by joining a piece of *p*-type material to a piece of *n*-type material. The result is the *junction diode.* After discussing why this *p-n* junction acts like a diode, we obtain the typical *IV* characteristics of a semiconductor diode. Our work in this chapter is concerned with understanding the important features of diode behavior. We need this for our later work in transistors.

2-1   The *p-n* Junction

We know that at room temperature a piece of *p*-type material has mostly holes produced by doping and only a small number of free electrons produced by thermal energy. Also, a piece of *n*-type material has mostly free electrons with only a small number of holes produced by thermal energy.

In Fig. 2-1*a* we have symbolically shown a piece of *p*-type material. The plus signs represent the holes, which are free to move around in the crystal. The circled minus signs represent the *atoms* associated with these

12

holes. Thus, if a hole moves away from the atom associated with it, that atom becomes negatively charged. Note that the negatively charged atom is not free to move around within the crystal. This atom is held in position because it is part of the crystal structure. Therefore, in Fig. 2-1a the plus signs represent positive charges that are free to move, and the circled minus signs represent negatively charged atoms that are immobile.

Fig. 2-1 Current carriers and im-mobile atoms. (_a_) _p_-type and (_b_) _n_-type material.

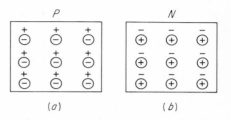

Similarly, in Fig. 2-1b we have a piece of _n_-type material. Here, the minus signs symbolize the free electrons, and the circled plus signs sym-bolize the atoms associated with these free electrons. Note that if a free electron moves away from its associated atom, it leaves a positively charged atom behind. Once again, this positively charged atom is not free to move; it is embedded at its particular position within the crystal structure.

For the moment we are disregarding the minority carriers in both types of material, and therefore we have not shown the small number of free electrons in the _p_-type material or the small number of holes in the _n_-type material. Let us remember that there are some thermally produced mi-nority carriers in both materials.

It is possible by various manufacturing techniques to produce a single crystal with _p_-type material on one side and _n_-type material on the other. Does anything unusual happen at the junction of the _p_- and _n_-type ma-terials? To answer this question, consider Fig. 2-2a. At the instant that the junction is formed, the holes are still in the _p_-type material and the free electrons are still in the _n_-type material. These charges are free to move; as a result, they do move randomly in all directions. Some of the free electrons and holes at the junction of the two materials will move across the junction and recombine. When this happens, the free charges disappear, since they neutralize each other. This recombination of free charges produces a narrow region at the junction called the _depletion region_ (see Fig. 2-2b). In this region there are essentially _no free electrons or holes;_ there are only positively and negatively charged atoms, which are not free to move.

As the depletion region builds up, a difference of potential builds up, simply because there are positively charged atoms on the right side of

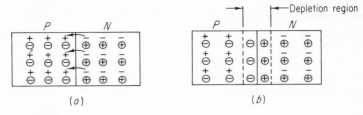

Fig. 2-2 A *p-n* junction. (*a*) At the instant of formation; (*b*) depletion region.

the junction and negatively charged atoms on the other side. Eventually, this potential becomes large enough to prevent further electron and hole movement across the junction. To understand why, note in Fig. 2-2*b* that an electric field exists at the junction; the direction of this field is from right to left. This means that when an electron tries to pass through the junction, it is repelled by the negative column of ionized atoms on the left and attracted by the positive column of ionized atoms on the right. In other words, a free electron is repelled into the *n*-type material. Similarly, any holes in the *p*-type material that try to move across the junction after the depletion region has formed will encounter a repelling force that drives them into *p*-type material.

The difference of potential at the junction is called the *barrier potential*. We find that at room temperature (about 25°C) the barrier potential is approximately 0.3 *volt for germanium and* 0.7 *volt for silicon.*

Let us summarize the main points of our discussion:

1. After the *p-n* junction is initially formed, free electrons and holes move across the junction and recombine.

2. A depletion region appears at the junction, in which there are essentially no free charges but only immobile charged atoms.

3. The charged atoms in the depletion region set up a barrier potential that prevents further movement of free electrons and holes across the junction.

(This summary of main points disregards the small number of minority carriers in each material, If they are taken into account, the first two steps of the summary are the same, but step 3 is slightly different. At equilibrium, a small number of minority carriers are swept across the junction by the barrier potential, while an equal number of majority carriers move across the junction in the opposite direction.)

2-2   The Rectifying Properties of a *p-n* Junction

A *p-n* crystal can be used as a diode because it allows current to flow more easily in one direction than in the other. To understand why this is so, consider Fig. 2-3, where we have shown a battery connected to a _p-n_ crystal. For the moment, disregard the minority carriers on either side of the junction. The barrier potential still tries to retard the movement of holes and free electrons across the junction. However, the battery drives holes and free electrons toward the junction. This means that all the free electrons in the _n_-type material move en masse to the left; as they move to the left, new _free_ electrons are injected by the battery into the right end of the crystal. Thus, a flow of free electrons is set up in the wire connected to the negative battery terminal.

The holes in the _p_-type material are also driven toward the junction. As they move en masse to the right, new holes are created at the left end of the crystal because _bound_ electrons leave the _p_-type material and enter the positive terminal of the battery. The important point to grasp here is that the battery potential has overcome the barrier potential and has established a flow of electrons in the external circuit. This flow is sustained because the holes and free electrons converging on the junction recombine with each other.

To better understand how the current flows in Fig. 2-3, let us follow one electron around the entire circuit. Here is approximately what happens. A free electron leaves the negative terminal of the battery and enters the _n_-type material. Once in the _n_-type material, this free electron is driven toward the junction by the battery potential. Somewhere in the vicinity of the junction this electron recombines with one of the holes from the _p_-type material. When this happens, the _free_ electron becomes a _bound_ electron. As a bound electron, it can continue drifting to the left by moving into an adjacent hole, and it now travels to the left through the _p_-type material until it reaches the left end of the crystal. When it leaves the crystal and enters the wire, the _bound_ electron becomes a _free_ electron, which then flows through the wire into the positive battery terminal. More or less, this is what happens to each of the electrons that participate in the total current flow.

Note that the current carriers inside the _p-n_ crystal are the holes and the free electrons. However, in the external circuit, that is, in the battery wires, _only free electrons are moving_. Also note that the conventional current is in the same direction as the holes. In drawing circuit diagrams _we will be using conventional current_, as shown in Fig. 2-3. This is a matter of convenience; there are many electronic devices whose schematic symbols are based upon conventional current; as a result, it will be easier to understand the meaning of these schematic symbols if we adopt the use of conventional current. Simply remember that conventional current flows in the same direction as the hole flow or opposite to the direction of the electron flow.

What happens if we reverse the polarity of the battery, as shown in

Fig. 2-4? The holes in the p-type material now move to the left, and the free electrons in the n-type material move to the right. The depletion layer widens as these carriers move away from the junction, and *momentarily* there will be a current in the external circuit. However, this current cannot continue indefinitely because there are no new holes and free electrons created by the battery, as in Fig. 2-3. The battery now aids the barrier potential in preventing further movement of majority carriers across the junction. Thus, for practical purposes we can say that after a momentary flow of current, the battery potential aids the barrier potential in preventing majority carriers from moving across the junction.

Actually, there is a small amount of current in the circuit of Fig. 2-4. Recall that we have shown only the majority carriers in Figs. 2-3 and 2-4.

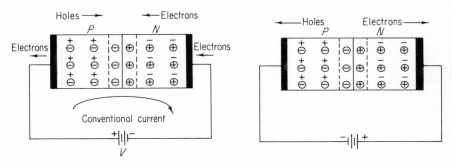

Fig. 2-3   Current in a diode.   **Fig. 2-4**   Reverse bias.

Because of thermal energy, there are also some holes in the n-type material and some free electrons in the p-type material. The battery drives these minority carriers across the junction, and therefore there is a *small* current in the circuit of Fig. 2-4.

Thus, the p-n crystal acts as a diode, since it allows current to flow easily in one direction only. To summarize the major points we note:

1. When the positive terminal of the battery is connected to the p-type material, current flows easily because the battery potential overcomes the barrier potential and drives majority carriers across the junction. The diode is then said to be *forward-biased*.

2. When the positive terminal of the battery is connected to the n-type material, very little current flows because the battery aids the barrier potential in preventing majority carriers from moving across the junction. The only current is the flow of the minority carriers. We call this condition *reverse bias* or *back bias*.

2-3   The *IV* Characteristics of a Semiconductor Diode

A *p-n* diode and its schematic symbol are shown in Fig. 2-5. From our
discussion of the preceding section we know that current flows easily when
the positive terminal of the battery is connected to the *p*-type material.

Fig. 2-5   Schematic symbol of a diode.

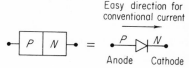

This means that conventional current flows easily from the *p*-type to the
n-type material. As a memory aid, note that the *triangle* of the schematic
symbol points in the *easy direction of conventional current*. In other words,
whenever a diode is used in a circuit where the conventional current is
trying to flow in the direction of the triangle, the diode offers a low-
impedance path. Whenever the conventional current is trying to flow
against the triangle, the diode offers a high-impedance path.

To get a more accurate idea of diode action, consider the following
hypothetical experiment. A battery is connected across a diode as shown
in Fig. 2-6a. If the battery is adjusted to 0 volts, we will find that there is

Fig. 2-6   The forward characteristic
of a diode.

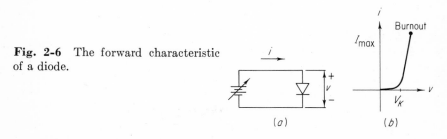

zero current in the diode. As we increase the battery voltage, current
begins to flow in the diode. The current will increase slowly at first, but
as we increase the battery voltage toward higher values, the current increases significantly. In other words, when the battery voltage is large
enough to overcome the barrier potential, current flows easily.

Figure 2-6b illustrates the current-voltage relation. The voltage V_K is
called the *knee* voltage; it simply refers to the approximate voltage above
which the diode current increases sharply. As an approximation, the knee
voltage is equal to the barrier potential. Thus, *for germanium diodes the
knee voltage is approximately equal to 0.3 volt, and for silicon diodes the
knee voltage is approximately equal to 0.7 volt.*

Of course, there is a limit to the amount of current that the diode can pass without burning out. When we increase the voltage well beyond the knee voltage, we eventually reach a burnout current. The diode will burn out simply because it has a maximum power dissipation. For instance, a typical semiconductor diode may have a maximum power rating of 0.5 watt. When the product of voltage and current exceeds 0.5 watt, the diode burns out (assuming d-c voltage and current).

What happens if we reverse the battery, as shown in Fig. 2-7a? With the battery reversed, we find that very little current flows. The actual conventional current flows opposite to the direction of i. Also, the actual voltage across the diode is opposite to the polarity of v. When we increase

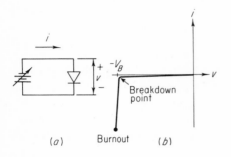

Fig. 2-7   The reverse characteristic of a diode.

the battery voltage, very little current flows, as shown in the reverse characteristic of Fig. 2-7b. This is because of the small number of minority carriers that are actually flowing in the diode. Note in Fig. 2-7b that there is a limit to the amount of reverse voltage that we can apply to the diode. When enough reverse voltage is applied, the diode current begins to increase sharply. The approximate voltage where this happens is called the *breakdown* voltage V_B of the diode (analogous to the peak inverse voltage of a vacuum-tube diode). If we continue to increase the battery voltage, more current flows, until eventually we reach a value of current that burns out the diode. Once again, this burnout is caused by exceeding the diode's maximum power rating. For instance, if the diode has a power rating of 0.5 watt, and if it breaks down at 100 volts, the maximum current is

$$I = \frac{P}{V} = \frac{0.5}{100} = 5 \text{ ma}$$

As long as we keep the current below this value, the diode is not destroyed. In other words, it is possible to break down a diode without destroying it, provided that the current is kept below the burnout value.

The breakdown phenomenon in a semiconductor diode is caused by either of two effects, *zener* or *avalanche*. In essence, what happens is

that bound electrons are being knocked out of outer shells and are then available for current flow. The breakdown voltage varies from one diode type to another and typically can occur in the range of a few volts to several hundred volts.

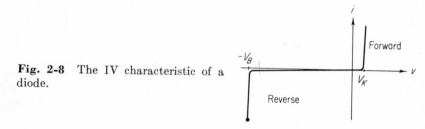

Fig. 2-8 The IV characteristic of a diode.

The overall *IV* characteristic of a typical semiconductor diode is shown in Fig. 2-8 (we have combined the forward and reverse characteristics).

To summarize our hypothetical experiment we note:

1. In the forward direction only a few tenths of a volt is needed to obtain significant values of current.

2. In the reverse direction very little current flows below the breakdown voltage.

3. Beyond the breakdown voltage, current increases sharply, but the diode is not necessarily destroyed.

4. In either the forward or the reverse direction, the diode can be burned out if its maximum power rating is exceeded.

Example 2-1

A semiconductor diode has a maximum power rating of 1 watt and a breakdown voltage of 150 volts. If the diode is operating in the breakdown region, what is the value of direct current that burns out the diode?

Solution

$$P = VI$$

or

$$I = \frac{P}{V} = \frac{1}{150} = 6.67 \text{ ma}$$

Example 2-2

The diode of the preceding example is forward-biased. When the voltage across the diode is 2 volts, the diode burns out. What was the value of the current at the burnout point?

SOLUTION

$$I = \tfrac{1}{2} = 0.5 \text{ amp}$$

SUMMARY

A p-n junction diode is a solid crystal with p-type material on one side of the junction and n-type material on the other side. After the junction is formed, majority carriers diffuse across the junction and recombine. This produces a depletion region containing immobile charged atoms, which in turn produce a barrier potential. For germanium the barrier potential is about 0.3 volt, and for silicon it is around 0.7 volt.

When the positive terminal of a battery is connected to the p side of the crystal, the battery can overcome the barrier potential and establish a current in the external circuit. We call this condition forward bias. When the negative terminal of the battery is connected to the p side of the crystal, the diode is reverse-biased, and only a small amount of current flows.

The IV characteristic of a p-n diode indicates that in the forward direction a large current can flow if the diode voltage is greater than the knee voltage. In the reverse direction only a small current flows unless the diode voltage exceeds the breakdown voltage. At breakdown the diode is not necessarily destroyed unless the maximum power dissipation of the diode is exceeded.

GLOSSARY

avalanche   At higher reverse voltages minority carriers can attain sufficient velocity to dislodge outer-shell electrons, which in turn can gain sufficient velocity to dislodge more outer-shell electrons, etc., with the result that there is a significant increase in reverse current.

barrier potential   The voltage across the p-n junction. This voltage is produced by the layer of charged atoms on both sides of the junction. Approximately 0.3 volt for germanium and 0.7 volt for silicon.

breakdown voltage (V_B)   That value of reverse voltage beyond which there is a significant increase in reverse current.

conventional current   Current that flows in the same direction as the holes and opposite to the direction of the electrons.

depletion region   A region on both sides of a p-n junction. It is relatively empty or depleted of free charges and primarily contains immobile ionized atoms.

forward bias Applying external voltage across a diode with a polarity such that the conventional current is trying to flow in the direction of the diode triangle, that is, from the *p*-type to the *n*-type material.

knee voltage (V_K) The approximate value of forward voltage across a diode beyond which the forward current increases sharply.

reverse bias Applying external voltage across a diode with a polarity such that conventional current is trying to flow against the diode triangle, that is, from the *n*-type to the *p*-type material.

zener effect In the back-bias condition outer-shell electrons can be dislodged by the electric field set up by the reverse voltage with the result that there is a significant increase in current.

REVIEW QUESTIONS

1. What is the depletion region of a diode?
2. What are the approximate values of the barrier potential in germanium and silicon diodes?
3. What effect does the barrier potential have upon the majority carriers that try to move across the junction?
4. What causes the barrier potential?
5. What are the majority carriers in the *p*-type material? In the *n*-type material? In the external wires of a battery connected to the diode?
6. What happens to the size of the depletion layer when the diode is back-biased?
7. What is the approximate value of the knee voltage for a germanium diode? For a silicon diode?
8. Does reverse breakdown immediately destroy the diode? Why?
9. When a diode is in the breakdown region, how are the current carriers produced?

PROBLEMS

2-1 A diode has a maximum power dissipation of 0.25 watt. What is the maximum direct current allowable in the forward direction if we allow an approximate voltage drop of 1 volt?

2-2 A diode has a breakdown voltage of 150 volts. If the maximum power dissipation is 0.25 watt, what is the approximate value of breakdown current that burns out the diode?

2-3 A diode with a maximum power rating of 0.5 watt burns out when the forward current is 400 ma. What was the d-c voltage across the diode at the burnout point?

3 | Large-signal Diode Approximations

Before we attempt to analyze transistor circuits, we must first be able to analyze diode circuits. When we can analyze diode circuits quickly and easily, we will find that transistor circuit analysis is only a step beyond.

We now work with the aim of obtaining *approximate* answers for diode and transistor circuits; this is essential to rapid, easy analysis of such circuits. In short, we are abandoning the quest for exact answers because such answers are found only after performing difficult and time-consuming calculations. Our intentions are to simplify diodes and transistors as much as possible in order to get at the essential ideas behind the use of these devices.

In this chapter we discuss some of the widely used approximations for the rectifier diode and for the zener (or avalanche) diode. These approximations are primarily for circuits driven by large-signal sources, that is, sources whose voltages are much larger than the diode knee voltage.

3-1 The Ideal Diode

As we saw in the last chapter, a typical semiconductor diode has the characteristic shown in Fig. 3-1. This characteristic is too complicated for

22

practical circuit analysis; we will therefore approximate it by a simpler graph.

The first (and simplest) approximation that we consider is the *ideal diode*. By this we mean a perfect diode. When we look at Fig. 3-1, it is clear that the real diode has imperfections. For instance, the breakdown

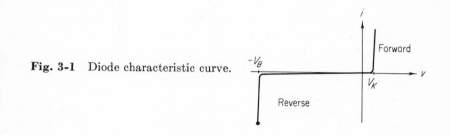

Fig. 3-1 Diode characteristic curve.

phenomenon is undesirable in any rectifier diode. Also, the small amount of reverse current below breakdown is undesirable. Finally, in the forward direction we see that a few tenths of a volt are needed before the diode conducts heavily. An ideal or perfect diode would have none of these obvious defects.

Figure 3-2a shows the characteristic of an ideal diode. There is no breakdown, no reverse current, and no forward voltage drop. Of course, such a diode cannot be built. It is only a theoretical approximation of a real diode. However, we will find that in well-designed rectifying circuits the behavior of real diodes approaches the behavior of an ideal diode.

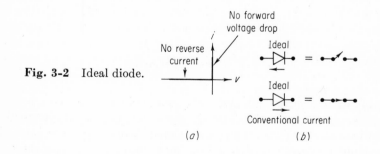

Fig. 3-2 Ideal diode.

In using the ideal-diode approximation, it is helpful to visualize the ideal diode as a switch, as shown in Fig. 3-2b. Note that these two properties apply to the ideal diode:

1. When *conventional current* is trying to flow *opposite* to the direction of the diode triangle, the diode is like an *open* switch.

2. When *conventional current* is trying to flow in the *same* direction as the diode triangle, the diode is like a *closed* switch.

To repeat, the ideal diode does not exist. It is only a convenient and simple approximation of the behavior of a real diode. We will use the ideal-diode approximation whenever we wish to obtain a basic idea of how rectifier circuits work. Occasionally, the answers obtained by using the ideal-diode approximation are grossly inaccurate. In these cases we will use better approximations to be developed in later sections.

As an illustration of using the ideal-diode approximation, consider the simple half-wave rectifier shown in Fig. 3-3a. How can we find the voltage waveform across the 10-kilohm resistor? First, note that during each positive half cycle the generator polarity is plus-minus, as indicated in Fig. 3-3b. Therefore, conventional current is trying to flow in the direction of the diode triangle. This means that the ideal diode is shorted. Hence, each positive half cycle must appear across the 10-kilohm resistor.

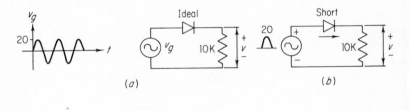

(a)   (b)

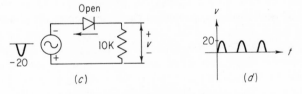

(c)   (d)

Fig- 3-3   Half-wave rectifier.

During each negative half cycle, the source polarity reverses, becoming minus-plus, as shown in Fig. 3-3c. Conventional current now tries to flow against the diode triangle; therefore the diode is open. With an open diode there can be no current through the 10-kilohm resistor; hence, there is no voltage across the resistor.

The final waveform is shown in Fig. 3-3d. This is the familiar half-wave-rectified sine wave found in some power supplies.

As another example of using the ideal-diode approximation, consider the circuit of Fig. 3-4a. Let us find the waveform of voltage across the diode. Again, the key to analysis is to determine when the ideal diode is

open and when it is shorted. During each positive half cycle the circuit
has the form shown in Fig. 3-4*b*. Conventional current is trying to flow
in the direction of the triangle; therefore the diode is shorted. The voltage
across a short, regardless of how much current is flowing, must be zero.
All the source voltage is dropped across the 10-kilohm resistor. Therefore,
throughout each positive half cycle the voltage across the diode is zero.

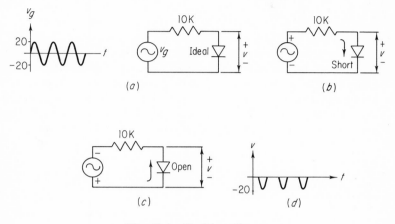

Fig. 3-4   Positive clipper.

During each negative half cycle, the circuit has the form shown in
Fig. 3-4*c*. Conventional current tries to flow against the triangle, and
therefore the diode is open. With an open diode there can be no current
through the 10-kilohm resistor, and hence there can be no voltage drop
across the resistor. From Kirchhoff's voltage law we know that the voltage across the diode must equal the source voltage. Stated another way,
the voltage across the diode must equal the source voltage minus the
voltage across the 10-kilohm resistor. With no voltage drop across the
10-kilohm resistor, all the source voltage appears across the diode. Thus,
each negative half cycle appears across the diode.

The final waveform is shown in Fig. 3-4*d*. Note that all the positive
portions of the source voltage have been removed. We call a circuit that
removes the positive parts of an input signal a *positive clipper*. If a circuit
clips off the negative parts of an input signal, we call it a *negative clipper*.
The circuit of Fig. 3-4*a* can be made into a negative clipper by reversing
the direction of the diode.

EXAMPLE 3-1

Sketch the waveform for *v* in the circuit of Fig. 3-5*a*.

SOLUTION

We must determine when the ideal diode is shorted and when it is open. First, note that as long as the source voltage is less than 10 volts, the battery voltage exceeds the source voltage, and therefore conventional current tries to flow against the triangle, as shown in Fig. 3-5b. Hence, the ideal diode is open. With an open diode, no voltage can appear across the 10-kilohm resistor. Therefore, the output voltage v must equal the source voltage.

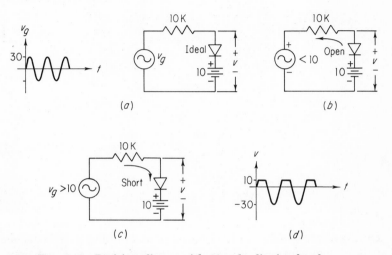

Fig. 3-5   Positive clipper with 10-volt clipping level.

Whenever the source voltage exceeds 10 volts, conventional current will try to flow in the direction of the triangle, and the ideal diode will appear shorted, as in Fig. 3-5c. With the diode shorted, the output voltage v must equal 10 volts, the value of the battery voltage.

We conclude, therefore, that whenever the source voltage is less than 10 volts, the output voltage v follows the waveform of the source voltage. Whenever the source voltage is greater than 10 volts, the output is held fixed at 10 volts. Because of these conclusions we can draw the final waveform shown in Fig. 3-5d.

We can think of the circuit of Fig. 3-5a as a positive clipper with a clipping level of 10 volts. All parts of the input signal above 10 volts have been clipped off. Note that the clipping level is equal to the battery voltage. In other words, if we change the battery voltage to another value, say 18 volts, the clipping level will be changed to 18 volts.

EXAMPLE 3-2

Sketch the output waveform for the circuit of Fig. 3-6a.

SOLUTION

By inspection, the diode-battery combination on the left clips off all parts of the input signal that are greater than 10 volts (discussed in Example 3-1). The diode-battery combination on the right is a negative clipper with a clipping level of -10 volts (the reader should be able to work this out, if in doubt). Thus, all parts of the input signal above $+10$ volts are clipped off, and all parts below -10 volts are clipped off. The final output waveform is shown in Fig. 3-6b.

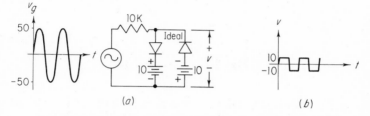

(a)   (b)

Fig. 3-6   Positive- and negative-clipper combination.

Note that this is one way of obtaining square waves (approximate) from sine waves. Also note that the clipping action takes place at $+10$ and -10 volts, regardless of the shape of the input waveform. Any input waveform—triangular, sawtooth, etc.—may be used, and if it exceeds the clipping levels, all positive parts above $+10$ volts and all negative parts below -10 volts will be clipped off.

EXAMPLE 3-3

Sketch the output waveform for the circuit of Fig. 3-7a.

SOLUTION

During each positive half cycle the ideal diode is shorted. Therefore during each of these positive half cycles, the circuit behaves like the simple voltage divider of Fig. 3-7b. From this circuit it is clear that the output voltage v must equal one-half the input voltage. Thus, the output will be a triangular wave with a peak value of 25 volts.

During each negative half cycle the ideal diode is open, and the circuit becomes equivalent to that shown in Fig. 3-7c. As noted in earlier examples, no current can flow through the 10-kilohm resistor. Therefore, the output voltage must follow the waveform of the input voltage.

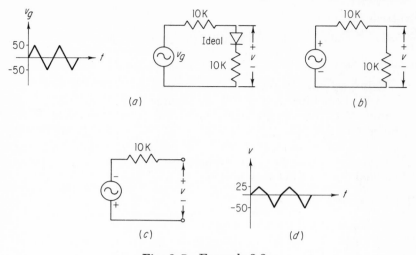

Fig. 3-7   Example 3-3.

We can now draw the final waveform of the output voltage, as shown in Fig. 3-7*d*.

3-2   The Second Approximation of a Real Diode

The ideal diode is the simplest but crudest approximation of a real diode. The answers we obtain using the ideal-diode approach provide us with an initial idea of how rectifier circuits operate.

To improve our approximation of the real diode we can take into account the forward voltage drop across the real diode. A simple way to do this is to allow a forward voltage drop equal to the knee voltage of the diode. For instance, in Fig. 3-8*a* we have shown the characteristic of the second approximation of a real diode. In this case our viewpoint is that the diode does not conduct until the voltage across the diode reaches the knee voltage.

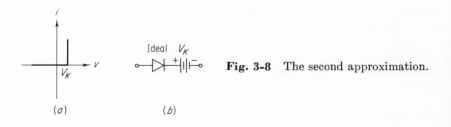

Fig. 3-8   The second approximation.

The equivalent circuit for the second approximation is given in Fig. 3-8*b*. There is an ideal diode in series with a battery whose voltage equals the knee voltage of the real diode. Our idea of the circuit action is simply this: whenever conventional current tries to flow in the direction of the triangle, the ideal diode is shorted, and the net voltage across the terminals of the combination becomes equal to the knee voltage. In other words, in the second approximation we allow a voltage drop of 0.3 or 0.7 volt across the real diode when it is conducting in the forward direction. (Remember: 0.3 volt for germanium and 0.7 for silicon.)

EXAMPLE 3-4

For the simple half-wave rectifier of Fig. 3-9*a*, sketch the waveform of the output voltage *v* by:

(*a*) Replacing the silicon diode by an ideal diode.
(*b*) Replacing the silicon diode by its second approximation.

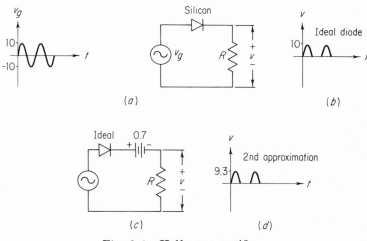

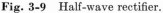

Fig. 3-9 Half-wave rectifier.

SOLUTION

(*a*) The ideal-diode approach simply gives us the standard half-wave-rectified sine wave shown in Fig. 3-9*b*.

(*b*) To use the second approximation we visualize the silicon diode as an ideal diode in series with a 0.7-volt battery, as shown in Fig. 3-9*c*. As the source voltage builds up from 0 to 0.7 volt, conventional current tries to flow against the triangle, so that the diode is open. Thus, as long as the source voltage is less than 0.7 volt, the output voltage remains at zero. However, once the source voltage is greater than 0.7 volt, the knee voltage is overcome, and the diode is turned on. The output voltage now begins to build up, following the waveform of the source. At the instant that the source voltage equals the peak voltage of 10 volts, the output must equal 10 volts minus the 0.7-volt drop. Thus, the peak value of output voltage is 9.3 volts.

The final output waveform is shown in Fig. 3-9d. Note that this waveform is almost the same as the waveform obtained by the ideal-diode approach (Fig. 3-9b).

EXAMPLE 3-5

Use the second approximation to find the output waveform for the circuit of Fig. 3-10a.

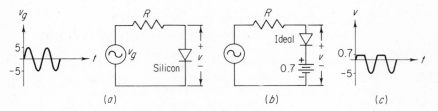

Fig. 3-10   Positive clipper.

SOLUTION

First, note that an ideal-diode approach would simply give us an output waveform that is positively clipped at the 0-volt level.

In using the second approximation of the silicon diode, we visualize the circuit as shown in Fig. 3-10b. The simplest way to analyze this circuit is to realize that it is a positive clipper with a 0.7-volt clipping level (similar to Example 3-1). Therefore, we conclude that the output waveform is that of Fig. 3-10c.

3-3   The Third Approximation of a Real Diode

Still another approximation can be made for a real diode to account more accurately for its forward voltage drop. We recall that the forward characteristic of a real diode is not vertical above the knee but actually slopes upward to the right. This means that as more current flows through the real diode, more voltage is dropped across it.

Figure 3-11a shows the characteristic of the third approximation of a real diode. By inspection, this characteristic still does not give the exact forward behavior of a real diode, but it does represent a more accurate model than our first two approximations. Our interpretation of this graph is that the diode begins to conduct above V_K (0.3 or 0.7 volt). Once the diode is conducting, it acts like a resistor, because the change in voltage is directly proportional to the change in current. The value of this resistance is called the *forward* or *bulk* resistance of the diode, and we will use the notation r_B to represent this resistance.

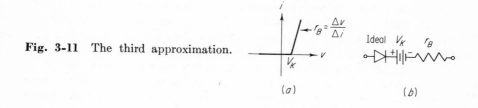

Fig. 3-11 The third approximation.

(a)   *(b)*

The equivalent circuit for the third approximation is shown in Fig. 3-11b. Our viewpoint here is that the real diode acts like an ideal diode in series with a battery of value V_K and a resistor of value r_B. Whenever the external circuit tries to force conventional current in the direction of the triangle, the ideal diode is shorted. The voltage drop across the terminals of the combination is then the sum of V_K and the drop across the r_B resistor. In other words, in the third approximation it takes at least 0.3 or 0.7 volt even to turn the diode on. The diode then acts like a resistor of value r_B, which drops additional voltage depending upon how much current is flowing.

A word or two on finding the value of r_B is in order. First, if an IV curve tracer is available, the diode characteristic can be displayed. From this graph we need only select two points well above the knee of the curve where the characteristic is almost linear. The change in voltage between the two points divided by the change in current is the approximate value of r_B. For instance, suppose the curve-tracer display of a diode is that shown in Fig. 3-12a. We would select two points well above the knee of the curve. Two such points are shown. To find the bulk resistance r_B we would divide the change in voltage by the change in current between the

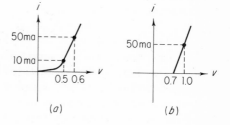

Fig. 3-12 Estimating the bulk resistance r_B.

(a)   *(b)*

two points. That is,

$$r_B = \frac{0.6 - 0.5}{50(10^{-3}) - 10(10^{-3})} = \frac{0.1}{40(10^{-3})} = 2.5 \text{ ohms}$$

Another approach is to find the approximate value of bulk resistance directly from the manufacturer's data sheet for the particular diode. On the data sheet one of the quantities normally specified is the forward current at 1 volt. Knowing whether the diode is germanium or silicon, we can subtract the knee voltage from 1 volt and divide this result by the forward current. For instance, suppose that a data sheet for a particular silicon diode indicates a forward current of 50 ma at 1 volt. In effect, we are being given one point on the forward characteristic of the silicon diode, as shown in Fig. 3-12b. By using the third approximation of the diode, we can use the knee as the second point. The change in voltage between the two points is

$$\Delta v = 1 - 0.7 = 0.3 \text{ volt}$$

The change in current between these two points is

$$\Delta i = 50 \text{ ma}$$

Therefore the bulk resistance is approximately

$$r_B \cong \frac{\Delta v}{\Delta i} = \frac{0.3}{50(10^{-3})} = 6 \text{ ohms}$$

The third approximation of a real diode can be used to refine the answers obtained by the simple ideal-diode approach.

EXAMPLE 3-6

Sketch the output voltage v for the circuit of Fig. 3-13a by using the third approximation of the germanium diode. This diode has a forward current I_F of 28 ma at 1 volt.

SOLUTION

First, calculate the value of bulk resistance

$$r_B = \frac{\Delta v}{\Delta i} = \frac{1 - 0.3}{28(10^{-3})} = 25 \text{ ohms}$$

Next, replace the germanium diode by its third approximation, as shown in Fig. 3-13b. From this circuit it is clear that the ideal diode cannot turn on until the source voltage is greater than 0.3 volt. Whenever the source voltage exceeds 0.3 volt, the ideal diode is shorted; the 25- and 75-ohm resistors then form a voltage divider, so that the out-

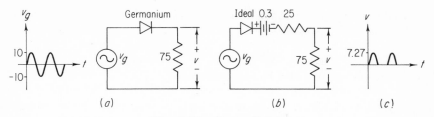

Fig. 3-13 Example 3-6.

put voltage is a reduced version of the positive half cycle. To find the peak value of the output voltage during the positive half cycle, we can find the peak current in the circuit and multiply it by 75 ohms. At the instant when the source reaches its peak value of 10 volts, the current will reach a peak value of

$$i_p = \frac{10 - 0.3}{100} = 97 \text{ ma}$$

The peak output voltage is

$$v_p = 97(10^{-3})(75) = 7.27 \text{ volts}$$

Whenever the source is less than 0.3 volt, the ideal diode is open, and there is no current through the 75-ohm resistor; therefore the output voltage is zero.

The sketch of the total waveform is shown in Fig. 3-13c.

3-4 Using the Diode Approximations

The diode approximations discussed so far can considerably shorten the amount of time required to analyze various diode circuits; they also are the basis of transistor circuit analysis. The ideal-diode approximation is by far the simplest and most often used approximation in transistor circuit analysis. Occasionally, we will want to refine our answers by using the second and third approximations.

Let us summarize the use of these approximations:

1. In analyzing any rectifier-diode circuit, start with the ideal-diode approach. This yields a basic idea of how the circuit operates and is adequate for most situations.

2. If the answers obtained by the ideal-diode approach indicate that 0.3 or 0.7 volt is significant, reanalyze the circuit using the second approximation.

3. If the external resistance in series with the diode is not large compared to the bulk resistance of the diode, use the third approximation.

3-5   Approximating the Reverse Current

In the reverse direction below breakdown, a small amount of current does flow through the diode. Up to now, we have completely disregarded the reverse current. In some circuits the reverse current can be a problem. Therefore, we need an approximation for a reverse-biased diode operating below the breakdown point. We want as simple an approximation as possible; therefore, we will view the diode as a large resistance whose value equals the reverse voltage V_R divided by the reverse current I_R. For instance, if a manufacturer's data sheet indicates that a particular diode has a reverse current of 10 μa for a reverse voltage of 50 volts, then we calculate a reverse resistance R_R of

$$R_R = \frac{V_R}{I_R} = \frac{50}{10(10^{-6})} = 5 \text{ megohms}$$

A point worth making at this time is that silicon diodes have much less reverse current than comparable germanium diodes. It is not at all uncommon for a silicon diode to have a reverse resistance that is 1000 or more times larger than that of a comparable germanium diode. For instance, a 1N277 is a germanium diode with a reverse current of 0.25 ma for a reverse voltage of 50 volts. Therefore it has a reverse resistance of

$$R_R = \frac{50}{0.25(10^{-3})} = 200 \text{ kilohms}$$

An SG1825 is a comparable silicon diode; however, it has a reverse current of only 10 na at 120 volts. Therefore it has a reverse resistance of

$$R_R = \frac{120}{10(10^{-9})} = 12{,}000 \text{ megohms}$$

Note that the higher the reverse resistance of a diode, the more closely it approaches the ideal, or perfect, diode. Generally speaking, silicon diodes and transistors are far superior to germanium diodes and transistors in this respect. Originally, the germanium diodes and transistors were less expensive than silicon devices. This is no longer true; comparably priced silicon diodes and transistors are now available.

The use of a resistance to represent the diode in the reverse region yields reasonably accurate results in low-frequency circuits, provided that the diode remains below the breakdown voltage. If the diode breaks down, we must adopt a different viewpoint, as discussed in Sec. 3-6.

EXAMPLE 3-7

Sketch the waveform of the output voltage v in the circuit of Fig. 3-14a. Neglect the forward voltage drop but take reverse current into account. The diode has a reverse current of 1 μa for a reverse voltage of 50 volts.

SOLUTION

The reverse resistance is

$$R_R = \frac{50}{10^{-6}} = 50 \text{ megohms}$$

During the positive half cycle the diode is shorted, and the output voltage follows the source voltage.

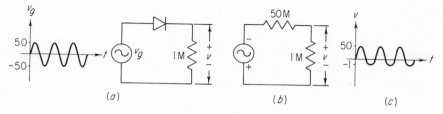

Fig. 3-14   Effect of reverse resistance.

During the negative half cycle the diode acts like a 50-megohm resistor, as shown in Fig. 3-14b. This circuit is a voltage divider, so that the output voltage is about $\frac{1}{50}$ of the source voltage. At the negative peak the source voltage is 50 volts, and the output voltage is about 1 volt.

The final waveform is shown in Fig. 3-14c. If the 1-volt level is objectionable on the negative half cycle, then either of two changes is possible to remedy the situation. First, the 1-megohm resistor can be reduced to a lower value, like 100 kilohms. In this case, only about $\frac{1}{500}$ of the source voltage will appear at the output during the negative half cycle. Second, we can change diode types to obtain a much larger reverse resistance. For instance, we can easily obtain a diode with a reverse resistance of 500 megohms. In this case, the output voltage will be only about $\frac{1}{500}$ of the source voltage during the negative half cycle.

3-6   Zener Diodes

When using the diode as a rectifying device we generally make sure that the driving voltage across the diode does not exceed the breakdown volt-

age. On data sheets the breakdown voltage V_B is often designated by
either PIV (peak inverse voltage) or by BV_R (reverse breakdown voltage).
In typical rectifying and detecting applications the PIV of the diode
should be sufficiently large compared to the driving voltage to prevent
any possibility of breakdown.

We might be tempted to think that diodes are never used in the breakdown region; this is not true. There definitely are uses for the breakdown
phenomenon, as we shall see shortly.

By careful manufacturing techniques the breakdown can be made very
sharp and almost vertical, as shown in Fig. 3-15a. Diodes exhibiting this
sharp knee at the breakdown point are called *zener* diodes. The voltage
V_Z is the approximate voltage where the zener diode breaks down. The
amount of current flowing in the breakdown region will depend upon the
external circuit driving the diode. There is, of course, a maximum value
of current at which the zener diode burns out. This value of current is
determined by the zener voltage and the maximum power dissipation of
the diode. An important point to realize is that the diode is not immediately destroyed just because it has entered the breakdown region. As long
as the external circuit connected to the diode limits the diode current to
less than the burnout current, the diode will not burn out.

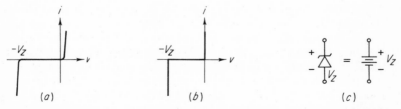

Fig. 3-15   Zener diode. (*a*) Typical characteristic; (*b*) ideal characteristic; (*c*)
equivalent circuit.

To enable us to analyze zener-diode circuits quickly and easily, we will
approximate the graph of Fig. 3-15a by redrawing it as shown in Fig.
3-15b. We call this the characteristic of an ideal zener diode. Note that
in the forward direction the diode acts like a short. In the reverse direction the diode is open until we reach the breakdown voltage. Beyond the
breakdown point the diode voltage remains *constant*, even though the
current can change considerably, depending upon the external circuit connected to the diode. This constant-voltage characteristic is the most useful property of a zener diode.

Our circuit viewpoint of a diode in the breakdown region is shown in
Fig. 3-15c. *An ideal zener diode looks like a battery of V_Z volts*, because
an ideal battery is a device whose voltage remains constant even though

the current through it changes. Remember we are not saying that the zener diode is a battery; we are only saying that in the breakdown region it acts like a battery. The usual schematic symbol for a zener diode is also shown in Fig. 3-15c. Memorize the polarity of voltage and the direction of the conventional current; this is essential for the analysis of zener-diode circuits. Note that in the breakdown region the conventional current flows against the triangle and the voltage is plus-minus as shown.

The breakdown phenomenon is actually a combination of two effects: zener effect and avalanche effect. The zener effect refers to removing bound electrons from outer shells by means of an electric field. In other words, as the reverse voltage is applied to a diode, an electric field appears at the junction. When this field is intense enough, outer-shell electrons are dislodged, resulting in a significant increase in reverse current. The avalanche effect is different. In this case, when the diode is reverse-biased, minority carriers are flowing. For higher reverse voltages these minority carriers can attain sufficient velocity to knock bound electrons out of their outer shells. These released electrons then attain sufficient velocity to dislodge more bound electrons, etc. The process is well named, since it is suggestive of an avalanche.

When a diode breaks down, both zener and avalanche effects are present, although usually one or the other predominates. It has been found experimentally that below 6 volts the zener effect is predominant; above 6 volts the avalanche effect is predominant. Strictly speaking, diodes with breakdown voltages greater than 6 volts should be called avalanche diodes, and sometimes they are so called. However, the general practice is to refer to diodes exhibiting either effect as *zener diodes*.

EXAMPLE 3-8

Find the current through the zener diode in the circuit of Fig. 3-16a. Use the ideal-zener-diode approximation.

SOLUTION

Note that the zener diode is back-biased by a source that exceeds the breakdown voltage of the diode. Therefore, the zener diode must be in the breakdown region, and we can visualize it as a 30-volt battery, as shown in Fig. 3-16b. The difference of potential across the 2-kilohm

Fig. 3-16   Example 3-8.

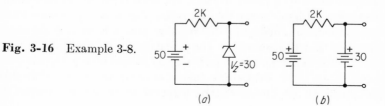

resistor must be the difference of 50 and 30 volts, that is, 20 volts. The current through the 2-kilohm resistor is

$$I = \frac{20}{2000} = 10 \text{ ma}$$

Since we have a series circuit, 10 ma must also flow through the zener diode. Thus, the zener diode is operating in the breakdown region with a voltage of 30 volts and a current of 10 ma.

EXAMPLE 3-9

In Fig. 3-17a, use the ideal-zener-diode approximation to find the following:

(a) The current through the zener diode when $R = 30$ kilohms.
(b) The current through the zener diode when $R = 4$ kilohms.

SOLUTION

(a) When $R = 30$ kilohms, there is more than enough voltage appearing across the diode to cause breakdown, and we can think of the zener diode as a 30-volt battery (Fig. 3-17b).

The voltage across the 2-kilohm resistor is still the difference between the source voltage of 50 volts and the zener voltage of 30 volts. Therefore, there is still 20 volts across the 2-kilohm resistor, and a current of 10 ma flows through it, as shown in Fig. 3-17b. This 10 ma of current splits at the junction of the zener diode and the 30-kilohm resistor.

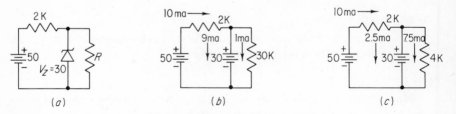

Fig. 3-17   A simple voltage regulator.

To find how this current divides, we note that the voltage across the 30-kilohm resistor must be 30 volts, the zener voltage. Therefore, there is 1 ma of current in this resistor. From Kirchhoff's current law, we know that the current in the zener diode must equal the difference between 10 and 1 ma, that is, 9 ma, as shown in Fig. 3-17b.

(b) When $R = 4$ kilohms, more current must flow through this resistor. With 30 volts across the zener diode, there must also be 30 volts across the 4-kilohm resistor, and therefore there is a current in the resistor of

$$I = \frac{30}{4000} = 7.5 \text{ ma}$$

The current in the zener diode must be the difference between the input 10 ma and the 7.5 ma flowing in the 4-kilohm resistor. Therefore, the zener-diode current is 2.5 ma, as shown in Fig. 3-17c.

Note what has happened. The load resistance R has changed from 30 to 4 kilohms, and yet the voltage across this resistor has been held constant at 30 volts by the zener diode. This is one of the major uses of zener diodes, namely, to hold the voltage across a load resistance constant, even though the load changes.

In Fig. 3-17a regulation is lost when R is less than 3 kilohms, because for this value, the load current has just reached 10 ma, and the zener current has reached zero; the diode is on the verge of coming out of the breakdown region, and any further reduction in the size of R will result in a voltage of less than 30 volts.

In general, there is a limit on the minimum value of R. If R is made too small, the zener diode will come out of the breakdown region, and regulation will be lost. To ensure that the diode is in the breakdown region, we must have at least a small amount of zener current.

EXAMPLE 3-10

Find the value of v in the circuit of Fig. 3-18a. Use the ideal-zener-diode approximation. Also, find the minimum and maximum value of zener-diode current.

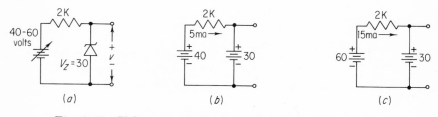

Fig. 3-18   Voltage regulation for a changing source voltage.

SOLUTION

The source voltage varies from 40 to 60 volts. The equivalent circuits for both of these conditions are shown in Fig. 3-18b and c. In both cases, note that there is enough source voltage to cause breakdown.

When the source is at its minimum value of 40 volts, there must be 10 volts across the 2-kilohm resistor, and therefore there is a current of 5 ma flowing in the zener diode. When the source voltage equals 60 volts, there must be 30 volts across the 2-kilohm resistor, and a current of 15 ma flows through the zener diode.

In either case, the voltage across the zener-diode terminals is 30 volts. The point of this example is to show how the voltage across the zener diode remains constant in spite of changes in the source voltage.

Thus, zener diodes can be used to regulate voltage under conditions of changing source voltage and changing load resistance (Example 3-9).

3-7 The Second Approximation of a Zener Diode

In the preceding section we discussed the ideal-zener-diode approximation, in which we think of the zener diode as a battery whenever it is in the breakdown region. This simple model is adequate for most troubleshooting and preliminary design.

To improve our analysis of zener-diode circuits we can take into account the slope of the breakdown characteristic. In other words, for the second approximation we will use the IV characteristic shown in Fig. 3-19a; note that the breakdown region is not vertical but actually has a slope, so that it more closely resembles the breakdown characteristic of a real zener diode. Our interpretation of this not quite vertical breakdown region is simply this: when more current flows through the diode, the voltage does not remain exactly constant but increases slightly.

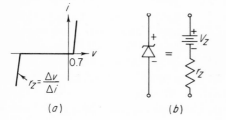

Fig. 3-19 Second approximation of zener diode. (a) Characteristic curve; (b) equivalent circuit.

In other words, once the diode is in the breakdown region, it resembles a resistor as far as changes in voltage and current are concerned. The size of this resistor can be found by taking the ratio of a change in voltage to a change in current between any two points on the breakdown characteristic. That is,

$$r_Z = \frac{\Delta v}{\Delta i}$$

where Δv is the change in voltage between two points, and Δi is the change in current between the same two points.

The resistance r_Z is called the *zener* resistance and is normally given on the data sheet for the particular diode. The circuit model that we use for the second approximation is shown in Fig. 3-19b. In the breakdown region we think of a zener diode as a battery in series with a resistor. Thus, the voltage across the zener diode is

$$V_Z + ir_Z \tag{3-1}$$

where V_Z is the voltage right at the knee of the breakdown and ir_Z is the additional voltage drop across the zener diode produced by the zener resistance and the current. The use of Eq. (3-1) is straightforward. For instance, suppose that a particular zener diode has the following values: $V_Z = 30$ volts, $r_Z = 20$ ohms. When the diode just breaks down, there is no current flowing, and therefore the total voltage across the diode is simply 30 volts. When there is 1 ma of current through the diode, the voltage across the diode is the sum of V_Z and the additional drop across r_Z, that is,

$$V_Z + ir_Z = 30 + 10^{-3}(20) = 30.02 \text{ volts}$$

If we increase the current from 1 to 2 ma, the voltage across the zener diode becomes

$$V_Z + ir_Z = 30 + 2(10^{-3})(20) = 30.04 \text{ volts}$$

The voltage across the zener diode has progressively changed from 30 to 30.02 to 30.04 volts as we changed the current from 0 to 1 to 2 ma. Thus, we see that all the second approximation does is to take into account the small additional voltage drop across the diode that occurs when we increase the amount of current through the diode. This means that in a voltage regulator using a zener diode (see Examples 3-8 to 3-10) the output voltage of the regulator is not exactly constant but changes slightly when the current through the diode changes.

Note in Fig. 3-19a that the forward characteristic of the zener diode shows the knee voltage of 0.7 volt. The reason for this is that all zener diodes are made out of silicon; germanium diodes have too much reverse current below breakdown, which prevents them from having a sharp knee at the breakdown point; the silicon diodes, on the other hand, have such low reverse current below breakdown that a very sharp knee can be produced at the breakdown point.

SUMMARY

The ideal diode is the simplest and most useful approximation of a rectifier diode. There is no breakdown, no reverse current, and no forward voltage drop. Our circuit model for the ideal diode is a switch that is closed whenever conventional current flows in the direction of the triangle and open whenever conventional current tries to flow against the triangle.

The second and third approximations refine the ideal diode by taking into account the forward voltage drop across a diode. The second approximation allows 0.3 volt for germanium diodes and 0.7 volt for silicon diodes. The third approximation allows for an additional drop by taking the bulk resistance of the diode into account.

A real diode does have some reverse current through it when it is back-biased. Below breakdown we think of a diode as being a large resistance R_R. A very important difference between germanium and silicon diodes is that silicon diodes have much larger reverse resistances than comparable germanium diodes.

With enough voltage applied to the back-biased diode, the breakdown point is reached. Zener diodes have an extremely sharp knee at the breakdown point and an almost vertical breakdown region. The ideal-zener-diode approximation simply views a zener diode in the breakdown region as a battery with a voltage equal to the breakdown voltage V_Z. To refine this simple approximation we can put a small resistance r_Z in series with the battery to account for the not quite vertical breakdown characteristic.

GLOSSARY

avalanche   A breakdown phenomenon based upon minority carriers dislodging outer-shell electrons, which in turn dislodge more outer-shell electrons.

bulk resistance   The resistance of a diode well above the knee of the forward characteristic. This is the ohmic resistance of the p-type and n-type materials.

ideal diode   The first approximation of an ordinary rectifier diode. The circuit model is a switch.

negative clipper   A circuit that removes the negative parts of an input signal.

positive clipper   A circuit that removes the positive parts of an input signal.

zener diode   A specially processed silicon diode that has an extremely sharp breakdown point and an almost vertical breakdown region.

REVIEW QUESTIONS

1. When visualizing the ideal diode as a switch, what determines whether the switch is closed or open?
2. What is a positive clipper? A negative clipper? How can the clipping level be changed?
3. What is the equivalent circuit for the second approximation of a real diode? What does the IV characteristic look like?
4. Name one approach in obtaining square waves (approximately square) from sine waves.
5. What is the equivalent circuit for the third approximation of a real diode? What does the IV characteristic look like?
6. What does the forward, or bulk, resistance of a diode refer to? Name two ways of finding the approximate value of r_B.
7. As a general rule, when can we neglect the knee voltage of a diode? When can we neglect the bulk resistance of the diode?
8. How do we find the approximate value of the reverse resistance of a diode that is not operating in the breakdown region?
9. What is the outstanding advantage that silicon diodes have over germanium diodes?
10. What is a zener diode? What circuit device do we use to represent the ideal zener diode operating in the breakdown region?
11. What does the zener effect refer to? What does avalanche refer to? For breakdown voltages greater than about 6 volts, which effect is dominant?
12. What is one of the major uses of zener diodes?

PROBLEMS

3-1   In Fig. 3-20a, use the ideal-diode approximation to find the value of direct current I.

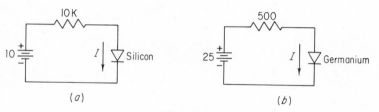

(*a*)   (*b*)

Fig. 3-20

3-2 In Fig. 3-20b, use the ideal-diode approximation to find I.

3-3 In Fig. 3-21a, sketch the waveform of v_{out}.

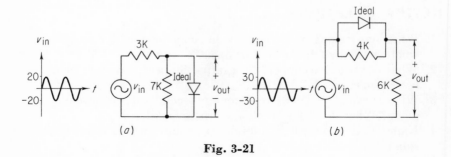

Fig. 3-21

3-4 In Fig. 3-21b, sketch the waveform of v_{out}.

3-5 Sketch the waveform of v_{out} in Fig. 3-22a.

3-6 Sketch the waveform of v_{out} in Fig. 3-22b.

3-7 Find the direct current I in Figs. 3-20a and b by using the second approximation.

3-8 Instead of using an ideal diode in Fig. 3-21a, use the second approximation of a silicon diode and sketch the waveform of v_{out}.

3-9 In Fig. 3-21b, replace the ideal diode by the second approximation of a silicon diode and sketch the waveform of v_{out}.

3-10 In Fig. 3-22a, use the second approximation of a silicon diode and sketch v_{out}.

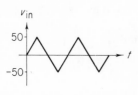
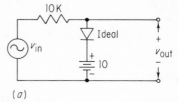

(a)

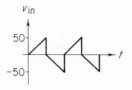
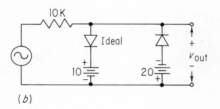

(b)

Fig. 3-22

3-11 In Fig. 3-22b, sketch v_{out} using the second approximation of a silicon diode in the place of the ideal diode.

3-12 In Fig. 3-20a, the silicon diode has a forward current I_F of 50 ma at 1 volt. Compute the approximate value of bulk resistance r_B and state why it is negligible in this circuit.

3-13 In Fig. 3-20b, the germanium diode has a forward current I_F of 10 ma at 1 volt. Compute the bulk resistance r_B and the value of direct current I.

3-14 In Fig. 3-23a, the silicon diode has a forward current I_F of 20 ma at 1 volt.

- (a) Compute the bulk resistance r_B.
- (b) Sketch the waveform of the current i using the ideal-diode approximation.
- (c) Sketch the waveform of the current i using the third approximation of the silicon diode.

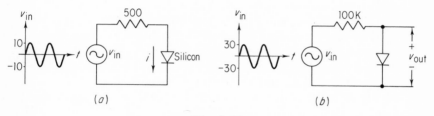

(a) (b)

Fig. 3-23

3-15 In the circuit of Fig. 3-23b, sketch the waveform of v_{out} for the following diodes:

- (a) A germanium diode with a reverse current of 0.125 ma for a reverse voltage of 50 volts. Neglect forward voltage drop.
- (b) A silicon diode with a reverse current of 1.25 μa for a reverse voltage of 50 volts. Neglect forward voltage drop.

3-16 In Fig. 3-24a, find the minimum and maximum current through the zener diode. Use the ideal-zener-diode approach.

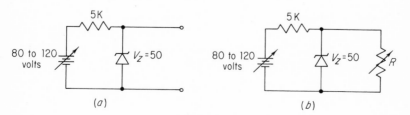

(a) (b)

Fig. 3-24

3-17 In Fig. 3-24b, use $R = 10$ kilohms. Find the minimum and maximum value of zener-diode current.

3-18 In Fig. 3-24b, find the value of R that causes the zener diode to come out of the breakdown region for the following source voltages:

(*a*) Source voltage equals 120 volts.

(*b*) Source voltage equals 80 volts.

3-19 In Fig. 3-24b, what is the maximum power dissipation in the 5-kilohm resistor for the given range of source voltage? What is the maximum power dissipation in the zener diode for any source or load condition?

3-20 In Fig. 3-24a, the zener diode has an $r_Z = 90$ ohms. Compute the minimum and maximum voltage appearing across the zener diode for the range of source voltage. Use the second approximation.

4 | Small-signal Diode Approximations

In the previous chapter we discussed large-signal diode approximations, that is, approximations that are suitable whenever the signal driving the diode is larger than the knee voltage. There are times, however, when the driving signal is smaller than the knee voltage; in this case we must use the small-signal diode approximations that will be developed in this chapter. In addition, we will review the superposition theorem, a theorem of great importance in transistor-circuit analysis.

4-1 The Superposition Theorem

The superposition theorem is widely used in science and engineering, as well as in more liberal subjects like economics and philosophy. To understand this important theorem, consider Fig. 4-1a. We have shown a linear system in which several causes are acting simultaneously to produce a net effect. This net effect is the result of all the causes acting together. The superposition theorem tells us that one approach to finding the net effect is the following: determine the individual effect produced by each cause acting by itself; all the individual effects added together then give the net effect. In other words, to find the net effect produced by all causes

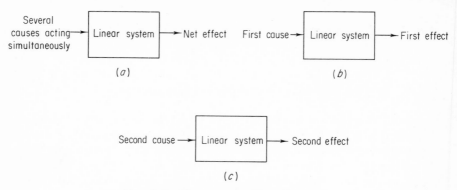

Fig. 4-1   The superposition theorem.

acting simultaneously in Fig. 4-1*a*, we single out any one cause and determine the effect it produces, as in Fig. 4-1*b*. Next, we select another cause and determine the effect it produces, as in Fig. 4-1*c*. We continue in this manner, finding the individual effect produced by each cause; finally, we add all the individual effects to obtain the net effect produced by all the causes acting simultaneously.

The superposition theorem sounds quite simple, and it is. Whenever many causes are acting together to produce a total effect, we can find this effect by isolating the causes, one at a time, to find the individual effects. Then by adding the individual effects we get the total effect. Remember, however, that we can apply the superposition theorem only to linear systems. A *linear system* is one in which the effect is directly proportional to the cause; in other words, if a given cause is producing an effect, doubling the size of the cause will double the size of the effect. If a system is nonlinear, there will not be a direct proportion between cause and effect, and therefore we cannot use superposition theorem.

The general proof of the superposition theorem is straightforward. Consider Fig. 4-2*a*. There is an effect y being produced by a cause x. In a linear system y is directly proportional to x; that is,

$$y = mx \tag{4-1}$$

where m is a constant of proportionality. Now suppose that the input is actually several causes acting simultaneously, as in Fig. 4-2*b*. In other words, suppose that

$$x = x_1 + x_2 + x_3 + \cdots$$

Then by substituting into Eq. (4-1) we get

$$y = m(x_1 + x_2 + x_3 + \cdots)$$

or

$$y = mx_1 + mx_2 + mx_3 + \cdots \tag{4-2}$$

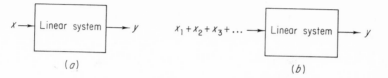

Fig. 4-2 General proof of superposition.

Examine this equation carefully; the proof of the superposition theorem is implied in it. Note that y is the total effect produced by all causes acting together. Also, on the right-hand side of this equation we have the individual effect produced by each cause acting by itself. In other words, mx_1 is the effect produced by the first cause; mx_2 is the effect produced by the second cause, and so on. Equation (4-2) tells us that we can add the individual effects to find the total effect.

To summarize the all-important idea of the superposition theorem we note:

1. The system must be linear.
2. The individual effect produced by each cause is found.
3. All the individual effects are added to find the total effect produced by all causes acting simultaneously.

4-2 Superposition in Electric Circuits

We have discussed the superposition theorem in its most general terms in order to establish the underlying notion behind this theorem. With the fundamental idea in mind, we now turn our attention to how the superposition theorem is applied to electric circuits. Specifically, we are interested in circuits in which two or more sources (causes) are acting simultaneously to produce a net voltage or current (effect). To find this voltage or current by superposition we find the component produced by each source and add all the components to obtain the net effect. Of course, the circuit must be linear, meaning that the currents produced are directly proportional to the sources causing them. A simple way to recognize a linear circuit is to determine whether or not the resistors, inductors, and capacitors remain fixed in value as the voltage across them changes. For instance, suppose a circuit contains a 1-kilohm resistor, a 1-henry inductor, and a 1-μf capacitor. If the values of these circuit elements remain at 1 kilohm, 1 henry, and 1 μf for different terminal voltages, the circuit is linear, and we can apply the superposition theorem to it.

In analyzing electric circuits we find the superposition theorem quite useful in determining the voltage or current in any part of a linear circuit driven by two or more sources. Let us summarize the superposition theorem as it applies in circuit analysis:

1. Compute the current (or voltage) produced by each source *with all other sources reduced to zero.*

2. Add the individual currents to find the net current produced by all sources acting simultaneously.

In applying step 1, reducing all other sources to zero means that voltage sources are shorted and current sources are opened. In applying step 2, adding the individual currents means *algebraic addition;* that is, if currents flow in the same direction, the magnitudes are added, but if the currents flow in opposite directions, the magnitudes are subtracted.

To bring out the full meaning of the superposition theorem, we will consider several examples. The circuit of Fig. 4-3a is a linear circuit with two voltage sources. What is the value of I_T in this circuit? One way to solve this problem is by applying superposition. We proceed as follows. First, determine how much current is produced by the left battery with the right one shorted, as in Fig. 4-3b. The current I_1 is the individual current produced by the left battery acting by itself. It is obvious that this current is

$$I_1 = \frac{45}{10 + 10\|10} = \frac{45}{15} = 3 \text{ amp to the right}$$

Incidentally, note the use of the vertical parallel lines in this equation. This will be our shorthand notation for two resistors in parallel. In

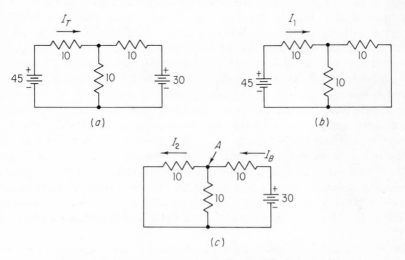

(a)

(b)

(c)

Fig. 4-3 Solving a circuit problem with superposition.

general, when we have two resistors R_1 and R_2 in parallel, we will indicate this by using $R_1 \| R_2$.

Next, we find the current produced by the right battery with the left one shorted, as shown in Fig. 4-3c. It is clear that the current I_B out of the battery will split when it reaches junction A. The current that we are after is I_2. From the circuit it is apparent that

$$I_B = \frac{30}{10 + 10 \| 10} = 2 \text{ amp}$$

and

$$I_2 = \frac{I_B}{2} = 1 \text{ amp to the left}$$

We now find the total current in the original circuit of Fig. 4-3a by algebraically adding the individual currents I_1 and I_2. Since the currents flow in opposite directions,

$$I_T = 3 - 1 = 2 \text{ amp to the right}$$

This is the current that will actually flow in the circuit when both batteries are acting together. This same result could have been obtained by using other methods, such as those derived from Kirchhoff's laws. For instance, we could have written two loop equations and solved them to find I_T. However, this latter approach is usually more difficult. The really important point here is that the superposition theorem offers us an alternate approach in the analysis of multisource circuits.

As another example of using the superposition theorem, consider the circuit of Fig. 4-4a. Again, there are two sources. How can we find the

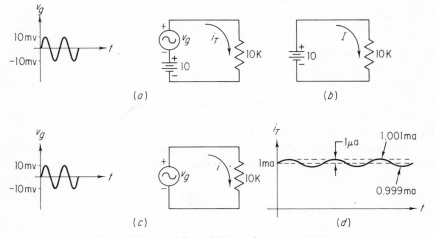

Fig. 4-4 Superposition of d-c and a-c components.

current i_T in the 10-kilohm resistor? We begin by finding the current produced by the battery, as shown in Fig. 4-4b. Obviously, the battery alone will produce a direct current of

$$I = \frac{10}{10^4} = 1 \text{ ma}$$

Next, we find the current produced by the a-c source with d-c source shorted, as shown in Fig. 4-4c. The signal out of the generator is a sine wave with a peak voltage of 10 mv. This voltage will produce a sine wave of current with a peak value of

$$I_p = \frac{10^{-2}}{10^4} = 10^{-6} = 1 \text{ } \mu\text{a}$$

To find the total current in the original circuit of Fig. 4-4a, we combine the a-c and the d-c components. The total current waveform is shown in Fig. 4-4d. Note that the current is a fluctuating current that varies from a low of 0.999 ma to a high of 1.001 ma.

We will use the superposition theorem frequently to analyze different transistor circuits, especially those circuits containing d-c and a-c sources. In drawing the equivalent circuits for the d-c and a-c sources it is important to remember the following:

1. Direct current cannot flow through a capacitor; therefore, *all capacitors look like open circuits in the d-c equivalent circuit.*

2. When a-c signals are involved, capacitors are generally used to couple or bypass the a-c signal. In order to accomplish this, the designer deliberately selects capacitors that are large enough to appear as *short circuits* to the a-c signal. Therefore, *when we draw the a-c equivalent circuit, we will show all capacitors as short circuits*, unless otherwise instructed.

As an example of using these two guides, consider Fig. 4-5a. What is the total voltage v_T simultaneously produced by the a-c and d-c sources?

The d-c equivalent circuit is shown in Fig. 4-5b. Since the capacitor is open to direct current, there can be no direct current in either 10-kilohm resistor. Therefore, the entire battery voltage must appear across the output terminals, that is, $V = 10$ volts.

The a-c equivalent circuit is shown in Fig. 4-5c. We will assume that the capacitor is large enough to appear essentially as a short circuit to the a-c signal. (The reader may verify that the capacitor does look like a very low impedance compared to 10 kilohms by calculating the capacitive reactance at 10 kHz.) Note that as far as the a-c signal is concerned, the circuit acts like a simple voltage divider. Since 10 kilohms is in series with 10 kilohms, the a-c output voltage v is one-half of the

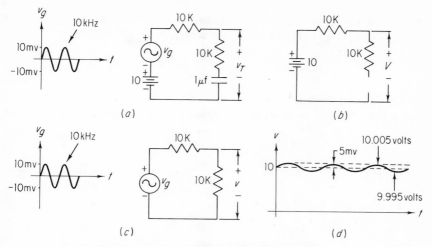

Fig. 4-5 A-c and d-c equivalent circuits.

a-c source voltage. In other words, the output voltage v is a sine wave with a peak value of 5 mv.

The total voltage v_T produced by both sources acting simultaneously is the sum of the a-c and d-c components. We have shown this voltage in Fig. 4-5d. Note carefully that it is a fluctuating voltage with a low of 9.995 volts and high of 10.005 volts. In other words, it is a d-c voltage of 10 volts with a 5-mv-peak sine wave superimposed on the d-c level.

A word about notation is appropriate at this time. In order to keep the d-c and a-c components distinct in the various formulas to be developed, we will use the following rules:

1. All d-c or fixed quantities will be denoted by capital letters. For instance, to represent a d-c voltage or current we will use V and I, respectively.

2. All a-c or varying quantities will be designated by lowercase letters. Thus, we will use v and i to represent a changing voltage or current.

Further refinements in our notation will be introduced as the need arises.

EXAMPLE 4-1

Find the voltage v_T appearing across the 10-ohm resistor in Fig. 4-6a.

SOLUTION

The d-c equivalent circuit is shown in Fig. 4-6b. The d-c voltage appearing across the 10-ohm resistor is approximately 10 mv, because the 10-ohm resistor and the 10-kilohm resistor form a voltage divider that divides the battery voltage by a factor of 1000. That is,

$$V = \frac{10}{10,010} \, 10 \cong \frac{1}{1000} \, 10 = 10 \text{ mv}$$

The a-c equivalent circuit is shown in Fig. 4-6c (the battery and capacitor have been shorted according to the usual rules). Note that

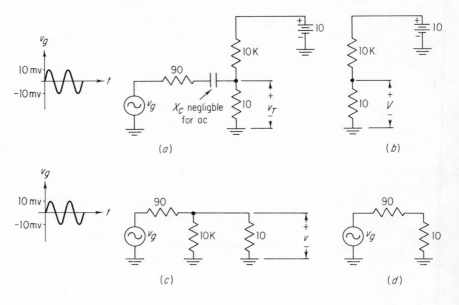

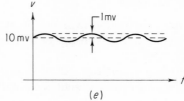

Fig. 4-6 Example 4-1.

for practical purposes the 10-ohm resistor in parallel with the 10-kilohm resistor is essentially 10 ohms; therefore we can redraw the a-c equivalent circuit, as shown in Fig. 4-6d. We can see that the a-c voltage v must be one-tenth of the a-c source voltage because of the 10:1 voltage divider. In other words, the a-c output voltage v is a sine wave with a peak value of about 1 mv.

The total voltage v_T produced by both sources acting simultaneously is the sum of the a-c and d-c components; this total voltage is shown in Fig. 4-6e. Note that it has an average value of 10 mv with a 1-mv-peak sine wave superimposed on this 10-mv level.

EXAMPLE 4-2

The reactance of the capacitor in Fig. 4-7a is very small as far as the a-c signal is concerned. Sketch the voltage v_T across the 10-kilohm resistor.

SOLUTION

The d-c equivalent circuit is shown in Fig. 4-7b. Since the capacitor is open to direct current, the d-c voltage V is equal to zero.

The a-c equivalent circuit is shown in Fig. 4-7c. Since the d-c source has been shorted, the two 10-kilohm resistors are in parallel as far as the a-c signal is concerned. The a-c equivalent circuit can be redrawn as shown in Fig. 4-7d. In this figure it is clear that the a-c voltage

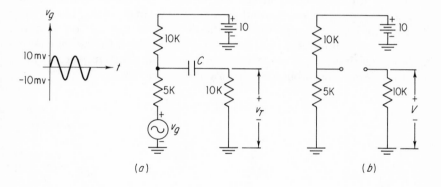

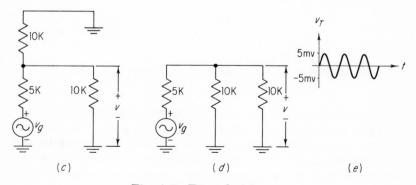

Fig. 4-7 Example 4-2.

across the output is one-half of the a-c source voltage. Therefore, the a-c voltage across the output is a sine wave with a peak value of 5 mv.

The total voltage v_T equals the sum of the d-c and a-c components, and is shown in Fig. 4-7e. In this case, there is no d-c component. In fact, coupling capacitors are generally used for this very purpose, namely, to pass the a-c component but to block the d-c component.

4-3   The A-C Resistance of a Diode

In order to apply the superposition theorem to diode and transistor circuit analysis we must discuss how a diode acts as far as a-c signals are concerned. We will see that if the a-c signal is *very* small, the diode resembles a resistance whose value is given by the ratio of the a-c voltage across the diode to the alternating current through the diode.

Let us begin our discussion by considering the circuit in Fig. 4-8a. A d-c source is in series with a *small* a-c source. What happens is quite simple: the d-c source establishes the average voltage across the diode, while the a-c source causes small changes above and below this average voltage. For instance, suppose that the d-c source voltage is 1 volt and the a-c source voltage is a 1-mv-peak sine wave. Then, the voltage across the diode will have an average value of 1 volt; in addition, there will be a fluctuation of 1 mv above and below this 1-volt level.

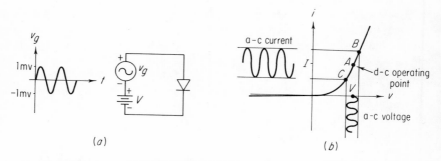

Fig. 4-8   The a-c resistance of a diode above the knee.

How much current flows through the diode? To answer this question, we draw a typical IV characteristic, as shown in Fig. 4-8b. Assume that we have adjusted the battery voltage so that the d-c operating point is well above the knee of the diode characteristic. The average operating point is point A; the d-c voltage and current at this operating point are V and I, respectively. We have shown a small a-c signal in Fig. 4-8b along the v axis. This a-c voltage causes the instantaneous current in the diode to change above and below the average value of I. On the positive half cycle the a-c voltage causes the diode current to change from point A to point B, and on the negative half cycle the current changes from A to C. If the a-c voltage is very small, the changes in current will be very small. In fact, notice that for small excursions, the instantaneous operating point of the diode will be moving along a segment of the curve that is *almost linear*. This means that the change in current is almost directly proportional to the change in voltage. For instance, suppose that a change of 1 mv produces a change of 0.1 ma; then a change of 2 mv will cause a change of about 0.2 ma.

The almost linear relation between small changes in voltage and current allows us to think of a diode as a *resistance* as far as *small a-c signals* are concerned. The value of this resistance is simply

$$r_{ac} = \frac{\Delta v}{\Delta i}$$

where Δv and Δi represent small changes in voltage and current about the d-c operating point. As an example, suppose that in Fig. 4-8b the changes in voltage and current between points B and C are $\Delta v = 1$ mv and $\Delta i = 0.1$ ma. As far as the a-c signal is concerned, the diode appears to be a resistance of

$$r_{ac} = \frac{\Delta v}{\Delta i} = \frac{10^{-3}}{0.1(10^{-3})} = 10 \text{ ohms}$$

What happens to the a-c resistance of the diode when we change the battery voltage? Suppose we adjust the battery voltage to a smaller value; then the d-c operating point will be lower down on the diode curve, as shown in Fig. 4-9a. Again there is an average voltage V and an average current I flowing through the diode. With the same small a-c voltage as before, the changes in current will be less than before as shown

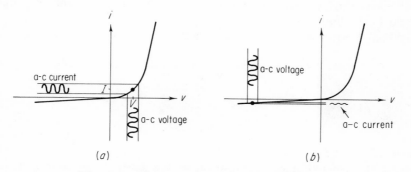

(a)   (b)

Fig. 4-9   The a-c resistance below the knee.

in Fig. 4-9a. Therefore, the a-c resistance of the diode is larger than it was before. As a matter of fact, it is clear that as we reduce the d-c current I through the diode, the a-c resistance r_{ac} will increase.

We can reverse-bias the diode to obtain the d-c operating point shown in Fig. 4-9b. In this case, the small a-c voltage produces extremely small changes in current. In other words, the a-c resistance of a diode is quite high in the reverse direction.

Let us summarize the key points of our discussion:

1. The d-c source establishes the operating point about which the a-c excursions take place.

2. For small a-c excursions the changes in voltage and current are almost linear (directly proportional).

3. As far as small a-c voltages and currents are concerned, the diode looks like a linear resistance whose value is given by

$$r_{ac} = \frac{\Delta v}{\Delta i}$$

4. In the forward direction the a-c resistance decreases when the direct current is increased.

4-4   Formulas for the A-C Resistance of a Diode

When a diode is *turned on hard*, that is, when it is operating well above the knee of the diode characteristic, the only opposition to the current is the bulk resistance of the diode (discussed in Chap. 3). In other words, well above the knee of the diode curve, only the ohmic resistance of the p- and n-type material remains to impede the current, as illustrated by Fig. 4-10a. Note that the ohmic resistance of the p- and n-type material is lumped into a single resistance called the bulk resistance r_B. Thus, well above the knee we can say that the a-c resistance of a diode is simply equal to the bulk resistance r_B.

When the operating point of the diode is *below* the knee of curve, the

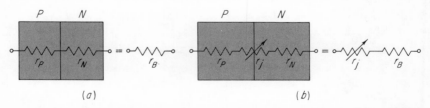

Fig. 4-10   A-c resistance. (a) Well above the knee; (b) junction and bulk resistance.

barrier potential also becomes important in retarding current. We can indicate this junction effect as shown in Fig. 4-10b, where we have shown an *additional* resistance r_j, the junction resistance of the diode. Hence, below the knee of the diode curve, we say that the a-c resistance of the diode is the sum of the bulk resistance and the junction resistance.

The value of junction resistance for any particular diode is not usually published on the data sheet for that diode. However, there are some approximations that are widely used for the value of junction resistance. Theoretically, it can be shown that at room temperature a perfect junction diode has a junction resistance of

$$r_j = \frac{25 \text{ mv}}{I} \tag{4-3}$$

where I is the d-c (average) value of current through the diode. For instance, suppose there is a direct current of 1 ma through the diode. Then the junction resistance is

$$r_j = \frac{25 \text{ mv}}{1 \text{ ma}} = 25 \text{ ohms}$$

If the direct current is changed to 2 ma, the junction resistance is changed to

$$r_j = \frac{25 \text{ mv}}{2 \text{ ma}} = 12.5 \text{ ohms}$$

Equation (4-3) gives the value of junction resistance for a *perfect* junction diode. *In practice,* we find that most junction diodes will fall in the range of

$$\frac{25 \text{ mv}}{I} < r_j < \frac{50 \text{ mv}}{I} \tag{4-4}$$

For instance, when there is 1 ma of direct current, the junction resistance of most diodes will fall in the range of 25 to 50 ohms. If the current is changed to 0.1 ma, the junction resistance will then be about 250 to 500 ohms.

When the diode is reverse-biased, it simply looks like a large resistance of R_R (discussed in Chap. 3). Recall that R_R is the reverse resistance and is calculated by taking the ratio of any reverse voltage to the corresponding current.

The main points of this section are simply this:

1. When the diode is reversed-biased, it has an a-c resistance of

$$r_{\text{ac}} = R_R$$

2. When the diode is forward-biased, it has an a-c resistance of

$$r_{\text{ac}} = r_j + r_B$$

3. As an approximation for most junction diodes we will use

$$\frac{25 \text{ mv}}{I} < r_j < \frac{50 \text{ mv}}{I}$$

EXAMPLE 4-3

A silicon diode has a forward current of 100 ma at 1 volt and a reverse current of 0.1 μa for a reverse voltage of 50 volts. Find the value of bulk resistance and reverse resistance.

SOLUTION

Using the method of Sec. 3-3, we get

$$r_B = \frac{1 - V_K}{I_F} = \frac{1 - 0.7}{10^{-1}} = 3 \text{ ohms}$$

And the reverse resistance is

$$R_R = \frac{V_R}{I_R} = \frac{50}{10^{-7}} = 500 \text{ megohms}$$

Incidentally, these two values r_B and R_R bracket the value of a-c resistance of the diode. In other words, the a-c resistance must be between 3 ohms and 500 megohms, depending upon the value of direct current through the diode.

EXAMPLE 4-4

For the diode of Example 4-3 find the a-c resistance in the forward region for the following direct currents:

(a) 0.1 ma.
(b) 50 ma.
Use Eq. (4-3).

SOLUTION

(a) The a-c resistance in the forward region is simply

$$r_{ac} = r_j + r_B$$

From the preceding example we already know that the diode has a bulk resistance of 3 ohms.

Next, we use Eq. (4-3) to find the junction resistance.

$$r_j = \frac{25 \text{ mv}}{I} = \frac{25 \text{ mv}}{0.1 \text{ ma}} = 250 \text{ ohms}$$

Hence, the a-c resistance for a d-c operating current of 0.1 ma is

$$r_{ac} = r_j + r_B = 250 + 3 = 253 \text{ ohms}$$

(b) When the direct current is increased to 50 ma, we get a new junction resistance of

$$r_j = \frac{25 \text{ mv}}{50 \text{ ma}} = 0.5 \text{ ohm}$$

Therefore, the a-c resistance becomes

$$r_{ac} = 0.5 + 3 = 3.5 \text{ ohms}$$

EXAMPLE 4-5

A germanium diode has a forward current of 35 ma at 1 volt and a reverse current of 100 μa for a reverse voltage of 50 volts. Find the following:

(a) The reverse resistance and the bulk resistance.

(b) The a-c resistance in the forward region for direct currents of 0.1, 1, 10, and 100 ma. Use Eq. (4-3).

SOLUTION

(a) The reverse resistance is

$$R_R = \frac{50}{100(10^{-6})} = 500 \text{ kilohms}$$

The bulk resistance is

$$r_B = \frac{1 - 0.3}{35(10^{-3})} = 20 \text{ ohms}$$

(b) To find the a-c resistances we first calculate the junction resistances for each direct current.

When $I = 0.1$ ma $\qquad r_j = \dfrac{25 \text{ mv}}{0.1 \text{ ma}} = 250 \text{ ohms}$

When $I = 1$ ma $\qquad r_j = \dfrac{25 \text{ mv}}{1 \text{ ma}} = 25 \text{ ohms}$

When $I = 10$ ma $\qquad r_j = \dfrac{25 \text{ mv}}{10 \text{ ma}} = 2.5 \text{ ohms}$

When $I = 100$ ma $\qquad r_j = \dfrac{25 \text{ mv}}{100 \text{ ma}} = 0.25 \text{ ohm}$

The value of a-c resistance is

$$r_{ac} = r_j + r_B$$

Thus, we need to add 20 ohms of bulk resistance to each of the junction resistances to find the a-c resistances. For direct currents of 0.1, 1, 10, and 100 ma, we get a-c resistances of 270, 45, 22.5, and 20.25 ohms, respectively.

Thus, we see that as we increase the direct current through the diode, the amount of resistance offered to a small a-c signal decreases from 270 to 20.25 ohms.

4-5   Applying the Superposition Theorem to Diode Circuits

Diodes and transistors are nonlinear devices. Nevertheless, when they are driven by small a-c signals, they operate over an almost linear part of the *IV* characteristic. Because of this, we can use the superposition theorem to analyze diode and transistor circuits driven by small a-c signal sources. Of special importance in our work are diode circuits in which there are large d-c sources and small a-c sources. For these circuits we can apply superposition as follows:

1.   Draw the d-c equivalent circuit. Compute the d-c component of the desired voltage or current. Also, calculate the amount of direct current *I* through the diode using the large-signal approximations of the preceding chapter (ideal-diode, second, or third approximations).

2.   Draw the a-c equivalent circuit, replacing the diode by its a-c resistance. Calculate the a-c component of the desired voltage or current.

3.   Combine the d-c and a-c components to obtain the total voltage or current produced by all sources acting together.

By a large d-c source we mean one whose voltage is large compared to the knee voltage of the diode. This allows us to use the large-signal approximations in computing the direct current *I* in the diode.

By a small a-c source we mean one that causes only a small excursion from the d-c operating point. As a guide, we will consider the a-c source as small if the peak alternating current is less than about 10 percent of the direct current. This rule of thumb is quite arbitrary and is intended only to give us a working criterion throughout this book. As an example, suppose that the direct current in the diode is 1 ma; we consider the a-c signal small if the peak alternating current is less than about 0.1 ma. As implied in the preceding section, the reason for requiring a small a-c signal is that the a-c resistance of the diode remains fixed only when the excursions from the operating point are small.

The following examples are important; understanding the use of superposition in these examples is essential to our later work in transistor circuit analysis.

EXAMPLE 4-6

The silicon diode shown in Fig. 4-11a has a bulk resistance of 1 ohm. The reactance of the coupling capacitor is very low at the frequency of the a-c source. Sketch the approximate waveform of the total voltage v_T across the diode. Use Eq. (4-3).

SOLUTION

First, we draw the d-c equivalent circuit as shown in Fig. 4-11b. It is clear from this circuit that the diode is forward-biased. For a silicon diode we can allow about 0.7 volt across it. The direct current through the diode is

$$I \cong \frac{30 - 0.7}{30(10^3)} \cong 1 \text{ ma}$$

Next, we draw the a-c equivalent circuit by shorting the capacitor and the d-c source (see Fig. 4-11c). Note that the junction resistance of the diode is about

$$r_j = \frac{25 \text{ mv}}{1 \text{ ma}} = 25 \text{ ohms}$$

and that the a-c resistance is

$$r_{ac} = r_j + r_B = 25 + 1 = 26 \text{ ohms}$$

In the a-c equivalent circuit (Fig. 4-11c) we see that the 30-kilohm resistor is so large compared to the 26 ohms of a-c resistance that we can neglect it. In other words, the a-c circuit is essentially a voltage

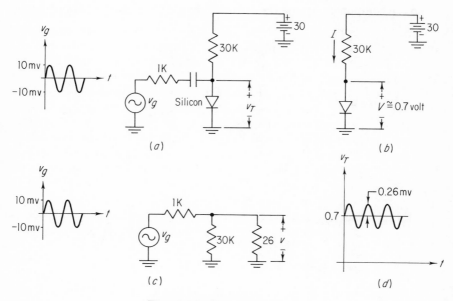

Fig. 4-11 Example 4-6.

divider consisting of a 1-kilohm resistor in series with a 26-ohm resistor. Therefore, the a-c component of voltage across the diode will have a peak value of approximately

$$v_{\text{peak}} \cong \frac{26}{1000} \, 10 \text{ mv} = 0.26 \text{ mv}$$

To find the total voltage across the diode we superimpose the d-c and a-c components. The waveform is shown in Fig. 4-11d. As indicated, the waveform has a d-c (average) value of 0.7 volt plus an a-c voltage with a peak value of 0.26 mv.

Note that if we were to reduce the value of the d-c voltage source, this would result in less direct current through the diode; the a-c resistance of the diode would increase, which, in turn, would produce a larger a-c component across the output. Thus, by varying the value of the d-c voltage source the diode becomes a voltage-controlled resistance.

Example 4-7

The germanium diode in Fig. 4-12a has a bulk resistance r_B of 3 ohms. The capacitors have extremely small reactance to the a-c signal. Sketch the output voltage waveform. Use Eq. (4-3).

Solution

First, visualize the d-c equivalent circuit; notice that there can be no d-c component across the output because the capacitor appears open

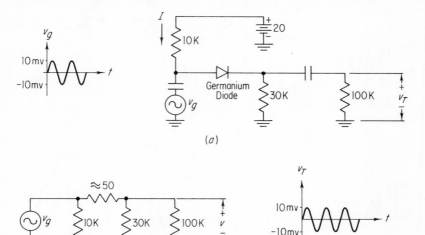

Fig. 4-12   Example 4-7.

to direct current. The direct current flowing through the diode passes
from the battery through the 10-kilohm resistor, through the diode,
and through the 30-kilohm resistor. Therefore, we can compute the
direct current through the diode as

$$I = \frac{20 - 0.3}{(10 + 30)(10^3)} \cong \frac{20}{40(10^3)} = 0.5 \text{ ma}$$

Next, we can draw the a-c equivalent circuit, as illustrated by Fig.
4-12b. The a-c resistance of the diode is approximately

$$r_{ac} = r_j + r_B = \frac{25 \text{ mv}}{0.5 \text{ ma}} + 3 \cong 50 \text{ ohms}$$

In Fig. 4-12b, the 50-ohm diode resistance is in series with the 30 kilohms shunted by 100 kilohms. This means that only a small part of the
a-c source voltage is dropped across the diode; therefore, almost all the
source voltage appears across the 100-kilohm resistor.

The final output waveform is given in Fig. 4-12c. For practical purposes, this waveform is the same as that of the a-c source.

EXAMPLE 4-8

Find the total current i_T in the diode of Fig. 4-13a. The bulk resistance and the knee voltage are negligible; the reactance of the capacitor
is very small to the a-c signal.

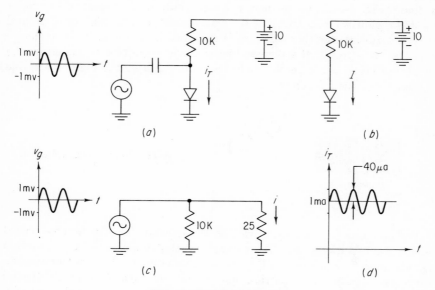

Fig. 4-13 Example 4-8.

SOLUTION

In the d-c equivalent circuit of Fig. 4-13b we can see that the approximate value of the direct current is

$$I \cong \frac{10}{10(10^3)} = 1 \text{ ma}$$

The a-c resistance of the diode is about 25 ohms if we use Eq. (4-3). In the a-c equivalent circuit of Fig. 4-13c we can see that the alternating current in the diode is a sine wave with a peak value of

$$i_{\text{peak}} = \frac{1 \text{ mv}}{25 \text{ ohms}} = 0.04 \text{ ma} = 40 \text{ } \mu\text{a}$$

The total current through the diode is the sum of the d-c and a-c components. The current waveform is given in Fig. 4-13d, where we see that the current has an average value of 1 ma and an a-c component with a peak value of 40 μa.

4-6 Diode Capacitance in the Reverse Region

We know that in the reverse region a diode acts like a large resistance R_R. There is also some capacitance that must be taken into account at higher frequencies. Recall that there is the so-called depletion region or layer in a diode (Fig. 4-14a). Since there are essentially no free electrons or holes in this region, we can think of it as an insulator. The regions of p- and n-type material on either side of this depletion layer contain many charge carriers. As a result, the reverse-biased diode resembles a capacitor: the depletion layer acts like the dielectric and the p and n regions are like the plates of the capacitor.

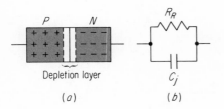

Fig. 4-14 Junction capacitance.

We can now use an improved approximation for the reverse-biased diode. Such a diode acts like a large resistance shunted by a junction capacitance C_j, as shown in Fig. 4-14b. The value of the junction capacitance (also called the *depletion-layer* or *barrier capacitance*) will depend upon the size of the reverse voltage. When the reverse voltage is increased, the depletion layer becomes wider because charges move away from the junction. This is analogous to the plates of a capacitor moving further apart and means that the diode capacitance decreases with an increase in reverse voltage. (Recall that a parallel-plate capacitor has a capacitance given by $C = \epsilon A/d$.)

Two widely used formulas for finding the approximate value of the junction capacitance are the following.

For junction diodes of the alloy type,

$$C_j = \frac{C_0}{\sqrt{V_R + V_K}} \tag{4-5}$$

and for junction diodes of the grown type,

$$C_j = \frac{C_0}{\sqrt[3]{V_R + V_K}} \tag{4-6}$$

where C_j is the capacitance seen by a small a-c signal
V_R is the magnitude of the reverse voltage
V_K is the magnitude of the knee voltage
C_0 is a reference value of capacitance

The a-c equivalent circuit of Fig. 4-14b is a useful approximation of a back-biased diode. Whether or not the capacitance is important depends upon the frequency of operation. Specifically, when the frequency is so low that the capacitive reactance is much higher than the reverse resist-

Fig. 4-15 Equivalent circuits. (a) Very low frequency; (b) very high frequency.

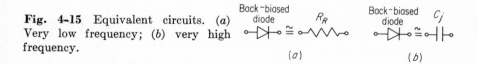

ance, we can disregard the capacitance and use the equivalent circuit of Fig. 4-15a. On the other hand, when the frequency is so high that the capacitive reactance is much smaller than the reverse resistance, we can use the equivalent circuit of Fig. 4-15b.

EXAMPLE 4-9

A silicon diode of the alloy type has a reverse current of 1 μa when the reverse voltage is 50 volts. Find the reverse resistance. Also, find the junction capacitance for reverse voltages of 5 and 10 volts. The value of C_0 is 10 pf.

SOLUTION

First, we find R_R.

$$R_R = \frac{V_R}{I_R} = \frac{50}{10^{-6}} = 50 \text{ megohms}$$

Next, we get the junction capacitance using Eq. (4-5) since the diode is an alloy type. When $V_R = 5$ volts

$$C_j = \frac{10(10^{-12})}{\sqrt{5 + 0.7}} = 4.18 \text{ pf}$$

When $V_R = 10$ volts,

$$C_j = \frac{10(10^{-12})}{\sqrt{10 + 0.7}} = 3.06 \text{ pf}$$

The a-c equivalent circuits for each value of reverse voltage are shown in Fig. 4-16. These circuits are the way that a diode looks to a small a-c signal.

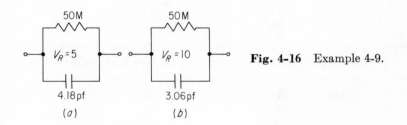

Fig. 4-16 Example 4-9.

EXAMPLE 4-10

The data sheet for a silicon diode indicates that it is an alloy type and has a capacitance of 50 pf for a reverse voltage of 4 volts. Find the value of C_0 and then find the value of C_j for a reverse voltage of 20 volts.

SOLUTION

(a) First, we substitute $V_R = 4$ and $C_j = 50$ pf into Eq. (4-5).

$$C_j = \frac{C_0}{\sqrt{V_R + V_K}}$$

$$50(10^{-12}) = \frac{C_0}{\sqrt{4 + 0.7}}$$

By solving this equation we get $C_0 = 108$ pf.

(b) Now we can find the value of junction capacitance for a reverse voltage of 20 volts.

$$C_j = \frac{108(10^{-12})}{\sqrt{20 + 0.7}} = 23.8 \text{ pf}$$

Note how the junction capacitance has changed from 50 pf (reverse voltage of 4 volts) to 23.8 pf (reverse voltage of 20 volts). In effect, we have a voltage-controlled capacitance. This ability to change the diode capacitance by varying the reverse voltage leads to a number of interesting applications in frequency modulation and control.

SUMMARY

A linear circuit is one whose resistors, capacitors, and inductors maintain constant values even though the voltage across them changes.

The superposition theorem allows us to analyze linear circuits containing more than one source. The basic approach in using superposition is to compute the voltage or current produced by one source at a time. The sum of the individual voltages and currents then gives the total effect produced by all sources.

Circuits containing a d-c source and an a-c source are of special importance in transistor circuit analysis. In applying superposition to these circuits we draw a d-c equivalent and an a-c equivalent circuit. In the d-c equivalent circuit all capacitors are open circuits. In the a-c equivalent circuit the capacitors normally look like short circuits.

The a-c resistance of a diode is the resistance that the diode presents to a small a-c signal. This resistance depends upon the amount of direct current flowing through the diode.

The superposition theorem can be applied to diode circuits provided we follow the modified procedure discussed in Sec. 4-5.

The capacitance of a reverse-biased diode appears in shunt with the reverse resistance. Since the depletion layer widens when the reverse voltage is increased, the diode capacitance decreases. At extremely low frequencies the diode acts like a resistance because the capacitance effects are negligible, whereas at very high frequencies the diode acts primarily like a capacitance.

GLOSSARY

a-c equivalent circuit   The circuit used in computing the a-c component. This circuit is obtained by reducing all d-c sources to zero, replacing all diodes by their a-c resistances, and replacing all coupling capacitors by short circuits.

a-c resistance   The resistance that a diode presents to a small a-c signal. The value of this resistance can be found by computing the ratio of a change in voltage to the change in current about the d-c operating point.

bulk resistance   The ohmic resistance of the *p*- and *n*-type material. The bulk resistance is the only resistance well above the knee of the diode curve.

d-c equivalent circuit   The circuit used in computing the d-c component. This circuit is obtained by reducing all a-c sources to zero and replacing all capacitors by open circuits.

junction capacitance   This is the capacitance produced by the depletion layer and the *p* and *n* materials on each side of the depletion layer.

junction resistance   The effects of barrier potential can be handled by means of a resistance as far as small a-c signals are concerned. This resistance is called the junction resistance and can be approximated by Eqs. (4-3) and (4-4).

linear system   One in which effects are directly proportional to causes.

superposition   In a linear system where several causes are acting simultaneously to produce an effect, this effect can be found by adding the individual effects produced by all the causes considered one at a time.

REVIEW QUESTIONS

1. What is the superposition theorem? To what kind of circuits can we apply it?
2. What is a linear circuit? What can be said about the values of resistors, capacitors, and inductors in a linear circuit?
3. How do we treat a capacitor when considering the d-c equivalent circuit? How do we usually visualize capacitors when drawing the a-c equivalent circuit?
4. We use capital letters to designate what kind of quantities? Lowercase letters are used for what?
5. How did we define the a-c resistance of a diode?
6. What happens to the size of the a-c resistance r_{ac} when the direct current in the diode is increased?
7. What is the formula for the junction resistance of a diode? How do we find the a-c resistance of the diode when it is forward-biased? Reverse-biased?

8. Describe our procedure for applying superposition to diode circuits containing large d-c and small a-c sources.
9. What is our rule for determining whether or not an a-c signal is small?
10. When the reverse voltage is increased, what happens to the width of the depletion layer? And to the junction capacitance?
11. Is the diode capacitance important at low or high frequency? Why?

PROBLEMS

4-1 Use the superposition theorem to find the current in the 10-ohm resistor of Fig. 4-17.

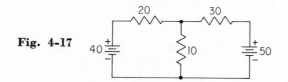

Fig. 4-17

4-2 Use superposition to find the current in the 20-ohm resistor of Fig. 4-17.

4-3 In Fig. 4-18a, sketch the waveform of current in the 30-kilohm resistor. Sketch the waveform of voltage across the 30-kilohm resistor.

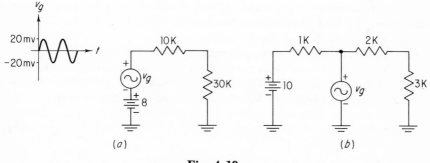

Fig. 4-18

4-4 In Fig. 4-18b, the a-c source is generating a sine-wave voltage with a peak value of 50 mv. Sketch the waveform of voltage across the 3-kilohm resistor.

4-5 Sketch the voltage waveform across the 1-kilohm resistor of Fig. 4-19a. The reactance of the capacitor is very small.

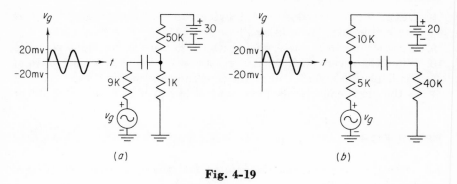

Fig. 4-19

4-6 Sketch the voltage waveform across the 40-kilohm resistor of Fig. 4-19b. The reactance of the capacitor to the a-c signal is very small.

4-7 A diode has a current of 1 ma flowing through it when the voltage across the diode is 0.71 volt. If the voltage is increased to 0.715 volts, the current becomes 1.1 ma. Find the a-c resistance of the diode.

4-8 A germanium diode has a forward current of 55 ma at 1 volt. What is the approximate value of bulk resistance r_B?

4-9 A silicon diode has a forward current of 80 ma at 1 volt. What is the approximate value of bulk resistance?

4-10 A diode has a bulk resistance of 2 ohms. Calculate the junction resistance and the a-c resistance for the following direct currents: 0.1, 0.5, 1, and 5 ma. Use Eq. (4-3).

4-11 What is the a-c resistance of the silicon diode of Prob. 4-9 when a direct current of 0.75 ma flows through the diode?

4-12 In Fig. 4-20a find the following:

    (a) The approximate direct current in the diode.

    (b) The approximate peak value of the alternating current in the diode.

4-13 If the d-c supply in Fig. 4-20a is increased to 60 volts, what will the direct current become? What will the peak current become?

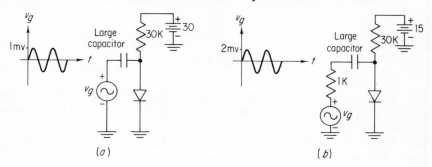

Fig. 4-20

4-14 In Fig. 4-20*b*, what is the direct current approximately? The approximate peak value of the alternating current?

4-15 In Fig. 4-20*a*, what happens to the alternating current in diode if the 30-kilohm resistor is changed to a 60-kilohm resistor?

4-16 In Fig. 4-20*b*, how much a-c voltage appears across the diode when the 30-kilohm resistor is changed to a 15-kilohm resistor?

4-17 In Fig. 4-21, find:

(*a*) The direct current in each diode.

(*b*) The peak value of the a-c voltage *v* across the output terminals.

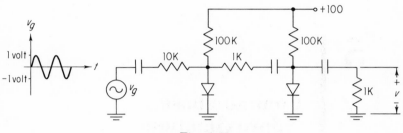

Fig. 4-21

4-18 A reverse voltage of 25 volts is applied to a grown type of silicon diode. What is the junction capacitance if the diode has a $C_0 = 75$ pf? What is the capacitive reactance at 1 kHz? At 1 MHz?

5 | Common-base Approximations

In its physical appearance the transistor is nothing more than two back-to-back diodes; however, because the spacing between these diodes is so small, a new phenomenon takes place in a transistor. This phenomenon makes it possible for us to obtain one of the most important effects in electronics, namely, amplification.

In this chapter we study the common-base connection of a transistor. After discussing the basic idea behind transistor action, we develop a transistor approximation called the *ideal transistor*, which makes it possible to analyze transistor circuits rapidly and easily. Even though the ideal transistor is only a simple approximation of an actual transistor, we find in practice that the ideal transistor is adequate for most everyday needs; it is quite useful for troubleshooting and initial design of transistor circuits.

There are more exact methods than the ideal transistor; we discuss these in later chapters after the basic idea of the transistor has become fixed.

5-1 Terminology and Schematic Symbols

A transistor is made by *growing, alloying,* or *diffusing* pieces of p-type and n-type materials together. A *p-n-p* transistor is made by placing

n-type material between two pieces of p-type material, as symbolized in Fig. 5-1a. The larger region of p-type material is called the *collector*, and the other region of p-type material is called the *emitter*. The region in the middle is called the *base*. Note in Fig. 5-1a that the transistor is like two back-to-back diodes.

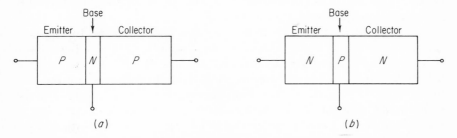

Fig. 5-1   (a) Structure of a p-n-p transistor; (b) structure of an n-p-n transistor.

Of course, we can put a piece of p-type material between two pieces of n-type material, as indicated in Fig. 5-1b. This would be an n-p-n transistor.

The relative sizes of the emitter, base, and collector are not accurately shown in Fig. 5-1. Of special importance is the fact that the base region is actually very *thin*. The reason for this will be brought out shortly. Also, the actual shape of the transistor can be different from the symbolic sketch of Fig. 5-1; the important idea is that no matter what the actual shape of the pieces, there is a piece of material between two regions of the opposite type of material.

In Fig. 5-2a and b we have shown the schematic symbols commonly used to represent transistors (sometimes the circle is omitted). An arrowhead is placed on the emitter but not on the collector. The direction of

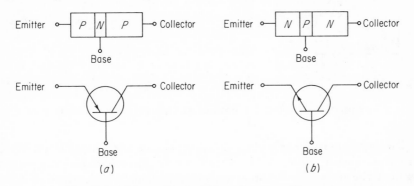

Fig. 5-2   Schematic symbols. (a) p-n-p; (b) n-p-n.

the arrowhead, like the triangle in a diode, points in the easy direction of *conventional current*, that is, *from the p- to the n-type material*. For instance, in Fig. 5-2a the *p-n* diode on the left conducts conventional current easily from the emitter to the base; in the schematic symbol, therefore, we show an arrowhead from the emitter to the base. Similarly, in Fig. 5-2b conventional current would flow easily from base to emitter, and we therefore show an arrowhead from base to emitter.

The collector-base part of a transistor also forms a diode. In Fig. 5-2a the easy direction of conventional current is from collector to base. Even though it is not customary to show an arrowhead on the collector, it is helpful to *visualize* an arrowhead pointing from the collector into the base in Fig. 5-2a. In Fig. 5-2b we can visualize an arrowhead pointing from the base to the collector. Thus, whenever we see the schematic symbol of transistor, we can visualize an arrowhead on the collector pointing in the same direction as the emitter arrowhead.

5-2   Biasing the Transistor

What happens when we apply voltages to the transistor? Let us consider an *n-p-n* transistor driven by two d-c supplies, as shown in Fig. 5-3a. Note that the base is grounded; this configuration is called the *grounded-base* or *common-base* connection (the base is common to both loops). As already indicated, the transistor is like two back-to-back diodes. For convenience, we will call the diode on the left, formed by the emitter and the base, the *emitter diode*. The diode on the right, formed by the collector and the base, will be called the *collector diode*.

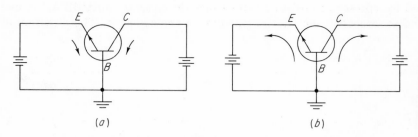

Fig. 5-3   Biasing. (*a*) Both diodes off; (*b*) both diodes on.

By inspection of Fig. 5-3a, both the emitter and the collector diodes are back-biased, since the batteries try to force conventional current against the direction of the arrowheads (visualize an arrowhead out of the collector). Therefore, only a small reverse current flows in each diode.

Suppose that we reverse both batteries as indicated in Fig. 5-3b. What happens now? In this case, both diodes are forward-biased, and therefore a large current can flow in each diode.

In Fig. 5-3a and b nothing of any consequence is taking place. Either both diodes are *off*, or both diodes are *on*. These results are of little importance because we can obtain the same results by using two separate p-n diodes instead of a transistor.

What makes the transistor different? Consider Fig. 5-4. In this case, *the emitter diode is forward-biased, and the collector diode is back-biased.* Our instinct tells us that there should be a large emitter current and a small collector current. *This is not what happens!* What actually happens

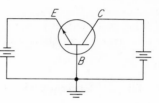

Fig. 5-4 Emitter diode forward-biased and collector diode reversed-biased.

is that there is a large emitter current and an almost equally large collector current. This unexpected phenomenon makes the transistor the important device that it is. Instead of having a small collector current because the collector diode is back-biased, we have a large collector current.

Here is the reason for the large collector current. In Fig. 5-5a (equivalent to Fig. 5-4) there is an excess of free electrons in the n-type emitter region. Since the emitter diode is forward-biased, these free electrons move to the right and enter the base region. Because the base region is deliberately made *very thin* and is *very lightly doped*, most of these free electrons do not recombine; instead, they diffuse into the collector-base depletion region, where they are swept across the junction into the col-

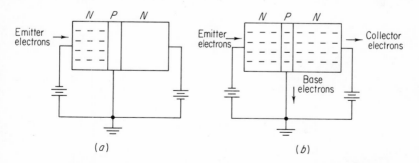

Fig. 5-5 Emitter electrons captured by the collector.

lector. They are then attracted and collected by the positive terminal of the collector supply, as shown in Fig. 5-5b.

Thus we see that the emitter injects free electrons into the base. Because the base is extremely thin and lightly doped, these electrons pass into the collector region, where they are immediately attracted by the positive terminal of the collector supply. *Almost all the free electrons that enter the base pass through to the collector.*

To summarize the circuit action for Fig. 5-4:

1. Under normal conditions we *forward-bias the emitter diode and back-bias the collector diode.*
2. The size of the collector current is *almost equal* to the size of the emitter current ($i_C \cong i_E$).
3. The base current is very small and equals the difference of the emitter current and the collector current ($i_B = i_E - i_C$).

5-3 The *IV* Characteristics of a Common-base Transistor

In order to obtain a fuller idea of how the currents and voltages are related in a common-base (CB) connection, let us consider a hypothetical experiment. A transistor is connected as shown in Fig. 5-6a. Note that the emitter diode is forward-biased and the collector diode is back-biased.

What is the relation between the emitter current and the emitter voltage? The current-voltage relation in the emitter diode depends to some extent upon the value of the collector voltage. Suppose that arbitrarily we set the collector supply to 1 volt. In the emitter circuit here is what we would find. When we increase the emitter battery supply, the emitter current will increase slowly at first; however, after v_{BE} has reached a few tenths of a volt, the emitter current will increase significantly with a further increase in voltage.

The graph for i_E vs. v_{BE} is shown in Fig. 5-6b. Note that this graph is

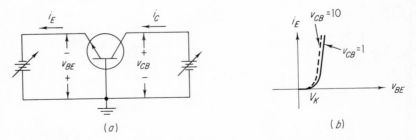

Fig. 5-6 (*a*) Obtaining *IV* curves; (*b*) emitter-diode curve.

the typical graph of a semiconductor diode. The emitter current is small until reaching the knee voltage, and then it turns up sharply above the knee. As observed in our discussions of diodes, the knee voltage is about 0.3 volt for germanium and 0.7 volt for silicon.

What effect does collector voltage have upon emitter current? If we increased the collector voltage from 1 to 10 volts, the relation between emitter current and voltage would change slightly, as indicated by the dashed curve of Fig. 5-6b. This suggests that there is a feedback effect from the collector to the emitter; however, this feedback effect is small, as implied by the small separation between the two graphs. *As a first approximation we can definitely say that the emitter-base part of a transistor acts like an ordinary semiconductor diode.*

Now, we turn our attention to the collector circuit. How is collector current related to collector voltage? From our discussion of Sec. 5-2 we know that almost all the electrons leaving the emitter pass through the base into the collector. In other words, *collector current almost equals emitter current.* In order to get a graph of i_C vs. v_{CB} we must specify a particular value of emitter current. Arbitrarily, suppose that the emitter supply is adjusted to produce an emitter current of 1 ma. In the collector circuit here is what we would find. When we increase the collector voltage, the collector current will increase only slightly because almost all the emitter electrons are captured by the collector; increasing the collector voltage cannot significantly increase the collector current because it is more or less fixed by the size of the emitter current.

Figure 5-7a graphically illustrates what takes place in the collector circuit. Note that the collector current remains fixed at about 1 ma even though the collector voltage is increased. Of course, there is a limit; when the breakdown voltage of the collector diode is exceeded, a significant increase in current can take place. Normally, the transistor is operated below this breakdown voltage.

The graph of Fig. 5-7a below the breakdown point suggests the concept of an ideal current source. An ideal current source is simply a hypothetical device whose current is independent of the voltage across it. In

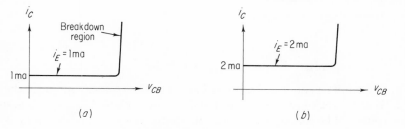

Fig. 5-7 Collector curves.

other words, below breakdown the collector current remains at about 1 ma even though the collector voltage is being increased.

If the emitter current is changed, the collector current will change. For instance, if we increase the emitter supply so that 2 ma of emitter current flows, we will find that the collector current almost equals 2 ma. Further, when we increase the collector voltage, very little increase occurs in the collector current until we reach the breakdown voltage, as indicated by Fig. 5-7b. Again note that the collector acts like an ideal current source below the breakdown voltage. That is, below the breakdown point the collector current remains at about 2 ma even though we increase the collector voltage.

The graphs of Fig. 5-7 suggest that the collector diode is a *controlled current source* for any collector voltage between zero and the breakdown voltage. In other words, the collector current is controlled by the emitter current. When we change the emitter current to a new value, the collector current will change to this new value. Further, changing collector voltage has no significant effect on collector current.

If we continue to obtain graphs like those of Fig. 5-7 for new values of emitter current, we can construct the typical composite characteristic shown in Fig. 5-8. This characteristic shows the relation of i_C to v_{CB} below the breakdown voltage. Note that for $i_E = 0$, there is a small amount of collector current. This small amount of current is the reverse current of the back-biased collector diode. Note also that for any value of emitter current it is necessary to reduce the collector voltage to slightly less than zero in order to shut off the collector current.

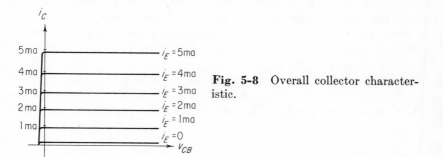

Fig. 5-8 Overall collector characteristic.

Let us summarize the key points of our discussion:

1. The emitter diode acts almost like an ordinary semiconductor diode.

2. Below breakdown the collector diode acts almost like an ideal current source. The value of this current source is controlled by, and is almost equal to, the emitter current ($i_C \cong i_E$).

3. The collector diode will break down if its breakdown voltage is exceeded. Normally a transistor is operated well below the breakdown voltage.

5-4 The Alpha of a Transistor

One of the important transistor quantities is what is called the α of a transistor. Actually, there are both a d-c α and an a-c α. By definition, the d-c α is

$$\alpha_{dc} = \frac{i_C}{i_E} \tag{5-1}$$

For instance, in Fig. 5-9a there is an emitter current of 1 ma and a collector current of 0.98 ma. According to Eq. (5-1), the d-c α is nothing more than the ratio of these currents. That is,

$$\alpha_{dc} = \frac{0.98 \text{ ma}}{1 \text{ ma}} = 0.98$$

The α_{dc} is actually a measure of the quality of a transistor. Ordinarily, the higher the α_{dc}, the better the transistor, in the sense that the collector current more closely equals the emitter current. For a perfect transistor the collector current equals the emitter current, and therefore the α_{dc} equals unity. In practice we find that almost all transistors have an α_{dc} in the range of 0.95 to 0.999 . . . . In other words, the collector current is usually no lower than about 95 percent of the emitter current and often much closer to 98 or 99 percent of the emitter current.

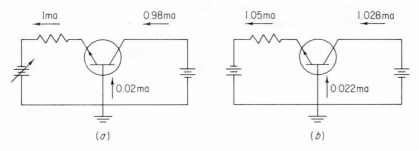

Fig. 5-9 D-c and a-c α.

There is also an a-c α for a transistor. This refers to the ratio of a *change* in collector current to the corresponding *change* in emitter current. For example, suppose that we change the emitter supply V_{EE} in Fig. 5-9a and that we then have currents of 1.05 and 1.028 ma, as shown in Fig. 5-9b. By definition, the a-c α is

$$\alpha = \frac{\Delta i_C}{\Delta i_E} \qquad (5\text{-}2)$$

where Δi_C is a small change in collector current and Δi_E is a small change in emitter current. In our example the change in collector current is

$$\Delta i_C = 1.028 - 0.98 \text{ ma} = 0.048 \text{ ma}$$

and the corresponding change in emitter current is

$$\Delta i_E = 1.05 - 1 \text{ ma} = 0.05 \text{ ma}$$

Hence, we calculate an α of

$$\alpha = \frac{0.048 \text{ ma}}{0.05 \text{ ma}} = 0.96$$

Often the values of the d-c and a-c α's are almost equal. In general, we find in practice that the a-c α also is typically in the range of 0.95 to 0.999 . . . .

5-5   The Ideal Transistor

In Chap. 3 we idealized the diode by simple approximations that retained the essential features of the diode while discarding the less important qualities. These approximations allowed us to analyze diode circuits easily and rapidly. We now wish to approximate the transistor in a similar way.

First, consider the emitter-base part of a transistor. We know that a change in collector voltage causes only a slight feedback into the emitter circuit. As an ideal approximation of the transistor we disregard this small amount of interaction between collector and emitter and say that for practical purposes the emitter diode acts like a typical semiconductor diode with the characteristic shown in Fig. 5-10a.

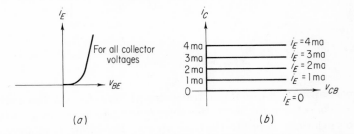

Fig. 5-10   Ideal transistor. (a) Emitter curve; (b) collector curves.

Next, consider the collector-base part of the transistor. We can idealize the characteristics of the collector by using the graphs of Fig. 5-10b. Note that there is no breakdown. Each curve is perfectly horizontal, and collector current equals emitter current. Of course, this is an ideal approximation; nevertheless, it does represent the most important features of transistor action, namely, that the collector is a controlled current source.

The circuit interpretation of the ideal n-p-n transistor is shown in Fig. 5-11a. We treat the emitter diode as being just that, a diode. However, the collector diode is represented by a current source (the circle with the arrow through it is the most common schematic symbol for a current source). Remember that whenever we encounter the schematic symbol of the current source as shown in Fig. 5-11a, we understand by definition that we have a device whose current is independent of the voltage across it. In Fig. 5-11a the current flowing in the collector is equal to i_E.

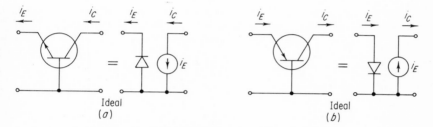

Fig. 5-11 Equivalent circuits for ideal transistor.

Analogously, the ideal p-n-p transistor is represented by a diode and a current source of opposite polarity from the n-p-n, as shown in Fig. 5-11b.

Here. are the key ideas for the *ideal-transistor* approximation. As long as the emitter diode is forward-biased and the collector diode is back-biased, then:

1. The emitter diode acts like an ordinary semiconductor diode.

2. The collector diode acts like an ideal current source whose value equals the emitter current ($i_C = i_E$).

EXAMPLE 5-1

Find the value of collector current i_C in the circuit of Fig. 5-12a.

SOLUTION

First, we visualize the circuit as shown in Fig. 5-12b, where we have replaced the transistor by an ideal transistor. In this circuit it is clear that the emitter diode is forward-biased. We know that only a few tenths of a volt appear across the emitter diode; therefore, we can say that practically the entire 10 volts from the supply appears across the 10-kilohm resistor. Thus, the emitter current is

$$i_E \cong \frac{10}{10(10^3)} = 1 \text{ ma}$$

Since the collector and emitter currents are almost equal, the collector current must equal about 1 ma.

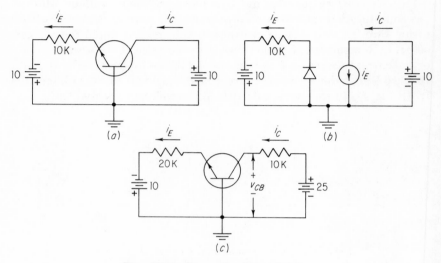

Fig. 5-12   Examples 5-1 and 5-2.

EXAMPLE 5-2

Find the collector-base voltage v_{CB} in the circuit of Fig. 5-12c.

SOLUTION

First, find the emitter current. It is approximately

$$i_E \cong \frac{10}{20(10^3)} = 0.5 \text{ ma}$$

The collector current is therefore about 0.5 ma. This 0.5 ma flows from right to left through the 10-kilohm resistor and produces a voltage of

$$0.5 \ (10^{-3})(10)(10^3) = 5 \text{ volts}$$

To find v_{CB} we apply Kirchhoff's voltage law to the collector loop circuit. In other words, v_{CB} must equal the supply voltage minus the voltage drop across the 10-kilohm resistor. That is,

$$v_{CB} = 25 - 5 = 20 \text{ volts}$$

This type of problem is important in troubleshooting because one of the first checks that should be made on a questionable circuit is to measure the collector-ground voltage.

EXAMPLE 5-3

In the circuit of Fig. 5-13a, what value of R_L causes $v_{CB} = 10$?

SOLUTION

The schematic drawing of Fig. 5-13a is the usual way of indicating power-supply voltages. The other terminal (not shown) on each power supply is grounded. For instance, the 10-kilohm resistor is connected to the negative terminal of a d-c supply, and it is understood by definition that the positive terminal of this supply is grounded even though it is not shown.

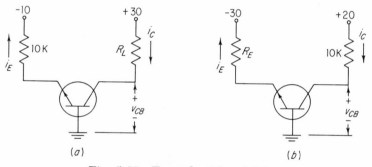

Fig. 5-13   Examples 5-3 and 5-4.

By inspection of the circuit the emitter diode is forward-biased, and therefore we have

$$i_E \cong \frac{10}{10(10^3)} = 1 \text{ ma}$$

Since the collector current approximately equals the emitter current, there is about 1 ma flowing through the load resistor R_L. It should be clear from the circuit that in order to have $v_{CB} = 10$ there must be a voltage drop of 20 volts across R_L. To find the size of R_L that produces this 20-volt drop we use Ohm's law.

$$R_L = \frac{20}{10^{-3}} = 20 \text{ kilohms}$$

EXAMPLE 5-4

For the circuit of Fig. 5-13b, find the value of R_E that causes v_{CB} to equal 10 volts.

SOLUTION

In order for v_{CB} to equal 10 volts there must be a voltage drop of 10 volts across the 10-kilohm load resistor. In order to have this 10-volt drop there must be a collector current of

$$i_C = \frac{10}{10(10^3)} = 1 \text{ ma}$$

The emitter current controls the collector current; thus, the emitter current must be made equal to 1 ma. This can be done by choosing a value of R_E that sets up 1 ma of emitter current. Using Ohm's law, we get

$$R_E = \frac{30}{10^{-3}} = 30 \text{ kilohms}$$

EXAMPLE 5-5

In Fig. 5-14a, find the collector-base voltage by the following approaches:

(a) Neglect the voltage drop across the emitter diode.
(b) Allow 0.7-volt drop across the emitter diode.

SOLUTION

(a) First, note that we are using a p-n-p transistor, instead of an n-p-n. Transistor action is essentially the same in both types of transistors except that the holes are the majority carriers in the p-n-p transistor. We still must forward-bias the emitter diode and back-bias the collector diode to obtain normal transistor action; therefore, we connect the d-c sources as shown in Fig. 5-14a.

In this circuit it is clear that the emitter diode is forward-biased and that the emitter current is approximately

$$i_E \cong \frac{10}{10(10^3)} = 1 \text{ ma}$$

The collector current is therefore almost equal to 1 ma and produces a voltage drop of about 5 volts across the 5-kilohm resistor with the polarity shown.

From Kirchhoff's law we know that the collector-base voltage is the difference between the collector supply and the drop across the 5-kilohm resistor. That is,

$$v_{CB} = 10 - 5 = 5 \text{ volts}$$

This is the magnitude of the collector-base voltage. The collector diode of a p-n-p transistor is back-biased by the negative d-c source; thus, the actual voltage across the collector-base part of the transistor is negative, as shown in Fig. 5-14a.

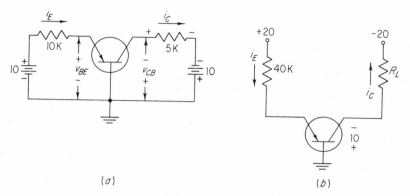

Fig. 5-14 Examples 5-5 and 5-6.

(b) If we want a more accurate answer, we can allow 0.7 volt drop across the emitter diode; this means that the voltage across the 10-kilohm resistor in the emitter circuit will be 10 volts minus 0.7 volt. Therefore, the emitter current must be

$$i_E = \frac{10 - 0.7}{10(10^3)} = 0.93 \text{ ma}$$

The voltage drop across the 5-kilohm load resistor is

$$0.93(10^{-3})(5)(10^3) = 4.65 \text{ volts}$$

and the magnitude of the collector-base voltage is

$$v_{CB} = 10 - 4.65 = 5.35 \text{ volts}$$

EXAMPLE 5-6

In Fig. 5-14b, what value of R_L produces a collector-base voltage of -10 volts?

SOLUTION

By inspection of the emitter circuit we see that the emitter current is approximately

$$i_E \cong \frac{20}{40(10^3)} = 0.5 \text{ ma}$$

In order to have a collector-base voltage of -10 volts, there must be a voltage drop of 10 volts across R_L. Therefore, R_L must equal

$$R_L = \frac{10}{0.5(10^{-3})} = 20 \text{ kilohms}$$

5-6   Using Superposition to Analyze CB Circuits

In the preceding section and in Examples 5-1 to 5-6 we analyzed circuits containing only d-c sources. Now we wish to analyze circuits that contain both d-c and a-c sources.

Recall that in Chap. 4 we discussed the use of superposition in analyzing diode circuits containing large d-c sources and small a-c sources. In analyzing these circuits we found the d-c component using the d-c equivalent circuit and the a-c component using the a-c equivalent circuit, and then we added these two components to find the total voltage or current that we wanted. When we analyze CB transistor circuits, we will use the same basic approach, namely, we will first find the d-c component and then the a-c component, and finally we will add these components.

In our early work in transistors we will concentrate upon the ideal-transistor approach because this simple approach will be adequate for most of our needs in the areas of troubleshooting and initial design. Later on, we will discuss more exact methods. For the moment, then, let us make sure that we understand how to use the ideal-transistor approach in d-c and a-c circuit analysis.

To begin with, in the d-c equivalent circuit we view the ideal transistor as nothing more than a rectifier diode in the emitter and a current source in the collector. The d-c equivalent circuit for the n-p-n transistor is shown in Fig. 5-15a and that for the p-n-p transistor in Fig. 5-15b. In finding the direct current that flows in the emitter diode, we can use any of the large-signal diode approximations developed in Chap. 3. In other words, we can use an ideal diode for the emitter diode, or if more accuracy is required, we can use the second or third approximation of a diode. Once we have found the d-c emitter current, we immediately know that this same value of d-c collector current is flowing.

As far as a *small* a-c signal is concerned, *the emitter diode does not rectify;* instead, it looks like a resistance (the a-c resistance of the diode discussed in Chap. 4). Therefore, we visualize the a-c equivalent circuit as a resistor and a current source, as shown in Fig. 5-15c. (This equivalent circuit is also valid for the p-n-p transistor.)

As an example of using superposition to analyze a CB circuit driven by

a large d-c source and a small a-c source, consider the circuit of Fig.
5-16a. The d-c sources set up direct currents in the transistor; the small
a-c source causes the transistor currents to fluctuate slightly. In order to
find the total voltage v_T appearing from the collector to ground, we first
find the d-c component by drawing the d-c equivalent circuit as in Fig.
5-16b. It is clear in this circuit that the emitter diode is forward-biased.

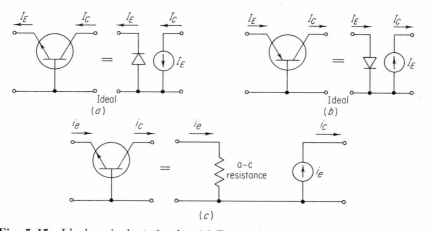

Fig. 5-15 Ideal equivalent circuits. (a) D-c equivalent circuit for $n\text{-}p\text{-}n$; (b) d-c
equivalent circuit for $p\text{-}n\text{-}p$; (c) a-c equivalent circuit for both.

By using an ideal diode for the emitter diode, we can see that the d-c
emitter current is about 1 ma. (If a more accurate answer were required,
we would allow 0.3 or 0.7 volt for the emitter-base voltage, depending on
whether the transistor is germanium or silicon.) With 1 ma of emitter
current there is about 1 ma of collector current, which produces a voltage drop of 5 volts across the 5-kilohm resistor. Therefore, the d-c voltage V_C from collector to ground is 15 volts (the power-supply voltage of
20 volts less the drop across the 5-kilohm resistor).

Next, we draw the a-c equivalent circuit as shown in Fig. 5-16c. The
coupling capacitor is shown as a short, and both d-c supplies are shorted to
ground. The emitter diode acts like a resistance whose value is given by
the sum of the junction resistance and bulk resistance. We will assume
that the junction resistance is much larger than the bulk resistance, so
that

$$r_{\text{ac}} \cong r_j \cong \frac{25\text{mv}}{I_E}$$

In the d-c analysis we found that the emitter current I_E was about 1 ma.

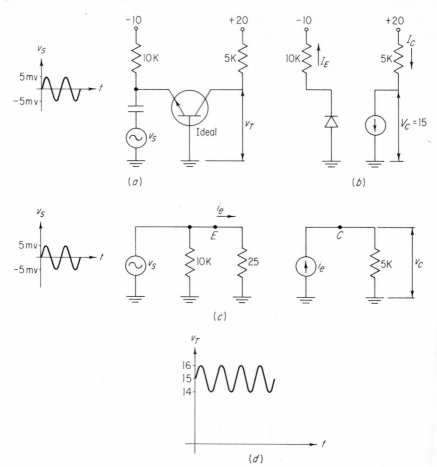

Fig. 5-16   Applying superposition and the ideal-transistor approximation.

Thus,

$$r_{ac} \cong \frac{25 \text{ mv}}{1 \text{ ma}} = 25 \text{ ohms}$$

We can now find the amount of alternating current flowing in the emitter. By inspection of Fig. 5-16c we can see that the a-c emitter current equals the source voltage divided by the a-c resistance of the emitter diode. That is, the current in the emitter is a sine wave with a peak value of

$$i_p = \frac{5 \text{ mv}}{25 \text{ ohms}} = 0.2 \text{ ma}$$

The a-c collector current is approximately equal to the a-c emitter current. Therefore, the a-c voltage appearing from collector to ground must be sine wave with a peak value of

$$v_p = 0.2(10^{-3})(5)(10^3) = 1 \text{ volt}$$

The total voltage v_T is the sum of the d-c and a-c components and is shown in Fig. 5-16d. In other words, there is an average voltage of 15 volts appearing from collector to ground. Superimposed on this average voltage, there is a sinusoidal variation from 14 to 16 volts.

Let us summarize the use of superposition in transistor circuits. As with diode circuits, we use a modified form of the superposition theorem. Our approach is:

1. Draw or visualize the d-c equivalent circuit by shorting all a-c sources and opening all capacitors. The transistor is replaced by a rectifier diode in the emitter and by a current source in the collector. Compute the desired d-c component of current or voltage.

2. Draw or visualize the a-c equivalent circuit by shorting all d-c sources and capacitors (we are assuming that capacitors are large enough to look like very low impedances to the a-c signal). Compute the desired a-c component of current or voltage using the a-c resistance of the emitter diode and a current source for the collector.

3. Add the d-c and a-c components to obtain the total voltage on current.

5-7   A Complicated A-C Equivalent Circuit

The simple a-c equivalent circuit of a transistor shown in Fig. 5-15c will lead to errors in some analysis problems because this model of the transistor is incomplete. A very accurate a-c equivalent circuit for a transistor is shown in Fig. 5-17a. This rather complicated circuit does take into account a number of transistor effects that we are neglecting for the moment. For instance, there is a capacitance across each p-n junction in the transistor; these capacitances are designated by C_e and C_c, the emitter and collector capacitance, respectively.

There is also a resistance r_c' across the collector current source. This resistance is usually several megohms and is equal to the inverse slope of the collector current-voltage characteristics.

There is a generator, designated by $\mu_{ec}v_c'$, which accounts for the small amount of feedback that takes place from the collector to the emitter. Recall that this feedback has the effect of producing a slight shift in the emitter-diode characteristic (see Fig. 5-6b).

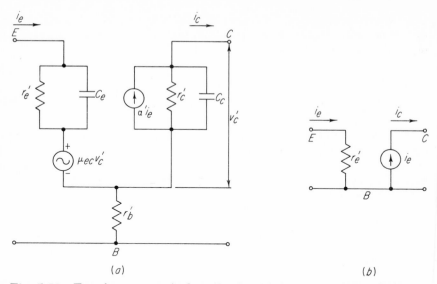

Fig. 5-17   Transistor a-c equivalent circuits. (*a*) Complicated; (*b*) idealized.

The α' quantity is almost identical to the α discussed in Sec. 5-4. For practical purposes α' is almost equal to unity.

The resistance r_b' is called the *base spreading resistance;* it is caused by the ohmic resistance of the base region.

Finally, the resistance r_e' is the junction resistance of the emitter diode. At room temperature the perfect junction diode has a junction resistance given by

$$r_e' = \frac{25 \text{ mv}}{I_E} \tag{5-3}$$

where r_e' is the resistance seen by a small a-c signal and I_E is the direct current flowing into the emitter diode.

Clearly, the equivalent circuit of Fig. 5-17a is much too complicated for practical circuit analysis. Various methods (*h* parameters, *r* parameters, etc.) have been evolved in an attempt to simplify the accurate model of Fig. 5-17a. In our work, especially at the beginning, we want as simple a model of the transistor as possible without losing the essential features. Therefore, in our ideal transistor the following approximations have been made:

1. We have neglected C_e and C_c because at low frequencies the reactances produced by these capacitances are negligible. Later on when discussing the high-frequency limits of a transistor, we will consider these capacitances.

2. We have neglected r_c' because it is on the order of megohms.

3. Since α' is normally between 0.95 and 0.999, we have rounded off this value to unity.

4. The quantity μ_{ec} is typically between 10^{-3} and 10^{-4}, small enough to neglect in a first approximation.

5. The base spreading resistance r_b' is small enough to neglect in a first approximation.

The only quantities that remain are r_e' and a current source in the collector, as shown in Fig. 5-17b. Admittedly, we have disregarded many of the effects in a transistor; yet we will find that as a first approximation, the ideal-transistor equivalent circuit is adequate in most initial analysis and design.

EXAMPLE 5-7

Use the ideal-transistor approximation to find the total voltage v_T across the 10-kilohm resistor in Fig. 5-18a.

SOLUTION

First, we visualize the d-c equivalent circuit; it is clear that the coupling capacitor on the output side is open to direct current. Therefore, there is no d-c component across the 10-kilohm resistor.

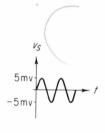
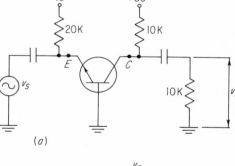
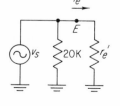
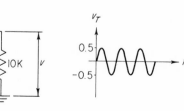

Fig. 5-18 Example 5-7.

Next, we short the d-c supplies and the coupling capacitors, and we replace the transistor by its ideal a-c equivalent circuit to get the a-c equivalent circuit of Fig. 5-18b. The a-c emitter current equals the a-c voltage across the emitter divided by the emitter resistance r'_e. To find r'_e we can use Eq. (5-3).

$$r'_e = \frac{25 \text{ mv}}{I_E}$$

where I_E is the d-c emitter current. By inspection of the original circuit, Fig. 5-18a, the d-c emitter current is

$$I_E \cong \frac{10}{20(10^3)} = 0.5 \text{ ma}$$

Now we can find r'_e.

$$r'_e = \frac{25 \text{ mv}}{0.5 \text{ ma}} = 50 \text{ ohms}$$

Now that we have the value of the a-c emitter resistance r'_e, we can find the a-c emitter current. In Fig. 5-18b with a 5-mv-peak sine wave voltage appearing across the emitter resistance, we will get an emitter current that is a sine wave with a peak value of

$$i_p = \frac{5(10^{-3})}{50} = 0.1 \text{ ma}$$

The a-c collector current will therefore be a sine wave with a peak of 0.1 ma. This collector current flows through two 10-kilohm resistors in parallel. Hence, the voltage appearing across the output will be a sine wave with a peak value of 0.1 ma times 5 kilohms (two 10-kilohm resistors in parallel). That is,

$$v_p = 0.1(10^{-3})(5)(10^3) = 0.5 \text{ volt}$$

The total voltage appearing across the output is simply the a-c component shown in Fig. 5-18c. Remember that the d-c component was blocked by the coupling capacitor.

Another point worth mentioning is that we used Eq. (5-3) to find r'_e; this equation is for a perfect diode. In practice, we find that most transistors have emitter resistances that fall within a 2:1 range, that is,

$$\frac{25 \text{ mv}}{I_E} < r'_e < \frac{50 \text{ mv}}{I_E} \tag{5-4}$$

In Example 5-7 we found that the a-c voltage across the output was a sine wave with a peak value of 0.5 volt based on an r'_e given by 25 mv/I_E.

By using Eq. (5-4) we would calculate an r'_e between 50 and 100 ohms, which would then produce an output voltage with a peak value between 0.25 and 0.5 volt.

EXAMPLE 5-8

Find the total voltage appearing across the 1-megohm resistor of Fig. 5-19a. Use 25 mv/I_E to find r'_e.

SOLUTION

First, note that the output coupling capacitor blocks the d-c component of voltage. Thus, there is only an a-c component of voltage across the 1-megohm resistor.

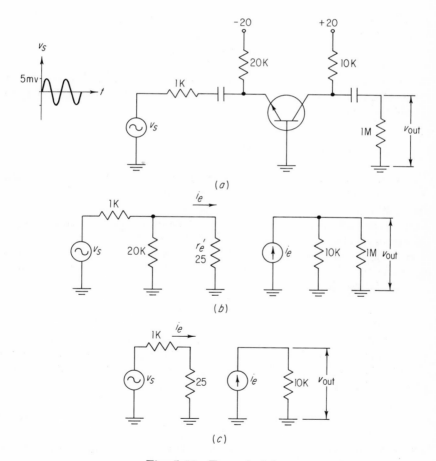

Fig. 5-19 Example 5-8.

The a-c equivalent circuit is shown in Fig. 5-19b. The value of r'_e is

$$r'_e = \frac{25 \text{ mv}}{I_E} = \frac{25 \text{ mv}}{1 \text{ ma}} = 25 \text{ ohms}$$

We can simplify the circuit of Fig. 5-19b by noting that 25 ohms of emitter resistance in shunt 20 kilohms is essentially 25 ohms. Also, on the collector side, 10 kilohms in shunt with 1 megohm is essentially 10 kilohms. The simplified a-c equivalent circuit is shown in Fig. 5-19c.

Clearly, from Fig. 5-19c we can see that the alternating current in the emitter must be a sine wave with a peak value of

$$i_p = \frac{5 \text{ mv}}{1000 + 25} \cong 5 \text{ } \mu\text{a}$$

The a-c collector current equals the a-c emitter current, and therefore the output voltage must be a sine wave with a peak value of

$$v_p = 5(10^{-6})(10)(10^3) = 50 \text{ mv}$$

Thus, the total voltage appearing across the 1-megohm resistor in the original circuit of Fig. 5-19a is simply a sine wave with a peak value of 50 mv.

5-8   Formulas for CB Analysis

Up to this point we have applied the superposition theorem to specific examples. Let us now apply superposition to the general CB circuit of Fig. 5-20a.

First, let us obtain the important formulas that describe the d-c operation. In Fig. 5-20a it is clear that the coupling capacitors are open circuits as far as d-c voltages and currents are concerned. We therefore can draw the d-c equivalent circuit as in Fig. 5-20b. The d-c emitter current I_E equals

$$I_E = \frac{V_{EE} - V_{BE}}{R_E} \tag{5-5}$$

The d-c voltage V_{BE} across the emitter diode is only a few tenths of a volt (approximately 0.3 for germanium and 0.7 volt for silicon). In most circuits the supply voltage V_{EE} is much larger than V_{BE}, and therefore we approximate Eq. (5-5) by neglecting V_{BE}.

$$I_E \cong \frac{V_{EE}}{R_E} \tag{5-6}$$

This is one of the important d-c quantities because we use I_E when we find the a-c resistance r'_e of the emitter diode.

Another important d-c quantity that we often need is the collector-ground voltage V_C. This d-c voltage equals the collector supply voltage minus the voltage drop across the load resistor R_L. That is,

$$V_C = V_{CC} - I_C R_L \qquad (5\text{-}7)$$

where V_C is the collector-ground d-c voltage
$\qquad V_{CC}$ is the collector-supply voltage
$\qquad I_C$ is the d-c collector current
$\qquad R_L$ is the resistance between the collector supply and the collector

In using Eq. (5-7) we note that I_C essentially equals I_E, provided that the transistor is operating under normal conditions, that is, with the emitter diode forward-biased and the collector diode back-biased.

In applying Eq. (5-7) to p-n-p transistor circuits we note that there is a sign reversal. In other words, for p-n-p transistors we use Eq. (5-7) to find the magnitude of the collector voltage; then we merely add a minus

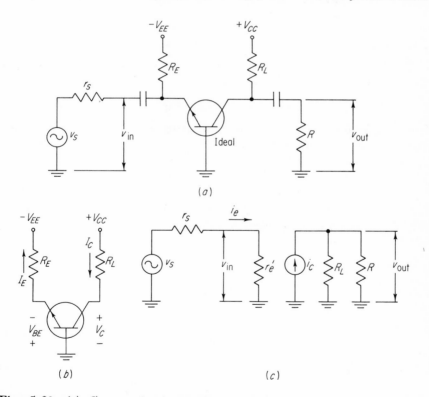

Fig. 5-20 (a) Common-base amplifier. (b) D-c equivalent circuit; (c) a-c equivalent circuit.

sign because we know that the collector voltage of a p-n-p transistor is negative with respect to ground. Example 5-11 illustrates the use of Eq. (5-7) for a p-n-p transistor.

The a-c operation of the CB transistor circuit can be determined by first drawing the a-c equivalent circuit as in Fig. 5-20c. The coupling capacitors are shorted under the assumption that their reactances are very small compared to the resistances in series with them (this is reasonable because otherwise the capacitors would not be coupling the signal properly). The emitter biasing resistor R_E is much larger than r'_e in almost all practical circuits; because R_E appears in shunt with r'_e, we can neglect R_E.

In Fig. 5-20c we can see that the a-c emitter current equals

$$i_e = \frac{v_s}{r_s + r'_e} \tag{5-8}$$

where i_e is the alternating current in the emitter
  v_s is the a-c source voltage
  r_s is resistance in series with the a-c source
  r'_e is the a-c resistance of the emitter diode

The a-c output voltage equals the a-c collector current times the a-c resistance seen by the collector. That is,

$$v_{out} = i_c r_L \tag{5-9}$$

where v_{out} is the a-c voltage from collector to ground
  i_c is the a-c collector current
  r_L is the a-c resistance seen by collector, in this case,

$$r_L = R_L \| R$$

To find an expression for the voltage gain from the source to the output we note that in an ideal transistor

$$i_c = i_e$$

Therefore,

$$v_{out} = i_c r_L = i_e r_L = \frac{v_s}{r_s + r'_e} r_L$$

or

$$\frac{v_{out}}{v_s} = \frac{r_L}{r_s + r'_e} \tag{5-10}$$

Examine this equation carefully. It tells us that the voltage gain from the source to the output equals the a-c load resistance divided by the sum of the source resistance and the emitter resistance. For instance, suppose in Fig. 5-20c that $r_L = 10$ kilohms, $r_s = 75$ ohms, and $r'_e = 25$ ohms.

Then we calculate

$$\frac{v_{\text{out}}}{v_s} = \frac{10,000}{75 + 25} = 100$$

Thus, we would have a voltage gain of 100 from the source to the output. A 1-mv-peak signal at the source would be amplified and appear as a 100-mv-peak signal at the output.

There are two special cases of importance implied in Eq. (5-10). First, note that when r_s is much smaller than r_e', we have approximately

$$\frac{v_{\text{out}}}{v_{\text{in}}} = \frac{r_L}{r_e'} \tag{5-11}$$

where v_{in} is the a-c voltage appearing across the emitter diode. Also, when r_s is much larger than r_e', we get

$$\frac{v_{\text{out}}}{v_s} = \frac{r_L}{r_s} \qquad \text{when } r_s \gg r_e' \tag{5-12}$$

Equation (5-12) has great practical value. We know that the value of r_e' is theoretically given by 25 mv/I_E. In practice, however, most transistors have emitter resistances that fall within the range of 25 to 50 mv/I_E. As we change from one transistor to another of the same type, the value of r_e' will change. These possible changes in r_e' mean that the voltage gain can change unless we somehow eliminate the effect of a change in r_e'. One standard method used in practice to eliminate the effects of r_e' is to use a source resistance r_s that is much larger than r_e'. Thus, in Eq. (5-10) if r_e' is small compared to r_s, changes in r_e' will change the value of the voltage gain only slightly. Making r_s much larger than r_e' is called *swamping out* the emitter diode.

Let us summarize the important formulas for CB transistor operation (Fig. 5-20a). For d-c operation we have

$$I_E \cong \frac{V_{EE}}{R_E} \qquad \text{provided that } V_{EE} \gg V_{BE}$$

$$V_C = V_{CC} - I_C R_L$$

For a-c operation we have

$$\frac{v_{\text{out}}}{v_s} = \frac{r_L}{r_s + r_e'}$$

$$\frac{v_{\text{out}}}{v_{\text{in}}} \cong \frac{r_L}{r_e'}$$

$$\frac{v_{\text{out}}}{v_s} \cong \frac{r_L}{r_s} \qquad \text{when } r_s \gg r_e'$$

These formulas are very useful approximations for the analysis of CB transistor circuits. In spite of the fact that we used an ideal transistor in deriving these formulas, we will find that they are adequate for most initial analysis and design of CB transistor circuits.

EXAMPLE 5-9

Find the approximate voltage gain from source to output for the circuit of Fig. 5-21.

SOLUTION

The a-c load resistance r_L seen by the collector is 10 kilohms in shunt with 1 megohm. Therefore,

$$r_L = 10(10^3) \| 10^6 \cong 10 \text{ kilohms}$$

The theoretical value of r'_e is

$$r'_e = \frac{25 \text{ mv}}{I_E} = \frac{25 \text{ mv}}{1 \text{ ma}} = 25 \text{ ohms}$$

We can expect the actual r'_e to be somewhere in the range of 25 to 50 ohms. Note that r_s is 1000 ohms and is much larger than the value of r'_e.

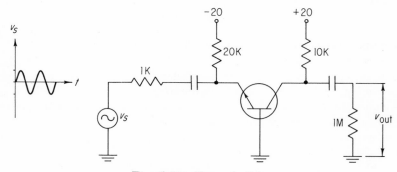

Fig. 5-21   Example 5-9.

Thus, r'_e is swamped out because its value is negligible in Eq. (5-10). Using Eq. (5-12), we get

$$\frac{v_{\text{out}}}{v_s} = \frac{r_L}{r_s} = \frac{10,000}{1,000} = 10$$

If we had used the more accurate formula given by Eq. (5-10) we would have calculated as follows:

When $r'_e = 25$ ohms $\dfrac{v_{\text{out}}}{v_s} = \dfrac{10,000}{1025} = 9.75$

When $r'_e = 50$ ohms $\dfrac{v_{\text{out}}}{v_s} = \dfrac{10,000}{1050} = 9.52$

The point is simply this: even though r'_e can change over a 2:1 range, the use of a large r_s has swamped out the effect of changes in r'_e so that the voltage gain only changes from 9.75 to 9.52 when r'_e changes from 25 to 50 ohms. This *swamping-out* technique is widely used in industry whenever it is desired to have an almost fixed value of voltage gain from source to output; temperature changes, aging of the transistor, or for that matter changing the transistor has virtually no effect on voltage gain once r'_e has been swamped out. In fact, once the emitter diode has been swamped out, there is little point in even using more exact transistor approaches (h parameters, r parameters, etc.), because the voltage gain is then almost independent of the transistor characteristics.

EXAMPLE 5-10

In the circuit of Fig. 5-22 find the approximate a-c output voltage v_{out}.

SOLUTION

By inspection of the circuit there is a d-c emitter current of

$$I_E \cong \frac{10}{20(10^3)} = 0.5 \text{ ma}$$

The a-c resistance of the emitter diode is in the vicinity of

$$r'_e = \frac{25 \text{ mv}}{I_E} = \frac{25 \text{ mv}}{0.5 \text{ ma}} = 50 \text{ ohms}$$

Since r_s is much larger than r'_e (1000 compared to 50), we can use Eq. (5-12) to find the approximate voltage gain from source to output.

$$\frac{v_{\text{out}}}{v_s} \cong \frac{r_L}{r_s} = \frac{10(10^3)\|30(10^3)}{10^3} = \frac{7.5(10^3)}{10^3} = 7.5$$

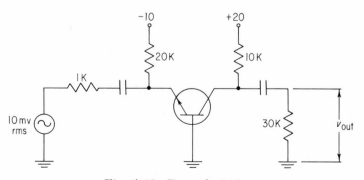

Fig. 5-22 Example 5-10.

Note that the a-c load resistance seen by the collector is 10 kilohms in parallel with 30 kilohms. By the product-over-sum rule we get 7.5 kilohms for the value of r_L.

To find the output voltage, simply realize that the voltage gain from source to output is 7.5, meaning that the source voltage is amplified by a factor of 7.5. That is,

$$v_{out} = 7.5v_s = 7.5(10 \text{ mv}) = 75 \text{ mv rms}$$

EXAMPLE 5-11

In Fig. 5-23 find the following:

(a) The d-c collector-to-ground voltage V_C.
(b) The a-c output voltage v_{out}.

SOLUTION

(a) The magnitude of the d-c voltage from collector to ground is given by Eq. (5-7)

$$V_C = V_{CC} - I_C R_L$$

V_{CC} is the magnitude of the collector-supply voltage, which in this case is 20 volts. The d-c collector current I_C equals the d-c emitter current, which by inspection of Fig. 5-23 is simply

$$I_E \cong \frac{20}{20(10^3)} = 1 \text{ ma}$$

Since there is about 1 ma of collector current through a d-c load of 10 kilohms, there is a voltage drop of about 10 volts across this d-c load. Therefore, the d-c voltage from the collector to ground is −10 volts.

(b) To find the a-c output voltage v_{out} we first need to find the volt-

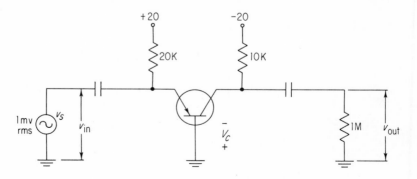

Fig. 5-23   Example 5-11.

age gain from source to load. Since $r_s = 0$, we can use Eq. (5-11):

$$\frac{v_{out}}{v_{in}} = \frac{r_L}{r'_e}$$

The a-c load resistance r_L is 10 kilohms in shunt with 1 megohm, which is essentially 10 kilohms. The theoretical value of r'_e is

$$r'_e = \frac{25 \text{ mv}}{I_E} = \frac{25 \text{ mv}}{1 \text{ ma}} = 25 \text{ ohms}$$

The practical range of r'_e is therefore 25 to 50 ohms. Hence, the minimum value of voltage gain is

$$\frac{v_{out}}{v_{in}} = \frac{10(10^3)}{50} = 200$$

and the maximum value is

$$\frac{v_{out}}{v_{in}} = \frac{10(10^3)}{25} = 400$$

Hence, the voltage gain of the circuit in Fig. 5-23 is somewhere in the range of 200 to 400.

The output voltage is simply the input voltage times the gain. With 1 mv rms input, the output voltage must be in the range of 200 to 400 mv rms.

EXAMPLE 5-12

In the circuit of Fig. 5-24 find the following:

(a) The voltage gain from the source to the output.
(b) The voltage gain from the emitter to the output.
(c) The approximate value of v_{in}.

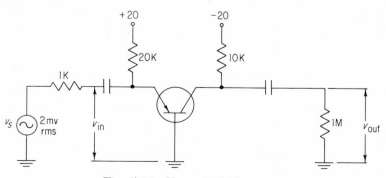

Fig. 5-24   Example 5-12.

SOLUTION

(a) The voltage gain from source to output is approximately

$$\frac{v_\text{out}}{v_s} \cong \frac{r_L}{r_s} = \frac{10(10^3)}{10^3} = 10$$

(b) The voltage gain from the emitter to the output is

$$\frac{v_\text{out}}{v_\text{in}} \cong \frac{r_L}{r_e'} = \frac{10(10^3)}{25} = 400$$

(For convenience, we used the theoretical value of 25 ohms for r_e'.)

(c) To find v_in, we can first find v_out, and then divide by 400. The output voltage is

$$v_\text{out} = 10v_s = 10(2 \text{ mv}) = 20 \text{ mv rms}$$

Therefore, the input voltage v_in appearing across the emitter diode is

$$v_\text{in} = \frac{20 \text{ mv rms}}{400} = 0.05 \text{ mv rms} = 50 \ \mu\text{v rms}$$

5-9 Notation for Voltages and Currents

In Chap. 4 we indicated that whenever possible we would use capital letters to represent d-c or fixed quantities and lowercase letters for a-c or varying quantities. To this basic rule we now wish to add the following:

1. When a current or voltage in a transistor is a d-c or fixed quantity, we will use capital letters on both the quantity and its subscript. For instance, to represent the d-c emitter current we use I_E (both the quantity I and its subscript E are capitalized). As another example, to represent the d-c collector-to-base voltage we use V_{CB}.

2. When the current or voltage is an a-c quantity obtained from an a-c equivalent circuit, we will use lowercase letters for both the quantity and its subscript. For instance, the a-c current in the emitter is designated by i_e (both the quantity i and its subscript e are lowercase letters). As another example, to represent the a-c voltage from collector to base we would use v_{cb}.

3. When we wish to represent the total voltage or current, that is, the sum of both the d-c and a-c components, we will use a hybrid notation, with a lowercase letter for the quantity and a capital letter for its subscript. For instance, to represent the total current into the emitter, we use i_E. To represent the total collector-to-base voltage we use v_{CB}.

Whenever possible, we will follow the above rules of notation; this will make it much easier for us to understand the meaning of various transistor formulas.

SUMMARY

A transistor is like two back-to-back diodes. There are two basic types, the n-p-n and the p-n-p transistor.

For normal transistor operation the emitter diode is forward-biased, and the collector diode is back-biased. Because of the thin and lightly doped base region most of the carriers pass from the emitter to the collector. As a result, the collector current is almost equal to the emitter current. The small base current is the difference of the emitter and collector currents.

The IV characteristics of a transistor indicate that the emitter diode acts essentially like a diode, whereas the collector diode acts like a current source whose value equals the emitter current. If the reverse voltage across the collector diode becomes too large, breakdown can occur. The collector diode is normally operated well below the breakdown voltage.

The ideal transistor is an approximation of any real transistor. In the ideal transistor we disregard a number of effects in order to obtain a simple model for preliminary transistor circuit analysis.

In analyzing CB circuits we use the concept of the ideal transistor in conjunction with the superposition theorem. In the d-c equivalent circuit, all a-c sources are shorted and all capacitors are opened. The direct currents and voltages can then be found by using the large-signal diode approximations of Chap. 3. In the a-c equivalent circuit, all d-c sources and all coupling capacitors are shorted. The a-c emitter current can then be found by using the various small-signal diode approximations of Chap. 4.

Of special importance is the fact that the voltage gain from source to output can be made almost independent of the transistor characteristics by swamping out the emitter diode. In other words, when the source resistance is much larger than the emitter-diode resistance, the voltage gain from source to output is approximately equal to the a-c load resistance divided by the source resistance.

GLOSSARY

alpha (α)   This a-c quantity is defined as the ratio of a change in collector current to the corresponding change in emitter current. There is also a d-c α, designated α_{dc}, defined as the total collector current divided by the total emitter current.

base spreading resistance (r_b')   This is the bulk or ohmic resistance of that part of the base region in which the base current flows.

collector capacitance (C_c) This is the depletion-layer capacitance of the back-biased collector-base junction.

collector resistance (r_c') This is the resistance that appears across the collector-current source. The value of this resistance is quite high, usually several megohms.

common base (CB)   One of the ways of connecting a transistor. In a CB connection the base is at a-c ground.

coupling capacitor   A capacitor whose purpose is to block the d-c component and pass the a-c component. Coupling capacitors are deliberately chosen large enough in size to offer very little reactance to the lowest frequency that is to be passed.

emitter resistance (r_e') The effective junction resistance of the emitter diode as seen by a small a-c signal. As a theoretical guide, this resistance equals 25 mv divided by the value of the direct current I_E in the emitter diode.

swamping   With respect to the emitter diode, this means making value of r_e' negligible as far as voltage gain is concerned.

REVIEW QUESTIONS

1. What are the two kinds of transistors? Name the different parts of a transistor.
2. Under normal conditions, is the emitter diode forward- or back-biased? Is the collector diode forward- or back-biased?
3. When a transistor is operating under normal conditions, the collector current is almost equal to the emitter current. Why is this so?
4. Is the base current large or small compared to the emitter current? How can we find the base current knowing the emitter and collector current?
5. The emitter-base part of a transistor acts essentially like what kind of device? The collector-base part of transistor acts like what kind of device?
6. What is an ideal current source?
7. Define the two types of α. What is the α of an ideal transistor?
8. What is the formula for the theoretical value of the emitter resistance r_e'? What is the range of r_e' for most transistors?
9. What does *swamping out* the emitter diode mean?

PROBLEMS

5-1   In a transistor the collector current is 4.9 ma, and the emitter current is 5 ma. What is the α_{dc} for this condition?

When the emitter current is increased to 10 ma, the collector current becomes 9.7 ma. What is the value of α_{dc} for this new condition?

5-2 When the emitter current changes from 2 to 2.25 ma, the collector current changes from 1.95 to 2.195 ma.

   (a) Find α_{dc} for an emitter current of 2 ma.

   (b) Find α.

5-3 In Fig. 5-25a, find the approximate emitter current. Also, find the voltage that appears from collector to base.

5-4 In Fig. 5-25b, find the following:

   (a) The emitter current and the collector-base voltage when $R_E = 40$ kilohms.

   (b) The emitter current and the collector-base voltage when $R_E = 20$ kilohms.

5-5 In Fig. 5-25b, what value of R_E produces a collector-base voltage of 15 volts?

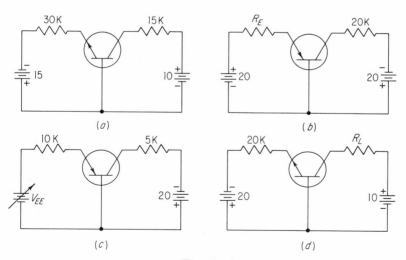

Fig. 5-25

5-6 In Fig. 5-25c, find the following:

   (a) The emitter current and the collector-base voltage when $V_{EE} = 10$ volts.

   (b) The emitter current and the collector-base voltage when $V_{EE} = 40$ volts.

5-7 In Fig. 5-25c, how much does the collector-base voltage change when V_{EE} is changed from 10 to 11 volts?

5-8   In Fig. 5-25d, find the following:

(a) The collector-base voltage when $R_L = 5$ kilohms.

(b) The collector-base voltage when $R_L = 10$ kilohms.

5-9   What value of R_L in Fig. 5-25d causes the collector-base voltage to equal 7.5 volts?

5-10   Find the theoretical value of emitter resistance using Eq. (5-3) for the following d-c emitter currents: 0.01, 0.05, 0.1, 0.5, and 1 ma.

5-11   Sketch the total voltage v_T from collector to ground in Fig. 5-26a. Show the d-c and a-c components. Use Eq. (5-3).

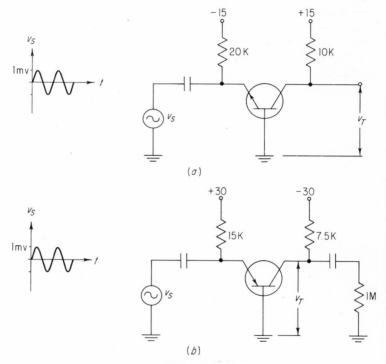

Fig. 5-26

5-12 In Fig. 5-26b, sketch the total voltage v_T that appears from collector to ground. Use Eq. (5-3).

5-13 In Fig. 5-27a, find:

(a) The d-c voltage from collector to ground.

(b) The a-c voltage v_{out} (approximately).

5-14 If the voltage gain from source to output in Fig. 5-27a is to be approximately 7.5, what size should r_s be?

5-15 In Fig. 5-27b, what is approximate value of v_{out}? (Neglect r'_e.)

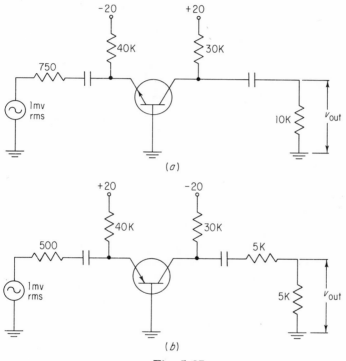

Fig. 5-27

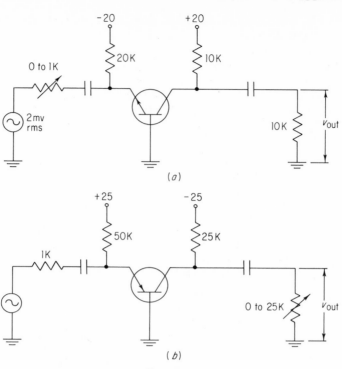

Fig. 5-28

5-16 In Fig. 5-28a, what is the maximum and minimum value of v_{out} that can be obtained by changing r_s? Use 25 mv/I_E to find the value of r'_e.
5-17 In Fig. 5-28b, approximately what are the minimum and maximum values of v_{out}?

6 | Common-emitter Approximations

In this chapter we will discuss the common-emitter connection, undoubtedly the most widely used of the three basic transistor connections. As we did with the CB connection, we will idealize the common-emitter connection in order to obtain a first approximation for the behavior of a transistor. This approximation is adequate for most initial analysis and design; furthermore, the first approximation allows us to become familiar with the essential features of the transistor before we attempt a more thorough analysis.

6-1 The IV Characteristics of the Common-emitter Connection

A transistor can be connected with the emitter grounded instead of the base, as shown in Fig. 6-1a; this connection is called a *common-emitter* or *grounded-emitter* connection. The base-emitter diode is forward-biased, and the collector diode is back-biased.

How are the voltages and currents related in a common-emitter (CE) connection? If we were to run a typical experiment in the laboratory, here is what we would find. First, imagine that the collector supply is adjusted to 1 volt. If we now vary the base supply V_{BB}, different values of base current i_B will flow. Specifically, when we increase V_{BB} from 0 volts toward higher positive voltages, the base current will increase slowly at first; after reaching a few tenths of a volt, however, the base current will increase sharply, as shown in Fig. 6-1b. Note how this curve (solid line) rises slowly until we reach the knee voltage and then turns up steeply beyond the knee voltage; this is the usual characteristic for a diode, and we certainly expect this kind of graph because the base-emitter part of a transistor is essentially a diode. As before, the knee voltages are around 0.3 volt for a germanium transistor and 0.7 volt for a silicon transistor.

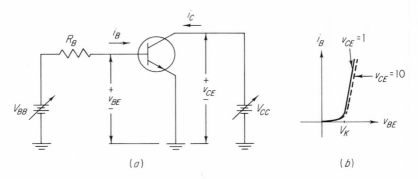

Fig. 6-1   (*a*) Obtaining CE curves; (*b*) base-diode curves.

The collector voltage does have some influence on the shape of the base characteristic. Assume that we change V_{CC} to 10 volts. When we return to the base circuit, we find that varying V_{BB} from 0 volts toward higher voltages now results in a different base characteristic, as shown by the dashed curve of Fig. 6-1b. The idea here is simply that there is a small amount of feedback from the collector to the base. For a first approximation, however, we can disregard the small gap between the two curves of Fig. 6-1b and say that the base-emitter part of a transistor acts like a diode. We will refer to the base-emitter diode simply as the *base diode*.

To find the collector characteristics, we can fix the base current at some value and then measure the collector current for different collector voltages. Specifically, in Fig. 6-1a imagine that we adjust and hold the base current at exactly 0.01 ma. If we now vary the collector voltage, different values of collector current occur. Figure 6-2a shows a typical collector curve. Note that when we increase the collector-emitter voltage v_{CE} from 0 volts upward, the collector current i_C increases sharply at first; however, after v_{CE} reaches a few tenths of a volt, the collector current levels off, becoming almost constant. When we continue to increase v_{CE}, the collector current i_C remains almost fixed until a breakdown occurs. (This breakdown is the usual avalanche effect that takes place at higher reverse voltages across a diode.) Normally, the transistor is operated well below the breakdown point.

In Fig. 6-2a the collector current above the first knee is about 1 ma, compared to a base current of 0.01 ma. Thus, the collector current is about 100 times larger than the base current. Of course, we are hypothesizing a typical experiment. In practice, we find that the collector current may be anywhere in the range of 20 to 200 times larger than the base current. The important point here is that the collector current is much larger than the base current; this is related to the fact that almost all the emitter carriers reach the collector, and only a few of the emitter carriers actually reach the external base terminal.

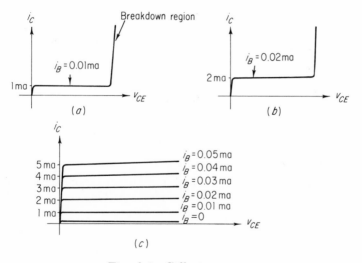

Fig. 6-2 Collector curves.

Suppose that we change the base current to a new value like 0.02 ma. In the collector circuit we will find that as we increase the collector voltage from 0 volts upward, the collector current will increase very sharply at first but then will reach an almost constant value, as shown in Fig. 6-2b. Once again, if we increase the collector voltage too much, we find a breakdown point, where the collector current suddenly increases. Above the first knee the collector current remains almost constant up to the breakdown voltage. Note that the collector current in Fig. 6-2b is around 2 ma, compared to a base current of 0.02 ma.

For each new value of base current that we use, we will get a new collector curve. When we plot several collector curves on a single set of axes, we get the typical CE characteristics shown in Fig. 6-2c. (We have omitted the breakdown region for convenience.) Note that even when there is zero base current, there is a small amount of collector current caused by the reverse current in the collector diode. Note also that each time we change the base current, there is a new value of collector current that is significantly larger than the base current.

Here are the most important features of Figs. 6-1b and 6-2c:

1. The base diode acts almost like an ordinary diode.

2. Above the knee and below breakdown the collector current is almost constant and is controlled by the base current.

6-2   The Beta of a Transistor

In analyzing the common-emitter connection we will be using d-c and a-c equivalent circuits. One of the important quantities that we will use in the d-c equivalent circuit of a transistor is the d-c beta, written β_{dc}. This is defined as

$$\beta_{dc} = \frac{I_C}{I_B} \tag{6-1}$$

where β_{dc} is the d-c β of a transistor
I_C is the d-c collector current
I_B is the d-c base current

When we analyze the a-c operation of transistor circuits, we will need a quantity called the a-c β, written simply as β. This is defined as

$$\beta = \frac{i_c}{i_b} \qquad \text{for a fixed } v_{CE} \tag{6-2}$$

where β is the a-c β of a transistor
i_c is the small-signal a-c collector current
i_b is the small-signal a-c base current

As an example of using Eqs. (6-1) and (6-2), consider the circuit shown in Fig. 6-3a. In the base circuit there is a d-c and a-c source. The d-c source sets up a d-c base current I_B. This d-c base current in turn produces a d-c collector current I_C. In addition to these d-c components, there are also a-c components. There is an alternating current in the base of i_b, which in turn produces an alternating current in the collector of i_c. For the sake of illustration, suppose that the total currents in the base and the collector are the waveforms shown in Fig. 6-3b and c.

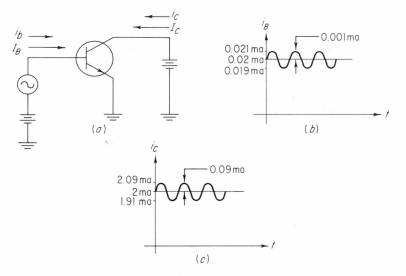

Fig. 6-3   D-c and a-c β.

By inspection of Fig. 6-3*b* the d-c component of base current I_B is 0.02 ma. The a-c component i_b, which is superimposed on this d-c level, is a sine wave with a peak value of 0.001 ma. By inspection of Fig. 6-3*c* the d-c component of collector current I_C is 2 ma; the a-c component i_c is a sine wave with a peak value of 0.09 ma. Now we can calculate the two kinds of β as follows:

$$\beta_{\text{dc}} = \frac{I_C}{I_B} = \frac{2 \text{ ma}}{0.02 \text{ ma}} = 100$$

and

$$\beta = \frac{i_c}{i_b} = \frac{0.09 \text{ ma}}{0.001 \text{ ma}} = 90$$

In general, the d-c and a-c β's are not exactly equal; however, they usually are close to each other in value, and at times we will treat these two β's as equal.

Typically, the β's of transistors show a wide variation from about 20 to 200 or more.   The β is a very unstable quantity; it changes with temperature, with the d-c operating point, and from one transistor to another.

6-3   The Ideal CE Transistor

For our first approximation we will eliminate all but the most essential features of the CE connection. For instance, in the base diode we know that there is some feedback from collector to base as illustrated by the gap between the curves of Fig. 6-1b. We will disregard this feedback and treat the base diode as an ordinary semiconductor diode with the characteristics shown in Fig. 6-4a. As far as the collector diode is concerned we will:

1. Disregard the breakdown phenomenon.
2. Disregard the small collector current that occurs for $i_B = 0$ (see Fig. 6-2c).
3. Eliminate the slight upward slope in the collector curves.
4. Reduce the knee voltages to zero.
5. Make the d-c and a-c β's equal, that is, $\beta_{dc} = \beta$.

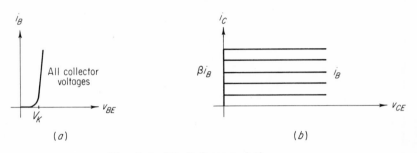

Fig. 6-4 Ideal characteristic curves.

Figure 6-4b summarizes these various approximations; for any value of base current, the collector current is β times larger. In other words, as long as the collector diode is back-biased, the collector current is controlled by the base current and is β times larger than the base current. This control that the base current has over the collector current holds for both direct and alternating currents. For instance, if the d-c and a-c β's equal 100, then 1 ma of d-c base current will produce 100 ma of d-c collector current; further, 0.02 ma of a-c base current will produce 2 ma of a-c collector current. We will call this first approximation the *ideal CE transistor.*

Example 6-1

In Fig. 6-5, the ideal CE transistor has a β of 100. Find the d-c collector current I_C and the d-c collector-ground voltage V_C.

Solution

First, find the d-c base current I_B.

$$I_B = \frac{10 - V_B}{10^6} \cong \frac{10}{10^6} = 10 \ \mu a$$

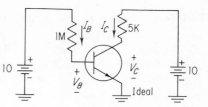

Fig. 6-5 Examples 6-1 and 6-2.

We neglected V_B because it is only around 0.3 or 0.7 volt, depending upon the material used.

Next, find the collector current, which is β times the base current.

$$I_C = \beta I_B = 100(10 \ \mu a) = 1000 \ \mu a = 1 \ ma$$

The collector-ground voltage is simply the supply voltage minus the voltage drop across the 5-kilohm load resistor. Thus,

$$V_C = 10 - I_C R_L = 10 - 10^{-3}(5)(10^3) = 5 \text{ volts}$$

EXAMPLE 6-2

If the transistor of Fig. 6-5 is made of silicon, find I_C and V_C by allowing for the base-diode voltage drop. Use a β of 100.

SOLUTION

$$I_B = \frac{10 - 0.7}{10^6} = 9.3 \ \mu a$$

$$I_C = \beta I_B = 100(9.3 \ \mu a) = 930 \ \mu a = 0.93 \ ma$$

$$V_C = 10 - 0.93(10^{-3})(5)(10^3) = 5.35 \text{ volts}$$

EXAMPLE 6-3

In Fig. 6-6 the ideal transistor has a β of 50. What value of R_B will produce a collector-ground voltage of 10 volts?

SOLUTION

In order for V_C to equal 10 volts, there must be a voltage drop of 10 volts across the 10-kilohm load resistor; the collector current,

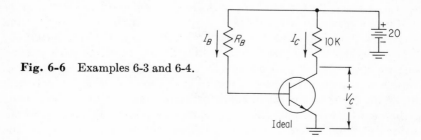

Fig. 6-6 Examples 6-3 and 6-4.

therefore, must be 1 ma. For a β of 50 we compute a base current of

$$I_B = \frac{I_C}{\beta} = \frac{1 \text{ ma}}{50} = 20 \ \mu a$$

We now must find the correct size of R_B that will produce a base current of 20 μa. Using Ohm's law, we get

$$R_B = \frac{20}{20(10^{-6})} = 1 \text{ megohm}$$

We disregard the small voltage drop across the base diode; therefore, all 20 volts appears across the R_B resistor.

EXAMPLE 6-4

Suppose that the transistor of Fig. 6-6 is replaced by another transistor with a β of 75. If $R_B = 1$ megohm, what will the new value of V_{CE} be?

SOLUTION

The base current is still

$$I_B \cong \frac{20}{10^6} = 20 \ \mu a$$

The collector current for the new transistor is different.

$$I_C = \beta I_B = 75(20 \ \mu a) = 1.5 \text{ ma}$$

With this new value of collector current the voltage from collector to ground becomes

$$V_C = 20 - 1.5(10^{-3})(10)(10^3) = 5 \text{ volts}$$

6-4   Base Bias of a Transistor

We already know that for normal operation the emitter diode is forward-biased and the collector diode is back-biased. When an a-c signal is injected into a transistor, there is the possibility that the signal may swing the emitter diode into the back-biased condition or perhaps swing the collector diode into the forward-biased condition. In either case, normal transistor action is lost, and clipping of the a-c signal results (see Chap. 8). In order to prevent this possibility, it is common practice to set up a suitable d-c operating point in collector current and voltage; the a-c signal then causes excursions from this operating point, and as long as the a-c signal is not too large, the emitter diode remains forward-biased and the collector diode remains back-biased throughout the entire a-c cycle. Setting up this d-c operating point in collector current and voltage is commonly called *biasing* the transistor.

In this section we discuss one of the ways to bias a transistor in the CE connection. Figure 6-7 illustrates what we will call *base bias*. Specific examples of this type of bias were examined in Examples 6-1 to 6-4. Now we analyze the general circuit of Fig. 6-7 to determine the bias formulas.

As shown in Fig. 6-7, the collector-emitter voltage V_{CE} is simply designated V_C and the base-emitter voltage V_{BE} is simply written as V_B. We already know that V_C is equal to the power-supply voltage minus the voltage drop across the load resistor R_L. That is,

$$V_C = V_{CC} - I_C R_L \tag{6-3}$$

where V_C is the d-c voltage from collector to ground

V_{CC} is the collector-supply voltage

I_C is the d-c collector current

R_L is the d-c load resistance seen from the collector

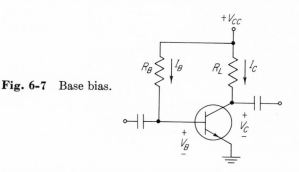

Fig. 6-7 Base bias.

The d-c collector current, of course, equals the β of the transistor times the base current. That is,

$$I_C = \beta I_B$$

where the d-c β will be used if there is a difference between the two β values.

By inspection of Fig. 6-7 we can see that the base current I_B is

$$I_B = \frac{V_{CC} - V_B}{R_B}$$

or for those circuits where the drop of a few tenths volt across the base diode is negligible, we have

$$I_B \cong \frac{V_{CC}}{R_B} \qquad \text{when } V_{CC} \gg V_B \tag{6-4}$$

The base-biased circuit of Fig. 6-7 is one of the simplest ways to bias a transistor. We set the base current I_B by choosing an appropriate size for R_B. This base current controls the size of the collector current I_C, which in conjunction with R_L determines the collector voltage V_C. For instance, in Fig. 6-8a, the base current is

$$I_B \cong \frac{V_{CC}}{R_B} = \frac{30}{10^6} = 30 \; \mu\text{a}$$

The β is given as 50, so that we immediately can calculate a collector current of

$$I_C = \beta I_B = 50(30 \; \mu\text{a}) = 1.5 \; \text{ma}$$

This collector current flows through an R_L of 10 kilohms and produces a voltage drop of 15 volts. Therefore, the collector-ground voltage is

$$V_C = V_{CC} - I_C R_L = 30 - 15 = 15 \; \text{volts}$$

Thus, the d-c operating point is set at $I_C = 1.5$ ma and $V_C = 15$ volts. When an a-c signal is coupled into the stage, it causes excursions about this operating point. As long as the a-c signal is not too large, the emitter diode remains forward-biased, and the collector diode remains back-biased throughout the entire a-c cycle.

The base-biased circuit of Fig. 6-7 is actually *the worst possible way to bias* a transistor from the standpoint of a stable operating point. The reason that the base-biased circuit is so poor can be understood by referring again to Fig. 6-8a. We have found that for this circuit with the given β of 50 we have a d-c operating point of

$$I_C = 1.5 \; \text{ma}$$
$$V_C = 15 \; \text{volts}$$

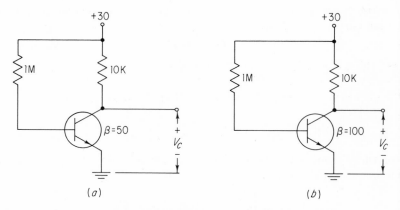

Fig. 6-8   Effect of β change in a base-biased circuit.

Suppose that for some reason or other the β of the transistor changes from 50 to 100 (a change of this size can occur when replacing transistors or when the ambient temperature changes over a large range). The new circuit is shown in Fig. 6-8b. In this circuit the base current is *still the same.*

$$I_B \cong \frac{V_{CC}}{R_B} = \frac{30}{10^6} = 30 \ \mu a$$

But the collector current is now

$$I_C = 100(30 \ \mu a) = 3 \ ma$$

This 3 ma of collector produces a collector voltage of

$$V_C = V_{CC} - I_C R_L = 30 - 3(10^{-3})(10)(10^3) = 0 \ volts$$

Therefore, the collector diode is no longer back-biased. If an a-c signal were coupled into the base, the signal at the collector would be clipped off on the negative-going half cycle. (Clipping is discussed further in Chap. 8.)

Let us summarize base bias:

1. The base current is essentially fixed by the value of V_{CC} and R_B.

2. The collector current is determined by I_B and β. Because β varies widely from one transistor to another and with temperature change, the collector current also varies widely with these changes.

3. Base bias is *the worst way* to bias a transistor from the standpoint of stability of the operating point.

6-5 Emitter Bias of a Transistor

Now that we have seen the worst way to bias a transistor, let us look at one of the best ways. The circuit of Fig. 6-9a illustrates what we will call *emitter bias.* The same circuit drawn in a more practical form is shown in Fig. 6-9b. The emitter-biased circuit of Fig. 6-9 is quite popular and is widely used whenever two power supplies (positive and negative) are available. Its popularity stems from the fact that the collector current is essentially independent of the β. In fact, we will show that the collector current is

$$I_C \cong \frac{V_{EE}}{R_E}$$

To prove this result we first write the Kirchhoff voltage equation around the loop containing R_E and R_B. If we start at the emitter and proceed in a clockwise direction, we get

$$I_E R_E - V_{EE} + I_B R_B + V_{BE} = 0$$

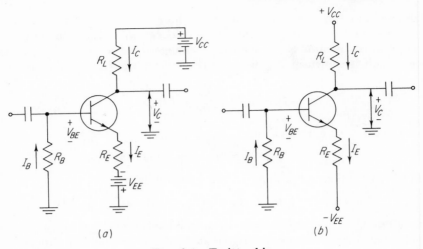

Fig. 6-9 Emitter bias.

By transposing V_{EE} and V_{BE} we obtain

$$I_E R_E + I_B R_B = V_{EE} - V_{BE} \qquad (6\text{-}5)$$

To simplify this expression recall that the emitter current is approximately equal to the collector current. Hence, β equals

$$\beta = \frac{I_C}{I_B} \cong \frac{I_E}{I_B}$$

or

$$I_B \cong \frac{I_E}{\beta}$$

If we substitute this expression for I_B into Eq. (6-5), we obtain

$$I_E R_E + \frac{I_E R_B}{\beta} = V_{EE} - V_{BE}$$

Next, we factor I_E to get

$$I_E \left(R_E + \frac{R_B}{\beta} \right) = V_{EE} - V_{BE}$$

Finally, we can divide to obtain

$$I_E = \frac{V_{EE} - V_{BE}}{R_E + R_B/\beta} \qquad (6\text{-}6)$$

Equation (6-6) is almost an exact expression for the d-c emitter current. A simpler and more useful expression for I_E can be obtained by realizing that in most circuits V_{BE} is negligible compared to V_{EE} (a few tenths of a volt compared to many volts). Also, in most circuits it is possible to choose R_B so that R_B/β is negligible compared to R_E. Therefore, an approximate expression for I_E that applies to most practical circuits is

$$I_E \cong \frac{V_{EE}}{R_E} \qquad (6\text{-}7)$$

provided that
$$V_{EE} \gg V_{BE} \qquad \text{(the usual case)}$$

and

$$R_E \gg \frac{R_B}{\beta} \qquad \text{(the usual case)}$$

Equation (6-7) tells us that the d-c emitter current in the emitter-biased circuit of Fig. 6-9 is essentially equal to the emitter-supply voltage V_{EE} divided by the emitter resistance R_E. For instance, in Fig. 6-9 if $V_{EE} = 10$ volts and $R_E = 10$ kilohms, the emitter current I_E is approximately 1 ma, and, of course, the collector current will be essentially 1 ma. Note that Eq. (6-7) does not contain β; in other words, *the emitter current is independent of β.* Herein lies the tremendous advantage of emitter bias over base bias; even though the β varies with temperature or transistor change, the amount of emitter current in the emitter-biased circuit remains essentially fixed and equal to V_{EE}/R_E.

A convenient way to remember emitter bias is to realize that it is actually a form of the CB connection, at least as far as the d-c equivalent circuit is concerned. Within the restrictions of Eq. (6-7) the emitter-biased circuit of Fig. 6-10a acts essentially the same as the CB circuit of Fig. 6-10b; the circuit of Fig. 6-10a has simply been redrawn, and R_B has

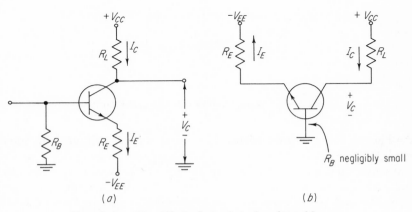

Fig. 6-10 Simplified viewpoint of emitter bias.

been shown as negligibly small. Thus, when we encounter the emitter-biased circuit of Fig. 6-10a, we can think of it as being like the CB circuit of Fig. 6-10b *as far as its d-c equivalent circuit is concerned*. The advantage of this viewpoint is that we already know from our earlier studies of the CB circuit that

$$I_E \cong \frac{V_{EE}}{R_E}$$

which is identical to Eq. (6-7).

The other formula of interest here is for the collector-ground voltage V_C. This voltage is equal to the collector supply minus the voltage drop across the load resistor. That is,

$$V_C = V_{CC} - I_C R_L \qquad (6\text{-}8)$$

Equations (6-7) and (6-8) are very useful in both analysis and design. Basically, they give us the d-c operating point of an emitter-biased transistor. These equations are summarized in Fig. 6-11a.

When a p-n-p transistor is used, the emitter-bias arrangement is quite similar, and the biasing formulas are identical. Figure 6-11b summarizes

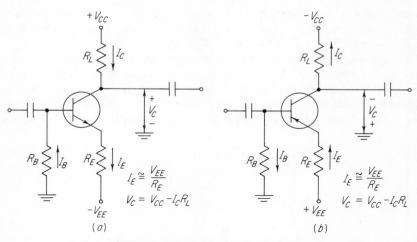

Fig. 6-11   Emitter-bias circuits and formulas.

the biasing of a p-n-p transistor. Note that the d-c voltage from the collector to ground is negative and its magnitude is given by Eq. (6-8). Note also that in a p-n-p circuit all d-c voltages and currents are in opposite directions from a similar n-p-n circuit. Therefore, all the d-c formulas that we develop for the n-p-n circuit also apply to the p-n-p circuit as far as magnitudes are concerned.

EXAMPLE 6-5

For the circuit of Fig. 6-12 the germanium transistor has a β of 50. Find:

(a) The approximate value of I_E.
(b) A more exact value of I_E by using Eq. (6-6).

SOLUTION

(a) We know that in an emitter-biased circuit almost all the emitter-supply voltage appears across the emitter resistor R_E. Hence, the emitter current is

$$I_E \cong \frac{V_{EE}}{R_E} = \frac{20}{20(10^3)} = 1 \text{ ma}$$

(b) When we use the more exact formula, Eq. (6-6), we get

$$I_E = \frac{20 - 0.3}{20(10^3) + 10(10^3)/50} = \frac{19.7}{20.2(10^3)} = 0.975 \text{ ma}$$

Note that the more exact answer of 0.975 ma is only 2.5 percent lower than the approximate answer of 1 ma. A small error of this size occurs in any well-designed emitter-biased circuit.

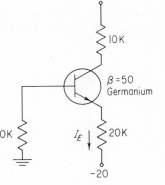

Fig. 6-12   Examples 6-5 and 6-6.

EXAMPLE 6-6

Suppose that we change transistors in the circuit of Fig. 6-12 and that the new β is 100. Find:

(a) The approximate value of I_E.
(b) The value of I_E by using Eq. (6-6).

SOLUTION

Once again, we note that for an emitter-biased circuit essentially all the emitter-supply voltage is dropped across the emitter resistor. Hence,

$$I_E \cong \frac{V_{EE}}{R_E} = \frac{20}{20(10^3)} = 1 \text{ ma}$$

When we use Eq. (6-6), we get

$$I_E = \frac{20 - 0.3}{20(10^3) + 10(10^3)/100} = \frac{19.7}{20.1(10^3)} = 0.98 \text{ ma}$$

Note carefully that even though β has changed from 50 to 100, the emitter current has changed only from 0.975 ma (Example 6-5) to 0.98 ma. This always occurs in a well-designed circuit because the designer makes sure that R_B/β is much smaller than R_E for the typical β range of the transistor being used.

EXAMPLE 6-7

In troubleshooting circuits one of the first measurements that should be made is to check the d-c collector-ground voltage V_C. In troubleshooting the circuit of Fig. 6-13a, what should the approximate value of V_C be?

SOLUTION

First, note that as far as the d-c operation of the circuit is concerned, all capacitors are open circuits. Hence, the circuit of Fig. 6-13a has

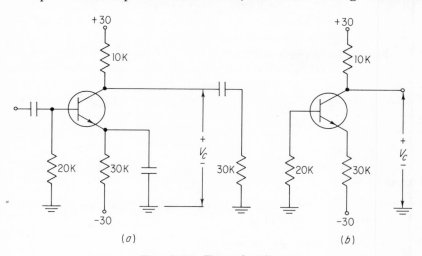

Fig. 6-13 Example 6-7.

the d-c equivalent circuit shown in Fig. 6-13*b*. It is now obvious that the emitter current is

$$I_E \cong \frac{V_{EE}}{R_E} = \frac{30}{30(10^3)} = 1 \text{ ma}$$

Next, we can see that the collector voltage should equal the collector supply voltage (30 volts) minus the voltage drop across the load resistor. Thus,

$$V_C = V_{CC} - I_C R_L = 30 - 10^{-3}(10^4) = 20 \text{ volts}$$

In troubleshooting a circuit like that shown in Fig. 6-13*a* the first important measurement to make is to check that the collector voltage is truly around 20 volts. This simple test verifies that three resistors, two power supplies, and one transistor are working properly as far as d-c voltages and currents are concerned.

6-6 Analyzing CE Transistor Circuits

In analyzing the complete operation of CE circuits driven by large d-c sources and small a-c sources we again will be using a modified form of the superposition theorem. We use the d-c equivalent circuit to find the d-c operating point of the transistor. We can then use the a-c equivalent circuit to find how the a-c signal is amplified or modified by the transistor circuit.

In the d-c equivalent circuit we will view the ideal transistor as a rectifier diode in the base circuit and a current source in the collector circuit. Figure 6-14 illustrates the d-c equivalent circuit. (For the *p-n-p* transistor we reverse the diode and the current source.)

In the a-c equivalent circuit we think of the ideal transistor as a resistance in the base and a current source in the collector, as shown in Fig. 6-15. Note that the a-c resistance looking into the base is $\beta r'_e$, where r'_e is theoretically given by 25 mv/I_E. The concept of a-c resistance looking into the base is quite similar to that developed for the CB connection in Chap. 5. Recall that the d-c sources establish the d-c operating

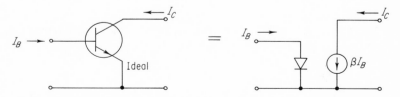

Fig. 6-14 Ideal d-c equivalent circuit of an *n-p-n* CE transistor.

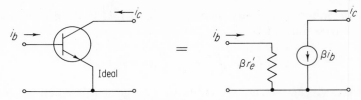

Fig. 6-15   Ideal a-c equivalent circuit of an n-p-n CE transistor.

point on both the collector and base characteristics; the a-c signal then causes small excursions from the operating point. For instance, in Fig. 6-16 the operating point on the base characteristic is shown at point Q. I_B is the d-c base current at point Q. When an a-c signal is applied to the base diode, there are excursions from the operating point. For a typical a-c signal the excursions might take place between points A and B. If the a-c signal is small, the changes in voltage and current are almost directly proportional because only a small part of the curve is being used. Because the changes are almost linear, the base diode looks like an ordinary resistor to the a-c signal.

The value of resistance seen by the a-c signal looking into the base shows a wide variation from one transistor to another. As a theoretical approximation, this a-c resistance is

$$r_{\mathrm{ac}} = \frac{25 \text{ mv}}{I_B} \tag{6-9}$$

where I_B is the value of the d-c base current. Thus, when $I_B = 10 \ \mu\mathrm{a}$, the a-c resistance is around

$$r_{\mathrm{ac}} = \frac{25 \text{ mv}}{10 \ \mu\mathrm{a}} \cong 2.5 \text{ kilohms}$$

Equation (6-9) should be easy to remember because it is analogous to Eq. (5-3). In Eq. (5-3) we saw that the a-c resistance *looking into the*

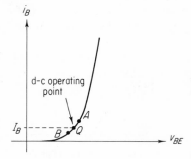

Fig. 6-16   A-c resistance of the base diode.

emitter is 25 mv/I_E. In Eq. (6-9) we see that the a-c resistance *looking into the base* is 25 mv/I_B. Both of these equations can be derived by applying calculus to an exponential equation relating current and voltage across a *p-n* junction; we will accept these results without derivation.

Equation (6-9) can be expressed in a more useful form. We can rearrange it as follows:

$$r_{ac} = \frac{25 \text{ mv}}{I_B} = \frac{25 \text{ mv}}{I_C/\beta} = \beta \frac{25 \text{ mv}}{I_C} \cong \beta \frac{25 \text{ mv}}{I_E}$$

or

$$r_{ac} \cong \beta r'_e \tag{6-10}$$

The significance of this result is important; it says that the a-c resistance looking into the base of a transistor is β times larger than the a-c resistance looking into the emitter of a transistor. This makes sense because we know that the base current is smaller than the emitter current by a factor of β; therefore, we should expect the resistance looking into the base to be larger by a factor of β.

The equivalent circuits of Figs. 6-14 and 6-15 should be memorized because they enable us to analyze CE emitter circuits quickly and easily. Of course, these equivalent circuits are for the ideal transistor; nevertheless, as pointed out before, the ideal-transistor approach is adequate for many of our needs in transistor circuit analysis and design.

EXAMPLE 6-8

Sketch the waveform of the total voltage v_C appearing from collector to ground in the circuit of Fig. 6-17a. Use a β of 50.

SOLUTION

First, draw or visualize the d-c equivalent circuit as shown in Fig. 6-17b. In this circuit it is immediately clear that the d-c base current is

$$I_B \cong \frac{V_{CC}}{R_B} = \frac{20}{10^6} = 20 \ \mu\text{a}$$

The d-c collector current is β times larger than the base current.

$$I_C = \beta I_B = 50(20 \ \mu\text{a}) = 1 \text{ ma}$$

The d-c collector-ground voltage is simply the collector-supply voltage minus the voltage drop across the 10-kilohm load resistor.

$$V_C = V_{CC} - I_C R_L = 20 - 10^{-3}(10^4) = 10 \text{ volts}$$

Next, we analyze a-c operation by means of the a-c equivalent circuit, which is shown in Fig. 6-17c. All d-c sources have been shorted; all coupling capacitors are assumed to have a low enough reactance to

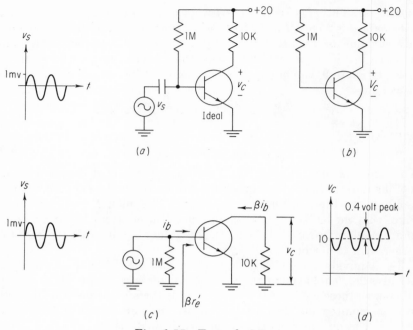

Fig. 6-17   Example 6-8.

act like short circuits as far as the a-c signal is concerned. Looking
into the base, the a-c signal sees a resistance of

$$\beta r'_e = \beta \frac{25 \text{ mv}}{I_E} \cong 50 \frac{25 \text{ mv}}{1 \text{ ma}} = 1250 \text{ ohms}$$

The source voltage is a 1-mv-peak sine wave. This voltage appears
directly across the base diode and produces a sine wave of base current
with a peak value of

$$i_{b(\text{peak})} = \frac{v_{s(\text{peak})}}{\beta r'_e} = \frac{0.001}{1250} = 0.8 \ \mu\text{a}$$

The a-c collector current is β times the base current; the collector
current, therefore, is a sine wave with a peak value of

$$i_{c(\text{peak})} = \beta i_{b(\text{peak})} = 50(0.8 \ \mu\text{a}) = 40 \ \mu\text{a}$$

In Fig. 6-17c it is clear that this a-c collector current flows through
the 10-kilohm resistor and develops a sine-wave voltage with a peak
value of

$$v_{c(\text{peak})} = 40(10^{-6})(10^4) = 0.4 \text{ volt}$$

Now that we have both the d-c and a-c components, we can super-pose them and obtain the total waveform shown in Fig. 6-17d.

Note two points about this waveform:

1. The a-c component is an amplified version of the source voltage. The voltage gain is the output voltage of 0.4 volt divided by the source voltage of 1 mv. Thus, the voltage gain is 400.

2. The output a-c signal is 180° out of phase with the source signal. The reason for this phase inversion is easily understood by referring to Fig. 6-17a. During the positive half cycle of source voltage, the a-c base current will aid the d-c base current, which means that the total base current is increased. This implies that the total collector current is increased, which in turn means a larger voltage drop across the load resistor. Therefore, the total collector voltage (which equals the supply voltage minus the drop across the load) must be smaller during the positive half cycle of source voltage. Thus, we have established that the total collector voltage is decreasing during the positive half cycle of source voltage, which immediately implies phase inversion. (For the reader familiar with vacuum-tube circuits, the CE transistor stage inverts the signal in the same way that a common-cathode tube connection inverts the signal at its grid.)

EXAMPLE 6-9

The circuit of Fig. 6-18a is driven by a 1-mv-rms signal. If the transistor has a β of 100, what is the rms value of the output voltage?

SOLUTION

When we visualize the d-c equivalent circuit, it is clear that the d-c component is blocked by the coupling capacitor on the output side. In other words, only the a-c component reaches the final 10-kilohm load.

We still must find the d-c emitter current because we will use it to find the a-c resistance of the base diode. It is clear that the circuit of Fig. 6-18a is emitter-biased. Using Eq. (6-7), we find that

$$I_E \cong \frac{V_{EE}}{R_E} = \frac{30}{30(10^3)} = 1 \text{ ma}$$

The a-c equivalent circuit is shown in Fig. 6-18b. Especially note that the *emitter is at a-c ground because the bypass capacitor looks like a short to the a-c emitter current*. The a-c resistance looking into the base diode is simply

$$\beta r'_e = \beta \frac{25 \text{ mv}}{I_E} = 100 \frac{25 \text{ mv}}{1 \text{ ma}} = 2500 \text{ ohms}$$

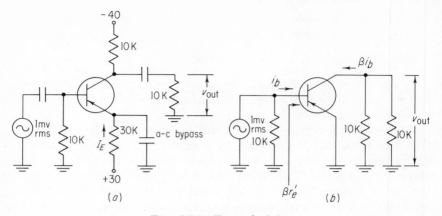

Fig. 6-18   Example 6-9.

In Fig. 6-18b, note that the a-c source voltage appears across the base diode; therefore, the a-c base current has an rms value of

$$i_b = \frac{v_s}{\beta r_e'} = \frac{0.001}{2500} = 0.4 \ \mu\text{a}$$

The a-c collector current has an rms value of

$$i_c = \beta i_b = 100(0.4 \ \mu\text{a}) = 40 \ \mu\text{a}$$

Finally, we see that as far as the a-c signal is concerned, the 10-kilohm resistors appear in parallel, and therefore the a-c load resistance is 5 kilohms. Thus, the output voltage has an rms value of

$$v_{\text{out}} = 40(10^{-6})(5)(10^3) = 200 \ \text{mv}$$

Note that the voltage gain from source to output is

$$\frac{v_{\text{out}}}{v_s} = \frac{200 \ \text{mv}}{1 \ \text{mv}} = 200$$

6-7   The Voltage Gain of an Emitter-biased Stage

In this section we will find the voltage-gain formula for the emitter biased circuit shown in Fig. 6-19a. This circuit is one of the widely used types of transistor amplifier, and therefore it will be worthwhile to have a formula for the voltage gain from input to output, that is, a formula for $v_{\text{out}}/v_{\text{in}}$.

Note that the transistor amplifier of Fig. 6-19a is analogous to the vacuum-tube amplifier of Fig. 6-19b. In the vacuum-tube circuit, bias

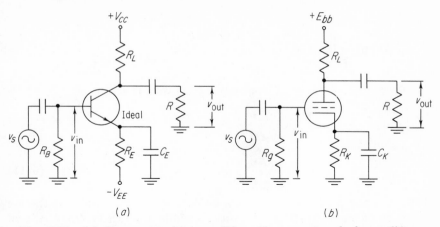

Fig. 6-19 (a) Common-emitter amplifier; (b) common-cathode amplifier.

voltage is developed across the cathode resistor R_K. Many readers have studied vacuum-tube circuits and recall that the purpose of the capacitor C_K is to prevent excessive degeneration. In a similar way, the emitter of the transistor is bypassed by ground by means of C_E. The purpose of C_E is similar to that of C_K in a vacuum-tube circuit: it prevents excessive degeneration from taking place.

How can we find the formula for the voltage gain of the transistor amplifier of Fig. 6-19a? First, we draw the a-c equivalent circuit of Fig. 6-20. We are, as usual, assuming that the amplifier is operating in its normal frequency range, where all capacitors are large enough to act like short circuits to the a-c signal. With the ideal-transistor approximation the base diode looks like a resistance of $\beta r'_e$. Also, in the collector circuit the parallel combination of R_L and R is simply a net resistance of r_L.

To find the voltage gain we proceed as follows. First, the a-c output

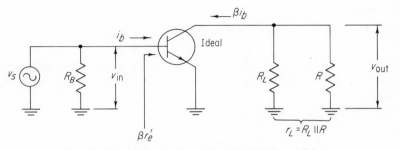

Fig. 6-20 A-c equivalent circuit of CE amplifier.

voltage is

$$v_{\text{out}} = \beta i_b r_L$$

The a-c input voltage is

$$v_{\text{in}} = i_b \beta r'_e$$

Therefore, the voltage gain from input to output is simply

$$\frac{v_{\text{out}}}{v_{\text{in}}} = \frac{\beta i_b r_L}{i_b \beta r'_e}$$

or

$$\frac{v_{\text{out}}}{v_{\text{in}}} = \frac{r_L}{r'_e} \tag{6-11}$$

where r_L is the a-c load resistance seen by the collector and r'_e is the a-c resistance of the emitter diode. Note carefully that the voltage gain of the ideal CE stage shown in Fig. 6-19a is exactly the same as the voltage gain from the emitter to the collector for a CB stage, Eq. (5-11).

Equation (6-11) is very useful in analyzing emitter-biased amplifiers. As usual, r'_e has a theoretical value of 25 mv/I_E, which can be used in preliminary analysis. If desired, we can allow for the typical range in r'_e by using

$$\frac{25 \text{ mv}}{I_E} < r'_e < \frac{50 \text{ mv}}{I_E}$$

EXAMPLE 6-10

In the circuit of Fig. 6-21 assume that all capacitors are a-c shorts. For a β of 100, find:

(a) The voltage gain from the base to the output.
(b) The output voltage for an input voltage of 1 mv rms.

SOLUTION

(a) The a-c load resistance in the collector circuit is 10 kilohms in parallel with 10 kilohms, which means that $r_L = 5$ kilohms. To find r'_e we can use

$$r'_e = \frac{25 \text{ mv}}{I_E} = \frac{25 \text{ mv}}{1 \text{ ma}} = 25 \text{ ohms}$$

(It should be apparent that the approximate value of d-c emitter current is about 1 ma for this emitter-biased circuit. If not, review Sec. 6-5.)

Therefore, the voltage gain is

$$\frac{v_{\text{out}}}{v_{\text{in}}} = \frac{r_L}{r'_e} = \frac{5000}{25} = 200$$

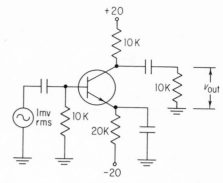

Fig. 6-21 Examples 6-10 to 6-12.

If we wish to allow for the range in r_e', we can observe that r_e' will be between 25 and 50 ohms; the voltage gain, therefore, will be between 100 and 200.

(*b*) To find the output voltage for an input voltage of 1 mv, we need only multiply by the voltage gain. Thus, the rms output is

$$v_{\text{out}} = 200\, v_{\text{in}} = 200(1 \text{ mv}) = 200 \text{ mv}$$

when r_e' is 25 ohms.

At the other extreme,

$$v_{\text{out}} = 100(1 \text{ mv}) = 100 \text{ mv}$$

when r_e' is 50 ohms.

Example 6-11

In the preceding example, what would happen to the voltage gain if the final 10-kilohm output resistor were changed to 30 kilohms?

Solution

The only change here is in the value of the a-c load resistance r_L. This resistance becomes 10 kilohms in parallel with 30 kilohms, which equals 7.5 kilohms (by the usual product-over-sum method). Thus, for an r_e' of 25 ohms the voltage gain becomes

$$\frac{v_{\text{out}}}{v_{\text{in}}} = \frac{r_L}{r_e'} = \frac{7500}{25} = 300$$

Example 6-12

In the circuit of Fig. 6-21, what happens to the voltage gain when the 20-kilohm emitter resistor is changed to a 40-kilohm resistor?

SOLUTION

First, notice that the d-c emitter current will change to

$$I_E \cong \frac{V_{EE}}{R_E} = \frac{20}{40(10^3)} = 0.5 \text{ ma}$$

With 0.5 ma of d-c emitter current the value of r'_e lies in the range of 50 to 100 ohms. Therefore, the voltage gain lies in the range of 50 to 100.

6-8   Effects of Source Resistance

In this section we want to find out what effect the source resistance r_s has on the voltage gain of a typical amplifier like that of Fig. 6-22a. In this circuit it should be immediately clear that some of the source voltage will be lost across r_s; only part of the source voltage v_s actually appears across the base diode of the transistor.

To find out how much effect r_s has, we first draw the a-c equivalent circuit for the input circuit, as shown in Fig. 6-22b. The input voltage v_{in}

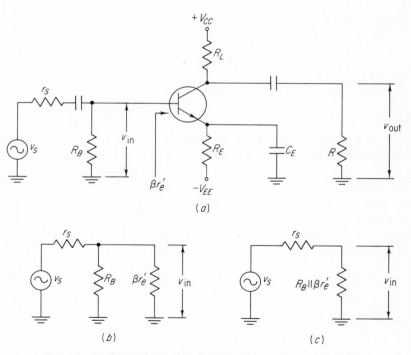

Fig. 6-22   Loss of a-c signal across the source resistance.

is the voltage that appears across the shunt combination of R_B and $\beta r'_e$. These two resistors can be lumped into a single resistor $R_B \| \beta r'_e$, as illustrated in Fig. 6-22c. The circuit of Fig. 6-22c is obviously a voltage divider, so that v_{in} is simply

$$v_{\text{in}} = \frac{R_B \| \beta r'_e}{r_s + (R_B \| \beta r'_e)}\, v_s \tag{6-12}$$

Note in Eq. (6-12) that when r_s is very small compared to $R_B \| \beta r'_e$, the expression becomes

$$v_{\text{in}} \cong v_s \qquad \text{for } r_s \ll (R_B \| \beta r'_e) \tag{6-13}$$

In other words, when the source resistance r_s is very small, almost no voltage is dropped across it; almost all the source voltage appears across the base diode.

In practice, we can encounter either situation. An amplifier may be driven from a very low-impedance source, in which case we use Eq. (6-13). On the other hand, if the source resistance r_s is not negligible, we must use Eq. (6-12) to determine how much of the source voltage actually appears across the base diode.

As far as the voltage gain from base to output is concerned, this is still given by

$$\frac{v_{\text{out}}}{v_{\text{in}}} = \frac{r_L}{r'_e}$$

Thus, given the source voltage v_s, we first find out how much of this voltage appears across the base diode. Then, to find the output voltage we simply multiply this voltage v_{in} by the voltage gain.

EXAMPLE 6-13

In Fig. 6-23, the transistor has a β of 50. Find the output voltage.

SOLUTION

We first must find how much of the 1-mv source voltage actually appears across the base diode. To do this, we must know the value of $\beta r'_e$. Using 25 mv/I_E for r'_e, we get

$$\beta r'_e = \beta\, \frac{25 \text{ mv}}{I_E} = 50\, \frac{25 \text{ mv}}{0.5 \text{ ma}} = 2500 \text{ ohms}$$

Next, we obtain the parallel resistance of R_B and $\beta r'_e$.

$$R_B \| \beta r'_e = 10{,}000 \| 2500 = 2000 \text{ ohms}$$

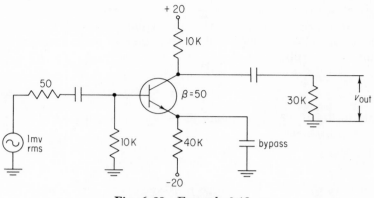

Fig. 6-23   Example 6-13.

Since 50 ohms of source resistance is much smaller than 2000 ohms, we can conclude that almost all the 1-mv source voltage appears across the base diode.

The voltage gain is

$$\frac{v_{\text{out}}}{v_{\text{in}}} = \frac{r_L}{r_e'} = \frac{10,000 \| 30,000}{50} = 150$$

And the output voltage is

$$v_{\text{out}} = 150(1 \text{ mv}) = 150 \text{ mv}$$

EXAMPLE 6-14

Suppose that the source resistance of the preceding example is changed from 50 ohms to 3 kilohms. Find the new output voltage.

SOLUTION

The voltage gain from base to output remains the same because r_L/r_e' is unchanged. What does change is the amount of voltage actually appearing across the base diode. We already know from Example 6-13 that the parallel combination of R_B and $\beta r_e'$ is 2000 ohms. Hence, by using Eq. (6-12) we can find the amount of voltage that actually reaches the base diode.

$$v_{\text{in}} = \frac{R_B \| \beta r_e'}{r_s + (R_B \| \beta r_e')} v_s = \frac{2000}{3000 + 2000} 1 \text{ mv} = 0.4 \text{ mv}$$

Thus, the output voltage is 150 times the actual base voltage.

$$v_{\text{out}} = 150(0.4 \text{ mv}) = 60 \text{ mv}$$

6-9   Tube-to-transistor Transformations

Many of us already have a knowledge of vacuum-tube circuits; it seems
worthwhile, therefore, to indicate that many of the formulas for vacuum-
tube circuits can be easily transformed into formulas for analogous
transistor circuits. In this section we show that a transistor has a g_m,
a μ, and an r_p and that the gain formulas for various tube circuits apply
to those transistor circuits which are the direct counterparts of the tube
circuits.

In Fig. 6-24a we have shown the a-c equivalent circuit of a vacuum
tube (biasing not shown). There is an a-c plate current i_{out} and an a-c
grid voltage of v_{in}. Recall that the g_m of a tube is defined as

$$g_m = \frac{i_{\text{out}}}{v_{\text{in}}} \qquad \text{for zero load resistance}$$

Basically, the g_m is the ratio of output current to input voltage; it tells us
how effective changes in the grid voltage are in changing the output
current.

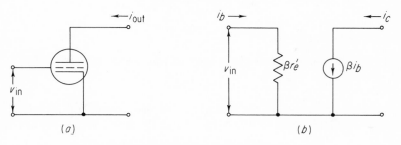

Fig. 6-24   Tube-transistor analogy.

In Fig. 6-24b, we have shown the a-c equivalent circuit for a transistor.
The output current is βi_b. The input voltage at the base is

$$v_{\text{in}} = i_b \beta r'_e$$

Therefore, the g_m of a transistor is

$$g_m = \frac{i_{\text{out}}}{v_{\text{in}}} = \frac{\beta i_b}{i_b \beta r'_e}$$

or

$$g_m = \frac{1}{r'_e} \qquad\qquad\qquad (6\text{-}14)$$

Next, recall that the r_p of tube is the dynamic, or a-c, resistance looking back into the plate. With respect to the tube curves, r_p is the inverse slope of the plate characteristics.

The collector characteristics of a transistor are quite similar to pentode characteristics. For the ideal transistor, the IV characteristics are horizontal; this means that the r_p is infinite for an ideal transistor.

Finally, recall that the μ equals the product of g_m and r_p. Because r_p is infinite, the μ of an ideal transistor is infinite.

What we can do with these results is simply the following: whenever we encounter a transistor circuit whose a-c configuration is the counterpart of a well-known tube circuit, we can transform the tube formula by replacing g_m by $1/r'_e$ and by replacing r_p and μ by ∞. That is, we transform the tube formula into a transistor formula by using the following transformations:

$$g_m \longrightarrow \frac{1}{r'_e}$$
$$r_p \longrightarrow \infty$$
$$\mu \longrightarrow \infty$$

As an example, consider the circuit of Fig. 6-25a. This is a well-known vacuum-tube amplifier and has a voltage gain of

$$\frac{v_{\text{out}}}{v_{\text{in}}} \cong g_m r_L \qquad \text{for pentodes}$$

where r_L is the a-c load resistance seen by the plate. In this case,

$$r_L = R_L \| R$$

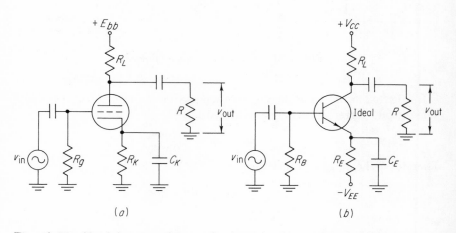

Fig. 6-25 Obtaining transistor gain formula from analogous vacuum-tube circuit.

The transistor circuit of Fig. 6-25b has the same a-c configuration as the tube circuit. Therefore, we can find the voltage gain of the transistor circuit by using the g_m of an ideal transistor. That is,

$$\frac{v_{\text{out}}}{v_{\text{in}}} \cong g_m r_L = \frac{1}{r'_e} r_L = \frac{r_L}{r'_e}$$

This result is identical to Eq. (6-11), which we derived in a completely different way.

The point here is simply that there is an analogy between the vacuum tube and the transistor. In a sense, the real transistor is like a pentode because it has a g_m, a very high r_p, and a very high μ. (Ideally, the r_p and μ are infinite.) One big difference, however, between the vacuum tube and the transistor is that the CE transistor has an input resistance of $\beta r'_e$, whereas the vacuum tube has an input resistance that approaches infinity. Nevertheless, as far as voltage gain from input to output is concerned, we can transform tube formulas into transistor formulas when analogous circuits are involved.

EXAMPLE 6-15

The vacuum-tube circuit of Fig. 6-26a is the well-known cathode follower. It has a voltage gain of approximately unity. Find the voltage gain of the transistor circuit shown in Fig. 6-26b.

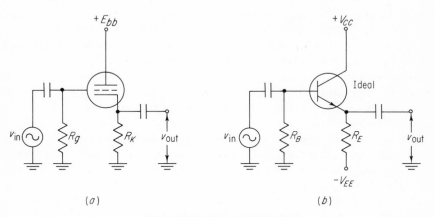

Fig. 6-26 Example 6-15.

SOLUTION

The transistor circuit of Fig. 6-26b is the transistor counterpart of the cathode follower; it is called an *emitter follower*. To find the voltage-gain formula for the emitter follower we will transform the vacuum-tube gain formula. The voltage gain of a cathode-follower is

$$\frac{v_{\text{out}}}{v_{\text{in}}} \cong \frac{g_m R_K}{1 + g_m R_K} \qquad \text{for a pentode}$$

Since the g_m of the ideal transistor is $1/r'_e$, and since R_E takes the place of R_K, we get

$$\frac{v_{\text{out}}}{v_{\text{in}}} = \frac{R_E/r'_e}{1 + R_E/r'_e}$$

This expression can be rearranged to obtain

$$\frac{v_{\text{out}}}{v_{\text{in}}} = \frac{1}{1 + r'_e/R_E} \cong 1 \qquad \text{when } \frac{r'_e}{R_E} \ll 1$$

In most emitter-follower circuits the condition $r'_e/R_E \ll 1$ is easily satisfied; therefore, the emitter follower has a voltage gain of approximately unity. We intend to study the emitter follower in more detail in the next chapter.

SUMMARY

The IV characteristics of the CE connection are similar to those of the CB connection. The base-emitter part of the transistor acts very much like an ordinary diode, while the collector resembles a current source.

The collector current is much larger than the base current. A figure of merit for a transistor is its β, which is the ratio of its collector current to its base current. The d-c β involves direct currents, whereas the a-c β involves alternating currents. Usually, these two β's are close to each other in value. The variation in β for various transistor types is roughly from 20 to 200 or more.

For our initial work in transistor circuit analysis we use a simple approximation called the ideal transistor. In the CE connection we treat the base diode as an ordinary diode and the collector diode as a current source with a value of βi_B.

Biasing a transistor refers to setting a d-c operating point in order to prevent an a-c signal from taking the emitter diode out of forward bias or the collector diode out of back bias. This is necessary to avoid clipping the a-c signal. From the standpoint of bias stability, base bias is the worst way to bias a transistor and emitter bias is the best way.

When the emitter of a CE stage is at a-c ground, the voltage gain from base to collector is simply r_L/r'_e (assuming an ideal transistor).

Unlike the grid of a vacuum tube, which normally offers a very high resistance to an a-c signal, the base of a transistor looks like a relatively low resistance of $\beta r_e'$. As long as the source resistance is very small, almost all the source voltage arrives at the base diode; when the source resistance is large, however, only part of the source voltage appears across the base diode.

The transistor is analogous to a pentode in its a-c operation. For an ideal transistor the $g_m = 1/r_e'$, $r_p = \infty$, and $\mu = \infty$. Any voltage-gain formula for a vacuum-tube circuit can be transformed to get the voltage gain of a corresponding transistor circuit.

GLOSSARY

a-c resistance The resistance seen by an a-c signal. When an a-c signal is driving the base of a transistor, it sees a resistance of $\beta r_e'$. But when it drives the emitter, it sees a resistance of r_e'.

base bias A biasing arrangement in which the d-c base current remains essentially fixed even though the β of the transistor changes.

bias Setting up direct currents and voltages in a transistor in order to prevent clipping of the a-c signal.

beta (β) The ratio of collector current to base current. The d-c β refers to the ratio of direct currents, whereas the a-c β refers to the ratio of alternating currents. The two β's are often quite close in value, and in our ideal-transistor approximation they are equal.

emitter bias A biasing arrangement in which the d-c emitter current remains essentially fixed even though the β changes.

g_m In a vacuum tube this is the ratio of a-c plate current to a-c grid voltage under the condition of fixed plate voltage. In a transistor it is the ratio of a-c collector current to a-c base voltage under the condition of fixed collector voltage. For an ideal transistor, $g_m = 1/r_e'$.

μ In a vacuum tube this is the ratio of a-c plate voltage to a-c grid voltage under the condition of fixed plate current.

r_p In a vacuum tube this is the ratio of the a-c plate voltage to the a-c plate current under the condition of fixed grid voltage.

REVIEW QUESTIONS

1. How are β_{dc} and β defined?
2. What is the typical range of β for different transistors?
3. In a base-biased circuit, which remains almost fixed when the β changes, the collector current or the base current?

4. What is one of the reasons that base bias is a very poor way to set a d-c operating point?
5. In an emitter-biased circuit, which remains almost fixed when β changes, the collector current or the base current?
6. Why is it usually necessary to set up a d-c operating point before applying an a-c signal to the transistor?
7. What is the d-c equivalent circuit for an ideal transistor? And the a-c equivalent circuit?
8. What is the formula for the resistance seen by an a-c signal when looking into the base diode?
9. What is the voltage-gain formula for a typical CE circuit like that shown in Fig. 6-19a?
10. If the source driving a CE circuit has a significant amount of source resistance, how do we take this into account?
11. What is the value of the g_m of an ideal transistor?

PROBLEMS

6-1 A transistor has a d-c base current of 0.02 ma and a d-c collector current of 1.5 ma. What is the β_{dc} for this condition?

6-2 The a-c base current in a transistor is a sine wave with a peak value of 1 μa. The β of the transistor is 200. Describe the waveform of collector current.

6-3 What is the base current in a transistor if the β equals 125 and the collector current equals 2 ma?

6-4 In Fig. 6-27a, the transistor has a β_{dc} of 50. Find the collector current and the collector-ground voltage. Neglect the voltage drop across the base diode.

6-5 Repeat Prob. 6-4, but allow 0.7 volt for the voltage across the base diode.

6-6 In Fig. 6-27b, the transistor has a β_{dc} of 100. What size should R_B be in order to have a collector-ground voltage of 5 volts? Neglect V_{BE}.

6-7 If the β_{dc} is 75 in Fig. 6-27c, what size should R_L be in order to have a collector-ground voltage of 10 volts? Neglect V_{BE}.

6-8 In Fig. 6-27d, an adjustable resistor is used in the base circuit so that V_C can be adjusted to 15 volts when different transistors are used in the circuit; however, there is a limit on the range of β_{dc} that can be compensated. In order to be able to adjust V_C to 15 volts, in what range must β_{dc} lie?

6-9 In Fig. 6-28a, the β_{dc} is 100. What is the collector-ground voltage? Suppose that we change transistors and that the new β_{dc} is 150. What is the new value of collector-ground voltage?

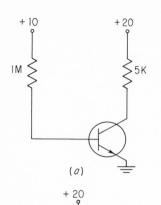

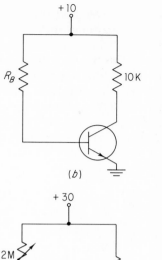

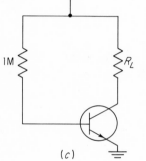

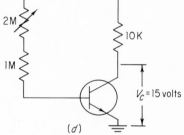

Fig. 6-27

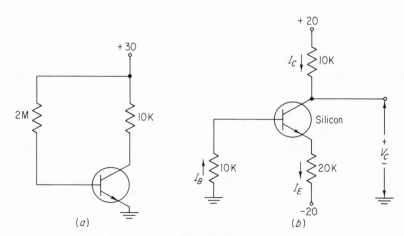

Fig. 6-28

6-10 In Fig. 6-28b, find the following:
(a) The approximate value of I_E using Eq. (6-7).
(b) The approximate value of V_C.
6-11 In Fig. 6-28b, find the value of I_E using Eq. (6-6) and a β of 100.
6-12 In Fig. 6-28b, find the approximate value of base current by using a β of 100. Also, what is the value of the d-c voltage from base to ground?
6-13 In Fig. 6-29, compute the following:
(a) The approximate value of emitter current.
(b) The approximate voltage from collector to ground.

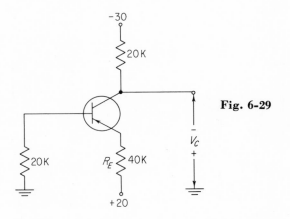

Fig. 6-29

6-14 In order to have a collector-ground voltage of -5 volts in Fig. 6-29, what size should R_E be approximately?
6-15 In Fig. 6-29, what value of R_E will cause the collector voltage to become approximately 0 volts?
6-16 In Fig. 6-30a, the transistor has a β of 75. Sketch the output waveform, using the theoretical value of 25 mv/I_E to find r'_e.
6-17 Repeat Prob. 6-16 but use a 2:1 range for r'_e; that is, compute r'_e by using

$$\frac{25 \text{ mv}}{I_E} < r'_e < \frac{50 \text{ mv}}{I_E}$$

6-18 The transistor of Fig. 6-30b has a β of 80. Find the following:
(a) The d-c voltage from collector to ground.
(b) The size of the output signal v_{out} (use 25 mv/I_E).
6-19 In Fig. 6-30b, what will happen to the d-c voltage from collector to ground and to the output voltage v_{out} if R_E is changed from 20 to 40 kilohms?

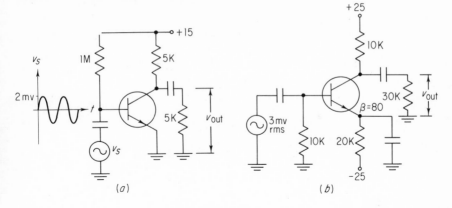

Fig. 6-30

6-20 In the circuit of Fig. 6-31a, the β of the transistor is 100, and r_s is 20 kilohms. Using 25 mv/I_E, find the value of v_{out}.

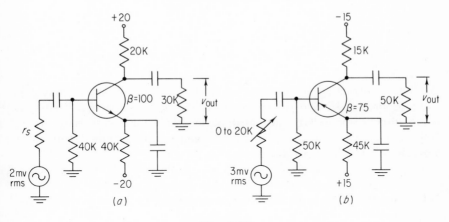

Fig. 6-31

6-21 Use a β of 75 for the transistor of Fig. 6-31b and use the theoretical value of 25 mv/I_E for r'_e. What is the maximum and minimum output voltage possible in this circuit?

6-22 A typical pentode like a 6AU6 has a g_m of 5000 μmhos. What is the g_m of an ideal transistor when the d-c emitter current is 1 ma? What must the value of d-c emitter current be in order to have a g_m of 500 μmhos?

7

Common-collector Approximations

We have now studied two basic transistor connections, namely, the common-base (CB) and the common-emitter (CE). Here we discuss the common-collector (CC), the third basic transistor connection. As we will see, the main advantage of the CC connection is that it transforms a given value of load resistance to a higher value.

7-1   The Basic Idea of the CC Connection

Figure 7-1 illustrates a CC stage. For a typical design, the circuit action is as follows. The input signal v_{in} is coupled through the capacitor into the base of the transistor. This signal causes the instantaneous value of the emitter current to increase on the positive half cycle and to decrease on the negative half cycle. This changing emitter current produces a voltage across the emitter resistor R_E as shown, and the signal is then coupled to the final load resistor R. For a typical CC stage, the output signal is almost equal to the input signal. For instance, if the source signal is a 1-mv-peak sine wave, the output will be almost a 1-mv sine wave. Note that the output signal is in phase with the input signal because on the positive half cycle of the input signal more base current flows; this increase in base current causes an increase in emitter current, which in turn produces a positive-going signal across R_E.

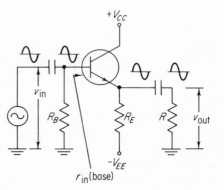

Fig. 7-1 The emitter follower.

In discussing the CC stage, we will use r_L to represent the a-c load resistance seen by the emitter. In Fig. 7-1, the a-c load resistance seen by the emitter is

$$r_L = R_E \| R \qquad (7\text{-}1)$$

For instance, in Fig. 7-1 if $R_E = 10$ kilohms and $R = 30$ kilohms, we would calculate an a-c load of

$$r_L = 10 \text{ kilohms} \| 30 \text{ kilohms} = 7.5 \text{ kilohms}$$

As we will show in the next section, the voltage gain of the CC stage of Fig. 7-1 is

$$\frac{v_{\text{out}}}{v_{\text{in}}} \cong \frac{1}{1 + r_e'/r_L} \qquad (7\text{-}2)$$

where r_e' is the emitter junction resistance and r_L is the a-c load resistance seen by the emitter. Note in this expression that if r_L is much greater than r_e', then r_e'/r_L is a small number, much less than unity, and the voltage gain becomes

$$\frac{v_{\text{out}}}{v_{\text{in}}} \cong 1 \qquad \text{when } r_e' \ll r_L \qquad (7\text{-}3)$$

In many CC circuits, r_e' is much smaller than r_L, so that for a first approximation we can say that the voltage gain of such circuits is essentially unity. In other words, whatever signal is coupled into the base appears across the final load resistor R.

A natural question to ask at this point is: Why use a CC stage if the voltage gain is unity or less? Now we come to the main reason for using a CC circuit. This circuit has the advantage that the a-c input resistance looking into the base of the transistor is much higher than the a-c load resistance seen by the emitter. In fact, we will show that the resistance looking into the base is

$$r_{\text{in(base)}} \cong \beta r_L \qquad \text{when } r'_e \ll r_L \tag{7-4}$$

This equation tells us that the load r_L seen by the emitter is stepped up to a new value of βr_L at the base. For instance, if $r_L = 1$ kilohm and $\beta = 100$, then looking into the base, the input resistance is

$$r_{\text{in(base)}} = 100(1 \text{ kilohm}) = 100 \text{ kilohms}$$

Thus, we see that the CC circuit is similar to a transformer in that it can be used to transform, or step up, the value of a load resistance; however, it is quite different from a transformer, because the output signal is almost equal to the input signal. The common collector is sometimes called an *emitter follower* because the emitter signal follows the signal at the base. For those readers who are familiar with the cathode follower, it is worth mentioning that the emitter follower is the analogous transistor circuit.

To summarize our discussion of the emitter follower, we note:

1. It has a voltage gain of unity or less.
2. It is primarily used to transform a load resistance to a much higher value.

7-2   Derivation of CC Formulas

In this section we want to prove Eqs. (7-2) to (7-4). Before we do this, however, let us find the important formulas that pin down the d-c operation of the emitter follower of Fig. 7-1. As usual, we first draw the d-c equivalent circuit by opening all capacitors and shorting all a-c sources. The d-c equivalent circuit is shown in Fig. 7-2a. This circuit is really a form of the emitter-biased circuit discussed in the last chapter. The only difference here is that there is no resistance in the collector circuit. In other words, we can visualize the d-c equivalent circuit as indicated in Fig. 7-2b, where we have shown an R_L of 0 ohms.

The formulas for emitter bias derived in Sec. 6-5 still apply. They are

$$I_E \cong \frac{V_{EE} - V_{BE}}{R_E + R_B/\beta}$$
$$V_C = V_{CC} - I_C R_L$$

As usual, we can simplify the first equation by noting that V_{BE} is usually much smaller than V_{EE} and that R_B/β is usually much smaller than R_E.

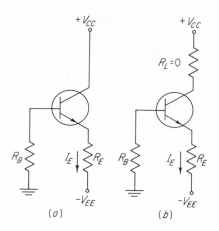

Fig. 7-2 Emitter bias of emitter follower.

Therefore, the first equation becomes simply

$$I_E \cong \frac{V_{EE}}{R_E} \qquad (7\text{-}5)$$

This equation says that the d-c emitter current is approximately equal to the emitter supply voltage divided by the value of the emitter resistor. Note also that with an R_L of zero, the d-c voltage from collector to ground becomes

$$V_C = V_{CC}$$

Now let us prove the a-c formulas given in the preceding section. When we draw the a-c equivalent circuit for Fig. 7-1, we short all d-c sources and capacitors, to obtain the circuit shown in Fig. 7-3a. By inspection, the a-c load resistance seen by the emitter is the parallel combination of R_E and R. If we let r_L represent this a-c load, we can redraw the circuit as in Fig. 7-3b. Next, to get approximate formulas for the a-c operation of the emitter follower we will replace the transistor by its ideal a-c equivalent circuit, as shown in Fig. 7-3c.

To find the voltage gain of the emitter follower we need only write expressions for v_{out} and v_{in} and take the ratio of these expressions. For instance, it is clear that the a-c output voltage must equal the a-c emitter current times the a-c load resistance. That is,

$$v_{\text{out}} = i_e r_L$$

Because the emitter current is almost equal to the collector current, we can write

$$v_{\text{out}} \cong i_c r_L = \beta i_b r_L$$

The input voltage v_{in} is the a-c voltage from base to ground. By inspection of Fig. 7-3c, v_{in} equals the a-c voltage across the base diode plus the

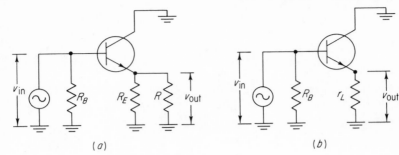

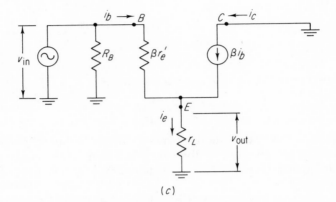

Fig. 7-3 Deriving gain and impedance formulas.

voltage across r_L. That is,

$$v_{in} = i_b \beta r'_e + i_e r_L$$

As already indicated, $i_e \cong i_c$, so that we can rewrite this expression as

$$v_{in} \cong i_b \beta r'_e + \beta i_b r_L \qquad (7\text{-}6)$$

The voltage gain is v_{out}/v_{in}.

$$\frac{v_{out}}{v_{in}} \cong \frac{\beta i_b r_L}{i_b \beta r'_e + \beta i_b r_L} = \frac{r_L}{r'_e + r_L}$$

By dividing numerator and denominator by r_L and rearranging we get

$$\frac{v_{out}}{v_{in}} \cong \frac{1}{1 + r'_e/r_L} \qquad (7\text{-}7)$$

It is immediately apparent from this result that when r'_e is much smaller than r_L, the voltage gain becomes

$$\frac{v_{out}}{v_{in}} \cong 1$$

Another a-c formula to prove is that the input resistance looking into the base is approximately β times the a-c load seen by the emitter. We do this as follows. The loading effect of the base can be found by taking the ratio of the input voltage to the input base current. That is,

$$r_{in(base)} = \frac{v_{in}}{i_b}$$

Recall that we have already found an expression for v_{in}. By using Eq. (7-6) we have

$$r_{in(base)} \cong \frac{i_b \beta r'_e + \beta i_b r_L}{i_b} = \beta r'_e + \beta r_L$$

Or we can write

$$r_{in(base)} \cong \beta(r'_e + r_L) \tag{7-8}$$

Often, r'_e is much smaller than r_L, and this equation reduces to

$$r_{in(base)} \cong \beta r_L \tag{7-9}$$

Thus, we see that to a first approximation *the input resistance looking into the base of an emitter follower is β times the a-c load seen by emitter.* In other words, the emitter follower transforms a load resistance r_L to a higher value of βr_L when viewed from the base.

Remember that the formulas we have derived are not exact formulas because we used an ideal transistor, in addition to other approximations. However, the formulas we have are adequate for preliminary analysis and design, and they certainly do describe the fundamental operation of the emitter follower to a good first approximation.

One more point. The total input resistance of a CC stage is actually the parallel combination of the base resistor and the input resistance looking into the base. This can be understood by referring to Fig. 7-4. As

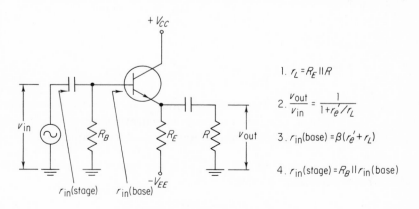

1. $r_L = R_E \| R$

2. $\dfrac{v_{out}}{v_{in}} = \dfrac{1}{1 + r'_e / r_L}$

3. $r_{in(base)} = \beta(r'_e + r_L)$

4. $r_{in(stage)} = R_B \| r_{in(base)}$

Fig. 7-4 Summary of emitter follower.

far as the source is concerned, it must provide current for both the base of the transistor and the base resistor. In other words, the source sees a total resistance of

$$r_{\text{in(stage)}} = R_B \| r_{\text{in(base)}} \tag{7-10}$$

The formulas for a-c operation are summarized in Fig. 7-4. As usual, if a p-n-p transistor is used instead of an n-p-n, the formulas are identical because the a-c equivalent circuit is the same for both types of transistors.

EXAMPLE 7-1

For the emitter follower shown in Fig. 7-5 find:

(a) The input resistance looking into the base.
(b) The input resistance looking into the stage.

SOLUTION

(a) Using Eq. (7-9), we can find the approximate input resistance looking into the base.

$$r_{\text{in(base)}} \cong \beta r_L$$

Note that r_L is 20 kilohms in parallel with 1 kilohm.

$$r_L = 20,000 \| 1000 \cong 950 \text{ ohms}$$

With a β of 50, we get

$$r_{\text{in(base)}} = 50(950) = 47.5 \text{ kilohms}$$

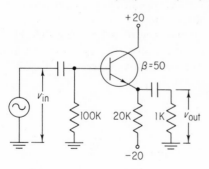

Fig. 7-5   Examples 7-1 and 7-2.

This is approximately the value of input resistance looking into the base. If we like, we can obtain a more accurate answer by using Eq. (7-8), which takes r'_e into account. According to this equation,

$$r_{\text{in(base)}} = \beta(r'_e + r_L)$$

The theoretical value of r'_e is

$$r'_e = \frac{25 \text{ mv}}{I_E} \cong \frac{25 \text{ mv}}{1 \text{ ma}} = 25 \text{ ohms}$$

(The d-c emitter current I_E equals 1 ma because the emitter supply voltage of 20 volts divided by the emitter resistance of 20 kilohms yields 1 ma.) Now, we compute the more accurate value of $r_{\text{in(base)}}$.

$$r_{\text{in(base)}} = \beta(r'_e + r_L) = 50(25 + 950) = 48.7 \text{ kilohms}$$

(Note that taking r'_e into account does not change the resistance very much.)

(b) Using Eq. (7-10), we can find the total input resistance of the stage. It is

$$r_{\text{in(stage)}} = R_B \| r_{\text{in(base)}} \cong 100 \text{ kilohms} \| 47.5 \text{ kilohms}$$
$$= 32.2 \text{ kilohms}$$

EXAMPLE 7-2

In the circuit of Fig. 7-5, suppose that v_{in} is a 3-mv-peak sine wave. Find the output voltage by using Eq. (7-7).

SOLUTION

We already know from the preceding example that $r'_e \cong 25$ ohms and that $r_L = 950$ ohms. Hence, the voltage gain is

$$\frac{v_{\text{out}}}{v_{\text{in}}} = \frac{1}{1 + r'_e/r_L} = \frac{1}{1 + 25/950} \cong 0.975$$

Therefore,

$$v_{\text{out}} = 0.975(3 \text{ mv}) = 2.92 \text{ mv}$$

Thus, the output voltage is a sine wave with a peak value of 2.92 mv. Obviously, this is quite close to 3 mv, and for a first approximation, we can say that the output voltage essentially equals the input voltage.

EXAMPLE 7-3

In Fig. 7-6, the β can be between 50 and 150. Find the following:

(a) The voltage gain.
(b) The input resistance looking into the base.
(c) The input resistance of the entire stage.

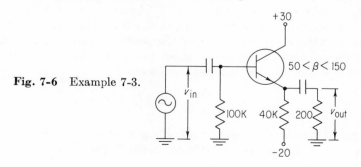

Fig. 7-6 Example 7-3.

SOLUTION

(a) First, let us find the theoretical value of r_e'.

$$r_e' = \frac{25 \text{ mv}}{I_E} \cong \frac{25 \text{ mv}}{0.5 \text{ ma}} = 50 \text{ ohms}$$

Next, we find r_L.

$$r_L = 40{,}000 \| 200 \cong 200 \text{ ohms}$$

Now, by using Eq. (7-7) we get

$$\frac{v_{\text{out}}}{v_{\text{in}}} \cong \frac{1}{1 + r_e'/r_L} = \frac{1}{1 + {}^{50}\!/_{200}} = 0.8$$

(b) The input resistance at the base will depend upon the β. For the minimum β of 50, we have

$$r_{\text{in(base)}} = \beta(r_e' + r_L) = 50(50 + 200) = 12.5 \text{ kilohms}$$

And for the maximum β of 150, we get

$$r_{\text{in(base)}} = 150(50 + 200) = 37.5 \text{ kilohms}$$

(c) The minimum input resistance of the stage occurs for the minimum β of 50. Using Eq. (7-10), we obtain

$$r_{\text{in(stage)}} = R_B \| r_{\text{in(base)}} = 100{,}000 \| 12{,}500 = 11.1 \text{ kilohms}$$

The maximum input resistance of the stage is

$$r_{\text{in(stage)}} = 100{,}000 \| 37{,}500 = 27.3 \text{ kilohms}$$

EXAMPLE 7-4

Suppose that we drive the emitter follower of Example 7-3 with a source that has an internal resistance of 10 kilohms, as shown in Fig. 7-7a. Find v_{out} for a β of 150.

SOLUTION

We already found in Example 7-3 that the input resistance of the stage is 27.3 kilohms when $\beta = 150$. Therefore, we can visualize the input side of the transistor circuit as illustrated in Fig. 7-7b. Since we have a voltage divider, some of the source signal is lost across the 10-kilohm resistor. The actual input voltage to the base of the transistor is a sine wave with a peak value of

$$v_{\text{in(peak)}} = \frac{27.3}{10 + 27.3} \, 50 \text{ mv} = 36.6 \text{ mv}$$

We already know from the preceding example that the emitter follower has a voltage gain of 0.8 from base to output. Therefore, the final

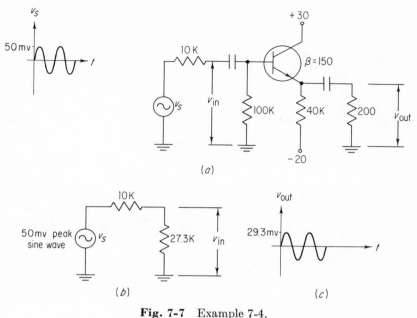

Fig. 7-7   Example 7-4.

output signal is a sine wave with a peak value of

$$v_{\text{out(peak)}} = 0.8(36.6 \text{ mv}) = 29.3 \text{ mv}$$

A sketch of the output waveform is shown in Fig. 7-7c. Thus, we see that if the source resistance is large enough, some of the source voltage can be lost before reaching the base of the transistor.

EXAMPLE 7-5

This particular example is included for the reader who is already familiar with the cathode-follower vacuum-tube circuit.

In Fig. 7-8a we have the conventional cathode-follower circuit. Recall that the voltage gain of this circuit is

$$\frac{v_{\text{out}}}{v_{\text{in}}} \cong \frac{1}{1 + 1/g_m r_L} \qquad \text{when } \mu \text{ and } r_p \text{ are very high}$$

where $r_L = R_K \| R$.

In Fig. 7-8b we have the conventional emitter follower. Notice that the cathode follower and emitter follower are almost identical in form. The only major difference is in the d-c operation, where it is necessary to use the V_{EE} supply to forward-bias the emitter diode. As far as a-c

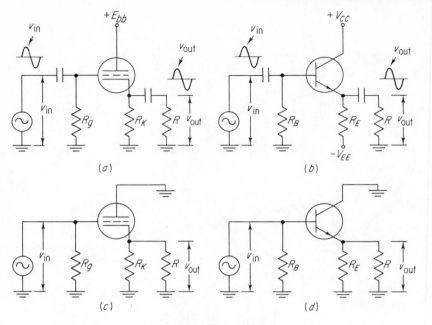

Fig. 7-8 Example 7-5.

equivalent circuits are concerned, the cathode and emitter followers are identical in form, as indicated by Fig. 7-8c and d.

Transform the voltage-gain formula for the cathode follower into the voltage-gain formula for the emitter follower by the methods of Sec. 6-9.

SOLUTION

The g_m of an ideal transistor is

$$g_m = \frac{1}{r_e'}$$

By substituting this value into the cathode-follower formula we get

$$\frac{v_{\text{out}}}{v_{\text{in}}} \cong \frac{1}{1 + 1/g_m r_L} = \frac{1}{1 + r_e'/r_L}$$

This equation is identical to Eq. (7-7), which gives the voltage gain of the emitter follower.

Thus, we have found a transistor formula by using the tube-transistor transformation of Sec. 6-9. This approach to finding transistor formulas is quite useful sometimes because it can save considerable time. Also, it can be used to check the results of a direct derivation of the transistor formula. For instance, in this example, we have checked the formula for the emitter-follower voltage gain that was derived earlier.

7-3 The Darlington Pair

As indicated in Sec. 6-2, the β of different transistors typically falls in the range of about 20 to 200. There may be times when we need a β that is much higher than 200. One way to get this is to connect two transistors together as shown in Fig. 7-9a. This particular connection is called a *Darlington pair*.

In Fig. 7-9a, note that the base current in the first transistor produces a collector current of βi_b in this transistor. Since the emitter and collector currents are almost equal, we see that the emitter current of this first transistor is approximately βi_b. Note that this emitter current drives the base of the second transistor; therefore, the collector current of the second transistor equals $\beta^2 i_b$ (assuming identical transistors). As a result, the emitter current of the second transistor is approximately equal to $\beta^2 i_b$.

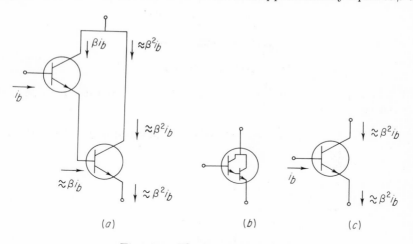

Fig. 7-9 The Darlington pair.

Transistor manufacturers sometimes put two transistors connected as a Darlington pair inside a single transistor housing, as shown in Fig. 7-9b. Thus, the Darlington pair acts like a single transistor (Fig. 7-9c) with an effective β of

$$\beta_{DP} = \beta^2 \qquad \text{for equal } \beta \text{ transistors}$$

where β_{DP} is the effective β of the Darlington pair. Of course, if the two transistors do not have equal β's, we must use the product of the β's.

That is,

$$\beta_{DP} = \beta_1 \beta_2$$

The important point here is that the Darlington pair can give us extremely high β's. For instance, if each transistor has a β of 100, the Darlington pair has an effective β of

$$\beta_{DP} = 100(100) = 10,000$$

Even for β's as low as 20 the Darlington pair has an effective beta of

$$\beta_{DP} = 20(20) = 400$$

EXAMPLE 7-6

For the circuit of Fig. 7-10 find the input resistance looking into the entire stage. Each transistor has a β of 50.

SOLUTION

The effective β of the Darlington pair is

$$\beta_{DP} = 50(50) = 2500$$

The a-c load seen by the second emitter is

$$r_L = 20,000 \| 500 \cong 500 \text{ ohms}$$

Using Eq. (7-9) we find that the resistance looking into the base of the first transistor is

$$r_{in(base)} = 2500(500) = 1.25 \text{ megohms}$$

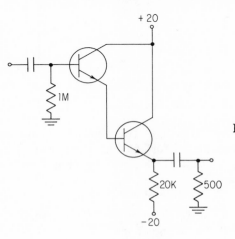

Fig. 7-10   Example 7-6.

The input resistance of the stage is the parallel combination of R_B and $r_{in(base)}$. Thus,

$$r_{in(stage)} = 1 \text{ megohm} \| 1.25 \text{ megohm} \cong 550 \text{ kilohms}$$

EXAMPLE 7-7

Find the voltage gain for the circuits shown in Fig. 7-11a and b.

SOLUTION

In Fig. 7-11a, we recognize this as a simple CE amplifier with a voltage gain of

$$\frac{v_{out}}{v_{in}} \cong \frac{r_L}{r'_e} = \frac{10,000}{25} = 400$$

Note that r_L in Fig. 7-11a consists only of the 10-kilohm resistor in the collector circuit; also, the theoretical value of r'_e is 25 ohms, obtained in the usual manner.

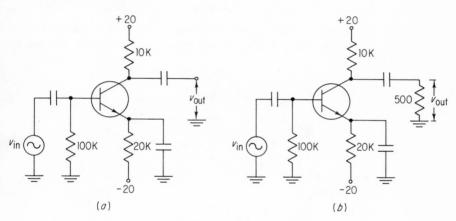

(a)   (b)

Fig. 7-11   Example 7-7.

In Fig. 7-11b, there is a 500-ohm resistor loading the stage. The new value of r_L becomes

$$r_L = 10,000 \| 500 \cong 500 \text{ ohms}$$

and the voltage gain becomes

$$\frac{v_{out}}{v_{in}} \cong \frac{500}{25} = 20$$

Obviously, coupling into the 500-ohm resistor has reduced the gain considerably (from around 400 to about 20). This kind of effect, where the gain is reduced by coupling the signal into an additional resistor, is called *loading down* the stage. One way to avoid the loss in gain is to step up the 500-ohm load to a much higher value, as illustrated in the next example.

EXAMPLE 7-8

In Fig. 7-12 we have cascaded the CE stage of the preceding example with an emitter follower using a Darlington pair. Find the following:

(a) The voltage gain for the first stage.
(b) The voltage gain for the total circuit.

SOLUTION

(a) Looking into the second stage we have an input resistance of $r_{in(stage)} = 550$ kilohms. (This result was worked out in Example 7-6.)
The effective r_L seen by the collector of the first stage is

$$r_L = 10 \text{ kilohms} \| 550 \text{ kilohms} \cong 10 \text{ kilohms}$$

In other words, the collector sees 10 kilohms in parallel with the 550-kilohm input resistance of the second stage. For practical purposes,

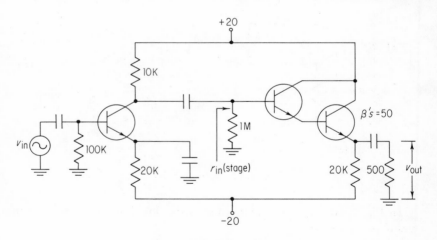

Fig. 7-12 Example 7-8.

this is 10 kilohms. Thus, the second stage hardly loads the first stage at all. Also, the voltage gain of the first stage goes back up to around 400, the result found in Example 7-7.

(b) The voltage gain of the entire circuit is simply the voltage gain of the first stage times the voltage gain of the second stage. Since the emitter follower has a voltage gain of approximately unity, we see that the overall gain is around 400.

SUMMARY

The common collector is also called an emitter follower. The voltage gain of the emitter follower is usually around unity but can be less, depending upon the relation between r_e' and r_L. The main reason for using the emitter follower is to increase impedances. As we have seen, a load of r_L can effectively be transformed to a higher value of βr_L by using the emitter follower.

The Darlington pair is a compound connection of two transistors; it has an effective β equal to the product of the individual β's.

GLOSSARY

common collector (CC)   One of the basic ways to connect a transistor. The input signal is applied to the base; the output is taken from the emitter. The CC is sometimes referred to as a grounded-collector circuit because the collector is at a-c ground.

Darlington pair   A connection of two transistors in such a way that the transistors act like a single equivalent transistor with an effective β equal to the product of the individual β's.

emitter follower   Another name for the common-collector circuit. The name is quite descriptive of the circuit because the emitter signal follows the signal applied to the base.

loading down a stage   Reducing the voltage gain of a stage by connecting the output of the stage into another stage or resistor.

REVIEW QUESTIONS

1. What is the approximate value for the voltage gain of the emitter follower? What is the approximate value of input resistance looking into the base?
2. In order for the voltage gain of the emitter follower to approximately equal unity, should r_e' be large or small compared to r_L?
3. What is the main reason for using an emitter follower?
4. For the emitter follower discussed in this chapter, how can we find the approximate value of the d-c emitter current?

5. What is a Darlington pair? Show the schematic for it.
6. What does loading down a stage mean?

PROBLEMS

7-1   An emitter follower is loaded by an a-c resistance of 1 kilohm. If the transistor has a β of 50, what is the a-c input resistance looking into base?
7-2   A transistor is used in an emitter follower that is loaded by an r_L of 500. If the transistor can have a β anywhere in the range of 50 to 200, what is the lowest value of a-c input resistance looking into the base? And the highest?
7-3   In Fig. 7-13, what is the approximate output voltage when the input voltage equals a 3-mv-peak sine wave?
7-4   In Fig. 7-13, what is the a-c input resistance looking into the base? What is the a-c input resistance of the stage?

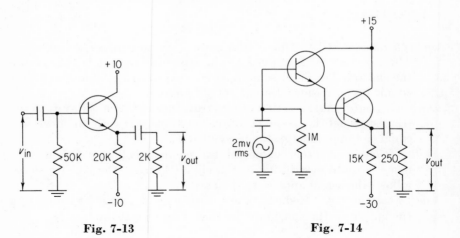

Fig. 7-13   Fig. 7-14

7-5   Suppose that the 2-kilohm resistor is actually a variable resistance in Fig. 7-13. For what value of resistance will the voltage gain of the emitter follower drop in half? (Use the theoretical value of r'_e.)
7-6   A Darlington pair has transistors whose β's equal 75. What is the effective β of the Darlington pair?
7-7   The β of the first transistor in a Darlington pair is twice as large as the β of the second transistor. The Darlington pair has an effective β of 10,000. Find the individual β's.
7-8   In Fig. 7-14 the transistors each have a β of 80. Find the approximate values of:

(a) The a-c resistance looking into the base.

(b) The a-c resistance looking into the entire stage.

(c) The output voltage.

7-9 Prove that when a third transistor is added to a Darlington connection the effective β is approximately β^3. (Use ideal transistors.)

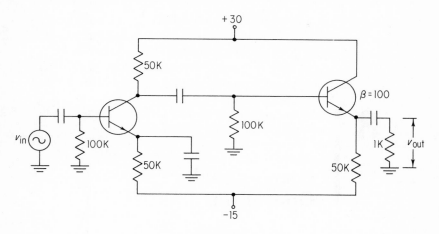

Fig. 7-15

7-10 For the two-stage circuit shown in Fig. 7-15 find the following:

(a) The a-c input resistance of the second stage (including the 100-kilohm base resistor).

(b) The overall voltage gain of the two-stage circuit.

8

Large-signal Operation

So far we have discussed only small-signal operation of the transistor, that is, operation in which the a-c currents and voltages are less than about 10 percent of the d-c currents and voltages.

Now our attention shifts to large-signal operation. Here we are interested in a-c signals that cause large changes in the total currents and voltages in transistor circuits. In this chapter, we discuss several concepts that are helpful in dealing with large signals, concepts like the d-c load line, the a-c load line, and maximum signal capability.

8-1 The D-C Load Line

Suppose that we have a common-base circuit like that shown in Fig. 8-1a. How is the collector current related to the collector voltage? From our discussion in Chap. 5 we know that

$$v_C = V_{CC} - i_C R_L \qquad (8\text{-}1)$$

In other words, the collector voltage equals the collector-supply voltage minus the voltage across the load resistor.

Equation (8-1) tells us that the collector voltage v_C is a function of the collector current i_C. When the collector current changes, we get different values of collector voltage. For instance, suppose that we adjust the emitter resistor R_E to a value of 20 kilohms. Then, the emitter current is approximately

$$i_E \cong \frac{V_{EE}}{R_E} = \frac{20}{20,000} = 1 \text{ ma}$$

This 1 ma of emitter current sets up a collector current of about 1 ma, and therefore the collector voltage is

$$v_C = V_{CC} - i_C R_L = 20 - 0.001(5000) = 15 \text{ volts}$$

Thus, when $i_C = 1$ ma, $v_C = 15$ volts. If we like, we can plot this pair of values as shown in Fig. 8-1b. The plotted point is at A.

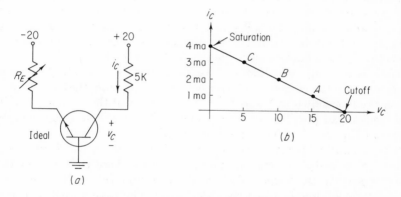

Fig. 8-1 Obtaining the d-c load line. (a) Circuit; (b) load line.

If we were to change the emitter resistor R_E, this would change the collector current and voltage to another set of values. For instance, if we make $R_E = 10$ kilohms, we get an emitter current of

$$i_E \cong \frac{20}{10,000} = 2 \text{ ma}$$

The collector current therefore changes to about 2 ma, and we get a collector voltage of

$$v_C = 20 - 0.002(5000) = 10 \text{ volts}$$

Therefore, the new d-c operating point is $i_C = 2$ ma, $v_C = 10$ volts. Again, we can plot this pair of values to obtain point B in Fig. 8-1b.

Suppose we change R_E until there is 3 ma of collector current. Under this condition, we get a collector voltage of

$$v_C = 20 - 0.003(5000) = 5 \text{ volts}$$

When we plot this pair of values, we obtain point C in Fig. 8-1b.

Suppose that we make $R_E = 5$ kilohms. Then, there is about 4 ma of collector current, which produces a collector voltage of

$$v_C = 20 - 0.004(5000) = 0 \text{ volts}$$

After plotting $i_C = 4$ ma, $v_C = 0$, we get the upper end of the line shown in Fig. 8-1b. Note that this point is called the *saturation point*. The reason for this name is that 4 ma is the largest value of collector current that we can get in the circuit of Fig. 8-1a. At this point, the transistor is said to be saturated because the collector diode is no longer back-biased. As we already know, we get normal transistor action only when the collector diode is back-biased. If we were to increase the emitter current above 4 ma, the collector current would not increase, since the collector current is controlled by the emitter current only when the collector diode is back-biased (see Sec. 5-2 if in doubt).

Here is an important idea: if we continued to plot all the possible pairs of collector current and voltage, we would find that these points lie on the line shown in Fig. 8-1b. This line is called the *d-c load line;* it is the locus of all possible operating points. [The d-c load line is simply a graph of Eq. (8-1), which is a linear equation.]

The saturation point on the d-c load line is one of the limits on the values of v_C and i_C in the circuit of Fig. 8-1a. Another limit on these values occurs at the lower end of the d-c load line. In Fig. 8-1b this lower end of the load line is called the *cutoff point*. The reason for this name is simply that at cutoff there is no collector current. One way to produce cutoff is to make $R_E = \infty$, that is, to open the emitter resistor. Under this condition, there is no emitter current and therefore no collector current.

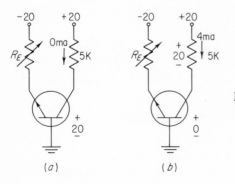

Fig. 8-2 (*a*) Cutoff; (*b*) saturation.

(In a real transistor there is a small reverse current through the back-biased collector diode, but we neglect this in our ideal-transistor approximation.) With no collector current, the collector voltage equals the collector supply voltage. In other words, with no current in the 5-kilohm resistor, there is no voltage drop across this resistor, and all the supply voltage appears from collector to ground.

In the future, we should remember that the d-c load line is drawn between two points, the cutoff point and the saturation point. At the cutoff point there is no collector current, and all the supply voltage appears across the collector diode, as shown in Fig. 8-2a. At the saturation point there is zero voltage across the collector diode, and all the supply voltage is dropped across the load resistor R_L, as illustrated in Fig. 8-2b.

In fact, we can generalize our results for any CB circuit of the form given in Fig. 8-3a. In this circuit, saturation occurs when all the supply voltage is dropped across R_L (Fig. 8-3b). Therefore, the saturation value

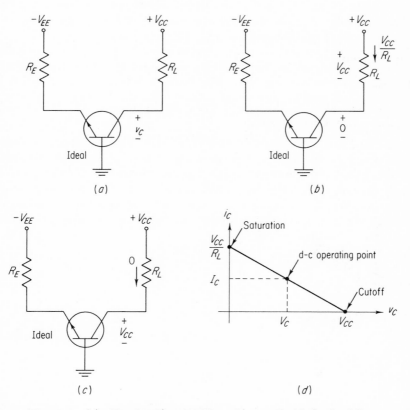

Fig. 8-3 (a) Circuit; (b) saturation; (c) cutoff; (d) d-c load line.

of collector current is

$$I_{C(\text{sat})} = \frac{V_{CC}}{R_L} \tag{8-2}$$

At cutoff there is no collector current, and all the supply voltage appears across the collector diode (Fig. 8-3c).

The d-c load line must pass through the saturation and cutoff points. Thus, we can show the d-c load line as in Fig. 8-3d. Whatever the values of collector current and voltage are, they must plot as a point somewhere along the d-c load line. As long as the collector current is between zero and the saturation value given by Eq. (8-2), we can find the approximate operating point by using

$$I_C \cong I_E \cong \frac{V_{EE}}{R_E} \tag{8-3}$$

and

$$V_C = V_{CC} - I_C R_L \tag{8-4}$$

EXAMPLE 8-1

For the circuit of Fig. 8-4a, draw the d-c load line and the d-c operating point.

SOLUTION

By inspection of the circuit, the cutoff voltage equals the collector supply voltage of 30 volts.

Also, the saturation value of collector current is

$$I_{C(\text{sat})} = \frac{V_{CC}}{R_L} = \frac{30}{10,000} = 3 \text{ ma}$$

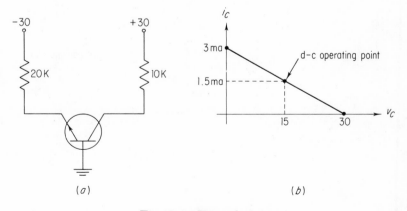

(a)   (b)

Fig. 8-4   Example 8-1.

The d-c load line can now be drawn as shown in Fig. 8-4b. The actual operating point of the transistor lies somewhere along this d-c load line, and it is easily found by Eqs. (8-3) and (8-4).

$$I_C \cong I_E \cong \frac{30}{20,000} = 1.5 \text{ ma}$$

and

$$V_C = 30 - 1.5(10^{-3})(10)(10^3) = 15 \text{ volts}$$

EXAMPLE 8-2

For the circuit of Fig. 8-5a, draw the d-c load line and locate the d-c operating point.

SOLUTION

Note that this circuit is similar to that of Fig. 8-4a; the only difference is that we are using an emitter supply of −50 volts instead of −30 volts. First, realize that this does not change the d-c load line at all because it still passes through a cutoff of 30 volts and a saturation point of 3 ma.

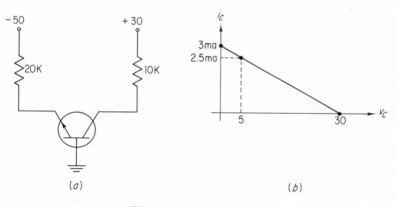

(a)   (b)

Fig. 8-5 Example 8-2.

The only change that takes place is in the d-c operating point. It is clear that the emitter current is

$$I_E \cong \frac{50}{20,000} = 2.5 \text{ ma}$$

The corresponding collector voltage is

$$V_C = 30 - 2.5(10^{-3})(10)(10^3) = 5 \text{ volts}$$

Thus, the d-c operating point shifts to a new location, as indicated in Fig. 8-5b.

EXAMPLE 8-3

Draw the d-c load line and find the d-c operating point for the circuit of Fig. 8-6a.

SOLUTION

This circuit is the same as that of Fig. 8-4a except that the collector supply voltage is now 50 volts instead of 30 volts. This causes the d-c load line to change because it passes through a cutoff point whose voltage is 50 volts. Also, the saturation current changes and becomes

$$I_{C(\text{sat})} = \frac{50}{10,000} = 5 \text{ ma}$$

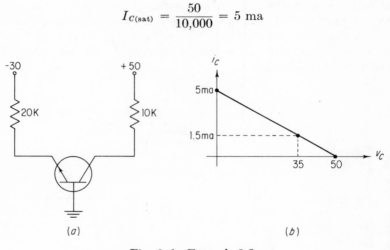

Fig. 8-6   Example 8-3.

The new d-c load line is shown in Fig. 8-6b. The actual d-c operating point is located at

$$I_C \cong I_E \cong \frac{V_{EE}}{R_E} = \frac{30}{20,000} = 1.5 \text{ ma}$$

and

$$V_C = V_{CC} - I_C R_L = 50 - 1.5(10^{-3})(10)(10^3) = 35 \text{ volts}$$

EXAMPLE 8-4

In Fig. 8-7a, draw the d-c load line and show the d-c operating point.

Solution

This circuit is the same as that of Fig. 8-4a except that we are using a load resistance of 5 kilohms instead of 10 kilohms. It should be clear that the cutoff point has a voltage of 30 volts, the collector supply voltage. Also, the saturation point has a current of

$$I_{C(\text{sat})} = \frac{30}{5000} = 6 \text{ ma}$$

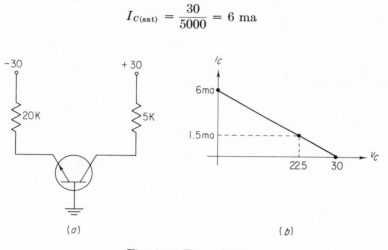

(a)   (b)

Fig. 8-7 Example 8-4.

The d-c load line is shown in Fig. 8-7b. The actual d-c operating point lies at

$$I_C \cong I_E \cong \frac{30}{20,000} = 1.5 \text{ ma}$$

and

$$V_C = 30 - 1.5(10^{-3})(5)(10^3) = 22.5 \text{ volts}$$

8-2 Load-line Interpretation of an A-C Signal

In Fig. 8-8a we have a CB circuit driven by d-c and a-c sources. We studied circuits of this type in Chap. 5; recall that voltage gain of such a circuit is

$$\frac{v_{\text{out}}}{v_s} \cong \frac{r_L}{r_s + r_e'}$$

In Fig. 8-8a it is obvious that the d-c emitter current is around 1 ma, and therefore the theoretical value of r_e' is about 25 ohms. Since r_s equals 1000 ohms, we can say that the emitter diode is swamped out (Sec. 5-8).

Thus, the voltage gain from source to output is approximately

$$\frac{v_{\text{out}}}{v_s} \cong \frac{10,000}{1000} = 10$$

Since v_s is shown as a 0.5-volt-peak sine wave in Fig. 8-8a, the a-c output voltage must be a 5-volt-peak sine wave.

The d-c output voltage is clearly equal to

$$V_C = 20 - 0.001(10,000) = 10 \text{ volts}$$

Hence, the total output waveform (sum of d-c and a-c components) is approximately that shown in Fig. 8-8b. It has an average or d-c value of

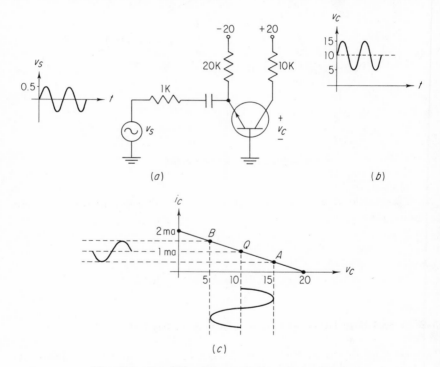

Fig. 8-8   Load-line interpretation of a-c signal.

10 volts; there is sine wave with a 5-volt peak superimposed on this 10-volt level, so that the total instantaneous voltage swings from a low of 5 volts to a high of 15 volts.

How is all this related to the load-line concept? First, we know that the d-c load line passes through a cutoff point with a voltage of 20 volts, the collector supply voltage. Also, we know that the saturation point on the d-c load line has a current of

$$I_{C(\text{sat})} \cong \frac{V_{CC}}{R_L} = \frac{20}{10,000} = 2 \text{ ma}$$

The actual d-c operating point is on the load line and is found by using Eqs. (8-3) and (8-4).

$$I_C \cong I_E \cong \frac{V_{EE}}{R_E} = \frac{20}{20,000} = 1 \text{ ma}$$
$$V_C = V_{CC} - I_C R_L = 20 - 0.001(10,000) = 10 \text{ volts}$$

Hence, we can draw the d-c load line as in Fig. 8-8c. The d-c or average operating point of the transistor is located at Q.

When the a-c signal is present, it causes excursions or changes to take place above and below point Q. These changes must take place along the d-c load line because this line is the graph of all possible pairs of i_C and v_C, as discussed in Sec. 8-1.

We found earlier that for the circuit of Fig. 8-8a, the total voltage at the collector swings sinusoidally from 5 to 15 volts, as shown in Fig. 8-8b. On the load line of Fig. 8-8c this means that the instantaneous operating point moves sinusoidally between points A and B.

A comment worth making at this time concerns the maximum signal that we get from the circuit before clipping occurs. Examine Fig. 8-8c and note that the maximum excursion on the positive peak is limited to the cutoff point on the d-c load line; on the negative peak the maximum excursion is limited by the saturation point. Therefore, in this particular circuit we can obtain an excursion of 10 volts on either side of the d-c operating point before clipping occurs. Thus, if we were to increase the source voltage, we would find that clipping would occur when the output signal reached a value of 20 volts peak to peak.

EXAMPLE 8-5

In the circuit of Fig. 8-9, find the following:

(a) The d-c load line and d-c operating point.
(b) The maximum peak-to-peak unclipped signal.
(c) The approximate value of source voltage that causes clipping to occur.

SOLUTION

(a) Note that this circuit is the same as the circuit we have been discussing (Fig. 8-8a), except that the emitter resistor R_E is 40 kilohms instead of 20 kilohms. Since the cutoff and saturation points on the d-c load line depend only on V_{CC} and R_L, the d-c load line will be the same as before, and is shown in Fig. 8-9b.

Of course, the d-c operating point will be different from before. The new values of collector current and voltage are

$$I_C \cong I_E \cong \frac{V_{EE}}{R_E} = \frac{20}{40,000} = 0.5 \text{ ma}$$
$$V_C = V_{CC} - I_C R_L = 20 - 5(10^{-4})(10)(10^3) = 15 \text{ volts}$$

(b) It is immediately clear in Fig. 8-9b that the positive swing can be from 15 to 20 volts but no more. On the negative swing, the output

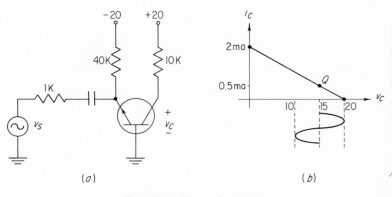

(a)   (b)

Fig. 8-9   Example 8-5.

signal can go from 15 volts down to 0 volts. Therefore, as the source signal is increased, clipping first occurs on the positive half cycle. As the source is increased further, clipping eventually takes place on the negative half cycle. The limiting factor, of course, is the cutoff that occurs on the positive half cycle. Therefore, the maximum unclipped signal that we can get is 10 volts peak to peak.

(c) Clearly the emitter diode is swamped out, so that the approximate voltage gain is

$$\frac{v_{\text{out}}}{v_s} \cong \frac{r_L}{r_s} = \frac{10,000}{1000} = 10$$

Therefore, clipping occurs when the source voltage is greater than

$$v_s = \frac{10 \text{ volts p-p}}{10} = 1 \text{ volt p-p}$$

8-3   The A-C Load Line

Suppose that the a-c load seen by the collector is different from the d-c load. What changes will this make in our load-line interpretation of an a-c signal?

Consider Fig. 8-10a. It is immediately clear that circuit has a d-c load line with a cutoff voltage of 20 volts and a saturation current of 2 ma. It is also clear that the d-c collector current is about 1 ma and the collector voltage is 10 volts. Therefore, we can draw the d-c load line and plot the d-c operating point as shown in Fig. 8-10b.

The a-c signal causes changes to take place in the collector current and voltage. However, the excursions from point Q no longer follow the d-c load line; instead the changes in current and voltage are along a new line, called the *a-c load line*. Basically, the reason for this new line is that the d-c load line only takes the d-c load resistance into account. We therefore would not expect a-c excursions along a line that does not account for the a-c load resistance.

To better understand why there is a new line called the a-c load line,

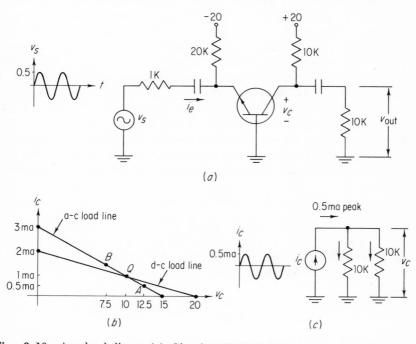

Fig. 8-10   A-c load line.   (*a*) Circuit; (*b*) load lines; (*c*) a-c load seen by collector.

consider the following discussion. In the circuit of Fig. 8-10a, the 0.5-volt-peak source produces a sine wave of current in the emitter. The peak value of this emitter current is simply

$$i_e \cong \frac{0.5}{1000} = 0.5 \text{ ma}$$

Since collector and emitter currents are almost equal, the a-c collector current is also a sine wave with a 0.5-ma peak value. The a-c equivalent circuit for the collector circuit is shown in Fig. 8-10c. From this circuit it is clear that the a-c load resistance is only 5 kilohms, and therefore the peak voltage at the collector is

$$v_c = 0.0005(5000) = 2.5 \text{ volts}$$

Now, here is the crucial point. The peak excursion from point Q in Fig. 8-10b must show a change of 0.5 ma and 2.5 volts. By inspection of Fig. 8-10b such a change is impossible along the d-c load line. When we plot these changes, we actually get two new points A and B, representing the positive and negative voltage peaks. Thus, when the a-c signal varies sinusoidally, excursions occur along the a-c load line between A and B.

Here are a few more interesting differences between the a-c and d-c load lines. As usual, if the a-c signal is large enough, clipping occurs. On the positive-going voltage swing, clipping occurs sooner on the a-c load line than on the d-c load line. In other words, cutoff on the d-c load line occurs at 20 volts; this, however, is no longer important as far as clipping is concerned. Since the actual changes in collector current and voltage take place along the a-c load line, we must use the a-c load line to find the maximum possible swings in either direction.

The cutoff voltage on the a-c load line is only 15 volts, because the maximum possible current change from the operating point is 1 ma. This means that the maximum positive voltage change from the operating point is

$$0.001(5000) = 5 \text{ volts}$$

Thus, we have shown the cutoff voltage at 15 volts in Fig. 8-10b.

The saturation point on the a-c load line is at 3 ma, because the maximum negative voltage change from the operating point is 10 volts. This means that the maximum possible current change from the operating point is

$$\frac{10}{5000} = 2 \text{ ma}$$

Therefore, we have shown the saturation current at 3 ma (1 ma operating current plus the 2 ma swing).

Let us extend the results of the foregoing discussion to the general CB circuit of Fig. 8-11a. The d-c load line passes through a cutoff voltage of V_{CC} and a saturation current of V_{CC}/R_L. The operating point Q has a d-c current I_C and a d-c voltage V_C which can be found by Eqs. (8-3) and (8-4).

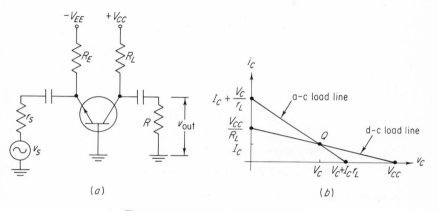

(a)   (b)

Fig. 8-11   Summary of load lines.

When the a-c signal is coupled into the emitter, changes in collector current and voltage take place along the a-c load line. The cutoff point on this a-c load line has a voltage of $V_C + I_C r_L$. In other words, the cutoff voltage must equal the d-c voltage at the operating point plus the maximum positive voltage change, which is $I_C r_L$. Also, the saturation current on the a-c load line equals the direct current at operating point plus the maximum positive current swing, which is V_C/r_L.

The two kinds of load lines with their cutoff and saturation points are summarized in Fig. 8-11b. Especially note on the a-c load line that:

1. The maximum positive swing of a-c collector voltage is limited to $I_C r_L$.

2. The maximum negative swing is limited to V_C.

In other words, the peak-signal-handling capacity is limited to $I_C r_L$ or V_C, whichever is smaller.

EXAMPLE 8-6

Draw the d-c and a-c load lines for the CB circuit of Fig. 8-12a.

SOLUTION

Clearly, the d-c load line passes through a cutoff voltage of 30 volts and a saturation current of 1 ma. The d-c operating point is $I_C = 0.5$ ma and $V_C = 15$ volts.

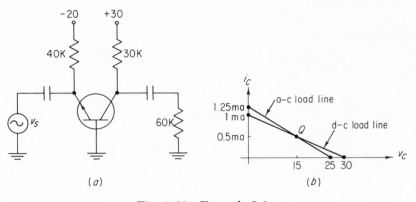

Fig. 8-12   Example 8-6.

The a-c load resistance seen by the collector is

$$r_L = 30(10^3)\|60(10^3) = 20 \text{ kilohms}$$

The cutoff voltage on the a-c load line is

$$V_C + I_C r_L = 15 + 0.5(10^{-3})(20)(10^3) = 25 \text{ volts}$$

The saturation current on the a-c load line is

$$I_C + \frac{V_C}{r_L} = 0.5(10^{-3}) + \frac{15}{20(10^3)} = 1.25 \text{ ma}$$

The d-c and a-c load lines are given in Fig. 8-12b. Note that clipping will occur if the a-c signal tries to exceed 10 volts on the positive voltage swing and 15 volts on the negative voltage swing.

EXAMPLE 8-7

In the circuit of Fig. 8-13a, what is the maximum unclipped output voltage? What approximate value of source voltage just causes clipping?

SOLUTION

By inspection of the circuit, we see that the d-c load line has a cutoff voltage of 20 volts, a saturation current of 2 ma, and a d-c operating point of $I_C = 1$ ma, $V_C = 10$ volts.

The a-c load seen by the collector is

$$r_L = 10,000\|30,000 = 7.5 \text{ kilohms}$$

Therefore, the cutoff voltage on the a-c load line is

$$V_C + I_C r_L = 10 + (10^{-3})(7.5)(10^3) = 17.5 \text{ volts}$$

and a saturation current of

$$I_C + \frac{V_C}{r_L} = 10^{-3} + \frac{10}{7.5(10^3)} = 2.33 \text{ ma}$$

The d-c and a-c load lines are drawn in Fig. 8-13b. It is clear that clipping first occurs on the positive-going excursion. The maximum a-c signal is limited to 7.5 volts peak.

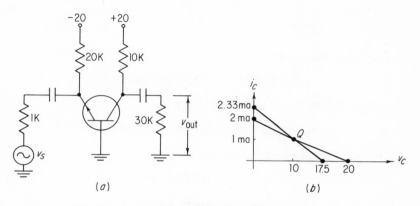

Fig. 8-13 Example 8-7.

The easiest way to find the value of source signal that just causes clipping is to compute the voltage gain from source to output and then divide 7.5 volts peak by this gain. The source-to-output gain is

$$\frac{v_L}{v_s} \cong \frac{r_L}{r_s} = \frac{10,000\|30,000}{1000} = 7.5$$

Therefore, the source voltage that just causes clipping to occur is

$$v_s = \frac{I_C r_L}{7.5} = \frac{7.5}{7.5} = 1 \text{ volt peak}$$

EXAMPLE 8-8

What is the maximum peak-to-peak signal that can be obtained from the circuit of Fig. 8-14?

SOLUTION

The d-c operating point is at

$$I_C \cong 0.333 \text{ ma} \qquad \text{and} \qquad V_C \cong 10 \text{ volts}$$

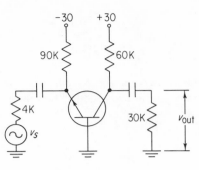

Fig. 8-14 Example 8-8.

The a-c load resistance is

$$r_L = 60,000\|30,000 = 20 \text{ kilohms}$$

Therefore, the maximum positive swing is

$$I_C r_L = 0.333(10^{-3})(20)(10^3) = 6.66 \text{ volts}$$

and the maximum negative swing is

$$V_C = 10 \text{ volts}$$

Clipping occurs first on the positive-going excursion. Hence, the maximum peak output signal is 6.66 volts, or 13.3 volts peak to peak.

8-4   Obtaining Maximum Unclipped Signal

In this section we discuss how to obtain the largest possible unclipped signal by biasing the transistor at the optimum operating point.

Specifically, consider the circuit of Fig. 8-15a. We already know that the maximum positive swing of collector voltage is limited to $I_C r_L$ and the maximum negative swing can be no more than V_C. In order to obtain the largest swing possible before clipping occurs, the a-c load line must be located so that clipping occurs for *equal excursions in either direction.* That is, for maximum unclipped output voltage,

$$V_C = I_C r_L$$

This optimum bias condition is depicted by the load lines of Fig. 8-15b. The a-c load line has been positioned to allow equal excursions above and below the d-c operating point. This particular position of the a-c load line yields the largest unclipped output signal because moving it either way along the d-c load line causes premature clipping.

In order to obtain a useful relation between supply voltages and load

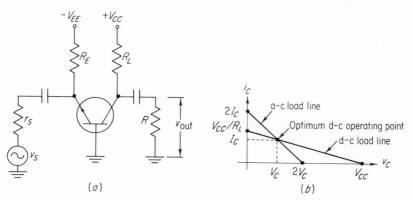

Fig. 8-15 Biasing to obtain maximum signal swing.

resistance, observe that the stage of Fig. 8-15a has a d-c voltage of

$$V_C = V_{CC} - I_C R_L$$

We have already said that for maximum unclipped signal we must have the condition

$$V_C = I_C r_L$$

By equating these expressions we get

$$I_C r_L = V_{CC} - I_C R_L$$

After solving for I_C, we have

$$I_C = \frac{V_{CC}}{r_L + R_L} \quad \text{for maximum unclipped signal} \quad (8\text{-}5)$$

where I_C is the d-c collector current at the optimum operating point
V_{CC} is the collector supply voltage
R_L is the d-c load resistance
r_L is the a-c load resistance

Equation (8-5) is quite useful; it tells us how to bias a stage to get the largest possible unclipped signal.

Also notice that when a stage is biased at the optimum operating point, the maximum available peak-to-peak output is

$$v_{\text{max(p-p)}} = 2V_C = 2I_C r_L \quad (8\text{-}6)$$

EXAMPLE 8-9

In Fig. 8-16, what value should R_E be in order to obtain maximum unclipped signal?

SOLUTION

It is obvious that $R_L = 10$ kilohms and $r_L = 5$ kilohms. Therefore, the correct amount of d-c collector current is

$$I_C = \frac{V_{CC}}{r_L + R_L} = \frac{30}{15,000} = 2 \text{ ma}$$

In order to have 2 ma of collector current, the emitter current must be set at approximately 2 ma. Thus

$$R_E \cong \frac{V_{EE}}{I_E} = \frac{10}{0.002} = 5 \text{ kilohms}$$

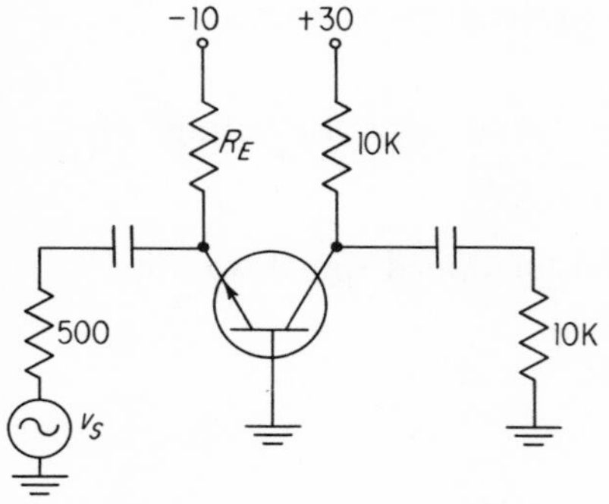

Fig. 8-16 Example 8-9. 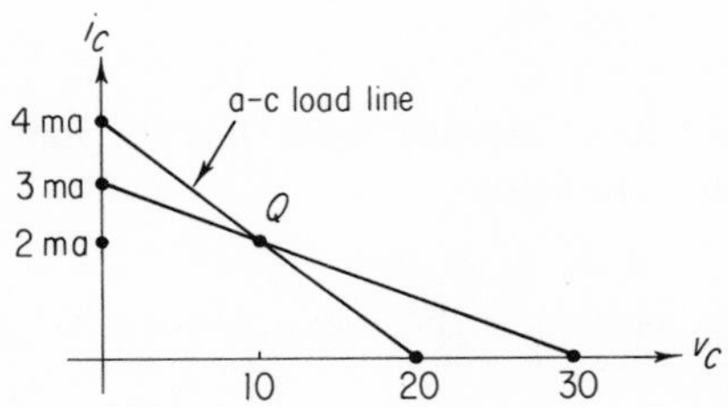   **Fig. 8-17** Example 8-10.

EXAMPLE 8-10

Draw the d-c and a-c load lines for the preceding example.

SOLUTION

For optimum bias we know that the collector current is set at 2 ma. This means that the d-c collector voltage is

$$V_C = 30 - 0.002(10,000) = 10 \text{ volts}$$

The cutoff voltage on the a-c load line is

$$V_C + I_C r_L = 10 + 0.002(5000) = 20 \text{ volts}$$

The d-c and a-c load lines are given in Fig. 8-17. Notice that the possible voltage swing in either direction is 10 volts. Therefore, we are at the optimum bias condition as far as maximum signal-handling capability is concerned.

EXAMPLE 8-11

In Fig. 8-18 the coil has essentially zero resistance. At the driving frequency, the reactance of the coil is so high that it acts like an open circuit to the a-c signal. The capacitors, as usual, appear as short circuits to the a-c signal. Determine whether or not the stage is at optimum bias.

SOLUTION

The d-c load resistance R_L is zero. The a-c load resistance is simply 10 kilohms, because the coil appears open to the a-c signal. Therefore, the optimum value of d-c collector current is

$$I_C = \frac{V_{CC}}{r_L + R_L} = \frac{30}{10,000} = 3 \text{ ma}$$

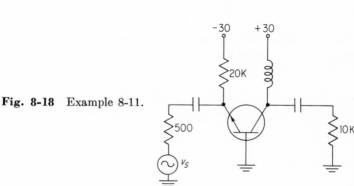

Fig. 8-18 Example 8-11.

The actual value of d-c collector current in Fig. 8-18 is

$$I_C \cong I_E \cong \frac{30}{20,000} = 1.5 \text{ ma}$$

Therefore, the stage is not at optimum bias. As it now stands, the maximum excursion on the positive half cycle is

$$I_C r_L = 1.5(10^{-3})(10)(10^3) = 15 \text{ volts}$$

and the maximum negative excursion is

$$V_C = 30 \text{ volts}$$

In order for the stage to have a maximum signal-handling capability, the d-c collector current must be increased to 3 ma. This is easily accomplished by making R_E equal to 10 kilohms. Once this is done, the stage can then deliver 60 volts peak-to-peak output before clipping.

8-5 p-n-p **Load Lines**

When a p-n-p transistor is used instead of an n-p-n, the d-c voltages and currents are reversed from those of the n-p-n transistor. How does this affect the load lines discussed so far?

As already indicated, all d-c formulas are exactly the same for p-n-p and n-p-n transistors if we use the *magnitudes* of voltages and currents. In other words, for the circuit of Fig. 8-19a, the emitter current is still given by

$$I_E \cong \frac{V_{EE}}{R_E}$$

and the collector voltage is still given by

$$V_C = V_{CC} - I_C R_L$$

where V_C is the magnitude of the collector-ground voltage and V_{CC} is the magnitude of the collector supply voltage.

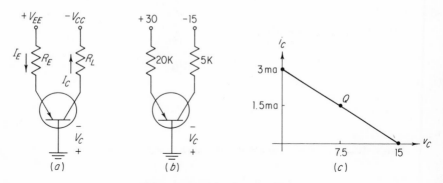

Fig. 8-19 p-n-p operation.

As an example, in the circuit of Fig. 8-19b, there is an emitter current of

$$I_E \cong \frac{30}{20,000} = 1.5 \text{ ma}$$

and the collector voltage is

$$V_C = 15 - 0.0015(5000) = 7.5 \text{ volts}$$

The polarity of the voltage is minus-plus, as shown in Fig. 8-19b. The corresponding d-c load line and operating point are shown in Fig. 8-19c.

Thus, there is no difference in the construction of load lines for p-n-p and n-p-n transistors if we use magnitudes of voltages and currents. However, there is another approach used in load-line construction that should be mentioned at this time. Consider the circuit shown in Fig. 8-20a; the direction of the d-c collector current and the polarity of the d-c collector voltage have been reversed from those shown in Fig. 8-19a. The true polarity of collector voltage and the true direction of collector current in a p-n-p transistor are opposite those shown in Fig. 8-20a. Nevertheless, if we insist on using the direction and polarity shown in Fig. 8-20a, we must change our load-line drawing. The correct load line for the circuit is shown in Fig. 8-20b. We have deliberately shown the load line in the third quadrant to reflect the reversal in current direction and voltage polarity.

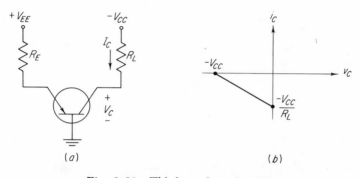

Fig. 8-20 Third-quadrant load line.

The use of a third-quadrant load line to compensate for a reversed current and polarity in Fig. 8-20a may seem to be an unnecessary complication, but there is a good reason for it in some applications. For instance, a typical transistor curve tracer uses the current direction and voltage polarity of an n-p-n transistor as a reference and the IV characteristics and the load line of the n-p-n transistor appear in the first quadrant. However, when a p-n-p transistor is used, the curve tracer displays the IV characteristics and load line in the third quadrant because the currents and voltages are reversed in p-n-p transistor.

In any event, either approach can be used in dealing with load lines. Throughout this book we will use the first method, that is, we will use magnitudes of voltage and current. This means that all d-c formulas and load lines developed for the n-p-n transistor will be the same for the p-n-p transistor. (Of course, any a-c formulas are identical for either transistor type, because each has the same a-c equivalent circuit.)

EXAMPLE 8-12

Draw the d-c and a-c load lines for the circuit of Fig. 8-21a. Use magnitudes of voltages and currents.

SOLUTION

The d-c load line must pass through a cutoff voltage of 30 volts and a saturation current of 3 ma. The d-c operating point is located at $I_C = 1$ ma and $V_C = 20$ volts.

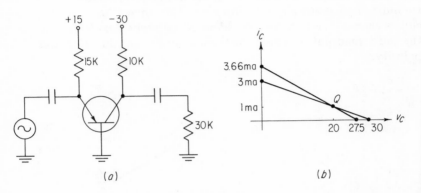

Fig. 8-21   Example 8-12.

The a-c load resistance seen by the collector is obviously 7.5 kilohms. Therefore, the cutoff point on the a-c load line is

$$V_C + I_C r_L = 20 + 0.001(7500) = 27.5 \text{ volts}$$

and the saturation current is

$$I_C + \frac{V_C}{r_L} = 0.001 + \frac{20}{7500} = 3.66 \text{ ma}$$

The d-c and a-c load lines are shown in Fig. 8-21b.

8-6   Load Lines for the CE Connection

When a CE connection is used, the load-line construction is the same as discussed for the CB connection. For instance, in Fig. 8-22a and b we have the base-biased and emitter-biased CE connections. The a-c signal drives the base, and the amplified output is taken from the collector.

To draw the d-c load line we merely draw a line through a cutoff voltage of V_{CC} and a saturation current of V_{CC}/R_L. In finding I_C and V_C we use either the base-bias or emitter-bias formulas, depending upon which circuit is being analyzed. In either case, we plot the values of I_C and V_C, thereby locating the d-c operating point, as in Fig. 8-22c.

The a-c load line is also drawn in the usual way; that is, it passes through the d-c operating point and has a cutoff voltage of $V_C + I_C r_L$; the upper end of the a-c load line passes through a saturation current of $I_C + V_C/r_L$, as shown in Fig. 8-22c.

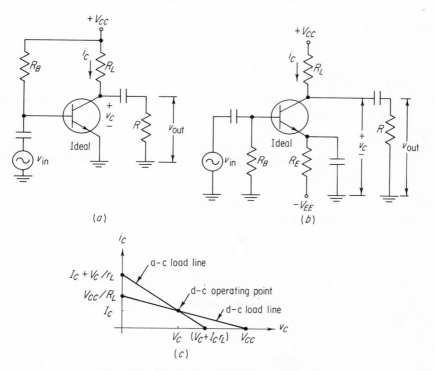

Fig. 8-22   Load lines for CE connections.

As observed with the CB circuit, clipping occurs when the a-c signal is too large. By inspection of Fig. 8-22c, it is clear that clipping occurs if the positive peak of the a-c signal tries to exceed $I_C r_L$; clipping also occurs if the negative peak of the a-c signal tries to exceed V_C. Thus, the maximum peak-to-peak unclipped signal for either CE circuit is

$$2I_C r_L \qquad \text{or} \qquad 2V_C$$

whichever is smaller.

Of course, the a-c load line can be located so that equal excursions occur in the positive and negative directions by making the d-c collector current equal to

$$I_C = \frac{V_{CC}}{r_L + R_L} \tag{8-7}$$

In this case, $I_C r_L = V_C$, so that the maximum unclipped peak-to-peak signal is simply $2V_C$ (or $2I_C r_L$).

All the foregoing results for the CE connections are the same as for the CB circuit.

EXAMPLE 8-13

Analyze the CE circuit of Fig. 8-23a by:

(a) Drawing the d-c load line and operating point.
(b) Drawing the a-c load line.
(c) Finding the maximum peak-to-peak unclipped output that can be obtained from this circuit.

SOLUTION

(a) The cutoff voltage on the d-c load line is 25 volts, and the saturation current is

$$I_{C(\text{sat})} = \frac{25}{20(10^3)} = 1.25 \text{ ma}$$

The d-c operating point is

$$I_C \cong I_E \cong \frac{16}{20(10^3)} = 0.8 \text{ ma}$$

and

$$V_C = 25 - 0.8(10^{-3})(20)(10^3) = 9 \text{ volts}$$

The d-c load line and operating point are drawn in Fig. 8-23b.

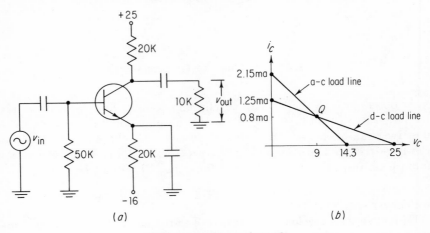

Fig. 8-23   Example 8-13.

(b) The a-c load resistance seen by the collector is

$$r_L = R_L \| R = 20(10^3) \| 10(10^3) = 6.67 \text{ kilohms}$$

Therefore, the cutoff voltage on the a-c load line is

$$V_C + I_C r_L = 9 + 0.8(10^{-3})(6.67)(10^3) = 14.3 \text{ volts}$$

and the saturation current on the a-c load line is

$$I_C + \frac{V_C}{r_L} = 0.8(10^{-3}) + \frac{9}{6.67(10^3)} = 2.15 \text{ ma}$$

The a-c load line can now be drawn as in Fig. 8-23b.

(c) Clipping occurs for $2I_C r_L$ or $2V_C$, whichever is smaller.

$$2I_C r_L = 2(0.0008)(6670) = 10.7 \text{ volts p–p}$$
$$2V_C = 2(9) = 18 \text{ volts p–p}$$

Hence, we see that the largest peak-to-peak unclipped output is about 10.7 volts.

EXAMPLE 8-14

For the preceding example, change the emitter resistor as needed to permit maximum signal-handling capability. What is the largest peak-to-peak signal available for this condition?

SOLUTION

The optimum value of d-c collector current is found by using Eq. (8-7).

$$I_C = \frac{V_{CC}}{r_L + R_L} = \frac{25}{6.67(10^3) + 20(10^3)} \cong 0.937 \text{ ma}$$

To get this value of d-c collector current we need to change R_E to a new value of

$$R_E \cong \frac{V_{EE}}{I_E} = \frac{16}{0.937(10^{-3})} \cong 17 \text{ kilohms}$$

The maximum unclipped signal under this condition is $2V_C$, or $2I_C r_L$, since these quantities are now equal. Hence, the maximum unclipped signal is

$$2I_C r_L = 2(0.937)(10^{-3})(6.67)(10^3) = 12.5 \text{ volts p–p}$$

8-7 The D-C Load Line for the CC Connection

The CC circuit (emitter follower) must be handled in a different way from the CB and CE circuits as far as load lines are concerned. In Fig.

8-24a, we have a typical CC circuit. How are the d-c and a-c load lines drawn for this circuit?

In Fig. 8-24b, we have shown the d-c equivalent circuit. Because the collector-ground voltage is fixed at V_{CC}, we will now use the collector-emitter voltage v_{CE} in our load-line graphs. By applying Kirchhoff's voltage law around the loop including the power supplies, the emitter resistor, and the transistor, we get

$$v_{CE} + i_E R_E - V_{EE} - V_{CC} = 0$$

After solving for v_{CE}, we have

$$v_{CE} = V_{EE} + V_{CC} - i_E R_E \qquad (8\text{-}8)$$

This is the equation we use for plotting the d-c load line. The cutoff voltage can be found by noting that at cutoff $i_E = 0$. Therefore, at cutoff

$$v_{CE} = V_{EE} + V_{CC}$$

In other words, at cutoff there is no current through the emitter resistor R_E. With no current through this resistor, there is no voltage drop across it, and the net voltage across the collector-emitter terminals is $V_{CC} + V_{EE}$.

At saturation, the voltage across the collector-emitter terminals drops to essentially zero, that is, $v_{CE} \cong 0$. Thus, at saturation, the current in the

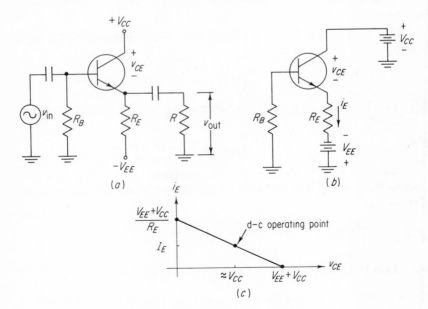

Fig. 8-24   D-c load line of emitter follower.

transistor is found as follows:

$$v_{CE} = V_{EE} + V_{CC} - i_E R_E$$
$$0 = V_{EE} + V_{CC} - i_E R_E$$
$$i_{E(\text{sat})} = \frac{V_{EE} + V_{CC}}{R_E} \tag{8-9}$$

The d-c load line is shown in Fig. 8-24c. Note that the d-c operating point of the emitter follower is located at a current of I_E and a collector-emitter voltage of approximately V_{CC}. The value of I_E is found in the usual way. That is,

$$I_E \cong \frac{V_{EE}}{R_E} \tag{8-10}$$

This formula assumes that $V_{EE} \gg V_{BE}$ and that $R_E \gg R_B/\beta$. These conditions are usually satisfied in any well-designed emitter follower. If necessary, the more accurate formula for I_E can be used, that is,

$$I_E \cong \frac{V_{EE} - V_{BE}}{R_E + R_B/\beta}$$

The collector-emitter voltage at the d-c operating point is approximately V_{CC} because the emitter voltage is usually only a few tenths of a volt with respect to ground. The actual voltage across the collector-emitter terminals equals

$$V_{CE} = V_{CC} - V_E \tag{8-11}$$

where V_E is the voltage from the emitter to ground. It is easily shown that

$$V_E = -V_{BE} - I_B R_B$$

V_{BE} is a few tenths of a volt; $I_B R_B$ is also small, being only a few tenths of a volt in a well-designed emitter follower. As a result, V_E is usually much smaller than V_{CC} and Eq. (8-11) simplifies to

$$V_{CE} \cong V_{CC} \tag{8-12}$$

Let us summarize the important points of our discussion.

1. The d-c load line of an emitter follower is a graph of

$$v_{CE} = V_{EE} + V_{CC} - i_E R_E$$

2. The d-c load line is a line passing through a cutoff voltage of $V_{EE} + V_{CC}$ and a saturation current of $(V_{EE} + V_{CC})/R_E$.

3. The d-c operating point of a typical emitter follower is located at

$$I_E \cong \frac{V_{EE}}{R_E} \qquad \text{and} \qquad V_{CE} \cong V_{CC}$$

EXAMPLE 8-15

Show the d-c load line and operating point for the emitter follower of Fig. 8-25a.

SOLUTION

Referring to Fig. 8-24c, it is clear that the cutoff voltage is

$$V_{EE} + V_{CC} = 20 + 30 = 50 \text{ volts}$$

(In using this formula, note that $V_{EE} = 20$ volts, not -20, because we are using magnitudes of voltages.)

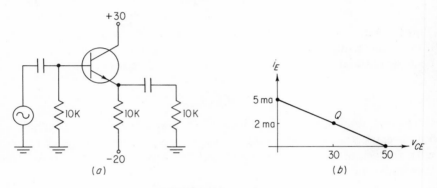

Fig. 8-25   Example 8-15.

The saturation current is

$$\frac{V_{EE} + V_{CC}}{R_E} = \frac{50}{10,000} = 5 \text{ ma}$$

The d-c operating point is at

$$I_E \cong \frac{20}{10,000} = 2 \text{ ma}$$

and

$$V_{CE} \cong V_{CC} = 30 \text{ volts}$$

The d-c load line and operating point are shown in Fig. 8-25b.

8-8   The A-C Load Line for the Emitter Follower

What is the a-c load line of a typical emitter follower like that of Fig. 8-26a?

First, realize that the d-c load resistance seen by the emitter is R_E, but the a-c load resistance is

$$r_L = R_E \| R$$

In other words, when a-c current leaves the emitter, it sees two paths that it can flow through. In effect, we lump these two paths into a single resistance designated r_L.

With an a-c signal present, excursions take place above and below the d-c operating point. With a d-c current of I_E, it is clear that the maximum positive voltage swing is

$$I_E r_L$$

Thus, the cutoff voltage on the a-c load line must be located at approximately

$$V_{CC} + I_E r_L$$

Also, the saturation current on the a-c load line is approximately

$$I_E + \frac{V_{CC}}{r_L}$$

The a-c load line is shown in Fig. 8-26b. As we observed with the CB and CE circuits, clipping occurs when the a-c signal is too large. Note

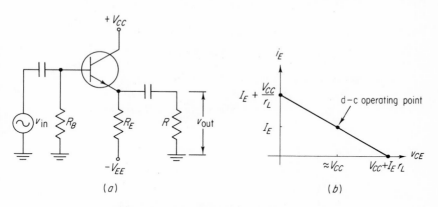

Fig. 8-26 A-c load line of emitter follower.

that the maximum positive voltage change from the operating point is

$$I_E r_L$$

and the maximum negative voltage change is approximately

$$V_{CC}$$

Also, note that the optimum bias point from the standpoint of largest unclipped signal occurs when both swings are equal, that is,

$$I_E r_L = V_{CC}$$

Therefore, the optimum d-c emitter current should be set at

$$I_E = \frac{V_{CC}}{r_L}$$

EXAMPLE 8-16

For the emitter follower of Fig. 8-27a, locate the d-c operating point and draw the a-c load line. For what peak-to-peak swing does clipping occur?

SOLUTION

It is clear that the d-c current is

$$I_E \cong \frac{V_{EE}}{R_E} = \frac{30}{30,000} = 1 \text{ ma}$$

and that

$$V_C \cong V_{CC} = 25 \text{ volts}$$

The a-c load resistance seen by the emitter is

$$r_L = R_E \| R = 30,000 \| 10,000 = 7500 \text{ ohms}$$

We can now find the cutoff voltage on the a-c load line.

$$V_{CC} + I_E r_L = 25 + 0.001(7500) = 32.5 \text{ volts}$$

Also, the saturation current on the a-c load line is

$$I_E + \frac{V_{CC}}{r_L} = 0.001 + \frac{25}{7500} = 4.33 \text{ ma}$$

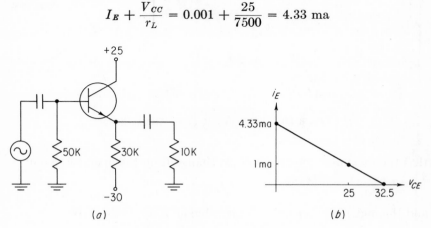

Fig. 8-27   Example 8-16.

We now draw the a-c load line as shown in Fig. 8-27b. From this load line, it is obvious that clipping occurs for a positive swing of

$$32.5 - 25 = 7.5 \text{ volts}$$

Therefore, the maximum peak-to-peak unclipped signal is 15 volts.

SUMMARY

The d-c load line is a locus or collection of all the possible d-c operating points of the transistor. The actual d-c operating point of the transistor must lie somewhere along the d-c load line.

When an a-c signal is coupled into a transistor, the currents and voltages in the transistor fluctuate. These fluctuations, or changes, take place along the a-c load line.

The maximum signal-handling capability of a transistor circuit is found by using the a-c load line. The excursions from the d-c operating point are limited by either the cutoff or the saturation of the transistor. By means of the a-c load line we can see which of these excursions is the limiting factor.

Optimum bias, in the sense used in this chapter, means locating the a-c load line so that equal excursions above and below the d-c operating point can occur. By doing this, the circuit has maximum signal-handling capability for the given supply voltages.

GLOSSARY

cutoff In this chapter, cutoff simply means no collector or emitter current.

d-c load line A graph of all the possible d-c operating points of a transistor.

magnitude The size of a voltage or current without regard to the actual polarity, or direction.

maximum unclipped signal The largest signal output that we can get from a transistor circuit without causing saturation or cutoff to occur.

saturation This refers to having essentially zero volts across the collector diode of a transistor.

REVIEW QUESTIONS

1. Where are the cutoff and saturation points on a load line?
2. For a CB circuit, how do you calculate the saturation current on the d-c load line?

3. Under what condition is the a-c load line the same as the d-c load line?
4. Why is the cutoff voltage on the a-c load line different from that on the d-c load line (assume $r_L \neq R_L$)?
5. For a CB or CE circuit, what are the formulas for the maximum positive and maximum negative voltage swings?
6. When a CB or CE stage is operating at optimum bias, what is the largest peak-to-peak signal that can be obtained?
7. What are the two basic ways of showing the d-c load line for a p-n-p transistor?
8. In an emitter follower, what is the maximum possible a-c swing in the positive direction? In the negative direction?

PROBLEMS

8-1   In Fig. 8-28a, draw the d-c load line and show the operating point for the following values of R_L:
   (a) $R_L = 1$ kilohm.
   (b) $R_L = 10$ kilohms.
   (c) $R_L = 20$ kilohms.

8-2   In Fig. 8-28b, draw the d-c load line and operating point for the following values of V_{CC}:
   (a) $V_{CC} = 10$ volts.
   (b) $V_{CC} = 20$ volts.
   (c) $V_{CC} = 40$ volts.

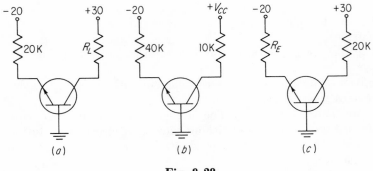

Fig. 8-28

8-3   Draw the d-c load line and operating point for the circuit of Fig. 8-28c for the following values of R_E:
   (a) $R_E = 40$ kilohms.
   (b) $R_E = 20$ kilohms.

8-4 In Fig. 8-29a, draw the d-c load line and operating point. Also, show the points along the d-c load line that represent peak excursions for the given 1-volt source signal.

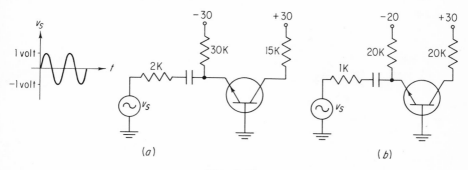

Fig. 8-29

8-5 In Fig. 8-29b, if the a-c signal is too large, clipping will occur. Does clipping first occur on the positive or on the negative swing? What is the approximate value of source voltage that just causes clipping to occur?

8-6 Draw the a-c load line for the circuit of Fig. 8-30a. What are the maximum possible voltage excursions in both directions? What is the largest unclipped peak-to-peak voltage that can be obtained from this circuit?

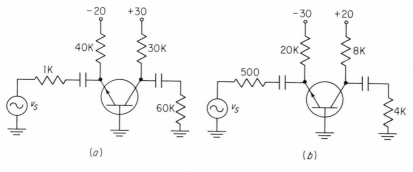

Fig. 8-30

8-7 What approximate size should the emitter resistor R_E of Fig. 8-30a be to have equal excursions above and below the d-c operating point?

8-8 In the circuit of Fig. 8-30b, what are the maximum positive and negative swings before cutoff or saturation is reached? What approximate size should R_E be to have the largest signal-handling capability?

8-9   Draw the d-c and a-c load lines for the circuit in Fig. 8-31.

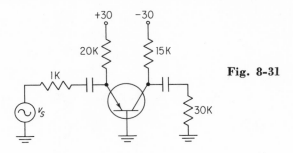

Fig. 8-31

8-10   What is the peak-to-peak value of the largest unclipped signal available from the circuit of Fig. 8-31 with the given bias conditions? If the emitter resistor were changed so as to produce the optimum operating point, what would the largest peak-to-peak output become?

8-11   Draw the d-c and a-c load lines for the CE circuit of Fig. 8-32a. What will happen to the d-c and a-c load lines if the β of the transistor changes to 50?

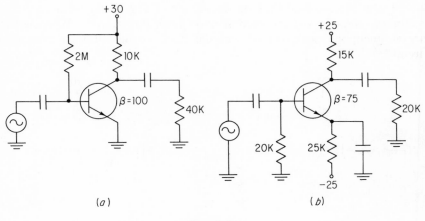

Fig. 8-32

8-12   Draw the a-c load line for the circuit of Fig. 8-32b. What happens to the location of the a-c load line if the β changes to 50? To 100?

8-13   In order to have optimum bias in the CE circuit of Fig. 8-32a, what size should the base resistor be?

8-14   Draw the d-c and a-c load lines for the emitter follower of Fig. 8-33a.

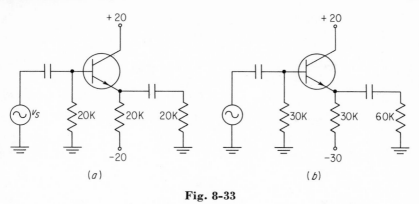

Fig. 8-33

8-15 In the emitter follower of Fig. 8-33a, for what values of a-c output voltage does clipping occur on each excursion?

8-16 Draw the d-c and a-c load lines for the emitter follower of Fig. 8-33b. What is the largest unclipped peak-to-peak signal that can be obtained from this circuit?

9 | Bias Arrangements

Up to now, we have discussed base bias and emitter bias. Recall that as far as setting and holding a d-c operating point is concerned, base bias is the worst way to bias, and emitter bias is the best way. In between these two extremes there are a number of widely used bias arrangements.

In this chapter we will study six of the most common ways to bias a transistor, emphasizing those concepts and formulas which are most useful in practice.

9-1   The Concept of β Sensitivity

The d-c operating point in some biasing arrangements shows a heavy dependence upon the exact value of β, whereas in others there is almost no dependence upon the β value. Generally speaking, it is far more desirable to have a biasing circuit in which the value of β does not matter; in this way, a change in the β value will not disturb the desired d-c operating point. (Changes in β can occur when the temperature changes or when the transistor is replaced.)

In this section we wish to discuss the concept of β *sensitivity*, that is, the influence that the β value has on the d-c operating point. To begin our discussion, consider the circuit of Fig. 9-1a. The base current in this circuit is clearly

$$I_B = \frac{V_{CC} - V_{BE}}{R_B} \cong \frac{V_{CC}}{R_B} = \frac{20}{10^6} = 20 \ \mu a$$

In Fig. 9-1a, the β is given as 100; therefore, the collector current is

$$I_C = \beta I_B = 100(20 \ \mu a) = 2 \ ma$$

The collector voltage with respect to ground equals the supply voltage minus the drop across the load resistor. That is,

$$V_C = 20 - 2(10^{-3})(5)(10^3) = 10 \ volts$$

Also, note that the cutoff voltage on the d-c load line is 20 volts, and the saturation current is 4 ma. Thus, we can draw the d-c load line and operating point as shown in Fig. 9-1b.

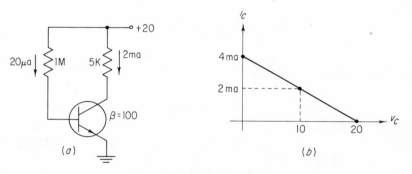

Fig. 9-1 Base-bias sensitivity.

From our earlier work with this base-bias circuit, we know that if for some reason the β changes, this will change the d-c operating point. For instance, suppose that the β changes from 100 to 110. We can write this as

$$\beta + \Delta\beta = 110$$

where β is the original value of β and $\Delta\beta$ is the change in the β value. Thus, in this case, the change $\Delta\beta$ in β is 10.

The percent change in β is defined as the change divided by the original value. That is,

$$\text{Percent change in } \beta = \frac{\Delta\beta}{\beta}$$

Therefore, when β changes from 100 to 110, we say that the percent change in β is

$$\frac{\Delta\beta}{\beta} = \frac{10}{100} = 0.1 = 10\%$$

We can also speak of the percent change in the collector current. In the circuit of Fig. 9-1a, when the β changes from 100 to 110, the base current remains essentially the same.

$$I_B \cong \frac{V_{CC}}{R_B} = 20 \ \mu a \qquad \text{as before}$$

The collector current, however, now becomes

$$I_C + \Delta I_C = 110(20 \ \mu a) = 2.2 \ \text{ma}$$

where I_C is the original value of collector current and ΔI_C is the change in collector current. In this particular case, the change in collector current is 0.2 ma; therefore, the percent change in collector current is

$$\frac{\Delta I_C}{I_C} = \frac{0.2 \ \text{ma}}{2 \ \text{ma}} = 0.1 = 10\%$$

Thus, we have seen a 10 percent change in β cause a 10 percent change in collector current. In other words,

$$\frac{\Delta I_C}{I_C} = \frac{\Delta\beta}{\beta} \qquad \text{for base bias}$$

This is quite bad; it means that the d-c operating point shifts significantly when the β changes.

There are other ways to bias a transistor, and we will find that the percent change in collector current can be less than the percent change in β for these circuits. In general, the percent change in collector current is

$$\frac{\Delta I_C}{I_C} = K\frac{\Delta\beta}{\beta} \qquad (9\text{-}1)$$

where K is a constant of proportionality. Equation (9-1) tells us that the percent change in the collector current equals a constant times the percent change in β. We will call K the β *sensitivity* because the value of K indicates how sensitive the collector current is to changes in β.

For the base-bias circuit of Fig. 9-1a, we have seen that K equals unity. In the remainder of this chapter we will discuss bias arrangements in which K is less than unity. In general, *the sensitivity K is between 0 and 1, with the least sensitive bias arrangements having K values approaching 0.* For instance, a good biasing circuit can have a K as low as 0.01. In a circuit like this, a change of 10 percent in β would cause a change of only 0.1 percent in collector current.

9-2 Base Bias

In this section we summarize the important formulas for the base-bias circuit of Fig. 9-2a. First, note that the saturation value of collector current occurs when the collector-emitter voltage is approximately zero. Thus, in Fig. 9-2a it is clear that

$$I_{C(\text{sat})} \cong \frac{V_{CC}}{R_L} \tag{9-2}$$

This is the maximum value of d-c collector current for the base-bias circuit. For normal operation the actual d-c current must be less than this value. The actual d-c collector current equals

$$I_C = \beta I_B \tag{9-3}$$

The base current, as already indicated, equals

$$I_B = \frac{V_{CC} - V_{BE}}{R_B} \cong \frac{V_{CC}}{R_B} \tag{9-4}$$

The collector-ground voltage V_C simply equals

$$V_C = V_{CC} - I_C R_L \tag{9-5}$$

Finally, we have seen that for a base-biased circuit the sensitivity is

$$K = 1 \tag{9-6}$$

Figure 9-2a summarizes the important biasing formulas.

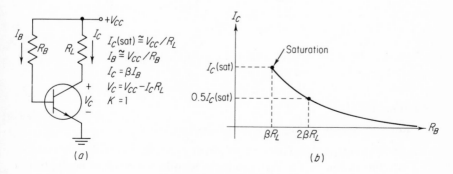

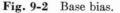

Fig. 9-2 Base bias.

Note that if we substitute Eq. (9-4) into (9-3), we get

$$I_C \cong \beta \frac{V_{CC}}{R_B}$$

or

$$I_C \cong \frac{V_{CC}}{R_B/\beta} \tag{9-7}$$

It is helpful to graph this equation for I_C vs. R_B, as shown in Fig. 9-2b. This graph tells us that when R_B is less than βR_L, the transistor is saturated; therefore, for normal operation R_B must be greater than βR_L. As shown in the graph, when $R_B = 2\beta R_L$, the d-c collector current is one-half of the saturation value.

EXAMPLE 9-1

In Fig. 9-3a, what value of β just causes saturation?

SOLUTION

By inspection of the graph in Fig. 9-2b we can see that saturation occurs when

$$R_B = \beta R_L$$

With $R_B = 50$ kilohms and $R_L = 1$ kilohm, we compute a β of

$$\beta = \frac{R_B}{R_L} = \frac{50(10^3)}{10^3} = 50$$

Thus, if the β is more than 50, the transistor will saturate.

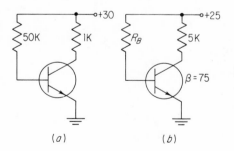

Fig. 9-3   Examples 9-1 to 9-3.

EXAMPLE 9-2

For the circuit of Fig. 9-3b, find the following:

(a) The saturation value of collector current.
(b) The value of R_B that produces a collector current equal to one-half the saturation value.

SOLUTION

(a) The saturation value of collector current is

$$I_{C(\text{sat})} \cong \frac{V_{CC}}{R_L} = \frac{25}{5000} = 5 \text{ ma}$$

(b) From the base-bias characteristic of Fig. 9-2b we see that the collector current is one-half the saturation value when

$$R_B = 2\beta R_L = 2(75)(5000) = 750 \text{ kilohms}$$

EXAMPLE 9-3

For the circuit of Fig. 9-3b, let $R_B = 1$ megohm and find the value of I_C and V_C.

SOLUTION

Using Eq. (9-7), we find that

$$I_C \cong \frac{V_{CC}}{R_B/\beta} = \frac{25}{10^6/75} = 1.88 \text{ ma}$$

The collector-ground voltage is

$$V_C = V_{CC} - I_C R_L = 25 - 1.88(10^{-3})(5)(10^3) = 15.6 \text{ volts}$$

9-3 Base Bias with Emitter Feedback

One way to reduce the sensitivity of collector current to changes in β is to use the circuit shown in Fig. 9-4a. The additional resistor in the emitter circuit causes degeneration to take place, thereby stabilizing the d-c operating point against changes in β. To understand the stabilizing action, assume that the β of the transistor increases for some reason. This increase in β will cause an increase in the emitter current, which, in turn, causes the voltage across R_E to increase. However, now that the voltage from the emitter to ground has increased, the voltage across the base resistor R_B will decrease, thereby reducing base current, which, in turn, partially compensates for the increase in β.

Some of the quantities that are useful in analysis and design are the following. First, the saturated value of collector current, which is found as follows. At saturation, v_{CE} is essentially zero, and the supply voltage is distributed across R_L and R_E. Since base current is much smaller than collector current, we have

$$I_{C(\text{sat})} \cong \frac{V_{CC}}{R_E + R_L} \qquad (9\text{-}8)$$

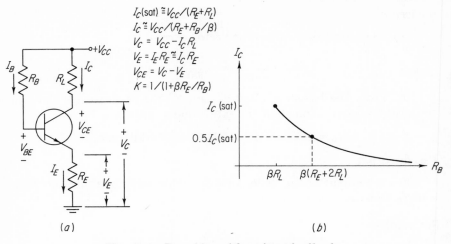

Fig. 9-4   Base bias with emitter feedback.

In the normal operating region of the transistor the collector current is less than the saturation value given by Eq. (9-8). We can find the formula for the actual collector current as follows. First, we write a voltage equation including the supply voltage, the drop across R_B, the V_{BE} drop, and the drop across R_E. That is,

$$V_{CC} = I_B R_B + V_{BE} + I_E R_E$$

Since $I_B = I_C/\beta$ and $I_E \cong I_C$, we can simplify to get

$$V_{CC} \cong \frac{I_C}{\beta} R_B + V_{BE} + I_C R_E$$

Solving for I_C, we obtain

$$I_C \cong \frac{V_{CC} - V_{BE}}{R_E + R_B/\beta}$$

As before, we take advantage of the fact that usually $V_{BE} \ll V_{CC}$. Hence we simply have

$$I_C \cong \frac{V_{CC}}{R_E + R_B/\beta} \qquad \text{for } V_{BE} \ll V_{CC} \qquad (9\text{-}9)$$

Remember that this formula is valid as long as the transistor is not saturated, that is, I_C must be less than $I_{C(\text{sat})}$.

The formulas for voltages are

$$V_C = V_{CC} - I_C R_L \qquad (9\text{-}10)$$

and

$$V_E = I_E R_E \cong I_C R_E \qquad (9\text{-}11)$$

By means of calculus, the sensitivity is found to be

$$K = \frac{1}{1 + \beta R_E/R_B} \tag{9-12}$$

Figure 9-4a summarizes the important biasing formulas.

As before, we can show a sketch of I_C vs. R_B (Fig. 9-4b). This graph tells us that when R_B is less than βR_L, the transistor is saturated. For normal operation, R_B must be greater than βR_L. In fact, note that if $R_B = \beta(R_E + 2R_L)$, the value of I_C equals one-half the saturation value.

EXAMPLE 9-4

For the circuit of Fig. 9-5a, find the saturation value of collector current and the actual value.

SOLUTION

The saturation value is

$$I_{C(\text{sat})} \cong \frac{V_{CC}}{R_E + R_L} = \frac{20}{3000} = 6.67 \text{ ma}$$

The actual value of collector current is

$$I_C \cong \frac{V_{CC}}{R_E + R_B/\beta} = \frac{20}{1000 + 300(10^3)/100} = 5 \text{ ma}$$

EXAMPLE 9-5

For the circuit of Fig. 9-5a, find V_C, V_E, and K.

SOLUTION

We found in Example 9-4 that the collector current in this circuit is $I_C = 5$ ma. Therefore, the collector-ground voltage is

$$V_C = 20 - 5(10^{-3})(2)(10^3) = 10 \text{ volts}$$

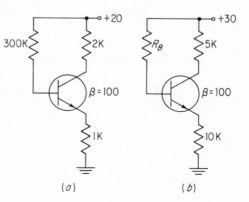

Fig. 9-5 Examples 9-4 and 9-6.

and the emitter-ground voltage is

$$V_E = I_E R_E \cong 5(10^{-3})(10^3) = 5 \text{ volts}$$

Using Eq. (9-12), we can find the sensitivity to changes in β.

$$K = \frac{1}{1 + 100(10^3)/300(10^3)} = 0.75$$

A sensitivity of 0.75 means that the circuit is less susceptible to changes in β than the ordinary base-bias circuit without feedback. For instance, if the β were to change 10 percent, the collector current in the circuit of Fig. 9-5a would change about 7.5 percent.

EXAMPLE 9-6

In Fig. 9-5b, use a β of 100 and find the following:

(a) The value of R_B that just causes saturation.
(b) The value of R_B that produces a collector current of one-half of the saturation value.
(c) The sensitivity K at one-half saturation value.

SOLUTION

(a) In the design characteristic of Fig. 9-4b we can see that saturation occurs when

$$R_B = \beta R_L = 100(5000) = 500 \text{ kilohms}$$

Thus, for normal operation R_B must be greater than 500 kilohms.

(b) Using the characteristic of Fig. 9-4b, we get

$$R_B = \beta(R_E + 2R_L) = 100(10{,}000 + 10{,}000) = 2 \text{ megohms}$$

(c) The sensitivity is

$$K = \frac{1}{1 + \beta R_E/R_B} = \frac{1}{1 + 100(10^4)/2(10^6)} = 0.667$$

9-4 Base Bias with Collector Feedback

Another common bias arrangement found in practice is the circuit shown in Fig. 9-6a. It is like base bias, except that the base resistor is returned to the collector instead of the V_{CC} supply. Because the voltage for the base resistor R_B is derived from the collector, there is a negative-feedback effect that tends to stabilize the collector current against changes in β. To understand the stabilizing action, assume that β increases. This will increase collector current, which then causes the collector voltage to drop.

However, with less collector voltage applied to R_B, the base current will decrease and partially compensate for the original change in β.

The important d-c operating formulas can be found as follows. First, we know that saturation occurs when v_{CE} is essentially zero. Under this condition, all the supply voltage appears across R_L. Note that the total current in R_L is the sum of collector and base current. Because the base current is much smaller than the collector current, however, we can neglect it and get a saturation value of

$$I_{C(\text{sat})} \cong \frac{V_{CC}}{R_L} \tag{9-13}$$

This represents the maximum value of collector current.

To find the actual collector current, we need to write some voltage equations. As usual, the collector voltage equals the supply voltage minus the drop across R_L. That is,

$$V_C = V_{CC} - (I_C + I_B)R_L \cong V_{CC} - I_C R_L$$

From the circuit of Fig. 9-6a, we note that the collector-ground voltage must also equal

$$V_C = I_B R_B + V_{BE}$$

Therefore, we can equate these last two expressions to obtain

$$I_B R_B + V_{BE} \cong V_{CC} - I_C R_L$$

Since $I_B = I_C/\beta$, we can rewrite this equation as

$$\frac{I_C}{\beta} R_B + V_{BE} \cong V_{CC} - I_C R_L$$

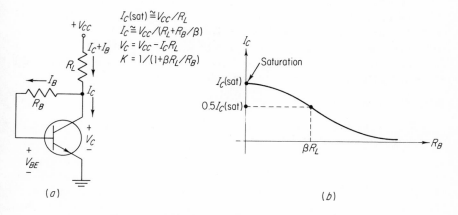

Fig. 9-6 Base bias with collector feedback.

Solving this equation for I_C, we get the desired result.

$$I_C \cong \frac{V_{CC} - V_{BE}}{R_L + R_B/\beta}$$

Again, we note that V_{BE} is usually small enough to neglect. Hence, our final practical formula for the collector current becomes

$$I_C \cong \frac{V_{CC}}{R_L + R_B/\beta} \qquad \text{for } V_{BE} \ll V_{CC} \qquad \textbf{(9-14)}$$

The circuit of Fig. 9-6a has a sensitivity of less than unity. By means of calculus, the sensitivity is found to be

$$K = \frac{1}{1 + \beta R_L/R_B} \qquad \textbf{(9-15)}$$

An alternate expression for the sensitivity is

$$K = 1 - \frac{I_C}{I_{C(\text{sat})}} \qquad \textbf{(9-16)}$$

Equation (9-16) is quite useful. It tells us how the sensitivity is related to the operating point. For instance, the limits on $I_C/I_{C(\text{sat})}$ are

$$0 < \frac{I_C}{I_{C(\text{sat})}} < 1$$

where the lower limit represents the cutoff condition and the upper limit represents saturation. Therefore, according to Eq. (9-16), the sensitivity at cutoff is 1; at saturation the sensitivity becomes 0. Thus, with the circuit of Fig. 9-6a, the lowest sensitivities occur when the transistor is almost saturated.

The biasing formulas are summarized in Fig. 9-6a.

The sketch of I_C vs. R_B is given in Fig. 9-6b. This characteristic tells us that the circuit of Fig. 9-6a does not saturate sharply, like the two preceding bias arrangements. As R_B is made smaller, the circuit approaches saturation, but it never quite saturates until $R_B = 0$. Note also that when $R_B = \beta R_L$, the collector current is one-half of the saturation value.

EXAMPLE 9-7

The transistor in Fig. 9-7a has a β of 50. Find the approximate value of collector current and voltage.

SOLUTION

The collector current is

$$I_C \cong \frac{V_{CC}}{R_L + R_B/\beta} = \frac{20}{10^3 + 10^5/50} = \frac{20}{3000} = 6.67 \text{ ma}$$

The collector voltage is

$$V_C = V_{CC} - I_C R_L = 20 - 6.67(10^{-3})(10^3) \cong 13.3 \text{ volts}$$

EXAMPLE 9-8

What is the value of K for the circuit of Fig. 9-7a?

SOLUTION

We can use either Eq. (9-15) or (9-16). If we use Eq. (9-15), we find

$$K = \frac{1}{1 + 50(10^3)/100(10^3)} = 0.667$$

Or, we can use Eq. (9-16), to find

$$K = 1 - \frac{I_C}{I_{C(\text{sat})}} = 1 - \frac{6.67 \text{ ma}}{20 \text{ ma}} = 0.667$$

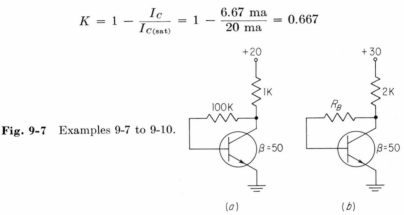

Fig. 9-7 Examples 9-7 to 9-10.

(a)   (b)

EXAMPLE 9-9

Suppose that R_B in Fig. 9-7b is equal to 10 kilohms. Find the value of $I_C/I_{C(\text{sat})}$ and the value of K.

SOLUTION

We can use Eq. (9-13) to find $I_{C(\text{sat})}$.

$$I_{C(\text{sat})} \cong \frac{V_{CC}}{R_L} = \frac{30}{2000} = 15 \text{ ma}$$

With Eq. (9-14) we can find I_C.

$$I_C \cong \frac{V_{CC}}{R_L + R_B/\beta} = \frac{30}{2000 + 10,000/50} = 13.6 \text{ ma}$$

Therefore,

$$\frac{I_C}{I_{C(\text{sat})}} = \frac{13.6 \text{ ma}}{15 \text{ ma}} = 0.907$$

A value of 0.907 means that the transistor is near the saturation point.

To find the sensitivity, we use Eq. (9-15) or (9-16). In this case, it is easier to use Eq. (9-16) because we have the value of $I_C/I_{C(\text{sat})}$ worked out.

$$K = 1 - \frac{I_C}{I_{C(\text{sat})}} = 1 - 0.907 = 0.093$$

This is a low value of sensitivity; therefore, the circuit of Fig. 9-7b is only slightly susceptible to changes in β. For instance, a 10 percent change in β will only cause a change of 0.93 percent in collector current; however, the transistor is almost at the saturation point, so that the signal-handling capability of the circuit is limited.

EXAMPLE 9-10

Using a β of 50, find the following for the circuit of Fig. 9-7b:

(a) The value of R_B that produces a collector current equal to one-half the saturation value.

(b) The sensitivity K at one-half saturation current.

SOLUTION

(a) Referring to Fig. 9-6b, we see that collector current equals one-half saturation current when

$$R_B = \beta R_L = 50(2000) = 100 \text{ kilohms}$$

(b) With the collector current at one-half the saturation value, we can find the sensitivity easily by using Eq. (9-16).

$$K = 1 - \frac{I_C}{I_{C(\text{sat})}} = 1 - 0.5 = 0.5$$

9-5 Base Bias with Collector and Emitter Feedback

There is one more variation of base bias that we want to discuss. The circuit of Fig. 9-8a uses both collector and emitter feedback in an attempt to lower the sensitivity to changes in β. In this circuit, an increase in β results in a larger emitter voltage and a smaller collector voltage. This means that the voltage across R_B is reduced, causing the base current to become smaller, thereby partially offsetting the increase in β.

To find the saturation current, we note that when v_{CE} is approximately zero, the supply voltage is distributed across R_L and R_E. Since I_B is much smaller than I_C, and since I_C is almost equal to I_E, we conclude that

$$I_{C(\text{sat})} \cong \frac{V_{CC}}{R_E + R_L} \tag{9-17}$$

The actual collector current I_C can be found by writing a voltage equation. Note that

$$V_{CC} = (I_C + I_B)R_L + I_B R_B + V_{BE} + I_E R_E$$

With our usual approximations, this equation becomes

$$V_{CC} \cong I_C R_L + \frac{I_C}{\beta} R_B + V_{BE} + I_C R_E$$

After solving for I_C, we have

$$I_C \cong \frac{V_{CC} - V_{BE}}{R_E + R_L + R_B/\beta}$$

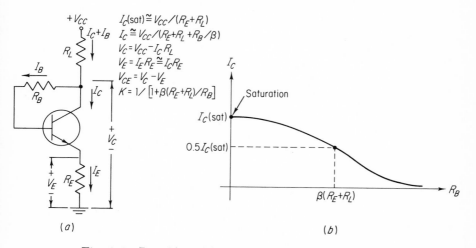

Fig. 9-8 Base bias with collector and emitter feedback.

When V_{BE} is negligible compared to V_{CC}, this becomes

$$I_C \cong \frac{V_{CC}}{R_E + R_L + R_B/\beta} \qquad \text{for } V_{BE} \ll V_{CC} \tag{9-18}$$

The collector-ground voltage V_C is approximately

$$V_C \cong V_{CC} - I_C R_L \tag{9-19}$$

and the emitter-ground voltage is

$$V_E \cong I_C R_E \tag{9-20}$$

A calculus derivation will show that the sensitivity is given by

$$K = \frac{1}{1 + \beta(R_E + R_L)/R_B} \tag{9-21}$$

A useful alternate formula for sensitivity is

$$K = 1 - \frac{I_C}{I_{C(sat)}} \tag{9-22}$$

The biasing formulas are summarized in Fig. 9-8a.

Finally, the sketch of I_C vs. R_B is shown in Fig. 9-8b. Again note that this graph implies a *soft* saturation, that is, the circuit does not completely saturate until R_B is zero.

EXAMPLE 9-11

For the circuit of Fig. 9-9a, find the following:

(a) $I_{C(sat)}$.
(b) V_C and V_{CE} for a β of 100.
(c) The percent change in I_C when β changes 10 percent.

SOLUTION

(a) At saturation, the supply voltage is distributed across R_L and R_E. Hence,

$$I_{C(sat)} = \frac{20}{10,000 + 10,000} = 1 \text{ ma}$$

(b) To find the collector current we use Eq. (9-18).

$$I_C \cong \frac{20}{10^4 + 10^4 + 5(10^5)/100} = 0.8 \text{ ma}$$

With 0.8 ma of collector current, there must be a drop of 8 volts across the 10-kilohm collector resistor. Therefore,

$$V_C = 20 - 8 = 12 \text{ volts}$$

The voltage from emitter to ground is simply

$$V_E \cong 0.8(10^{-3})(10)(10^3) = 8 \text{ volts}$$

The voltage from the collector to the emitter is the difference of V_C and V_E. Thus,

$$V_{CE} = V_C - V_E = 12 - 8 = 4 \text{ volts}$$

(c) We can find the sensitivity by using Eq. (9-22).

$$K = 1 - \frac{I_C}{I_{C(sat)}} = 1 - \frac{0.8 \text{ ma}}{1 \text{ ma}} = 0.2$$

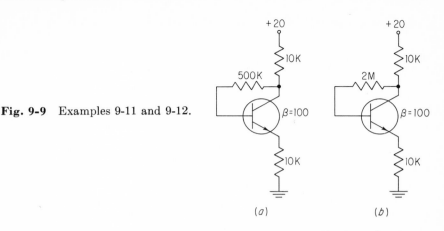

Fig. 9-9   Examples 9-11 and 9-12.

This value of sensitivity is fairly good; it means that a 10 percent change in β causes a change of about 2 percent in collector current.

EXAMPLE 9-12

When we change the base resistor of the preceding example from 500 kilohms to 2 megohms, we obtain the circuit of Fig. 9-9b. For this new circuit, find $I_{C(\text{sat})}$, V_{CE}, and K.

SOLUTION

The saturation current remains at 1 ma because R_L, R_E, and V_{CC} are the same as before.

The new collector current is

$$I_C \cong \frac{V_{CC}}{R_E + R_L + R_B/\beta} = \frac{20}{10^4 + 10^4 + 2(10^6)/100} = 0.5 \text{ ma}$$

Note that this collector current is one-half of saturation current.

The sensitivity of the new circuit is also different. Using Eq. (9-22), we find that

$$K = 1 - \frac{I_C}{I_{C(\text{sat})}} = 1 - \frac{0.5 \text{ ma}}{1 \text{ ma}} = 0.5$$

Note the degradation of sensitivity that has occurred by increasing the size of the base resistor. In the preceding example, $R_B = 500$ kilohms, and $K = 0.2$. In this example, $R_B = 2$ megohms, and $K = 0.5$.

9-6   Emitter Bias with Two Supplies

We have now discussed four variations of base bias. In all these circuits, the value of R_B is important in setting up the desired collector current.

For the simplest form of base bias (no feedback) the sensitivity equals unity; this represents the worst way to bias as far as stability of the d-c operating point is concerned. When feedback is added to the base-bias circuit, the sensitivity is reduced. We saw that the last two forms of base bias had sensitivities of

$$K = 1 - \frac{I_C}{I_{C(\text{sat})}}$$

Clearly, by almost saturating the transistor, we can get very low values of K; however, we pay the price of limited signal-handling capability when we do this because the possible a-c signal swing is limited.

What we really want is a bias circuit that shows almost no dependence upon the value of β, that is, a bias arrangement whose K is low no matter what the ratio of I_C to $I_{C(\text{sat})}$. The emitter-bias circuit discussed in Chap. 6 is such an arrangement.

In Fig. 9-10a, we have shown the d-c equivalent circuit for an emitter-biased circuit. Recall that the voltage from emitter to ground is approximately zero, provided that the V_{BE} and $I_B R_B$ voltages are small enough to neglect. (As already indicated, the designer deliberately makes sure that these conditions are met.) Therefore, at saturation the voltage from collector to ground is almost zero, and we have a current of

$$I_{C(\text{sat})} \cong \frac{V_{CC}}{R_L} \tag{9-23}$$

In Chap. 6 we showed that

$$I_C \cong I_E = \frac{V_{EE} - V_{BE}}{R_E + R_B/\beta} \tag{9-24}$$

The key to a good design, that is, one in which the collector current is only slightly dependent upon the transistor characteristics, is to make

$$V_{EE} \gg V_{BE}$$

and

$$R_E \gg \frac{R_B}{\beta}$$

By doing this, the collector current is essentially given by

$$I_C \cong \frac{V_{EE}}{R_E} \tag{9-25}$$

This last equation tells us that to a first approximation the value of I_C depends only upon V_{EE} and R_E; it does not depend upon the exact value of β. In other words, *by ensuring that $R_E \gg R_B/\beta$, we are freeing the collector current from a heavy dependence upon the value of β.* This, of course, is most desirable from the standpoint of a stable d-c operating point.

The expression for the collector-ground voltage is

$$V_C = V_{CC} - I_C R_L \tag{9-26}$$

As already indicated, the emitter-ground voltage is approximately zero for a well-designed circuit. If necessary, this low value of emitter-ground voltage can be found by using

$$V_E = -(V_{BE} + I_B R_B) = -\left(V_{BE} + I_C \frac{R_B}{\beta}\right) \tag{9-27}$$

For example, suppose that a germanium transistor is used and that $\beta = 100$ and $R_B = 10$ kilohms. For 1 ma of collector current, we calculate

$$V_E = -\left(0.3 + 10^{-3}\frac{10^4}{10^2}\right) = -0.4 \text{ volt}$$

Thus, the emitter is slightly negative with respect to ground.

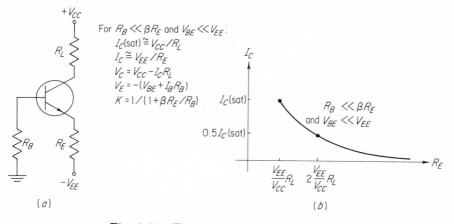

Fig. 9-10 Emitter bias with two supplies.

With calculus, the sensitivity can be derived.

$$K = \frac{1}{1 + \beta R_E/R_B} \tag{9-28}$$

As an example of using this equation, suppose that $R_B = R_E$; then the sensitivity is

$$K = \frac{1}{1 + \beta} \cong \frac{1}{\beta}$$

For a $\beta = 100$, $K \cong 0.01$. For β as low as 20, $K \cong 0.05$. Thus, we can get extremely low values of sensitivity using emitter-biased circuits.

Of course, if R_B is made too large, the sensitivity may become objectionable. For instance, suppose that $R_B = 10R_E$. Then,

$$K = \frac{1}{1 + \beta R_E/10R_E} = \frac{1}{1 + \beta/10}$$

For a β of 100, we get

$$K = \frac{1}{1 + 100/10} \cong 0.091$$

Or, if the β is as low as 20, we get

$$K = \frac{1}{1 + 20/10} = 0.333$$

Under this condition, the circuit is becoming too sensitive to changes in β; we are, in fact, defeating the whole purpose of the emitter-biased circuit if we make R_B too large. To avoid this, we simply need to satisfy the general rule already given for a well-designed emitter-bias circuit. That is,

$$R_E \gg \frac{R_B}{\beta}$$

By satisfying this inequality, we justify the use of Eq. (9-25) and ensure a low value of sensitivity.

A sketch of I_C vs. R_E is shown in Fig. 9-10b. Note that R_E is used instead of R_B because in a well-designed emitter-bias circuit, the collector current is controlled by R_E instead of R_B.

EXAMPLE 9-13

For the circuit of Fig. 9-11, find the approximate value of

(a) $I_{C(\text{sat})}$ and I_C.
(b) V_C, V_E, and V_{CE}.
(c) K for a β of 50.

SOLUTION

(a) Using Eq. (9-23), we get

$$I_{C(\text{sat})} \cong \frac{V_{CC}}{R_L} = \frac{20}{10(10^3)} = 2 \text{ ma}$$

With Eq. (9-25), we find that

$$I_C \cong \frac{V_{EE}}{R_E} = \frac{10}{20(10^3)} = 0.5 \text{ ma}$$

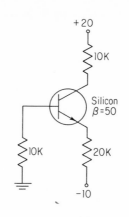

Fig. 9-11 Example 9-13.

(b) The collector voltage with respect to ground is

$$V_C = V_{CC} - I_C R_L = 20 - 0.5(10^{-3})(10)(10^3) = 15 \text{ volts}$$

The approximate value of the emitter-ground voltage is zero. If we like, we can use Eq. (9-27) to get a more accurate value.

$$V_E = -\left(V_{BE} + I_C \frac{R_B}{\beta}\right) = -\left(0.7 + 0.0005 \frac{10,000}{50}\right) = -0.8 \text{ volt}$$

The collector-emitter voltage is

$$V_{CE} = V_C - V_E = 15 - (-0.8) = 15.8 \text{ volts}$$

For practical purposes, we can neglect the emitter voltage with respect to ground and say that $V_{CE} \cong 15$ volts.

(c) To find the sensitivity, we use Eq. (9-28).

$$K = \frac{1}{1 + \beta R_E/R_B} = \frac{1}{1 + 10^6/10^4} \cong 0.01$$

EXAMPLE 9-14

In Fig. 9-12, find the value of R_E that produces a collector current of one-half the saturation value. Also, to ensure a low sensitivity select a value of R_B that is $\frac{1}{20}\beta R_E$. Use a β of 100.

SOLUTION

The characteristic of Fig. 9-10b tells us that I_C equals $\frac{1}{2}I_{C(\text{sat})}$ when

$$R_E = 2 \frac{V_{EE}}{V_{CC}} R_L = 2 \frac{20}{30} 5000 = 6.67 \text{ kilohms}$$

The value of R_B must be chosen so as to satisfy

$$R_E \gg \frac{R_B}{\beta}$$

or

$$R_B \ll \beta R_E$$

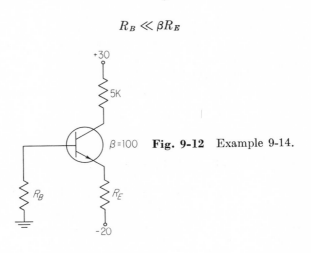

Fig. 9-12   Example 9-14.

Since $R_E = 6.67$ kilohms and we are given a β of 100, we must ensure that

$$R_B \ll 667 \text{ kilohms}$$

If we make R_B equal to $\frac{1}{20}\beta R_E$, we get

$$R_B = \frac{1}{20}(667 \text{ kilohms}) = 33.3 \text{ kilohms}$$

In a practical design, we would use the nearest standard values, that is, $R_E = 6.8$ kilohms and $R_B = 33$ kilohms.

Also, note that in a practical design we would take the β spread into account. In other words, for the transistor type that is being used, the β may be specified as between 50 and 150. In this case, we would use the worst case, which is a β of 50. If R_B is to remain less than $\frac{1}{20}\beta R_E$ for all transistors of the given type, we must reduce it to about 16.6 kilohms (15 kilohms for a standard value).

9-7   Emitter Bias with One Supply

The emitter bias circuit studied in the preceding section is an excellent low-sensitivity circuit, and is used whenever two power supplies are available. Note that both a positive and a negative supply are required. There are many occasions, however, when only a single power supply is available. In this case, the *modified form of emitter bias* shown in Fig. 9-13a can be used.

At saturation, the collector-emitter voltage drops to approximately zero, and all the supply voltage is distributed across R_L and R_E. Since the collector and emitter currents are essentially equal, we can write

$$I_{C(\text{sat})} \cong \frac{V_{CC}}{R_E + R_L} \tag{9-29}$$

When the circuit of Fig. 9-13a is well designed, it operates as follows. Resistors R_1 and R_2 form a voltage divider, so that the voltage from base to ground is approximately

$$V_B \cong \frac{R_2}{R_1 + R_2} V_{CC} \tag{9-30}$$

By inspection of the circuit we can see that

$$V_B = V_{BE} + V_E$$

Because V_{BE} is only a few tenths of a volt, it is usually negligible, and we can write

$$V_B \cong V_E$$

In other words, to a first approximation, the voltage across R_E is approximately equal to the voltage across R_2. Therefore, the emitter current is

$$I_E \cong \frac{V_B}{R_E}$$

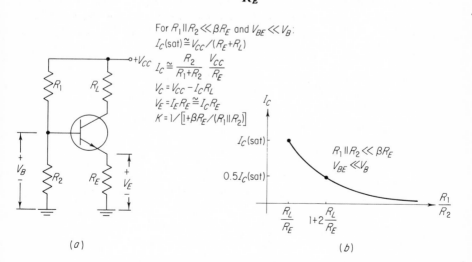

For $R_1 \| R_2 \ll \beta R_E$ and $V_{BE} \ll V_B$:

$I_C(\text{sat}) \cong V_{CC}/(R_E + R_L)$

$I_C \cong \dfrac{R_2}{R_1 + R_2} \dfrac{V_{CC}}{R_E}$

$V_C = V_{CC} - I_C R_L$

$V_E = I_E R_E \cong I_C R_E$

$K = 1 / \left[1 + \beta R_E / (R_1 \| R_2) \right]$

$R_1 \| R_2 \ll \beta R_E$

$V_{BE} \ll V_B$

(a)   (b)

Fig. 9-13 Emitter bias with one supply.

Finally, since the collector current almost equals the emitter current, we can write

$$I_C \cong \frac{V_B}{R_E} \tag{9-31}$$

Equation (9-31) is a simple approximation for the d-c collector current that flows in a circuit like that shown in Fig. 9-13a. It tells us that the collector current equals the ratio of the base voltage (developed by the voltage divider) to the emitter resistance R_E.

The collector-ground voltage is simply

$$V_C = V_{CC} - I_C R_L$$

and the emitter-ground voltage is

$$V_E = I_E R_E \cong I_C R_E$$

Calculus can be used to prove that the sensitivity is

$$K = \frac{1}{1 + \beta R_E / (R_1 \| R_2)} \tag{9-32}$$

where $R_1 \| R_2$ is the parallel resistance of R_1 and R_2.

Finally, a sketch of I_C vs. R_1/R_2 is shown in Fig. 9-13b.

All the foregoing results have assumed a well-designed circuit. What is a well-designed circuit? To answer this question, we must make a more accurate derivation for the collector current. The easiest way to do this is to replace the voltage divider in the base circuit by its Thévenin equivalent circuit, as shown in Fig. 9-14. Summing voltages around the base loop, we get

$$\frac{R_2}{R_1 + R_2} V_{CC} = I_B(R_1 \| R_2) + V_{BE} + I_E R_E$$

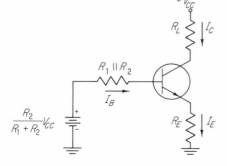

Fig. 9-14 Thévenin equivalent circuit.

If we substitute $I_C \cong I_E$ and $I_C/\beta = I_B$, we can solve for I_C, to get

$$I_C = \frac{V_{CC}R_2/(R_1 + R_2) - V_{BE}}{R_E + (R_1\|R_2)/\beta} \tag{9-33}$$

Equation (9-33) is more accurate than Eq. (9-31); however, the whole point of the circuit is that it should be insensitive to changes in β. To accomplish this, it is good design practice to make

$$R_E \gg \frac{R_1\|R_2}{\beta}$$

Also, when possible, V_{BE} is made negligible by ensuring that

$$\frac{R_2}{R_1 + R_2} V_{CC} \gg V_{BE}$$

(The left member of this inequality is simply V_B, the voltage from base to ground.)

To summarize these important results, refer to Fig. 9-15. In a circuit satisfying the two inequalities just given, we can say the following. The

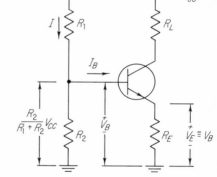

Fig. 9-15 Emitter bias with one supply.

amount of base current I_B is small compared to the current I flowing down through the voltage divider. Because of this, the voltage divider is lightly loaded by the base of the transistor. In other words,

$$V_B \cong \frac{R_2}{R_1 + R_2} V_{CC}$$

Further, since V_{BE} is small, almost all the base-ground voltage appears across the emitter resistor. That is,

$$V_E \cong V_B$$

Finally, the collector current approximately equals the emitter current, so that

$$I_C \cong \frac{V_B}{R_E}$$

The circuit of Fig. 9-15 is basically *a form of emitter bias* because we set the emitter current to an approximately fixed value of V_B/R_E. As far as sensitivity is concerned, this circuit can have a very low sensitivity. An inspection of Eq. (9-32) immediately shows that to have a low sensitivity, we need only make $R_1\|R_2$ comparable in size to R_E. For instance, for $R_1\|R_2 = R_E$ we get a sensitivity of

$$K = \frac{1}{1 + \beta R_E/(R_1\|R_2)} = \frac{1}{1 + \beta}$$

For a β of 100, $K \cong 0.01$. Thus, as long as the parallel combination of R_1 and R_2 is not too large compared to R_E, we will have a low sensitivity.

EXAMPLE 9-15

For the circuit of Fig. 9-16a, find the approximate value of collector current.

SOLUTION

By inspection of the circuit, we see that the voltage divider delivers a voltage of about 10 volts to the base. Most of the 10 volts appears across R_E because of the small V_{BE} drop. Therefore, the collector current is

$$I_C \cong \frac{10}{10,000} = 1 \text{ ma}$$

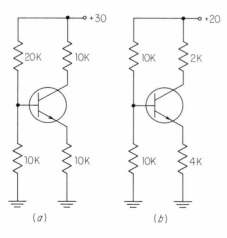

Fig. 9-16 Examples 9-15 and 9-16.

EXAMPLE 9-16

For the circuit of Fig. 9-16b, find the following:

(a) $I_{C(\text{sat})}$ and I_C.
(b) V_C, V_E, and V_{CE}.

SOLUTION

(a) Saturation occurs when the collector-emitter voltage is approximately zero. Thus,

$$I_{C(\text{sat})} \cong \frac{V_{CC}}{R_E + R_L} = \frac{20}{6000} = 3.33 \text{ ma}$$

To find the actual collector current, we note that the voltage divider in the base develops about 10 volts from base to ground. Most of this 10 volts appears across the 4-kilohm emitter resistor. Therefore, the approximate value of collector current is

$$I_C \cong \frac{10}{4000} = 2.5 \text{ ma}$$

(b) The collector-ground voltage is

$$V_C = V_{CC} - I_C R_L = 20 - 2.5(10^{-3})(2)(10^3) = 15 \text{ volts}$$

and the emitter-ground voltage is

$$V_E \cong V_B \cong 10 \text{ volts}$$

The collector-emitter voltage is the difference of V_C and V_E.

$$V_{CE} = V_C - V_E = 15 - 10 = 5 \text{ volts}$$

EXAMPLE 9-17

Find the collector current and the sensitivity of the circuit shown in Fig. 9-17a. Use a β of 50.

SOLUTION

The voltage divider develops about 5 volts from base to ground. Therefore, the emitter-ground voltage is about 5 volts, and the collector current is approximately

$$I_C \cong \frac{V_B}{R_E} = \frac{5}{5000} = 1 \text{ ma}$$

The sensitivity can be found by using Eq. (9-32).

$$K = \frac{1}{1 + \beta R_E/(R_1 \| R_2)} = \frac{1}{1 + 50(5000)/7500} \cong 0.0292$$

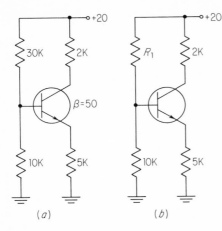

Fig. 9-17 Examples 9-17 and 9-18.

EXAMPLE 9-18

Find the value of R_1 in Fig. 9-17b that produces an I_C equal to $\frac{1}{2}I_{C(\text{sat})}$.

SOLUTION

We can easily find the correct value of R_1 by referring to Fig. 9-13b. To get an I_C of $\frac{1}{2}I_{C(\text{sat})}$, we need an R_1/R_2 ratio of

$$\frac{R_1}{R_2} = 1 + \frac{2R_L}{R_E} = 1 + \frac{4000}{5000} = 1.8$$

or

$$R_1 = 1.8R_2 = 1.8(10,000) = 18 \text{ kilohms}$$

9-8   A Comparison of Sensitivities

We have discussed six common ways of biasing a transistor. Generally speaking, the base-bias arrangements show much more sensitivity to changes in β than the emitter-bias arrangements. As already indicated, a low value of K is desirable if a stable d-c operating point is required.

In order to compare the various circuits with each other, look at Table 9-1. The various sensitivities have been calculated on the basis that all circuits are operated at one-half the saturation current. That is, in all circuits,

$$I_C = 0.5I_{C(\text{sat})}$$

Further, in those circuits having additional degrees of freedom, arbitrary conditions have been imposed. For instance, for emitter bias with two supplies, R_B has been arbitrarily set equal to R_E, and a β of 50 has been used.

Table 9-1 shows the overwhelming superiority of emitter-biased circuits over base-biased circuits insofar as stability of the operating point is concerned. This is quite important in class A amplifiers if we are to avoid clipping due to a shift in the d-c operating point. It is also important in d-c amplifiers, where a d-c shift caused by β changes is indistinguishable from an actual signal.

Table 9-1 Comparison of Beta Sensitivities*

Circuit	K	Conditions
Base bias	1	
Base bias with emitter feedback	0.75	$R_L = R_E$
Base bias with collector feedback	0.5	
Base bias with collector and emitter feedback	0.5	
Emitter bias with two supplies	0.02	$R_B = R_E, \beta = 50$
Emitter bias with one supply	0.02	$R_1 \| R_2 = R_E, \beta = 50$

* All circuits compared at $I_C = 0.5 I_{C(\text{sat})}$.

9-9 Location of the Ground Point

So far we have shown the ground point at a typical point in the biasing arrangement. There will be times, however, when we want the ground point at some other place in the circuit.

To show that we can move the ground point, consider the simple base-bias circuit of Fig. 9-18a. We already know that the base current is fixed in this circuit by the value of V_{CC} and R_B. The collector current simply equals β times the base current.

The circuit of Fig. 9-18a can be redrawn as in Fig. 9-18b. Realize that ground is only a reference point; the biasing of the transistor does not depend upon having a ground point. For instance, we can remove the ground altogether, as shown in Fig. 9-18c. In this case, the base diode is still forward-biased, the collector diode is still back-biased, and the value of collector current is exactly the same as before.

At times, we will want to locate the ground point on the end of the collector supply, as shown in Fig. 9-18d. Again note that the ground point has no effect on the collector current; the transistor is still biased to the same V_{CE}, I_C point as before.

We can redraw Fig. 9-18d as shown in Fig. 9-18e. This circuit has exactly the same value of collector current as the original circuit of Fig. 9-18a. The collector-emitter voltages in each circuit are also equal. In effect, all we have done is to locate the ground, or reference, point at another position in the circuit.

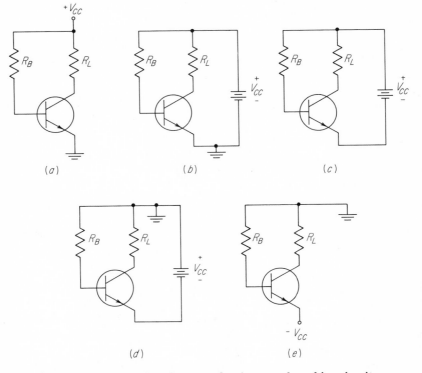

Fig. 9-18   Changing the ground point on a base-bias circuit.

Of the six biasing arrangements, five use a single supply. Up to now, we have grounded the negative end of this supply for n-p-n transistors. We can ground the other end of this supply as we have just done for the base-biased circuit. When this is done, the five single-supply bias circuits appear as shown in Fig. 9-19. In all these circuits, we can find the d-c collector current by using the formulas developed in earlier sections.

The collector-ground voltage is different from before because we have moved the ground point. By inspection of the circuits in Fig. 9-19 it is clear that the collector voltage in each circuit is negative with respect to

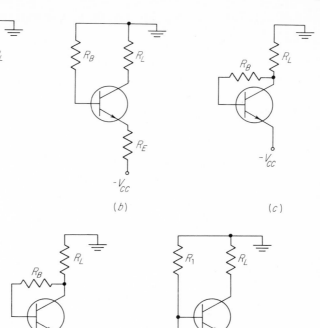

Fig. 9-19 Changing the ground point on all single-supply circuits.

ground, and the magnitude is given by

$$V_C \cong I_C R_L \tag{9-34}$$

EXAMPLE 9-19

Find the collector current and the collector-ground voltage for the circuit of Fig. 9-20a.

SOLUTION

The problem is similar to one we have already solved. In Example 9-7 we analyzed the circuit shown in Fig. 9-7a. Note that the only difference between Figs. 9-7a and 9-20a is the location of the ground point.

The collector current is the same in both circuits. We found in Example 9-7 that the collector current is

$$I_C = 6.67 \text{ ma}$$

With a different ground point, however, the collector-ground voltage is different from before. Clearly, the circuit of Fig. 9-20a has a voltage drop across the 1-kilohm resistor of

$$V_C = I_C R_L = 6.67(10^{-3})(10^3) = 6.67 \text{ volts}$$

This is the magnitude of the voltage from collector to ground. Because of the polarity, we would measure -6.67 volts from collector to ground.

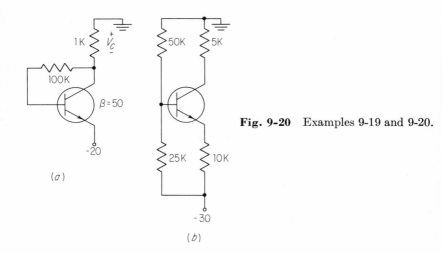

Fig. 9-20   Examples 9-19 and 9-20.

EXAMPLE 9-20

Find the value of the collector current and the collector-ground voltage in Fig. 9-20b.

SOLUTION

The voltage divider in the base will develop about 10 volts across the 25-kilohm resistor. Almost all this 10 volts appears across the 10-kilohm resistor. Therefore, the emitter current is about 1 ma.

The collector current is essentially 1 ma. This current flows down through the 5-kilohm resistor and establishes a 5-volt drop. Therefore, the collector-ground voltage is about -5 volts.

9-10 Biasing p-n-p Transistors

As we said before, when we use a *p-n-p* transistor instead of an *n-p-n*, we must reverse the polarity of all d-c sources. This, in turn, means that all d-c voltages and currents in the *p-n-p* circuit will be reversed. There is no need to have a separate group of formulas for *p-n-p* circuits; we can use the formulas developed for *n-p-n* circuits if we deal with *magnitudes* of voltages and currents.

For instance, in Fig. 9-21a, we have a base-biased circuit with collector feedback. Since a *p-n-p* transistor is used instead of an *n-p-n*, we make the collector supply voltage negative instead of positive. As a result, the base current and collector current flow in opposite directions from those of a similar *n-p-n* circuit. Also, the collector voltage is negative with respect to ground instead of positive. We can use the formulas given in Fig. 9-6a, provided we use magnitudes of voltages and currents.

Fig. 9-21 Biasing with *p-n-p* transistors.

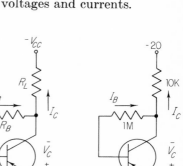

As a numerical example, consider the circuit of Fig. 9-21b. The magnitude of the collector current is easily found.

$$I_C = \frac{V_{CC}}{R_L + R_B/\beta} = \frac{20}{10^4 + 10^6/50} = 0.667 \text{ ma}$$

The magnitude of the collector voltage is

$$V_C = V_{CC} - I_C R_L = 20 - 0.667(10^{-3})(10^4) = 13.3 \text{ volts}$$

Note that we have used magnitudes throughout. In substituting for V_{CC}, we use the magnitude, which is 20, not −20, volts. Also, the magnitude of the collector-ground voltage is 13.3 volts; the actual voltage is −13.3 volts with respect to ground.

Thus, in analyzing the d-c operation of p-n-p circuits, we will use magnitudes of voltages and currents. After obtaining a magnitude of current or voltage, we will add the direction or polarity to this value. This approach avoids the unnecessary complication of having separate formulas for n-p-n and p-n-p circuits.

SUMMARY

The sensitivity K of a biasing arrangement tells us how sensitive the d-c operating point is to changes in β. As we have seen, base bias with no feedback has a sensitivity of unity, which means that the percent change in collector current equals the percent change in β.

By adding feedback to the simple base-bias circuit, we can reduce the sensitivity to some extent. The two forms of base bias with collector feedback (Secs. 9-4 and 9-5) have very low sensitivity provided that the transistor is biased near saturation; this, of course, limits the signal-handling capability of the transistor circuit.

The emitter-bias circuits are undoubtedly the best way to bias when stability of the operating point is the prime consideration.

GLOSSARY

base bias   A biasing arrangement in which the d-c base current remains essentially fixed even though the β changes.

class A amplifier   An amplifier in which collector current flows throughout the a-c cycle without the transistor saturating or cutting off.

emitter bias   A biasing arrangement in which the d-c emitter current remains essentially fixed even though the β changes.

negative feedback   In this chapter, this refers to feeding a signal back from either the collector or the emitter to the base to partially offset a change in β.

sensitivity (K)   The constant of proportionality between percent changes in d-c collector current and β.

REVIEW QUESTIONS

1. In a simple base-biased circuit without feedback, does the base current or collector current remain fixed when the β changes?
2. How is the β sensitivity defined?
3. The sensitivity K must lie between what two values?

4. What is the sensitivity of a base-biased circuit without feedback?
5. Describe the circuit arrangements of the four forms of base bias discussed in this chapter.
6. In the four forms of base bias, should the value of R_B be small or large to obtain a low sensitivity?
7. In a base-biased circuit using collector feedback, should the transistor be operated near saturation or cutoff to get a low sensitivity?
8. What is the approximate value of V_{CE} for any circuit in which the transistor is saturated?
9. In an emitter-biased circuit with two supplies, the d-c emitter current is approximately equal to V_{EE}/R_E, provided that two conditions are satisfied. What are these conditions?
10. In the emitter-biased circuit with one supply, how do we find the approximate value of the base-ground voltage? And how do we get the approximate value of collector current?
11. In emitter-biased circuits, does the sensitivity increase or decrease when we increase R_B (or $R_1 \| R_2$)?

PROBLEMS

9-1 A biasing arrangement has a sensitivity K equal to 0.35. If the β changes 7 percent, how much will the d-c collector current change?

9-2 When the β changes 12 percent, the d-c collector current changes 2 percent. What is the value of sensitivity K?

9-3 In Fig. 9-22a, find the approximate values of base current, collector current, and collector-ground voltage.

9-4 In Fig. 9-22b, what is the approximate value of R_B that just causes saturation? What value of R_B sets the d-c collector current to one-half the saturation value?

9-5 In Fig. 9-22b, $R_B = 5$ megohms. If β changes from 75 to 100, what is the new value of collector current and voltage?

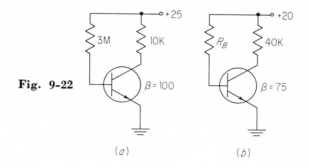

Fig. 9-22

(a)   (b)

9-6 For the circuit shown in Fig. 9-23a, find the following:
(a) The collector current I_C.
(b) The collector-ground voltage V_C.
(c) The collector-emitter voltage V_{CE}.

9-7 What is the value of sensitivity for the circuit in Fig. 9-23a? If β changes from 150 to 160, what is the percent change in collector current?

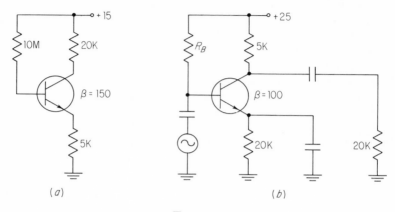

Fig. 9-23

9-8 The circuit of Fig. 9-23b is to be biased so that I_C equals $\frac{1}{2}I_{C(\text{sat})}$. For a β of 100, what approximate size should R_B be? With this value of R_B, what is the sensitivity of the circuit?

9-9 In the circuit of Fig. 9-24a, what is the value of collector current? Of collector-ground voltage? Of base current?

9-10 In Fig. 9-24a, find the sensitivity of the circuit to changes in β.

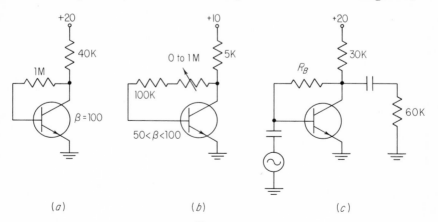

Fig. 9-24

9-11 The transistor of Fig. 9-24*b* can have a β anywhere in the range of 50 to 150. The base resistance R_B consists of a fixed 100 kilohms in series with a 1-megohm rheostat. Find the following:

(*a*) The smallest *possible* collector current.

(*b*) The largest possible value of collector current.

(*c*) The worst-case sensitivity.

(*d*) The smallest value of collector-ground voltage.

9-12 The β in Fig. 9-24*c* has a value of 100. What is the approximate size of R_B that produces a d-c collector current of one-half the saturation value? If this value of R_B is used in the circuit, what will the value of the d-c collector current become if β changes from 100 to 50?

9-13 In the circuit of Fig. 9-25*a*, find the value of:

(*a*) The collector-ground voltage.

(*b*) The emitter-ground voltage.

(*c*) The collector-emitter voltage.

9-14 What is the sensitivity of the circuit in Fig. 9-25*a*?

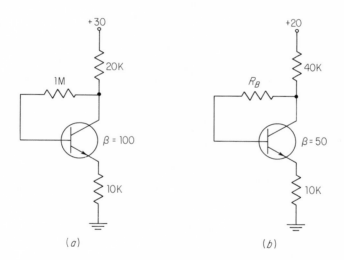

Fig. 9-25

9-15 In Fig. 9-25*b*, find the following:

(*a*) $I_{C(\text{sat})}$.

(*b*) I_C for an R_B of 1 megohm.

(*c*) The value of R_B that sets up an I_C of $\frac{1}{2}I_{C(\text{sat})}$.

9-16 In the emitter-biased circuit shown in Fig. 9-26*a*, find the approximate values of I_E, V_C, V_E, and V_{CE}.

9-17 What is the sensitivity of the circuit in Fig. 9-26*a*?

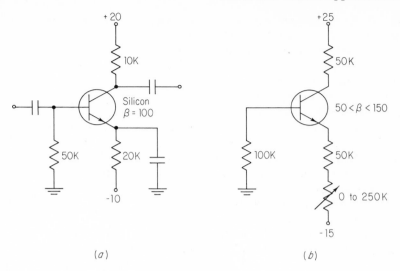

Fig. 9-26

9-18 In Fig. 9-26b, find the approximate values of the following quantities:

(a) The maximum emitter current.

(b) The minimum emitter current.

(c) The largest value of collector-ground voltage.

(d) The largest value of sensitivity.

9-19 For the emitter-biased circuit shown in Fig. 9-27a, find the following:

(a) The emitter current.

(b) The collector-ground voltage.

(c) The collector-emitter voltage.

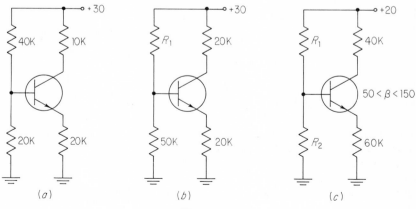

Fig. 9-27

9-20 In Fig. 9-27b, what approximate value of R_1 is required to set the collector-ground voltage at 20 volts? What is the sensitivity of the circuit for a β of 50? Of 150?

9-21 The values of R_1 and R_2 in Fig. 9-27c are to be such that:

(a) I_C will equal $\frac{1}{2}I_{C(\text{sat})}$.

(b) $R_1 \| R_2 = \frac{1}{20}$ the smallest value of βR_E.

What are the values of R_1 and R_2 that satisfy these requirements?

9-22 In Fig. 9-28a, find the collector current and the collector-ground voltage.

9-23 In Fig. 9-28b, find the collector-ground voltage.

9-24 Find the following for the circuit of Fig. 9-28c:

(a) The collector current.

(b) The collector voltage with respect to ground.

(c) The emitter voltage with respect to ground.

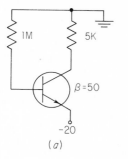

(a)

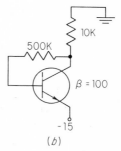

(b)

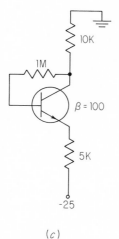

(c)

(d)

Fig. 9-28

9-25 In Fig. 9-28d, find the voltage from collector to ground and from emitter to ground.

9-26 Find the collector-ground voltage in Fig. 9-29a.

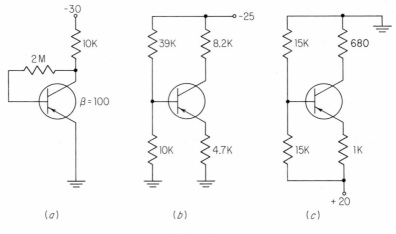

(a)   (b)   (c)

Fig. 9-29

9-27 Find the collector-ground voltage in Fig. 9-29b.

9-28 In Fig. 9-29c, find the following:
  (a) The emitter voltage with respect to ground.
  (b) The collector voltage with respect to ground.

10

A-C Operation

In the preceding chapter we discussed six common ways of biasing a transistor. After the transistor is biased, we can inject an a-c signal into one of the transistor terminals. This causes the transistor currents and voltages to fluctuate; we can then take a signal out of another of the transistor terminals.

In this chapter, we will discuss the a-c operation of the six biasing arrangements. By means of bypass capacitors, we can place any of the three transistor terminals at a-c ground. This gives rise to CB, CE, or CC operation. In addition, we will discuss how the voltage gain of a transistor circuit can be stabilized against changes in the transistor characteristics.

10-1 CE Operation

In the CE operation of a transistor, the a-c signal is coupled into the base, and an amplified signal is taken out of the collector. The *emitter operates at a-c ground*, and because of this, the CE circuit is often referred to as a grounded-emitter circuit.

241

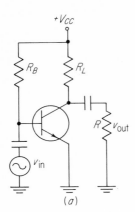
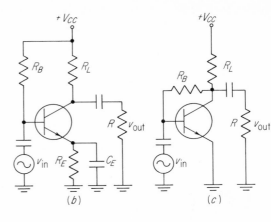

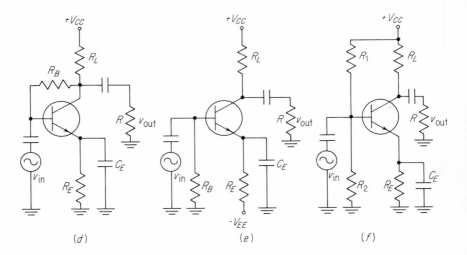

Notes:
1. All circuits have a voltage gain of $\dfrac{v_{out}}{v_{in}} \cong \dfrac{r_L}{r_e'}$

2. Circuits a, b, and e have an input resistance of $r_{in} \cong R_B \| \beta r_e'$

3. Circuits c and d have an input resistance of $r_{in} \cong \dfrac{R_B}{A} \| \beta r_e'$

4. Circuit f has an input resistance of $r_{in} \cong R_1 \| R_2 \| \beta r_e'$

Fig. 10-1   CE operation of the six bias circuits.

Figure 10-1 illustrates the correct use of coupling and bypass capacitors to get CE operation in each of the six biasing circuits. First, note that in each circuit the emitter is at a-c ground. In some of these circuits (Figs. 10-1a and c) the emitter is physically grounded, so that it is at both d-c and a-c ground. In the remaining bias arrangements, however, there is an R_E resistor. This resistor will develop an a-c voltage unless it is bypassed by a capacitor as shown in Fig. 10-1b and d to f.

The emitter capacitor C_E must be large enough to appear almost like a short circuit to the lowest-frequency signal to be amplified. The problem of calculating the size of this capacitor is discussed in the chapter on frequency response. Throughout this chapter we will treat all capacitors as a-c shorts. Thus, every circuit shown in Fig. 10-1 has an emitter that is grounded as far as the a-c signal is concerned.

The a-c signal is coupled into the base by means of the input coupling capacitor. The purpose of this capacitor is to appear as an open circuit to d-c voltage but as a short circuit to the a-c signal. As a result, the d-c voltages in each circuit are not shorted out through the low resistance of the a-c generators.

An inverted, amplified version of the input signal will appear at the collector of each circuit. This signal is coupled into a load of resistance R. Again, the purpose of the coupling capacitor is to pass the a-c signal but to block the d-c collector voltage.

Basically, all the circuits shown in Fig. 10-1 are examples of CE amplifiers. As far as d-c operation is concerned, the capacitors appear open, so that the circuits revert to the six biasing arrangements discussed in the last chapter. As far as the a-c operation is concerned, the capacitors look like short circuits. The a-c operation of these circuits is discussed in the next section.

10-2   A-C Analysis of CE Circuits

In applying the superposition theorem to find the a-c component, we short all d-c sources and capacitors (shorting the capacitors assumes they have reactances that are low enough to neglect). The a-c equivalent circuit for each circuit of Fig. 10-1 is shown in Fig. 10-2. Recall that r_L is the a-c load resistance seen by the collector. In each case, $r_L = R_L \| R$.

We already know from our earlier studies that the CE circuit inverts the signal; that is, the output signal is 180° out of phase with the input signal. Let us now find the magnitude of the voltage gain for each of the circuits shown in Fig. 10-2.

Note that the circuits shown in Fig. 10-2a, b, and e are identical; therefore, the voltage gain and input impedance of each of these circuits will

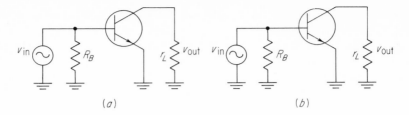

(a)   (b)

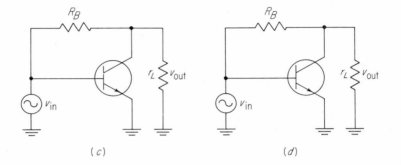

(c)   (d)

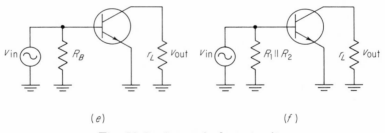

(e)   (f)

Fig. 10-2   A-c equivalent circuits.

be the same. By using the ideal-transistor approach, we can redraw the
a-c equivalent circuit as shown in Fig. 10-3. From this it is clear that

$$v_{\text{in}} = i_b \beta r'_e$$

Also, the magnitude of v_{out} is simply

$$v_{\text{out}} = \beta i_b r_L$$

Dividing v_{out} by v_{in}, we get the magnitude of the voltage gain.

$$\frac{v_{\text{out}}}{v_{\text{in}}} = \frac{\beta i_b r_L}{i_b \beta r'_e}$$

or

$$\frac{v_{\text{out}}}{v_{\text{in}}} = \frac{r_L}{r'_e} \tag{10-1}$$

In speaking of the input resistance, we must distinguish between the resistance looking directly into the base and the resistance seen by the

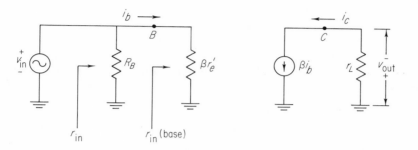

Fig. 10-3 Input resistance.

source. By inspection of Fig. 10-3, we can see that the input resistance looking into the base is simply

$$r_{\text{in(base)}} = \beta r'_e \tag{10-2}$$

The total input resistance seen by the source is

$$r_{\text{in}} = R_B \| \beta r'_e \tag{10-3}$$

The circuit of Fig. 10-2f is actually in the same form as those of Fig. 10-2a, b, and e. The only difference is that $R_1 \| R_2$ takes the place of R_B. The voltage gain is still given by r_L/r'_e, and the resistance looking into the base is still $\beta r'_e$. The resistance seen by the source, however, becomes

$$r_{\text{in}} = R_1 \| R_2 \| \beta r'_e \tag{10-4}$$

The two remaining circuits (Fig. 10-2c and d) have the resistor R_B connected from the collector back to the base. What effect does this have on the voltage gain and input resistance seen by the source? To answer this question, we will replace the transistor by its ideal approximation, as shown in Fig. 10-4. The alternating current in R_B must be the difference of the current source and the load current. That is, the current in R_B equals

$$\beta i_b - i_L$$

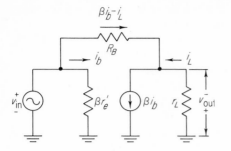

Fig. 10-4 A-c equivalent circuit for collector feedback.

Next, we can write a voltage equation around the outside loop that contains r_L, R_B, and v_{in}.

$$v_{in} + v_{out} - R_B(\beta i_b - i_L) = 0$$

or

$$v_{in} + v_{out} - R_B \beta i_b + R_B i_L = 0 \qquad (10\text{-}5)$$

By inspection of Fig. 10-4 we can see that

$$v_{in} = i_b \beta r_e'$$

or

$$i_b = \frac{v_{in}}{\beta r_e'}$$

Also, note that

$$v_{out} = i_L r_L$$

or

$$i_L = \frac{v_{out}}{r_L}$$

If we substitute these expressions for i_b and i_L into Eq. (10-5) and simplify, we get

$$v_{in} + v_{out} - \frac{R_B}{r_e'} v_{in} + \frac{R_B}{r_L} v_{out} = 0$$

After factoring and solving for v_{out}/v_{in}, we have

$$\frac{v_{out}}{v_{in}} = \frac{R_B/r_e' - 1}{R_B/r_L + 1} \qquad (10\text{-}6)$$

In most practical circuits, R_B must be much larger than r_e' or r_L to avoid saturating the transistor (see Secs. 9-4 and 9-5). Because of this, Eq. (10-6) simplifies to

$$\frac{v_{out}}{v_{in}} = \frac{R_B/r_e' - 1}{R_B/r_L + 1} \cong \frac{R_B/r_e'}{R_B/r_L} = \frac{r_L}{r_e'}$$

This final result simply tells us that the value of R_B is so large in most circuits that it has a negligible effect on the voltage gain.

What is the input a-c resistance seen by the source in Fig. 10-2c and d? One way to find this input resistance is as follows. Consider Fig. 10-5. The input resistance seen by the source is

$$r_{in} = \frac{v_{in}}{i_{in}}$$

Note carefully that i_{in} equals the sum of the alternating current in the base resistor R_B plus the current in the base diode. That is,

$$i_{in} = i_B + i_b$$

If the right end of R_B were at a-c ground, the input resistance would be the parallel combination of R_B and $\beta r'_e$. However, the right end of R_B is not at a-c ground, because there is a signal on the collector. To find the

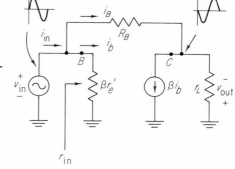

Fig. 10-5 Deriving the input resistance.

effective resistance that R_B presents to the source, we note that the current i_B must equal the voltage across R_B divided by the value of R_B. That is,

$$i_B = \frac{v_{in} - (-v_{out})}{R_B} = \frac{v_{in} + v_{out}}{R_B}$$

If we let A represent the voltage gain from base to collector, we can write

$$i_B = \frac{v_{in} + A v_{in}}{R_B} = \frac{v_{in}(1 + A)}{R_B}$$

By rearranging, we get

$$\frac{v_{in}}{i_B} = \frac{R_B}{1 + A} \cong \frac{R_B}{A} \qquad \text{for } A \gg 1 \qquad (10\text{-}7)$$

Equation (10-7) tells us that as far as the source is concerned, the effective resistance of R_B is given by R_B/A. In other words, we can redraw the circuit of Fig. 10-5 as shown in Fig. 10-6. The source sees an effective input resistance of

$$r_{\text{in}} = \frac{R_B}{A} \,\|\beta r_e' \tag{10-8}$$

The a-c equivalent circuit shown in Fig. 10-6 is quite accurate for most typical circuits of the form originally given in Fig. 10-1c and d. It only assumes that R_B is much greater than r_e' and r_L, a condition that almost always exists if saturation is to be avoided.

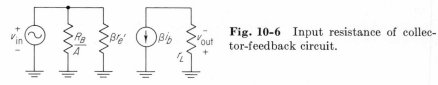

Fig. 10-6 Input resistance of collector-feedback circuit.

To summarize, we have seen that all CE circuits shown in Fig. 10-1 are quite similar as far as a-c operation is concerned. They all have a voltage gain from base to collector of approximately r_L/r_e'. The notes at the bottom of Fig. 10-1 summarize the important a-c formulas.

EXAMPLE 10-1

The β in Fig. 10-7a is 50. Find the following:

(a) The d-c collector-to-ground voltage.
(b) The voltage gain from base to collector.
(c) The input resistance of the entire stage.

SOLUTION

(a) The d-c base current is about 10 μa; therefore, the d-c collector current is 0.5 ma. This produces a 5-volt drop across the 10-kilohm resistor, so that

$$V_C = 10 - 5 = 5 \text{ volts}$$

(b) The voltage gain from base to collector is

$$\frac{v_{\text{out}}}{v_{\text{in}}} = \frac{r_L}{r_e'}$$

The theoretical value of r_e' is

$$r_e' = \frac{25 \text{ mv}}{I_E} = \frac{25 \text{ mv}}{0.5 \text{ ma}} = 50 \text{ ohms}$$

The a-c load resistance is

$$r_L = 10^4 \| 10^4 = 5 \text{ kilohms}$$

Therefore, the voltage gain from base to collector is

$$\frac{v_{\text{out}}}{v_{\text{in}}} = \frac{5000}{50} = 100$$

If we allow for the spread of $2:1$ in the value of r_e', we get a voltage gain between 50 and 100.

(c) The input resistance is

$$r_{\text{in}} = R_B \| \beta r_e'$$

By using the theoretical value of r_e', we get

$$r_{\text{in}} = 10^6 \| 50(50) \cong 2500 \text{ ohms}$$

If we allow for the $2:1$ spread in r_e', we get an input resistance between 2500 and 5000 ohms.

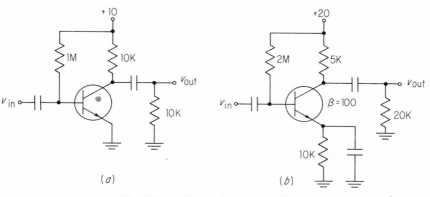

Fig. 10-7 Examples 10-1 and 10-2.

EXAMPLE 10-2

In Fig. 10-7b, find the voltage gain for:

(a) $r_e' = 25 \text{ mv}/I_E$.
(b) $r_e' = 50 \text{ mv}/I_E$.

SOLUTION

(a) In Fig. 10-7b, β is given as 100. This bias circuit was studied in Chap. 9.

$$I_C = \frac{V_{CC}}{R_E + R_B/\beta} = \frac{20}{10^4 + 2(10^6)/100} = 0.667 \text{ ma}$$

We can now find r_e'.

$$r_e' = \frac{25 \text{ mv}}{0.667 \text{ ma}} = 37.5 \text{ ohms}$$

The voltage gain is

$$\frac{v_{\text{out}}}{v_{\text{in}}} = \frac{r_L}{r_e'} = \frac{5000\|20{,}000}{37.5} = 107$$

(b) If we use $r_e' = 50 \text{ mv}/I_E$, we have an r_e' of 75 ohms. Hence, the voltage gain becomes 53.5.

EXAMPLE 10-3

The circuit of Fig. 10-8 has a β of 75. If $v_{\text{in}} = 5$ mv rms, find the approximate value of v_{out}.

SOLUTION

$$I_C = \frac{V_{CC}}{R_L + R_B/\beta} = \frac{15}{20(10^3) + 1.5(10^6)/75} = 0.375 \text{ ma}$$

Hence, we can compute the theoretical value of r_e'.

$$r_e' = \frac{25 \text{ mv}}{0.375 \text{ ma}} = 66.7 \text{ ohms}$$

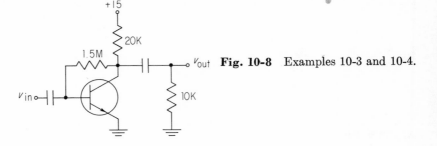

Fig. 10-8 Examples 10-3 and 10-4.

The voltage gain is

$$\frac{v_{\text{out}}}{v_{\text{in}}} = \frac{r_L}{r_e'} = \frac{20(10^3)\|10(10^3)}{66.7} = 100$$

Therefore,

$$v_{\text{out}} = 100v_{\text{in}} = 100(5 \text{ mv}) = 500 \text{ mv rms}$$

(Note that had we used $r_e' = 50 \text{ mv}/I_E$, we would have obtained an output voltage of 250 mv rms.)

EXAMPLE 10-4

What is the input resistance seen by the source in the preceding example?

SOLUTION

The source sees a resistance of

$$r_{in} \cong \frac{R_B}{A} \| \beta r_e' = \frac{1.5(10^6)}{100} \| 75(66.7) \cong 3.75 \text{ kilohms}$$

EXAMPLE 10-5

Find the voltage gain and the input resistance of the circuit shown in Fig. 10-9. The transistor has a β of 200, and r_e' is given by 25 mv/I_E.

SOLUTION

First, we need the approximate value of I_E. Recall that this circuit is a single-supply emitter-biased circuit. By inspection, we see that the

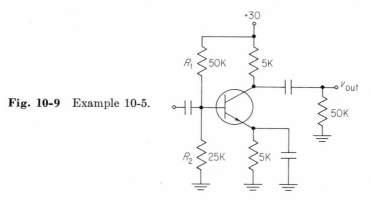

Fig. 10-9 Example 10-5.

d-c voltage developed from base to ground is about 10 volts. Hence, the d-c emitter-ground voltage is about 10 volts, and the emitter current is

$$I_E \cong \frac{10}{5000} = 2 \text{ ma}$$

The value of r_e' is

$$r_e' = \frac{25 \text{ mv}}{I_E} = \frac{25 \text{ mv}}{2 \text{ ma}} = 12.5 \text{ ohms}$$

The voltage gain is simply

$$\frac{v_{out}}{v_{in}} = \frac{r_L}{r_e'} = \frac{5000 \| 50,000}{12.5} \cong 360$$

The input resistance of the circuit is

$$r_{\text{in}} = R_1 \| R_2 \| \beta r'_e = 50(10^3) \| 25(10^3) \| 200(12.5) \cong 2.18 \text{ kilohms}$$

10-3   Emitter Feedback

Recall that in Sec. 5-8 we discussed the a-c operation of a CB circuit. In that section we showed that the voltage gain from source to output could be stabilized against variations in r'_e by *swamping* the emitter diode. Swamping simply means using a source resistance that is much larger

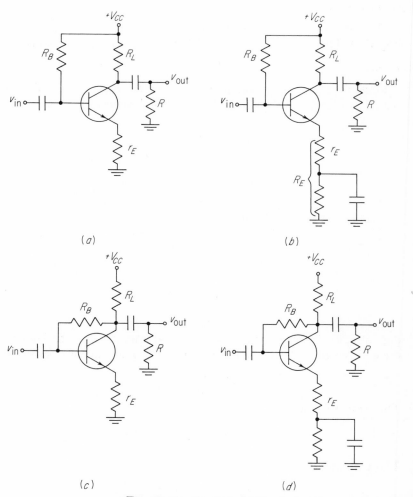

(a)   (b)

(c)   (d)

Fig. 10-10   Emitter-feedback circuits, to be visualized

than the r'_e of the transistor. In this way, the exact value of r'_e is un-important as far as the gain from source to output is concerned.

A similar technique is possible in CE circuits. We have just seen that the voltage gain of a CE circuit is given by r_L/r'_e. Because the value of r'_e varies with temperature, as well as with the particular transistor used, the voltage gain will vary along with r'_e. To stabilize the gain, we need to swamp out the emitter diode.

A widely used method for swamping out the emitter diode is shown in the circuits of Fig. 10-10. In each of the six biasing circuits a resistor r_E

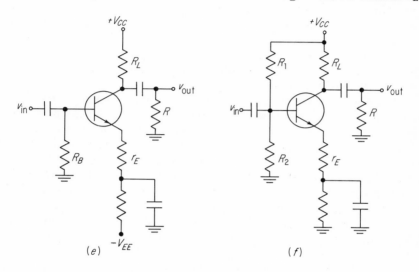

(e)   (f)

Notes:

1. All have a voltage gain of $\dfrac{v_{out}}{v_{in}} \cong \dfrac{r_L}{r_E + r_e'} \cong \dfrac{r_L}{r_E}$ when $r_E \gg r_e'$

2. All have an input resistance looking into the base of
$$r_{in} \text{ (base)} \cong \beta(r_E + r_e') \cong \beta\, r_E \quad \text{when} \quad r_E \gg r_e'$$

3. Circuits $a, b,$ and e, have an input resistance of
$$r_{in} \cong R_B \parallel r_{in} \text{ (base)}$$

4. Circuits c and d have an input resistance of
$$r_{in} \cong \dfrac{R_B}{A} \parallel r_{in} \text{ (base)}$$

5. Circuit f has an input resistance of
$$r_{in} \cong R_1 \parallel R_2 \parallel r_{in}\text{(base)}$$

as combination of emitter follower and CB amplifier.

has been added between the emitter and the a-c ground point. As far as d-c operation is concerned, the value of r_E is lumped into the total d-c resistance R_E seen by the emitter (Fig. 10-10b). The d-c voltages and currents can be found by the methods of Chap. 9.

The a-c operation of the circuits shown in Fig. 10-10 will be different from before, because the emitter is no longer at a-c ground. When an a-c signal is coupled into the base of the transistor, the emitter signal tends to follow this input signal (similar to the emitter-follower action). The a-c voltage developed across the r_E resistor sets up an a-c emitter current. The a-c collector current, which is almost equal to this emitter current, then develops an a-c voltage across the r_L seen by the collector.

(For those familiar with vacuum-tube circuits, the use of an unbypassed emitter resistance is analogous to leaving part of the cathode resistance unbypassed. This results in degeneration, which stabilizes the voltage gain of the circuit.)

A simple qualitative viewpoint of the circuits shown in Fig. 10-10 is just this: we can visualize these circuits as a combination of an *emitter follower* and a *CB amplifier*. The input signal is applied to the base; a signal is then developed across r_E because of the emitter-follower action of the circuit. When the circuit is well designed, the a-c voltage across r_E almost equals the a-c input voltage to the base. Since almost all the input voltage appears across r_E, the circuit now acts like a CB amplifier whose emitter diode has been swamped out. In other words, the a-c voltage across r_E sets up an a-c emitter current; the a-c collector current is almost equal to this emitter current; this is completely analogous to a CB circuit whose emitter diode has been swamped.

To find the voltage gain from base to collector for the circuits shown in Fig. 10-10, consider the simplified a-c equivalent circuit of Fig. 10-11a. This simplified circuit is applicable to all the circuits of Fig. 10-10, in-

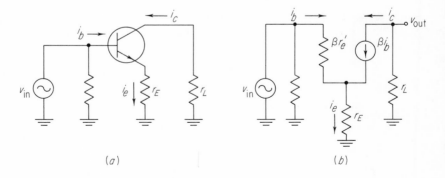

Fig. 10-11 Deriving the voltage gain of an emitter-feedback circuit.

cluding those in Figs. 10-10c and d, as long as R_B is large enough to neglect (discussed in Sec. 10-2).

The transistor in Fig. 10-11a can be replaced by its ideal approximation, as shown in Fig. 10-11b. If we write a voltage equation around the base loop, we get

$$v_{in} = i_b \beta r_e' + i_e r_E \cong i_b \beta r_e' + \beta i_b r_E = i_b \beta (r_e' + r_E)$$

The magnitude of the a-c output voltage developed across r_L is simply

$$v_{out} = i_c r_L = \beta i_b r_L$$

Dividing v_{out} by v_{in}, we obtain

$$\frac{v_{out}}{v_{in}} \cong \frac{r_L}{r_e' + r_E} \tag{10-9}$$

Usually the circuit designer deliberately makes r_E much greater than r_e' in order to swamp out the variations in r_e'. In fact, this is the whole point of using the r_E resistor. Under this condition, the voltage gain from base to collector becomes

$$\frac{v_{out}}{v_{in}} \cong \frac{r_L}{r_E} \qquad \text{for } r_E \gg r_e' \tag{10-10}$$

Equation (10-10) is *very important*. Whenever we analyze circuits like those shown in Fig. 10-10, we can easily find the voltage gain to a close approximation by calculating the ratio of the r_L to r_E (the unbypassed part of the emitter resistance). The condition $r_E \gg r_e'$ is usually satisfied; if there is any doubt, we can easily find the approximate value of r_e' and use the more accurate formula given in Eq. (10-9).

As an example, suppose that the a-c load resistance seen by the collector is 10 kilohms. If the d-c emitter current is 1 ma, the value of r_e' is in the range of 25 to 50 ohms. Hence, we can select an r_E that is 10 or more times greater than r_e'. For an r_E of 1 kilohm, we get a voltage gain from base to collector of

$$\frac{v_{out}}{v_{in}} \cong \frac{r_L}{r_E} = \frac{10,000}{1000} = 10$$

This voltage gain is quite stable; that is, the exact value of r_e' has little effect upon the voltage gain because it has been swamped out.

The a-c input resistance of the circuits shown in Fig. 10-10 is also important. The various a-c equivalent circuits are shown in Fig. 10-12. Note that in each of these variations the input resistance looking directly into the base is simply βr_E. The reason for this can be understood by referring again to Fig. 10-11b. In this figure it is clear that

$$v_{\text{in}} = i_b \beta r'_e + i_e r_E \cong i_b \beta (r'_e + r_E)$$

or

$$\frac{v_{\text{in}}}{i_b} = \beta (r'_e + r_E)$$

The quantity v_{in} divided by i_b is nothing more than the input resistance looking into the base. Hence,

$$r_{\text{in(base)}} \cong \beta (r'_e + r_E)$$

Once again we observe that the whole point of using the r_E resistor is to swamp out the value of r'_e. Under this condition, we get

$$r_{\text{in(base)}} \cong \beta r_E \qquad \text{for } r_E \gg r'_e \qquad \qquad (10\text{-}11)$$

Thus, to a first approximation, the input resistance looking into the base is β times larger than the value of r_E.

The actual input resistance seen by the source is the parallel combination of bias resistors and the input resistance looking into the base. Figure 10-12 illustrates the various input circuits. The a-c equivalent circuit of Fig. 10-12a (applicable to Fig. 10-10a, b, and e) has an input resistance of

$$R_B \| \beta r_E$$

This is what the source actually sees.

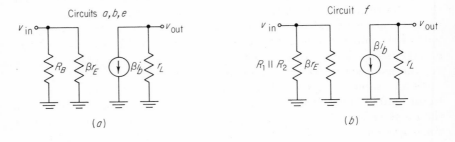

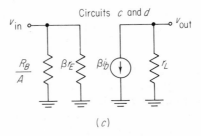

Fig. 10-12   The input resistance of emitter-feedback circuits.

The a-c equivalent circuit of Fig. 10-12*b* (applicable to Fig. 10-10*f*) has an a-c input resistance of

$$R_1\|R_2\|\beta r_E$$

In the a-c equivalent circuit of Fig. 10-12*c* (applicable to Fig. 10-10*c* and *d*), the R_B resistor appears as a resistance of R_B/A as far as the source is concerned. Therefore, the source sees an a-c input resistance of

$$\frac{R_B}{A}\,\|\beta r_E$$

where A is the voltage gain from base to collector.

A summary of the important formulas for voltage gain and input resistance is given at the bottom of Fig. 10-10; these will be quite useful for future reference.

EXAMPLE 10-6

The transistor in Fig. 10-13*a* has a β of 100. Find the voltage gain and the input resistance.

SOLUTION

The voltage gain is

$$\frac{v_{\text{out}}}{v_{\text{in}}} \cong \frac{r_L}{r_E} = \frac{10^4\|3(10^4)}{500} = 15$$

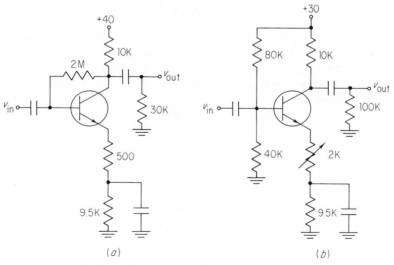

(*a*)   (*b*)

Fig. 10-13 Examples 10-6 and 10-7.

The input resistance consists of the resistance looking into the base in parallel with R_B/A.

$$r_{\text{in}} = \frac{R_B}{A} \, \| r_{\text{in(base)}} = \frac{2(10^6)}{15} \, \| 100(500) = 36.4 \text{ kilohms}$$

In both of the calculations we have assumed that $r_E \gg r'_e$. To check the validity of this, let us find I_E and then r'_e. In Chap. 9 we saw that a base-biased circuit with collector and emitter feedback has a d-c emitter current of

$$I_E \cong \frac{V_{CC}}{R_E + R_L + R_B/\beta} = \frac{40}{10^4 + 10^4 + 2(10^6)/10^2} = 1 \text{ ma}$$

Therefore, r'_e is in the range of 25 to 50 ohms. Obviously, r_E is much greater than r'_e.

EXAMPLE 10-7

The circuit of Fig. 10-13b has an adjustable r_E. Find the approximate range of voltage gain and input resistance. Use a β of 100.

SOLUTION

By inspection, r_L is 10 kilohms in parallel with 100 kilohms. By the product-over-sum rule, we get an r_L of 9.1 kilohms. When r_E is adjusted to its maximum value of 2 kilohms, the voltage gain is minimum and equals

$$\frac{v_{\text{out}}}{v_{\text{in}}} \cong \frac{r_L}{r_E} = \frac{9100}{2000} = 4.55$$

On the other hand, when r_E is turned down to zero, there is no emitter feedback, and the voltage gain is given by r_L/r'_e. A calculation will show that $I_E \cong 1$ ma, and so r'_e will be between 25 and 50 ohms. The maximum possible gain occurs if r'_e is as low as 25 ohms. This maximum gain is

$$\frac{v_{\text{out}}}{v_{\text{in}}} \cong \frac{r_L}{r'_e} = \frac{9100}{25} = 364$$

Thus, we have a variable gain that lies between 4.55 and 364, depending upon the r_E adjusment.

Since the β is 100, looking into the base with r_E at maximum, we get

$$r_{\text{in(base)}} \cong \beta r_E = 100(2000) = 200 \text{ kilohms}$$

This 200 kilohms is in parallel with 80 kilohms and 40 kilohms when viewed from the source. Hence,

$$r_{\text{in}} = 80(10^3) \| 40(10^3) \| 200(10^3) = 23.5 \text{ kilohms}$$

On the other hand, when r_E is at its minimum value, the input resistance looking into the base is only

$$r_{\text{in(base)}} \cong \beta r'_e = 100(25) = 2.5 \text{ kilohms}$$

The source sees 2.5 kilohms in parallel with 80 and 40 kilohms. For practical purposes, the source sees approximately 2.5 kilohms. Therefore, the range of input resistance as r_E is varied from minimum to maximum in 2.5 to 23.5 kilohms.

10-4   CC Operation

In the CC connection (emitter follower), we couple the input signal into the base and take an output signal from the emitter. The collector is deliberately placed at a-c ground. Because of this, there is no need to use a d-c load resistance R_L. In other words, we can connect the collector directly to the V_{CC} supply.

Of the six biasing arrangements studied in Chap. 9, there are only three distinct forms that we can use for emitter-follower circuits when $R_L = 0$. These forms are shown in Fig. 10-14.

The d-c operation of these circuits is straightforward. In all cases, $R_L = 0$. Therefore, in using the formulas developed in Chap. 9, we simply set R_L equal to zero. For instance, the circuit of Fig. 10-14a is a base-biased circuit with emitter feedback; its d-c operation is summarized by Fig. 9-4. Likewise, the two-supply emitter-bias circuit of Fig. 10-14b has direct currents and voltages that we can find by using the formulas of Fig. 9-10. Finally, we can analyze the d-c operation of the single-supply emitter-bias circuit of Fig. 10-14c by using the formulas of Fig. 9-13.

The circuits shown in Fig. 10-14 are emitter followers. To find the a-c equivalent circuit, we short all d-c supplies and capacitors. When we do this, we find that all these circuits reduce to the a-c equivalent circuit of Fig. 10-15. In Chap. 7, we discussed the emitter follower using the a-c equivalent circuit of Fig. 10-15. We saw that the voltage gain is

$$\frac{v_{\text{out}}}{v_{\text{in}}} = \frac{1}{1 + r'_e/r_L} \cong 1 \qquad \text{for } r_L \gg r'_e \tag{10-12}$$

The input resistance looking into the base is

$$r_{\text{in(base)}} \cong \beta(r'_e + r_L) \cong \beta r_L \qquad \text{for } r_L \gg r'_e \tag{10-13}$$

For the circuits of Figs. 10-14a and b the input resistance seen by the source is

$$r_{\text{in}} = R_B \| r_{\text{in(base)}} \tag{10-14}$$

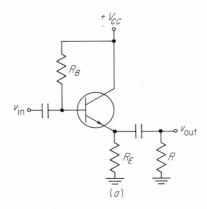

(a)

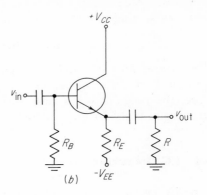

(b)

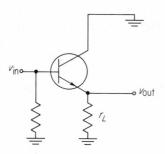

(c)

Notes :

1. $r_L = R_E \| R$

2. All have a voltage gain of

$$\frac{v_{out}}{v_{in}} \cong \frac{1}{1 + r_e' / r_L} \cong 1 \quad \text{when} \quad r_L \gg r_e'$$

3. Circuits a and b have an input resistance of

$$r_{in} \cong R_B \| \beta \, r_L$$

4. Circuit c has an input resistance of

$$r_{in} \cong R_1 \| R_2 \| \beta \, r_L$$

Fig. 10-14   Emitter-follower circuits.

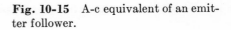

Fig. 10-15   A-c equivalent of an emitter follower.

Where $r_L = R_E \| R$

whereas the circuit of Fig. 10-14c has an input resistance of

$$r_{in} = R_1 \| R_2 \| r_{in(base)} \qquad (10\text{-}15)$$

These various results are summarized at the bottom of Fig. 10-14 and should be useful for future reference.

Recall the main idea behind the emitter follower: the circuit is used to increase the impedance level; the value of load resistance r_L seen by the emitter is stepped up by a factor of β when seen from the base.

EXAMPLE 10-8

Calculate the approximate input resistance of the emitter follower in Fig. 10-16a. Use a β of between 100 and 200.

SOLUTION

The a-c load resistance seen by the emitter is

$$r_L = R_E \| R = 10,000 \| 500 \cong 500$$

The resistance looking into the base is

$$r_{in(base)} \cong \beta(r'_e + r_L)$$

If we were to calculate the d-c collector current, we would find that it is 1 ma or more, depending upon the value of β; therefore, r'_e is in the range of 25 to 50 ohms. As a result, $r_L \gg r'_e$ (500 ohms compared to 25 or 50 ohms). Hence, we can say that

$$r_{in(base)} \cong \beta r_L$$

When $\beta = 100$,

$$r_{in(base)} \cong 100(500) = 50 \text{ kilohms}$$

Also, when $\beta = 200$,

$$r_{in(base)} \cong 200(500) = 100 \text{ kilohms}$$

The source sees 1 megohm in parallel with $r_{in(base)}$. Since 1 megohm is much larger than 50 to 100 kilohms, we can say that the source sees approximately 50 to 100 kilohms of resistance.

Note carefully the significance of this result: a 500-ohm load on the output side has been transformed so that it appears as 50 to 100 kilohms when seen by the source. This is the whole point of the emitter follower.

EXAMPLE 10-9

Find the voltage gain and the input resistance of the emitter follower in Fig. 10-16b. Use a β of 200 and an $r'_e = 25 \text{ mv}/I_E$.

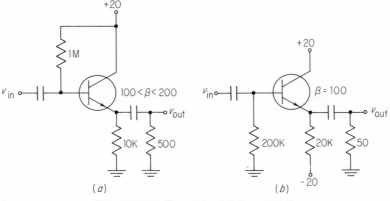

Fig. 10-16 Examples 10-8 and 10-9.

SOLUTION

The emitter sees an a-c load of 20 kilohms in parallel with 50 ohms. Therefore, r_L is approximately 50 ohms. Because this is so low, we will need to take r'_e into account. This means we need to first find I_E.

The circuit is a two-supply emitter-biased connection. We already know that in this kind of circuit almost all the emitter supply voltage appears across R_E. Therefore,

$$I_E \cong \frac{V_{EE}}{R_E} = \frac{20}{20,000} = 1 \text{ ma}$$

With 1 ma of emitter current, we find that

$$r'_e = \frac{25 \text{ mv}}{I_E} = \frac{25 \text{ mv}}{1 \text{ ma}} = 25 \text{ ohms}$$

The voltage gain of the circuit is

$$\frac{v_{\text{out}}}{v_{\text{in}}} = \frac{1}{1 + r'_e/r_L} = \frac{1}{1 + 25\!/_{50}} = 0.667$$

The resistance looking into the base is

$$r_{\text{in(base)}} = \beta(r'_e + r_L) = 200(25 + 50) = 15 \text{ kilohms}$$

This 15 kilohms of resistance is in parallel with the 200-kilohm base-to-ground resistor. For practical purposes, the source sees approximately 15 kilohms.

Again note how a relatively low value of load resistance has been transformed to a much higher value of resistance when viewed from the source.

Also, note that at times, the voltage gain can be quite a bit less than unity, as in this case; r_e' was not negligibly small compared to r_L.

10-5 CB Operation

In a CB connection, we couple the input signal into the emitter and take the output from the collector. The base is held at a-c ground, and as a result, the circuit is sometimes called a grounded-base circuit. The base does not have to be physically grounded. In other words, there may be a d-c voltage from base to ground; however, in this case, we must use a bypass capacitor to ensure that the base is at a-c ground.

When we examine the six biasing arrangements of Chap. 9, we find that two of these have the emitter connected directly to ground. Since the input signal is coupled into the emitter, we cannot use these two circuits for CB operation.

The four remaining bias arrangements are shown in Fig. 10-17, along with coupling and bypass capacitors. In each circuit, observe that the input signal is coupled into the emitter and the output signal is taken from the collector. In each case, the base is at a-c ground.

The d-c operation of these circuits is straightforward. All capacitors appear open to d-c voltage; therefore, these circuits revert to the standard biasing arrangements of Chap. 9. We can analyze the d-c operation of Fig. 10-17a by using the formulas of Fig. 9-4. Similarly, Fig. 10-17b is analyzed by using Fig. 9-8, Fig. 10-17c by using Fig. 9-10, and Fig. 10-17d by using Fig. 9-13.

By shorting all d-c supplies and capacitors, we get the a-c equivalent circuits. The circuits of Fig. 10-17a, c, and d have the same a-c equivalent circuit, which is shown in Fig. 10-18a. We found the voltage gain of this circuit in Chap. 5. It is

$$\frac{v_{\text{out}}}{v_{\text{in}}} \cong \frac{r_L}{r_e'} \tag{10-16}$$

Remember that this is the voltage gain from *emitter* to collector. [When there is source resistance, the voltage gain from *source* to collector becomes $r_L/(r_s + r_e')$. This was discussed in Sec. 5-8.]

By inspection of Fig. 10-18a, it is clear that the input resistance of the circuit is R_E in parallel with r_e'. That is,

$$r_{\text{in}} \cong R_E \| r_e' \cong r_e' \qquad \text{when } R_E \gg r_e' \tag{10-17}$$

Usually, in a CB circuit, R_E is much greater than r_e', so that the input resistance of the circuit is quite low, being equal to the r_e' of the transistor.

The CB circuit of Fig. 10-17b has an a-c equivalent circuit that is

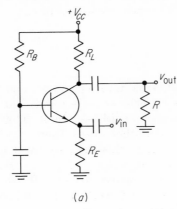

(a)

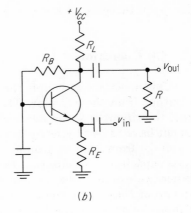

(b)

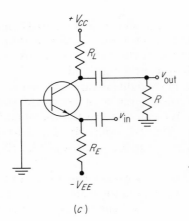

(c)

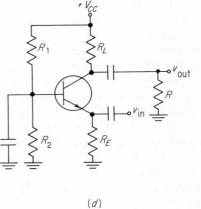

(d)

Notes:

1. $r_L = R_L \parallel R$

2. All have a voltage gain of

$$\frac{v_{out}}{v_{in}} \approx \frac{r_L}{r_e'}$$

3. All have input resistance of

$$r_{in} \approx R_E \parallel r_e' \approx r_e' \quad \text{when} \quad R_E \gg r_e'$$

Fig. 10-17 Common-base circuits.

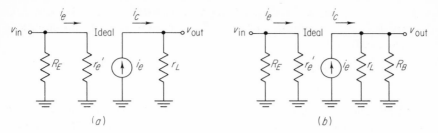

Fig. 10-18 A-c equivalent circuit for CB amplifiers.

slightly different from the other circuits in Fig. 10-17. Its equivalent circuit is shown in Fig. 10-18*b*. The collector sees an a-c load of three resistors in parallel. That is,

$$r_L = R_B \| R_L \| R$$

However, we observed in Chap. 9 that R_B must be much larger than R_L if we are to avoid saturation. Therefore, in most practical circuits, R_B is large enough to neglect, and we can say that the a-c load resistance is simply

$$r_L = R_L \| R$$

The circuit of Fig. 10-17*b* has essentially the same voltage gain and input resistance as the other circuits in this figure.

All the results are summarized by the notes at the bottom of Fig. 10-17.

There is an important result worth remembering. By using the ideal-transistor approximation, we have seen that the voltage gains of CB and CE circuits are equal, being given by r_L/r_e'. One important difference between these two connections is the input resistance. A CB circuit has an input resistance looking into the base of about r_e', whereas the CE circuit has an input resistance of $\beta r_e'$. Because of its higher resistance, the CE circuit is used more often; nevertheless, the CB circuit does have some use, especially at higher frequency. This is discussed in the chapter on frequency response.

EXAMPLE 10-10

A 2-mv-rms signal drives the emitter of the *p-n-p* transistor shown in Fig. 10-19. Find the approximate value of v_{out} and the input resistance looking into the emitter.

SOLUTION

As we already know, when a *p-n-p* transistor is used instead of an *n-p-n*, all d-c currents and voltages are reversed. The a-c operation, however, is identical for either type of transistor because the same a-c equivalent circuit applies to each. The voltage gain of the circuit is approximately

$$\frac{v_{\text{out}}}{v_{\text{in}}} \cong \frac{r_L}{r'_e}$$

To find r'_e, we first must find I_E, the d-c emitter current. Recall the d-c operation of the single-supply emitter-bias circuit. The voltage divider

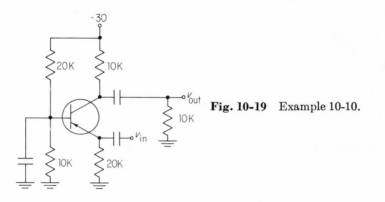

Fig. 10-19   Example 10-10.

in the base develops a voltage of about 10 volts. Almost all this 10 volts appears across the emitter resistor, so that

$$I_E \cong \frac{10}{20,000} = 0.5 \text{ ma}$$

With 0.5 ma of d-c emitter current, the value of r'_e is in the range of 50 to 100 ohms. Hence, for $r'_e = 50$ ohms,

$$\frac{v_{\text{out}}}{v_{\text{in}}} = \frac{10,000\|10,000}{50} = 100$$

If r'_e is as high as 100 ohms, the voltage gain becomes 50. Thus, the voltage gain is between 50 and 100.

Since the input signal is 2 mv rms at the emitter, the output signal will be between 100 and 200 mv rms.

The input resistance is the parallel combination of R_E and r'_e. Obviously, the 20-kilohm value of R_E is so much larger than r'_e that we have

$$r_{\text{in}} \cong r'_e = 50 \text{ to } 100 \text{ ohms}$$

10-6 The Effect of Source Resistance

Up to this point, we have been discussing the voltage gain from the input terminal of the transistor to the output. In this section, we want to study the effect that source resistance has on the overall voltage gain from source to output.

Consider Fig. 10-20a. We have shown a source with a resistance of r_s. The amplifier inside the box can be a CE, CC, or CB circuit. The voltage gain of the amplifier is A, where A is the ratio of v_{out} to v_{in}. Note carefully that v_{in} is the voltage appearing across the input of the amplifier. This input voltage does not equal the source voltage v_s because some signal is lost across the source resistor r_s.

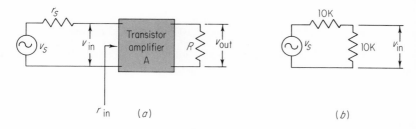

Fig. 10-20 The effect of source impedance.

How large is the actual signal appearing across the input terminals of the amplifier? The easiest way to find this is to apply the voltage-divider theorem. That is,

$$v_{in} = \frac{r_{in}}{r_s + r_{in}} v_s \qquad (10\text{-}18)$$

The use of this equation is straightforward. For instance, suppose the source has a resistance of 10 kilohms and the amplifier has an input resistance of 10 kilohms, as shown in Fig. 10-20b. Then the input voltage is

$$v_{in} = \frac{10,000}{10,000 + 10,000} v_s = \frac{v_s}{2}$$

In other words, the input voltage equals one-half of the source voltage when $r_s = r_{in}$.

It should be clear from Eq. (10-18) that if the source resistance is very small compared to the input resistance of the amplifier, almost all the source signal will appear across the amplifier input, and very little signal is lost across the source resistance. But when the source resistance becomes comparable to the input resistance of the amplifier, a significant part of the source signal is lost across the source resistance.

EXAMPLE 10-11

The transistor of Fig. 10-21a has a β of 100. Find the value of v_{in} and v_{out}.

SOLUTION

The input resistance looking into the base of the transistor (not including the bias resistors) is

$$r_{in(base)} \cong \beta r_E = 100(500) = 50 \text{ kilohms}$$

The biasing resistors (50 kilohms and 25 kilohms) are in parallel with $r_{in(base)}$. Therefore, the input resistance of the amplifier is

$$r_{in} = R_1 \| R_2 \| r_{in(base)}$$
$$= 50(10^3) \| 25(10^3) \| 50(10^3) = 12.5 \text{ kilohms}$$

Now we can find how much of the source signal actually reaches the input of the amplifier. Using Eq. (10-18), we get

$$v_{in} = \frac{12,500}{5000 + 12,500} \, 20 \text{ mv} = 14.3 \text{ mv rms}$$

We can find v_{out} by first finding the voltage gain A. Since part of the emitter resistance is unbypassed, we know that the approximate gain is

$$\frac{v_{out}}{v_{in}} \cong \frac{r_L}{r_E} = \frac{10,000 \| 30,000}{500} = 15$$

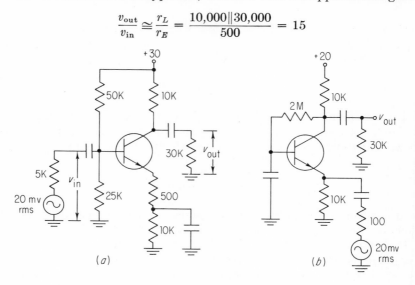

Fig. 10-21   Examples 10-11 and 10-12.

Therefore,
$$v_{\text{out}} = 15(14.3 \text{ mv}) = 214 \text{ mv rms}$$

Note that a significant part of the source signal is lost across the source resistor r_s. If the amplifier were driven by a very low impedance source (like 50 ohms), almost all the source signal would appear across the input terminals of the amplifier.

EXAMPLE 10-12

The transistor of Fig. 10-21*b* has a β of 100 and an r'_e of 100 ohms. Find the value of v_{out}.

SOLUTION

This is a CB stage with an input resistance of approximately r'_e; therefore,
$$r_{\text{in}} \cong r'_e = 100 \text{ ohms}$$

The source voltage is 20 mv rms. Since the source resistance is 100 ohms, only one-half of the source voltage reaches the emitter terminal. That is,
$$v_{\text{in}} = \frac{r_{\text{in}}}{r_s + r_{\text{in}}} v_s = \frac{100}{100 + 100} 20 \text{ mv} = 10 \text{ mv}$$

The voltage gain of the amplifier is
$$\frac{v_{\text{out}}}{v_{\text{in}}} \cong \frac{r_L}{r'_e} = \frac{10,000 \| 30,000}{100} = 75$$

Therefore, the output voltage is
$$v_{\text{out}} = 75(10 \text{ mv}) = 750 \text{ mv rms}$$

10-7 Stabilizing the Voltage Gain from Source to Output

In this section we discuss the conditions that are necessary to ensure a stable or fixed voltage gain from the source to the output in spite of changes in the transistor characteristics.

We already know that
$$v_{\text{out}} = A v_{\text{in}}$$

where A is the voltage gain from input to output. We have just seen that the actual input voltage at the amplifier input is
$$v_{\text{in}} = \frac{r_{\text{in}}}{r_s + r_{\text{in}}} v_s$$

By substituting this equation into the preceding one, we get

$$v_{\text{out}} = A \frac{r_{\text{in}}}{r_s + r_{\text{in}}} v_s$$

or

$$\frac{v_{\text{out}}}{v_s} = A \frac{r_{\text{in}}}{r_s + r_{\text{in}}} \qquad (10\text{-}19)$$

Equation (10-19) tells us how to find the voltage gain from *source* to output; it contains voltage gain A of the amplifier and the effect of the voltage divider formed by r_s and r_{in}.

In transistor work, it is often desirable to have a fixed voltage gain from source to output, a gain that remains constant even though the transistor characteristics change. How can we get this fixed value of voltage gain?

If the amplifier uses a CE circuit, the usual approach in getting stable voltage gain from source to output is to:

1. Fix A by using emitter feedback.
2. Make r_{in} much greater than r_s.

The reason for these two conditions is apparent by inspection of Eq. (10-19). When r_{in} is much greater than r_s, Eq. (10-19) reduces to

$$\frac{v_{\text{out}}}{v_s} \cong A$$

Since A is fixed because of emitter feedback, the voltage gain from source to output is fixed. We can summarize the situation as shown in Fig. 10-22. With r_{in} much greater than r_s, almost all the source voltage reaches the amplifier input. With emitter feedback, the amplifier has a gain of r_L/r_E, and the output voltage is simply

$$v_{\text{out}} \cong \frac{r_L}{r_E} v_s$$

or

$$\frac{v_{\text{out}}}{v_s} \cong \frac{r_L}{r_E} \qquad \text{for } r_{\text{in}} \gg r_s \qquad (10\text{-}20)$$

This approximate formula for the source-output voltage gain depends only upon the ratio of fixed external resistances; it does not depend upon the β or the r'_e of the transistor.

For a CB circuit, the situation is reversed; that is, to get stable voltage gain from source to output, we deliberately make r_s much greater than r'_e, the input resistance. This condition is illustrated in Fig. 10-23. The CB

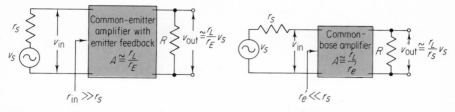

Fig. 10-22 Stabilizing the voltage gain of a CE circuit.

Fig. 10-23 Stabilizing the voltage gain of a CB circuit.

amplifier has a voltage gain of r_L/r'_e. To find the overall voltage gain we use Eq. (10-19).

$$\frac{v_{\text{out}}}{v_s} = A\,\frac{r_{\text{in}}}{r_s + r_{\text{in}}} = \frac{r_L}{r'_e}\,\frac{r'_e}{r_s + r'_e} = \frac{r_L}{r_s + r'_e}$$

By inspection of the result, it is clear that we can swamp out the emitter junction resistance by making r_s much greater than r'_e. Under this condition,

$$\frac{v_{\text{out}}}{v_s} \cong \frac{r_L}{r_s} \qquad \text{for } r_s \gg r'_e \qquad (10\text{-}21)$$

This same result was derived in Chap. 5 for a single-supply emitter-biased CB circuit. We have merely proved that the same result applies to any CB circuit, no matter what the particular biasing arrangement.

Fig. 10-24 Stabilizing the voltage gain of a CC circuit.

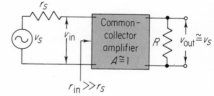

Finally, the voltage gain from source to output can be stabilized in a CC circuit, as shown in Fig. 10-24. The idea is to make r_{in} much greater than r_s, so that almost all the source voltage appears across the emitter-follower input. With a voltage gain of approximately unity, the emitter follower delivers an output signal almost equal to the source signal.

EXAMPLE 10-13

For the circuit of Fig. 10-25 verify that the voltage gain from source to output is essentially fixed even though β changes from 20 to 200.

SOLUTION

First, note that the amplifier uses emitter feedback so that the voltage gain from the base to output is

$$A = \frac{v_{\text{out}}}{v_{\text{in}}} \cong \frac{r_L}{r_E} = \frac{10,000 \| 10,000}{500} = 10$$

The input resistance looking into the base is

$$r_{\text{in(base)}} \cong \beta r_E$$

When $\beta = 20$,

$$r_{\text{in(base)}} = 20(500) = 10 \text{ kilohms}$$

When $\beta = 200$,

$$r_{\text{in(base)}} = 200(500) = 100 \text{ kilohms}$$

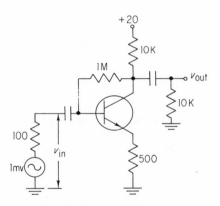

Fig. 10-25   Example 10-13.

The biasing resistor R_B appears as a resistance of

$$\frac{R_B}{A} = \frac{10^6}{10} = 100 \text{ kilohms}$$

The worst case, that is, the lowest value of input resistance for the amplifier, occurs when $\beta = 20$ and equals

$$r_{\text{in}} = \frac{R_B}{A} \| r_{\text{in(base)}} = 100(10^3) \| 10(10^3) = 9.1 \text{ kilohms}$$

Note that r_s is only 100 ohms compared to an r_{in} of 9.1 kilohms; therefore, almost all the source voltage reaches the amplifier input. With a 1-mv source, the final output voltage will be essentially 10 mv.

Thus, we have seen that the voltage gain from source to output is fixed even though the β changes from 20 to 200. In effect, the voltage gain is independent of the transistor characteristics.

10-8   *p-n-p* **Operation**

If *p-n-p* transistors are used instead of *n-p-n*, we need only change the polarity of the supply voltages. The a-c operation is the same, so that all the results of this chapter apply to *p-n-p* transistors.

As an example, consider the circuit of Fig. 10-26. A *p-n-p* transistor is used instead of an *n-p-n*; therefore, we must use a negative collector supply, as shown. All the d-c currents and voltages in this circuit are in the opposite direction from a comparable *n-p-n* circuit. The magnitudes of these d-c currents and voltages are easily found by the methods of Chap. 9. For instance, the biasing arrangement is single-supply emitter bias.

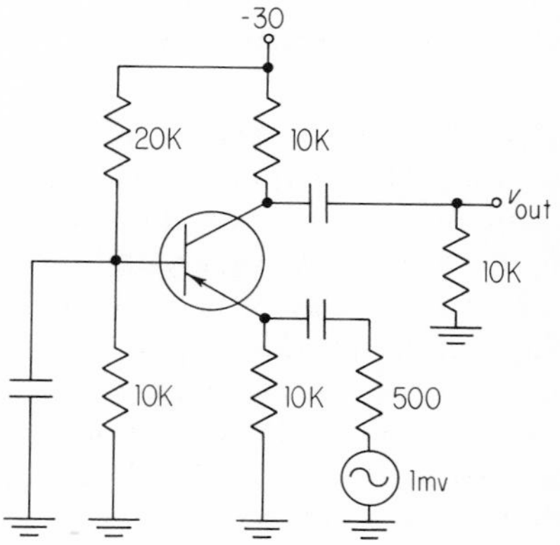

Fig. 10-26   Using a *p-n-p* transistor.

The voltage divider in the base develops about 10 volts across the 10-kilohm base resistor. This means that almost 10 volts appears across the 10-kilohm emitter resistor, thereby producing about 1 ma of d-c emitter current.

As far as the a-c operation is concerned, we have a CB circuit. The input signal is injected into the emitter; the output signal is taken from the collector; the base is at a-c ground. To find the voltage gain from emitter to output, we note that r'_e is between 25 and 50 ohms (we have already found that the d-c emitter current is about 1 ma). Therefore, the voltage gain from emitter to output is

$$\frac{v_{\text{out}}}{v_{\text{in}}} \cong \frac{r_L}{r'_e} = \frac{5000}{r'_e} = 100 \text{ to } 200$$

The voltage gain from the source to the output is

$$\frac{v_{\text{out}}}{v_s} \cong \frac{r_L}{r_s + r'_e}$$

Since r_s is 500 ohms and r_e' is in the range of 25 to 50 ohms, the emitter diode is swamped, and we get an approximate gain of

$$\frac{v_{\text{out}}}{v_s} \cong \frac{r_L}{r_s} = \frac{5000}{500} = 10$$

To generalize the operation of p-n-p circuits, note:

1. The n-p-n transistors in Figs. 10-1, 10-10, 10-14, and 10-17 can be replaced by p-n-p transistors provided we use a negative V_{CC} supply and a positive V_{EE} supply.

2. All the a-c formulas shown for n-p-n circuits apply to p-n-p circuits.

10-9   The Ground Point

As pointed out in Sec. 9-9, for single-supply biasing arrangements we can ground either end of the supply. Which end of the supply is grounded is unimportant as far as the a-c operation is concerned because both ends of the supply are a-c ground points.

If it is necessary to move the d-c ground point, we need only move those grounds which appear in the d-c equivalent circuit. For example, consider the circuit of Fig. 10-27a (this is the same as Fig. 10-1f). If the opposite end of the d-c supply is grounded, we merely redraw the circuit as shown in Fig. 10-27b. The a-c operation of Fig. 10-27b is identical to that of Fig. 10-27a.

As another example, consider the p-n-p circuit of Fig. 10-27c. If we wish to move the d-c ground point to the other end of the d-c supply, we simply draw the circuit as shown in Fig. 10-27d. The a-c operation of Fig. 10-27c and d is identical.

10-10   Maximum Signal-handling Capability

In Chap. 8, we discussed the load lines of simple CE, CB, and CC circuits. Recall that the d-c load line is a graph of all the possible d-c operating points. The actual d-c operating point is somewhere along this d-c load line and can be located by the methods of Chap. 9.

When an a-c signal drives a transistor, it causes changes in the transistor currents and voltages. These changes take place along the a-c load line instead of the d-c load line because the a-c load seen by the transistor can be different from the d-c load.

Of special importance is the maximum signal-handling capability, that

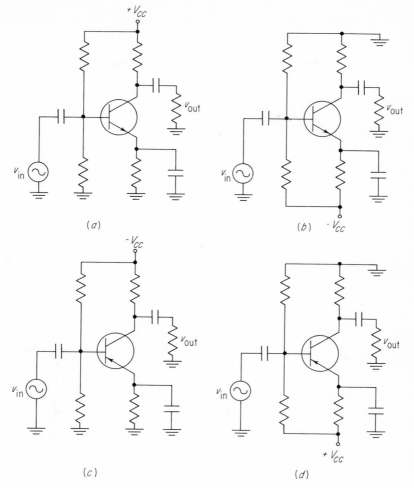

(a)

(b)

(c)

(d)

Fig. 10-27 Moving the ground point.

is, the largest unclipped signal that we can get from a transistor amplifier. Recall that clipping occurs at the saturation point and at the cutoff point on the a-c load line. As we saw in Chap. 8, the largest peak-to-peak unclipped signal is $2V_{CE}$ or $2I_C r_L$, whichever is smaller.

In this present chapter, we have discussed a number of different biasing arrangements and their use in CE, CC, and CB circuits. The a-c load-line analysis of these circuits is essentially the same as the a-c load-line analysis of Chap. 8. In other words, the a-c load line passes through the d-c operating point (V_{CE}, I_C) and has a cutoff voltage of $V_{CE} + I_C r_L$.

Thus, the maximum peak-to-peak unclipped signal that we can get is

$$V_{\text{p-p}} = 2V_{CE} \qquad\qquad (10\text{-}22)$$

or

$$V_{\text{p-p}} = 2I_C r_L \qquad\qquad (10\text{-}23)$$

whichever is smaller. In applying these formulas, remember that:

V_{CE} is the d-c collector-emitter voltage.
I_C is the d-c collector current.
r_L is the a-c load resistance seen by the output terminal of the transistor.

Equations (10-22) and (10-23) can be used to find the largest unclipped signal available from a transistor amplifier. The only exception worth mentioning is Fig. 10-10, where some of the emitter resistance is left unbypassed to get a stable voltage gain. Analysis shows that the largest unclipped signal for the circuits of Fig. 10-10 is the smaller of

$$V_{\text{p-p}} = 2I_C r_L \qquad\qquad (10\text{-}24)$$

and

$$V_{\text{p-p}} = 2V_{CE}\frac{1}{1 + r_E/r_L} \cong 2V_{CE} \qquad \text{for } r_E \ll r_L \qquad (10\text{-}25)$$

In most practical circuits, r_E is much smaller than r_L (otherwise, the voltage gain is very low). Thus, for a first approximation, we can say that all circuits in this chapter can deliver a maximum unclipped signal of $2I_C r_L$ or $2V_{CE}$, whichever is smaller.

EXAMPLE 10-14

The circuit of Fig. 10-7a was analyzed earlier in Example 10-1, where we found that $I_C = 0.5$ ma and $V_{CE} = 5$ volts (this was for a β of 50). Find the maximum signal-handling capability of the circuit in Fig. 10-7a.

SOLUTION

Equations (10-22) and (10-23) apply.

$$2I_C r_L = 2(0.5)(10^{-3})(5)(10^3) = 5 \text{ volts}$$

and

$$2V_{CE} = 2(5) = 10 \text{ volts}$$

Therefore, the largest unclipped peak-to-peak signal is 5 volts.

EXAMPLE 10-15

The circuit of Fig. 10-9 was analyzed in Example 10-5, where we found that the d-c emitter current equals 2 ma. Find the maximum signal-handling capability of this circuit.

SOLUTION

Referring to Fig. 10-9, we see that a d-c emitter current of 2 ma will produce a d-c voltage from the emitter to ground of

$$V_E = I_E R_E = 2(10^{-3})(5)(10^3) = 10 \text{ volts}$$

Further, the d-c collector current is approximately equal to the value of emitter current, so that the d-c collector-ground voltage is

$$V_C = V_{CC} - I_C R_L = 30 - 2(10^{-3})(5)(10^3) = 20 \text{ volts}$$

The d-c voltage from collector to emitter is

$$V_{CE} = V_C - V_E = 20 - 10 = 10 \text{ volts}$$

Thus, the d-c operating point is $V_{CE} = 10$ volts, $I_C = 2$ ma.

Now we can find the maximum signal-handling capability. Using Eqs. (10-22) and (10-23), we get

$$2I_C r_L = 2(0.002)(5000 \| 50,000) \cong 18 \text{ volts}$$

and

$$2V_{CE} = 2(10) = 20 \text{ volts}$$

The smaller value is the limitation, so that the circuit of Fig. 10-9 can deliver a maximum unclipped signal of 18 volts peak to peak.

EXAMPLE 10-16

Find the maximum unclipped signal available from the circuit of Fig. 10-13a. This circuit was analyzed in Example 10-6, where we found that $I_C = 1$ ma for a β of 100.

SOLUTION

First, find V_{CE}. With 1 ma of d-c collector current, the d-c voltage from collector to ground must be

$$V_C = V_{CC} - I_C R_L = 40 - 0.001(10,000) = 30 \text{ volts}$$

and the d-c voltage from emitter to ground must be

$$V_E = I_E R_E = 0.001(10,000) = 10 \text{ volts}$$

Therefore, the d-c voltage from collector to emitter is

$$V_{CE} = V_C - V_E = 30 - 10 = 20 \text{ volts}$$

The largest unclipped signal is the smaller of $2I_C r_L$ and $2V_{CE}$.

$$2I_C r_L = 2(0.001)(10,000 \| 30,000) = 15 \text{ volts}$$
$$2V_{CE} = 2(20) = 40 \text{ volts}$$

Therefore, the largest unclipped signal that we can get from the amplifier of Fig. 10-13a is 15 volts peak to peak.

EXAMPLE 10-17

What is the signal-handling capability of the circuit in Fig. 10-16b?

SOLUTION

This is an emitter follower using two-supply emitter bias. By inspection, almost all the emitter supply voltage is dropped across the 20-kilohm resistor, so that the d-c collector current is

$$I_C \cong \frac{V_{EE}}{R_E} = \frac{20}{20,000} = 1 \text{ ma}$$

We already know that in an emitter follower the d-c voltage from the collector to the emitter is approximately equal to the collector-ground voltage. Therefore, in Fig. 10-16b, $V_{CE} \cong 20$ volts.

Now, we calculate the maximum signal-handling capability using Eqs. (10-22) and (10-23).

$$2I_C r_L = 2(0.001)(20,000\|50) = 0.1 \text{ volt}$$

and

$$2V_{CE} = 2(20) = 40 \text{ volts}$$

Therefore, the circuit of Fig. 10-16b can only deliver a peak-to-peak voltage of 0.1 volt.

EXAMPLE 10-18

Find the largest unclipped signal available from the circuit of Fig. 10-19.

SOLUTION

By inspection, this is a single-supply emitter-biased arrangement. The d-c voltage from base to ground is about -10 volts. Almost all this voltage appears across the 20-kilohm emitter resistor, so that the d-c emitter current is about 0.5 ma.

The magnitude of V_{CE} is clearly 15 volts, since 5 volts is dropped across the 10-kilohm collector resistor and 10 volts is dropped across the 20-kilohm emitter resistor.

Thus,

$$2I_C r_L = 2(0.5)(10^{-3})(5)(10^3) = 5 \text{ volts}$$

and

$$2V_{CE} = 2(15) = 30 \text{ volts}$$

The maximum unclipped signal that can be delivered to the output is therefore 5 volts peak to peak.

SUMMARY

We have discussed CE, CC, and CB operation of the various bias arrange-ments of Chap. 9. A circuit arrangement is classified as CE, CC, or CB by determining which of the transistor terminals is at a-c ground.

For all CE circuits discussed in this chapter, the a-c voltage gain equals r_L/r'_e. The amplified signal at the collector is 180° out of phase with the input signal at the base.

The CE circuit can be stabilized by leaving some of the emitter resist-ance unbypassed. In this case, the circuit behaves like a combination of an emitter follower and a CB amplifier. The voltage gain is r_L/r_E, where r_E is the unbypassed part of the emitter resistance.

The CC circuit normally has a voltage gain of close to unity. The out-put signal appearing at the emitter is in phase with the input signal at the base. The main advantage of an emitter follower is to increase the load resistance by a factor of β.

The CB circuit has its base at a-c ground. The output signal at the collector is in phase with the input signal at the emitter. The voltage gain of a CB circuit is r_L/r'_e, the same as that for a CE circuit.

In stabilizing the source-output voltage gain of a CE circuit, the usual practice is to make the input resistance of the amplifier much larger than the source resistance. In addition, emitter feedback is used to fix the voltage gain from base to collector.

To stabilize the source-output voltage gain of a CB circuit, we deliber-ately make the source resistance much greater than r'_e, the input resistance of the CB amplifier. Under this condition, the voltage gain becomes r_L/r_s.

The source-output voltage gain of a CC circuit is stabilized by making the input resistance much larger than the source resistance. Under this condition, the overall voltage gain approximately equals unity.

GLOSSARY

a-c ground   A point that is either connected directly to ground or by-passed to ground through a capacitor.

biasing resistors   All resistors in the d-c equivalent circuit that set the d-c collector current.

degeneration   Synonymous with negative feedback. In this chapter, degeneration refers to the use of an unbypassed emitter resistance.

stabilizing   With respect to voltage gain, this means fixing the voltage gain at some constant value, so that changes in the transistor have no effect.

swamping   With respect to the emitter diode, this means making value of r'_e negligible as far as voltage gain is concerned.

REVIEW QUESTIONS

1. A CE circuit is also called a grounded-emitter circuit. Why?
2. Why are coupling capacitors used?
3. What is the input resistance looking directly into the base of a CE circuit whose emitter is at a-c ground?
4. In a CE circuit in which there is a biasing resistor R_B connected from collector back to base, what is the effective value of this resistance when viewed from the source?
5. A CE amplifier can be modified by leaving some of the emitter resistance unbypassed. What is the approximate voltage gain in this case? What should the relation between r_E and r'_e be to ensure that stable gain?
6. What is the main advantage of an emitter follower?
7. What condition must be satisfied if the emitter follower is to have a voltage gain of almost unity?
8. In a CB circuit, what is the approximate voltage gain from emitter to collector? If the source resistance driving the CB circuit is much larger than r'_e, what is the approximate voltage gain from source to collector?
9. To a first approximation, the voltage gains of the CE and CB circuits are the same. Why is the CE circuit more commonly used?
10. What effect does source resistance have upon the amount of signal actually reaching the input of the amplifier circuit? What relation must exist between the source resistance and the amplifier input resistance if almost all the source signal is to reach the amplifier input terminals?
11. To stabilize the voltage gain from source to output in a CB circuit, should r_s be much larger or much smaller than r_{in}? What should the relation be in a CE circuit?

PROBLEMS

10-1   In Fig. 10-28a, find the voltage gain and the value of v_{out}. Use a β of 50 and an r'_e of 50 mv/I_E.

10-2   Repeat Prob. 10-1 using a β of 150.

10-3   Find the voltage gain in Fig. 10-28b. Use an r'_e between 25 and 50 mv/I_E. Also find the input resistance of the entire stage.

10-4   The transistor in Fig. 10-28c has an $r'_e = 25$ mv/I_E. What is the minimum and maximum voltage gain for this amplifier?

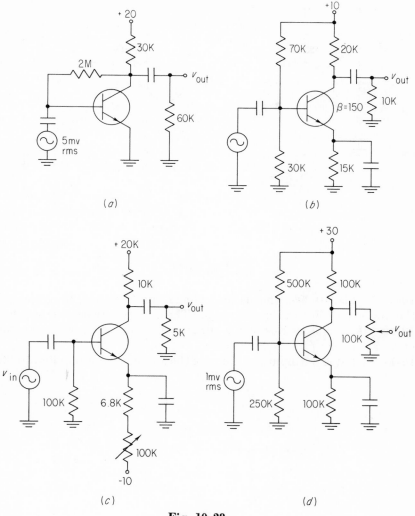

Fig. 10-28

10-5 What are the minimum and maximum values of v_{out} in Fig. 10-28d? Use an r'_e of 25 mv/I_E.

10-6 If $v_{in} = 500$ μv rms in Fig. 10-29a, what is the approximate value of v_{out}? What is the input resistance of the stage for a $β$ of 100?

10-7 If the voltage gain in Fig. 10-29a is to be 15, what size should r_E be?

10-8 In Fig. 10-29a, if $v_{in} = 2$ mv rms, what is the approximate value of the a-c voltage from emitter to ground?

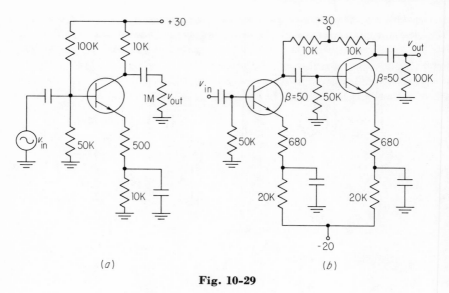

(a)   (b)

Fig. 10-29

10-9   In Fig. 10-29b, what is the voltage gain from base to collector for the first stage? For the second stage? The β of each transistor equals 50.
10-10   If $v_{in} = 5$ μv rms in Fig. 10-29b, what is the approximate value of v_{out}?
10-11   What is the input resistance of the amplifier shown in Fig. 10-30a?

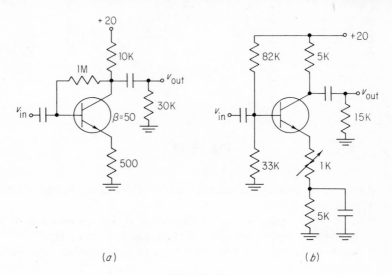

(a)   (b)

Fig. 10-30

10-12 In Fig. 10-30b, the value of r_E is adjustable from 0 to 1 kilohm. What is the minimum possible voltage gain (use $r'_e = 25$ mv/I_E).

10-13 The transistor in Fig. 10-30b has a β between 50 and 200. What is the highest possible input resistance for the entire circuit? What is the lowest possible input resistance (use $r'_e = 25$ mv/I_E)?

10-14 In Fig. 10-31a, what is the input resistance of the stage?

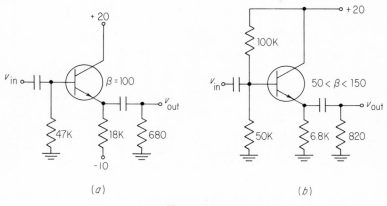

(a) (b)

Fig. 10-31

10-15 In Fig. 10-31b, what are the minimum and maximum values of input resistance of the stage?

10-16 In Fig. 10-32a, the input voltage is 3 mv rms. Find the approximate output voltage for an $r'_e = 25/I_E$.

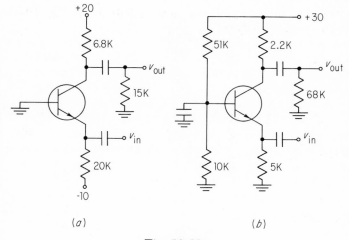

(a) (b)

Fig. 10-32

10-17   In Fig. 10-32b, the value of $v_{\text{in}} = 3$ mv rms. Find v_{out} for an $r'_e = 25$ mv$/I_E$ and for $r'_e = 50$ mv$/I_E$.

10-18   The transistor of Fig. 10-33a has a β between 30 and 100. What is the approximate value of v_{out}?

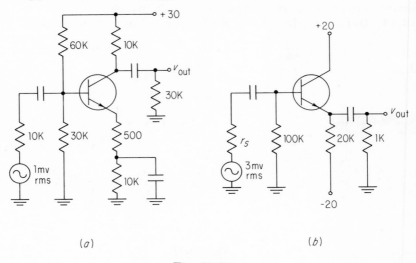

(a)   (b)

Fig. 10-33

10-19   In Fig. 10-33b, the transistor has a β between 40 and 120. What is the approximate output voltage for:

(a) An r_s of 600 ohms.

(b) An r_s of 30 kilohms.

10-20   What is the approximate output voltage in Fig. 10-34a for an input of 10 mv rms? Neglect r'_e.

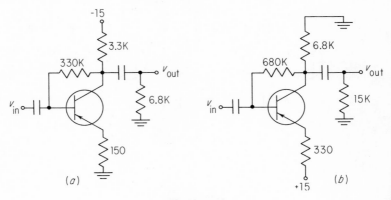

(a)   (b)

Fig. 10-34

10-21 In Fig. 10-34*b*, v_{in} is 5 mv rms. What is the approximate value of v_{out}?

10-22 What is the approximate output voltage in Fig. 10-35*a* for an input voltage of 200 μv rms?

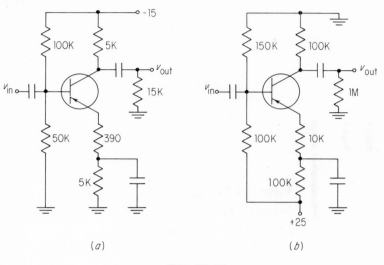

(*a*)   (*b*)

Fig. 10-35

10-23 If the input voltage in Fig. 10-35*b* is 500 μv rms, what is the approximate output voltage?

11 | Cascading Stages

Up to now, we have analyzed a number of basic transistor circuits. We have discussed the biasing problem, that is, setting the d-c operating point. Also, we have worked out the formulas for the a-c voltage gain of typical circuits.

However, we have confined our discussion to single stages. Now we want to turn our attention to the problem of cascading stages, that is, connecting the output of one transistor circuit to the input of another.

11-1 *RC* Coupling

The easiest and most widely used method of cascading stages is resistance-capacitance (*RC*) coupling. In this approach, the voltage developed across a resistance in one stage is coupled through a capacitor into the next stage. To make the discussion concrete, consider the two-stage *RC*-coupled amplifier shown in Fig. 11-1. A coupling capacitor is connected from the collector of the first transistor to the base of the second transistor. The purpose of this coupling capacitor is to appear as an open circuit to d-c voltage but as a short circuit to a-c voltage. As a result, there is no d-c interaction between stages; that is, the d-c voltage of the first stage does not disturb the d-c operating point of the second stage. On the other hand, any a-c voltage at the collector of the first transistor is coupled directly into the base of the second transistor. Thus, with this two-stage circuit, an a-c signal is amplified by both transistor stages.

Let us find the overall voltage gain of the two-stage amplifier shown in Fig. 11-1. First, note that the d-c voltage from the base to ground

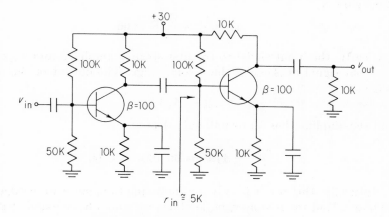

Fig. 11-1 *RC*-coupled amplifier.

in the second stage is about 10 volts. This will produce about 1 ma of d-c emitter current in the second transistor. The r'_e is therefore in the range of 25 to 50 ohms. Arbitrarily, we will use 50 ohms. The voltage gain of the second stage is

$$A_2 \cong \frac{r_L}{r'_e} = \frac{10,000\|10,000}{50} = 100$$

To find the voltage gain of the first stage, we must find the a-c load resistance r_L seen by the collector of the first stage. It is clear that looking out from the collector there is a 10-kilohm resistance in parallel with the input resistance of the second stage. As shown in Fig. 11-1, the r_{in} of the second stage is approximately 5 kilohms. This is found by the methods of Chap. 10; that is, we know that the input resistance of such a stage is

$$r_{in} = R_1\|R_2\|\beta r'_e = 100(10^3)\|50(10^3)\|100(50) \cong 5 \text{ kilohms}$$

(We are neglecting the effects of R_1 and R_2 because they are large compared to the 5 kilohms looking directly into the base of the second transistor.)

Here is an important point to remember. *The 5 kilohms looking into the second stage is part of the load seen by the first stage.* In other words, the first stage sees a load resistance of

$$r_L = 10(10^3)\|5(10^3) \cong 3.3 \text{ kilohms}$$

Now we can find the voltage gain of the first stage. There is also about 1 ma of d-c emitter current in the first stage, so that r'_e is in the range of 25 to 50 ohms. Again, we will use the upper limit of 50 ohms. The first-stage gain is

$$A_1 = \frac{r_L}{r'_e} = \frac{3300}{50} \cong 66$$

Clearly, the input signal to the first stage is amplified and appears as an input signal of $A_1 v_{\text{in}}$ to the second stage. The output of the second stage is

$$v_{\text{out}} = A_1 A_2 v_{\text{in}}$$

and the amplifier has an overall gain A of

$$\frac{v_{\text{out}}}{v_{\text{in}}} = A_1 A_2 = 66(100) = 6600$$

Naturally, this result is only an approximation, since we used an r'_e of 50 ohms. Had we used an r'_e of 25 ohms, we would have found that

$$A_1 = 80 \qquad A_2 = 200 \qquad \text{and} \qquad A = 16,000$$

Thus, the two-stage amplifier of Fig. 11-1 has a voltage gain in the range of 6600 to 16,000 for a β of 100 and an r'_e between 25 and 50 ohms.

Suppose that the β of the transistors were 50 instead of 100. How would this affect the voltage gain? Let us use an r'_e of 50 ohms for convenience. The voltage gain of the second stage is

$$A_2 = \frac{r_L}{r'_e} = \frac{10,000\|10,000}{50} = 100$$

Looking directly into the base of the second stage, we see

$$r_{\text{in(base)}} = \beta r'_e = 50(50) = 2500$$

Again, we can neglect R_1 and R_2, so that the input resistance of the second stage is approximately 2500 ohms.

The collector of the first stage sees 10 kilohms in parallel with the 2500-ohms input resistance of the second stage. Therefore, the voltage gain of the first stage is

$$A_1 = \frac{r_L}{r'_e} = \frac{10,000\|2500}{50} = 40$$

The overall voltage gain is

$$A = A_1A_2 = 40(100) = 4000$$

Thus, we have seen that for r_e' between 25 and 50 ohms and β between 50 and 100, the two-stage amplifier has a voltage gain between 4000 and 16,000.

The β and r_e' change significantly with temperature and with transistor replacement. Therefore, a two-stage amplifier like that of Fig. 11-1 is usable only in those situations where large variations in voltage gain are tolerable.

The voltage gain of the two-stage amplifier can be stabilized to some extent by using emitter feedback. For instance, suppose we add a 500-ohm resistor to each emitter, as shown in Fig. 11-2. Now the voltage gain of

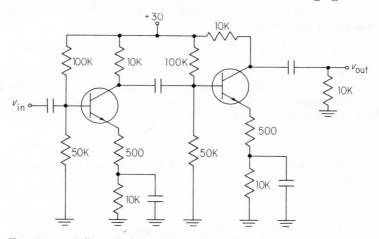

Fig. 11-2 *RC*-coupled amplifier with emitter feedback.

each stage is relatively free of the changes in r_e' since it has been swamped by the 500-ohm resistor in each emitter. The voltage gain of each stage is now given by

$$\frac{r_L}{r_E + r_e'} \cong \frac{r_L}{r_E} \qquad \text{for } r_E \gg r_e'$$

Thus, the voltage gain of the second stage is

$$A_2 \cong \frac{r_L}{r_E} = \frac{5000}{500} = 10$$

The input resistance of the second stage still is a function of β. When $\beta = 50$, we get

$$r_{\text{in(base)}} \cong \beta r_E = 50(500) = 25 \text{ kilohms}$$

The input resistance of the second stage is

$$r_{in} = R_1 \| R_2 \| r_{in(base)} = 100(10^3) \| 50(10^3) \| 25(10^3) = 14.3 \text{ kilohms}$$

The a-c load resistance seen by the first collector is

$$r_L = R_L \| r_{in} = 10(10^3) \| 14.3(10^3) \cong 5.9 \text{ kilohms}$$

and therefore the first-stage voltage gain is

$$A_1 \cong \frac{r_L}{r_E} = \frac{5900}{500} = 11.8$$

The overall voltage gain is

$$A = A_1 A_2 = 11.8(10) = 118$$

Remember this result is based on a β of 50. If we had used a β of 100, we would have found that

$$A_1 = 13.3 \qquad A_2 = 10 \qquad \text{and} \qquad A = 133$$

Thus, we have seen that with no feedback the overall voltage gain is in the range of 4000 to 16,000 for a $2:1$ spread in β and r'_e. With 500-ohm emitter feedback resistors, the voltage gain is in the range of 118 to 133 for the same spreads in β and r'_e.

EXAMPLE 11-1

Find the overall voltage gain and the input resistance of the three-stage amplifier of Fig. 11-3. Use a β of 100.

SOLUTION

The voltage gain of the third stage is

$$A_3 \cong \frac{r_L}{r_E} = \frac{10,000}{1000} = 10$$

and the input resistance of this stage is

$$r_{in} = \frac{R_B}{A_3} \| \beta r_E = \frac{10^6}{10} \| 100(10^3) = 50 \text{ kilohms}$$

The a-c load resistance seen by the collector of the second stage is

$$r_L = R_L \| r_{in} = 10(10^3) \| 50(10^3) = 8.33 \text{ kilohms}$$

Therefore, the voltage gain of the second stage is

$$A_2 \cong \frac{r_L}{r_E} = \frac{8330}{1000} = 8.33$$

and the input resistance of this stage is

$$r_{in} = \frac{R_B}{A_2} \| \beta r_E = \frac{10^6}{8.33} \| 100(10^3) = 54.5 \text{ kilohms}$$

The a-c load resistance seen by the collector of the first stage is

$$r_L = 10(10^3) \| 54.5(10^3) = 8.45 \text{ kilohms}$$

Therefore, the voltage gain of the first stage is

$$A_1 = \frac{8450}{1000} = 8.45$$

The overall voltage gain of the amplifier is

$$A = A_1 A_2 A_3 = 8.45(8.33)10 \cong 700$$

The input resistance of the three-stage amplifier is equal to the input resistance of the first stage.

$$r_{in} = \frac{R_B}{A_1} \| \beta r_E = \frac{10^6}{8.45} \| 100(10^3) \cong 54 \text{ kilohms}$$

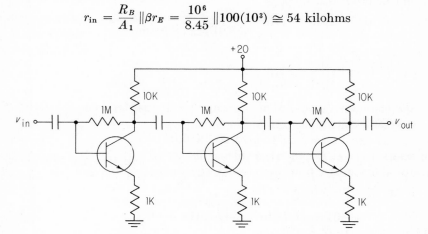

Fig. 11-3 Examples 11-1 and 11-2.

EXAMPLE 11-2

Suppose that the β is 50 instead of 100 in the three-stage amplifier of Fig. 11-3. What is the overall voltage gain and input resistance?

SOLUTION

The gain of the third stage still equals

$$A_3 \cong \frac{10,000}{1000} = 10$$

The input resistance, however, is lower.

$$r_{in} = \frac{10^6}{10} \,\|\, 50(10^3) = 33.3 \text{ kilohms}$$

The voltage gain of the second stage is now

$$A_2 = \frac{10(10^3)\,\|\,33.3(10^3)}{1000} \cong 7.7$$

and its input resistance is

$$r_{in} = \frac{10^6}{7.7} \,\|\, 50(10^3) = 36 \text{ kilohms}$$

The voltage gain of the first stage is

$$A_1 = \frac{10(10^3)\,\|\,36(10^3)}{1000} \cong 7.8$$

and its input resistance is

$$r_{in} = \frac{10^6}{7.8} \,\|\, 50(10^3) \cong 36 \text{ kilohms}$$

The overall gain is

$$A = A_1 A_2 A_3 = 7.8(7.7)(10) = 600$$

and the input resistance of the amplifier equals the input resistance of the first stage:

$$r_{in} = 36 \text{ kilohms}$$

Thus, we have seen that for β between 50 and 100, the three-stage amplifier of Fig. 11-3 has a voltage gain between 600 and 700, and an input resistance between 36 and 54 kilohms.

11-2 Two-stage Feedback

Up to this point, we have discussed single-stage feedback in the form of an unbypassed emitter resistor. It is also possible to use feedback around two stages. The most widely used two-stage feedback arrangement is shown in Fig. 11-4. The basic idea behind this amplifier is the following. The input signal v_{in} is amplified and inverted in the first stage. The output of the first stage is amplified and inverted again by the second stage. A portion of this second-stage output is fed back to the first stage via the voltage divider formed by r_F and r_E. This return signal v_F is applied to the emitter of the first stage, *thereby reducing the base-emitter a-c voltage of the first transistor*. In other words, we have negative feedback.

Most of us already know that negative feedback reduces the overall voltage gain. The resulting voltage gain is more stable than the gain without feedback. To understand why this is so, suppose that for some reason the β of the second stage becomes larger. The output signal will then try to increase; however, more signal will be fed back to the emitter of the first transistor, thereby reducing the base-emitter a-c voltage. This results in less output voltage from the first stage, which partially offsets the β increase in the second stage.

Similarly, if the output voltage of the second transistor tries to become smaller, less signal is fed back to the first stage, so that the output voltage of the first stage becomes larger. This will partially offset the original change in output voltage.

To find out how effective the feedback is in stabilizing the voltage gain, we must first discuss the *error voltage*. Note in Fig. 11-4 that the a-c

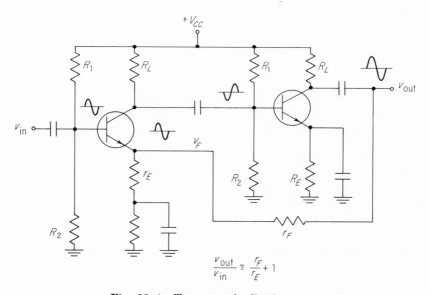

$$\frac{V_{out}}{V_{in}} \cong \frac{r_F}{r_E} + 1$$

Fig. 11-4 Two-stage feedback.

voltage at the base of the first transistor is v_{in} and that the a-c voltage at the emitter is v_F. The error voltage is simply the difference of these two voltages, that is,

$$v_{error} = v_{in} - v_F$$

This is the a-c voltage actually applied to the base-emitter terminals of the first transistor.

The error voltage is amplified by the first transistor to produce a collector signal of

$$v_{c1} = A_1 v_{\text{error}} = A_1(v_{\text{in}} - v_F)$$

where A_1 is the voltage gain of the first stage, r_L/r_e'.

The voltage out of the first stage is amplified by the second stage to produce a final output voltage of

$$v_{\text{out}} = A_1 A_2(v_{\text{in}} - v_F)$$

where A_2 is the voltage gain of the second stage, r_L/r_e'.

We can rearrange this equation to get

$$v_{\text{in}} - v_F = \frac{v_{\text{out}}}{A_1 A_2}$$

Note that $A_1 A_2$ is the product of the individual stage gains. Normally, this product is quite high, so that to a first approximation the right-hand side of the last equation is almost zero. That is,

$$v_{\text{in}} - v_F \cong 0$$

or

$$v_{\text{in}} \cong v_F$$

In other words, in a good feedback arrangement, the product of A_1 and A_2 is large enough for the error voltage to approach zero. This is equivalent to saying that the feedback voltage v_F is almost equal to the input voltage v_{in}.

To find an approximate formula for the voltage gain of Fig. 11-4, note that the output voltage is applied to a voltage divider consisting of r_E and r_F. Thus, to a first approximation

$$v_F \cong \frac{r_E}{r_F + r_E} v_{\text{out}}$$

We showed earlier that $v_{\text{in}} \cong v_F$. Therefore, we can rewrite the last equation as

$$v_{\text{in}} \cong \frac{r_E}{r_F + r_E} v_{\text{out}}$$

or

$$\frac{v_{\text{out}}}{v_{\text{in}}} \cong \frac{r_F + r_E}{r_E} = \frac{r_F}{r_E} + 1 \cong \frac{r_F}{r_E}$$

or

$$\frac{v_{\text{out}}}{v_{\text{in}}} \cong \frac{r_F}{r_E} \qquad \text{for } \frac{r_F}{r_E} \gg 1 \tag{11-1}$$

Equation (11-1) *is quite important.* It tells us that the voltage gain of the two-stage amplifier of Fig. 11-4 is essentially equal to the ratio of the feedback resistor r_F to the emitter resistor r_E. Since β and r_e' do not appear in this equation, we conclude that the amplifier gain is independent of the transistor characteristics. Thus, we have a voltage gain that is free of variations caused by temperature and transistor replacement.

Admittedly, the derivation of Eq. (11-1) was only an approximation. Still, in any well-designed two-stage feedback amplifier, Eq. (11-1) is quite accurate. If we were to make a more rigorous derivation, we would obtain this expression for the voltage gain:

$$A_{fb} = \frac{v_{out}}{v_{in}} = \left(\frac{r_F}{r_E} + 1\right) \frac{1}{1 + r_F/Ar_e' + (r_F + r_E)/Ar_E} \qquad (11\text{-}2)$$

where A_{fb} is the voltage gain with feedback, v_{out}/v_{in}

A is the product of stage gains, that is, A_1A_2

r_e' is the emitter junction resistance, 25 mv/I_E

An examination of Eq. (11-2) shows that the voltage gain depends upon r_e' and A. But the whole point of feedback is to swamp these quantities, that is, make them unimportant in determining the voltage gain. Therefore, by deliberate design we can make

$$\frac{r_F}{Ar_e'} \ll 1 \qquad \text{and} \qquad \frac{r_F + r_E}{Ar_E} \ll 1$$

In Eq. (11-2), note that when these inequalities are satisfied, the equation reduces to

$$A_{fb} \cong \frac{r_F}{r_E} + 1$$

This is precisely what is done in any good two-stage feedback amplifier; the inequalities are deliberately satisfied to make the voltage gain essentially independent of the transistor characteristics.

We can also show with a careful derivation that the input resistance looking into the base of the first transistor is

$$r_{in(base)} = \beta r_e' \left[1 + \frac{r_E}{r_F + r_E}\left(\frac{r_F}{r_e'} + A\right)\right] \qquad (11\text{-}3)$$

Again, we note that in a well-designed feedback amplifier the aforementioned inequalities are satisfied, so that Eq. (11-3) reduces to

$$r_{in(base)} \cong \frac{A}{A_{fb}} \beta r_e'$$

This last equation tells us that the input resistance looking into the base of the first transistor equals $\beta r_e'$ multiplied by A/A_{fb}. For instance suppose that the voltage gain A is

$$A = A_1A_2 = 10{,}000$$

and that the voltage gain with feedback is

$$A_{fb} = 100$$

Then $A/A_{fb} = 10,000/100 = 100$. Therefore, the input resistance is 100 times greater than $\beta r'_e$.

Let us summarize the important results of this section. For the two-stage feedback amplifier of Fig. 11-4:

1. $A = A_1 A_2$, where A_1 and A_2 are found by using the r_L/r'_e for each stage.

2. The necessary approximation conditions are

$$A \gg \frac{r_F}{r'_e} \qquad \text{and} \qquad A \gg A_{fb}$$

3. The voltage gain is

$$A_{fb} \cong \frac{r_F}{r_E} + 1 \cong \frac{r_F}{r_E} \qquad \text{for } r_F \gg r_E$$

4. The input resistance looking into the base is

$$r_{\text{in(base)}} \cong \frac{A}{A_{fb}} \beta r'_e$$

EXAMPLE 11-3

Suppose that the amplifier of Fig. 11-4 has an r_F of 10 kilohms and an r_E of 100 ohms. Find the approximate voltage gain.

SOLUTION

The voltage gain is the ratio of the feedback resistor to the emitter resistor.

$$A_{fb} \cong \frac{r_F}{r_E} = \frac{10,000}{100} = 100$$

EXAMPLE 11-4

Find the voltage gain and input resistance looking into the base of the first transistor in Fig. 11-5.

SOLUTION

$$A_{fb} \cong \frac{r_F}{r_E} = \frac{35,000}{250} = 140$$

The input resistance looking into the base is

$$r_{\text{in(base)}} = \frac{A}{A_{fb}} \beta r'_e$$

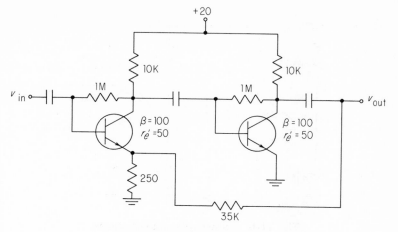

Fig. 11-5 Example 11-4.

We need to find A_1 and A_2.

$$A_2 \cong \frac{r_L}{r'_e} \cong \frac{10(10^3)\|35(10^3)}{50} = 155$$

and

$$A_1 \cong \frac{r_L}{r'_e} = \frac{10(10^3)\|10^6/155\|5(10^3)}{50} = 44$$

Therefore,

$$A = A_1 A_2 = 44(155) = 6820$$

and

$$r_{\text{in(base)}} = \frac{6820}{140}(100)(50) = 244 \text{ kilohms}$$

11-3 Inductive Coupling

Occasionally, transistor stages will use an inductor in the place of a resistor in the collector. Figure 11-6 illustrates a two-stage amplifier of this type. The analysis of such an amplifier is straightforward. First, note that such an amplifier is inherently a high-pass amplifier; that is, it is intended to amplify frequencies that are high enough for the inductors to appear as open circuits. In this case, the a-c load seen by the collector of the first stage is simply the input resistance of the second stage (the inductor looks open). The a-c load resistance seen by the second collector is simply 10 kilohms.

Let us find the voltage gain of the amplifier shown in Fig. 11-6. As already indicated, this amplifier is intended to operate at frequencies high

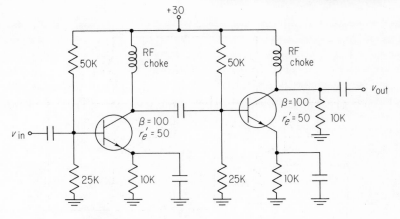

Fig. 11-6 Inductively coupled stages.

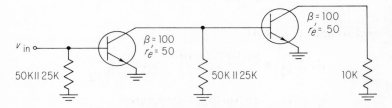

Fig. 11-7 A-c equivalent circuit.

enough for the inductors to look open. In this case, we can draw the a-c equivalent circuit as shown in Fig. 11-7. The voltage gain of the second stage is

$$A_2 = \frac{r_L}{r_e'} = \frac{10,000}{50} = 200$$

The a-c load resistance seen by the collector of the first stage is

$$r_L = R_1\|R_2\|\beta r_e' = 50(10^3)\|25(10^3)\|100(50) = 3.85 \text{ kilohms}$$

and the voltage gain of the first stage is

$$A_1 = \frac{r_L}{r_e'} = \frac{3850}{50} = 77$$

Therefore, the overall voltage gain is

$$A = A_1 A_2 = 77(200) = 15,400$$

The amplifier of Fig. 11-6 has limited use since it inherently has a high-pass filter response. Note that as the frequency is reduced, the reactance of the inductors eventually becomes so small that the inductors appear almost as short circuits. In this case, the circuit no longer amplifies.

EXAMPLE 11-5

Find the d-c voltage from collector to ground in the stages of Fig. 11-6. The r-f chokes have 10 ohms of d-c resistance.

SOLUTION

For practical purposes, the d-c resistance of the chokes is so small that there is a negligible d-c voltage drop across them. Therefore, almost all the 30 volts from the supply appears at the collector of each transistor.

Actually, there is a small d-c voltage drop across each choke. By inspection, the voltage divider in each base circuit develops about 10 volts with respect to ground. This sets up about 1 ma of d-c emitter current. In turn, the d-c collector current is about 1 ma, and this produces a d-c voltage drop of about 10 mv across the 10 ohms of resistance in each coil. Therefore, the d-c collector voltage is actually 10 mv less than 30 volts.

EXAMPLE 11-6

Suppose that the inductor in the second stage of Fig. 11-6 has an $L = 10$ mh. Find the frequency where the inductive reactance just equals 10 kilohms.

SOLUTION

$$X_L = 2\pi f L$$

or

$$f = \frac{10,000}{2\pi 10^{-2}} = 159 \text{ kHz}$$

This means that at 159 kHz (kilocycles) the reactance of the choke is too low to neglect. The a-c load seen by the collector of the second stage is 10 kilohms of inductive reactance in parallel with the 10-kilohm load resistance. Normally, the amplifier should be operated at a much higher frequency, so that the inductive reactance is much larger than the 10-kilohm load resistor.

11-4 Transformer Coupling

Sometimes, a load resistance is so small that voltage gain is impossible. For instance, consider the circuit of Fig. 11-8. The a-c load seen by the

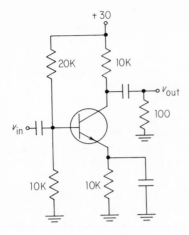

Fig. 11-8 Loading down a stage.

collector is 10 kilohms in parallel with 100 ohms, which is essentially 100 ohms.

There is about 1 ma of d-c emitter current, so that r'_e is in the range of 25 to 50 ohms. This means that the voltage gain r_L/r'_e will be very low, around 2 to 4. In addition, we know from Chap. 10 that the maximum peak-to-peak signal that can be obtained before clipping occurs is approximately $2V_{CE}$ or $2I_Cr_L$, whichever is smaller. In this case, $2I_Cr_L$ is smaller, so that the maximum peak-to-peak unclipped signal is

$$V_{\text{p-p}} = 2I_Cr_L = 2(0.001)(100) = 0.2 \text{ volts}$$

We can use a transformer in this situation like this to improve the voltage gain and the signal-handling capability. For instance, suppose we add a 10:1 transformer to the circuit, as illustrated in Fig. 11-9a. We are using an ideal transformer to simplify the analysis. Recall that for an ideal transformer whose primary-to-secondary turns ratio equals n, the impedance looking into the primary is n^2 times the load on the secondary.

In Fig. 11-9a, the load on the secondary is 100 ohms; therefore, looking into the primary there is a resistance of

$$r_L = n^2R = 10^2(100) = 10 \text{ kilohms}$$

The a-c equivalent circuit of the transistor stage is given in Fig. 11-9b. As already indicated, r'_e is in the range of 25 to 50 ohms, so that we have a voltage gain between 200 and 400. This is the base-to-collector voltage gain. To find the actual output voltage note that the voltage across the secondary is stepped down by a factor of 10. Thus, the overall voltage gain in Fig. 11-9a is between 20 and 40.

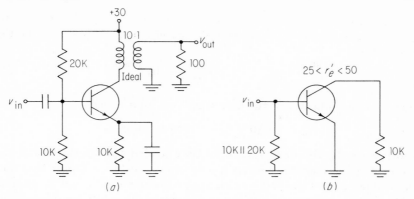

Fig. 11-9   Transformer coupling. (*a*) Circuit; (*b*) transformed collector load.

By using a transformer, we have not only increased the voltage gain, we have also increased the signal-handling capability. At the collector of Fig. 11-9a, the maximum peak-to-peak unclipped signal is

$$V_{\text{p-p}} = 2I_C r_L = 2(0.001)(10,000) = 20 \text{ volts}$$

(Note that $2V_{CE} = 40$ volts, so that $2I_C r_L$ is smaller and therefore is the limiting quantity.) With a 10:1 step-down in voltage, the secondary voltage can be as large as 2 volts peak to peak before clipping occurs.

Another possible use of transformers is in a cascade of CB stages. First, consider the two-stage amplifier of Fig. 11-10. Note that there is about 1 ma of d-c emitter current in each transistor; therefore, the a-c input

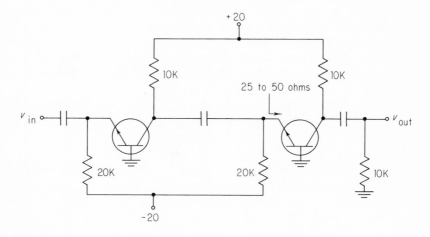

Fig. 11-10   Cascading CB stages.

resistance looking into each emitter is between 25 and 50 ohms. Let us use the upper limit of 50 ohms and compute the voltage gain of the second stage.

$$A_2 = \frac{r_L}{r'_e} = \frac{5000}{50} = 100$$

Note that the collector of the first stage sees an a-c load

$$r_L = 10(10^3)\|20(10^3)\|50 \cong 50 \text{ ohms}$$

In other words, the first stage is heavily loaded by the emitter of the second stage because the emitter has an input resistance of only 50 ohms. The voltage gain of the first stage is approximately unity, that is, no gain.

This is one reason that CB stages are almost never RC-coupled. Some form of impedance transformation must be used between the CB stages to permit a reasonable voltage gain to take place, as well as a higher signal-handling capability.

One way of transforming impedances is to use a transformer between stages, as shown in Fig. 11-11. The voltage gain of the second stage is still 100. The collector of the first stage, however, now sees an a-c load of

$$r_L \cong n^2 r'_e = 10^2(50) = 5 \text{ kilohms}$$

Now the voltage gain from the base to the collector of the first stage is

$$A_1 = \frac{5000}{50} = 100$$

Of course, there is a 10:1 voltage step-down in going from the primary

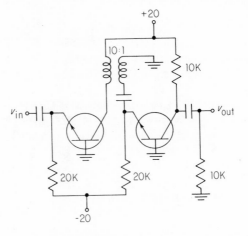

Fig. 11-11   Cascading CB stages with a transformer.

to the secondary, so that the voltage gain from the base of the first stage to the base of the second stage is about $^{100}\!/_{10}$, or 10. The overall voltage gain of the two stages is 1000.

In general, if a CB or CE stage uses a transformer to step up the impedance level, there is an improvement in the voltage gain. In Fig. 11-12, we see that the a-c load looking into the primary is

$$r_L = n^2 R$$

Therefore, the voltage gain of the stage is

$$A = \frac{r_L}{r'_e} = \frac{n^2 R}{r'_e}$$

The voltage is stepped down between the primary and secondary by a factor of n. Therefore, the overall voltage gain is

$$\frac{v_{\text{out}}}{v_{\text{in}}} = \frac{nR}{r'_e} \qquad\qquad (11\text{-}4)$$

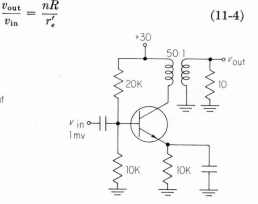

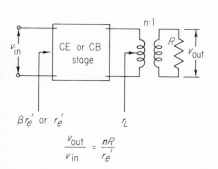

Fig. 11-12 Deriving the voltage gain of a transformer-coupled stage.

Fig. 11-13 Example 11-7.

EXAMPLE 11-7

Find v_{out} in the circuit of Fig. 11-13. Use an r'_e of 25 ohms.

SOLUTION

We get

$$\frac{v_{\text{out}}}{v_{\text{in}}} = \frac{nR}{r'_e} = \frac{50(10)}{25} = 20$$

and

$$v_{\text{out}} = 20(1 \text{ mv}) = 20 \text{ mv}$$

11-5   Tuned Amplifiers

Sometimes, the stages of an amplifier are designed to amplify only a narrow band of frequencies. A way of accomplishing this is shown in Fig. 11-14. The idea here is simple. At resonance, the impedance of each

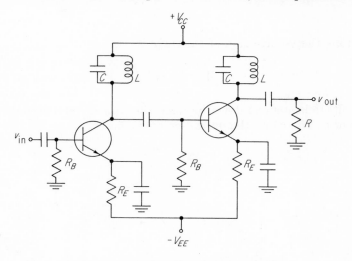

Fig. 11-14   A tuned amplifier.

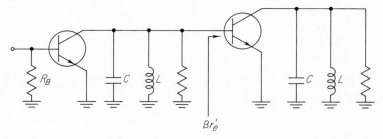

Fig. 11-15   A-c equivalent circuit.

LC tank circuit is high. Above and below the resonant frequency the impedance decreases. Therefore, the voltage gain is maximum at resonance because each collector load is maximum at resonance.

The approximate formula for the resonant frequency is

$$f_0 \cong \frac{1}{2\pi \sqrt{LC}}$$

The 3-db bandwidth of each resonant circuit is

$$\text{BW} = \frac{f_0}{Q}$$

where Q is the ratio of the a-c load resistance to the inductive reactance of the coil. That is,

$$Q = \frac{r_L}{X_L}$$

The a-c equivalent circuit is shown in Fig. 11-15. Each collector works into a parallel LC tank. At resonance, the inductive reactance cancels out the capacitive reactance, leaving a purely resistive load on each collector. Above resonance, the X_C becomes smaller than the X_L; the a-c load seen by the collector is therefore reduced, and this causes the voltage gain to become lower. Similarly, the voltage gain drops off below resonance because the X_L becomes smaller than the X_C.

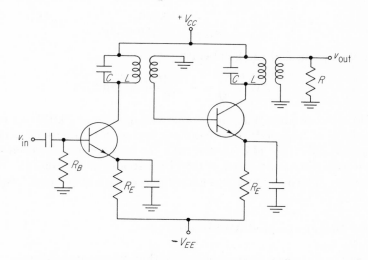

Fig. 11-16   Transformer-coupled tuned stages.

Another tuned amplifier is shown in Fig. 11-16. Again this is a bandpass amplifier. Transformers are used to improve the impedance match between stages. The voltage gain reaches a maximum value at the resonant frequency of the LC tank circuits.

EXAMPLE 11-8

In Fig. 11-14, $L = 100$ μh, and $C = 100$ pf. The a-c load resistance seen by each collector is 10 kilohms, and the r'_e of each transistor is

100 ohms. Find the following:

(a) The resonant frequency.
(b) The voltage gain at resonance.
(c) The bandwidth of each tuned tank circuit.

SOLUTION

(a) The resonant frequency is

$$f_0 \cong \frac{1}{2\pi \sqrt{100(10^{-6})(100)(10^{-12})}} = 1.59 \text{ MHz}$$

(b) The voltage gain at resonance is

$$A = A_1 A_2 = \frac{10{,}000}{100} \frac{10{,}000}{100} = 10{,}000$$

(c) To find the bandwidth, we need the Q.

$$Q = \frac{r_L}{X_L} = \frac{10{,}000}{2\pi(1.59)(10^6)(100)(10^{-6})} = 10$$

Now, we can find the bandwidth.

$$\text{BW} = \frac{f_0}{Q} = \frac{1.59(10^6)}{10} = 159 \text{ kHz}$$

Thus, the amplifier has a maximum voltage gain of 10,000 at a resonant frequency of 1.59 MHz. The bandwidth of each tank circuit is 159 kHz, or about 160 kHz. This means that the voltage gain of each stage is down 3 db when the frequency is 80 kHz greater or less than the resonant frequency. The overall voltage gain will be down 6 db at these frequencies.

11-6   Direct-coupled Amplifiers

There is one more type of coupling that we want to discuss. All the amplifiers discussed so far have been limited in the lowest frequency that can be amplified. In other words, as the frequency of operation is reduced, eventually we find that coupling and bypass capacitors no longer appear as short circuits. Similarly, if a transformer is used to couple between stages, there is a lower frequency limit at which its coupling properties fall off.

There are many applications in which an extremely low-frequency response is needed. The use of capacitors and transformers is out of the question for extremely low frequencies because the electrical sizes of these components become prohibitively large. For instance, we may want to amplify 0.01 Hz. In this case, the size of coupling and bypass capacitors becomes huge and impractical.

One approach in obtaining a frequency response that extends all the way to zero frequency is to direct-couple from one stage to another. Many circuit arrangements are possible in direct coupling. We will examine a few of them to convey the notion of how direct coupling is accomplished. The main idea is to leave out all coupling and bypass capacitors.

A two-stage circuit that uses direct coupling is shown in Fig. 11-17. Since there is no coupling capacitor between stages, there will be a d-c as well as an a-c interaction between stages. In the circuit of Fig. 11-17

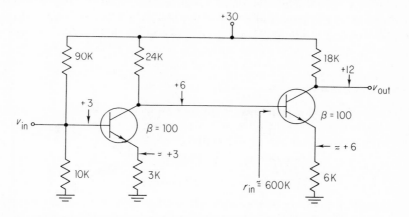

Fig. 11-17 Direct-coupled stages using n-p-n transistors.

note that the voltage divider in the first stage develops about 3 volts from base to ground. Almost all this 3 volts appears from the emitter to ground and sets up a current of about 1 ma. This 1 ma produces a voltage drop of 24 volts across the 24-kilohm collector resistor, so that the collector-ground voltage is about 6 volts. This 6 volts drives the base of the second transistor. Note that the second stage loads the first stage slightly because the input resistance of the second stage is around 600 kilohms. The loading effect is light, so that the base-ground voltage of the second transistor remains at about 6 volts. The emitter-ground voltage of the second transistor is approximately 6 volts, and this produces an emitter current of about 1 ma. In turn, there is a voltage drop of about 18 volts across the 18-kilohm collector resistor, so that the final output voltage is about 12 volts with respect to ground.

If we apply an input voltage v_{in}, this will change the currents and voltages throughout the two-stage amplifier of Fig. 11-17. Note that there is no lower frequency limit. The input voltage can be an extremely low frequency. In fact, the amplifier of Fig. 11-17 can amplify a d-c change at the input. For instance, suppose that the input voltage changes from 3 to 3.1 volts. This is a change of 0.1 volt. This change is amplified by a factor of 8 in the first stage (24 kilohms divided by 3 kilohms). Therefore, the change in the collector voltage of the first stage is about 0.8 volts in the negative direction. This change is now amplified by the second stage, whose voltage gain is about 3. Thus, the change in the output voltage is around 2.4 volts.

As another example of direct coupling, consider the circuit of Fig. 11-18. Note that the first stage uses an *n-p-n* transistor and the second stage uses a *p-n-p*. There is about 1 ma of current in the first transistor so that the emitter-ground voltage is about 3 volts, and the collector-ground voltage is about 24 volts. This 24 volts drives the base of the

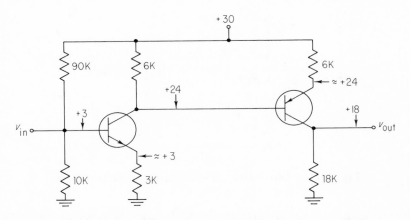

Fig. 11-18   Direct-coupled stages using complementary transistors.

second stage. The net voltage across the 6-kilohm emitter resistor of the second stage is about 6 volts (30 minus 24 volts). This means that the current in the second transistor is around 1 ma, and therefore the collector-ground voltage is about 18 volts.

The voltage gain of the two-stage amplifier of Fig. 11-18 is

$$A = A_1A_2 = \frac{6000}{3000}\frac{18,000}{6000} = 6$$

Thus, any change in the input voltage is amplified by a factor of 6.

If two power supplies are available, a direct-coupled circuit like that of Fig. 11-19 can be used. The first stage is emitter-biased; the emitter current is about 1 ma. This produces a collector voltage of about 3 volts,

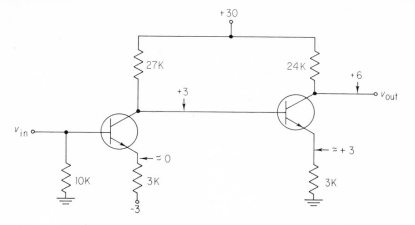

Fig. 11-19 Direct coupling with two supplies.

which drives the second stage. The current in the second transistor is about 1 ma, and the collector voltage is about 6 volts.

Note that the voltage gain of Fig. 11-19 is

$$A = A_1 A_2 = \frac{27,000}{3000} \frac{24,000}{3000} = 72$$

Probably one of the most important of the direct-coupled types of circuits is the so-called *difference amplifier* (also known as a differential amplifier). There are many forms of the difference amplifier and we will discuss only a few of the more important ones. One way to build a difference amplifier is the circuit of Fig. 11-20a. Note that there are two inputs; the output is taken between the collectors. What the circuit does is first to take the algebraic difference of the two inputs and then to amplify this difference. That is, the output of the difference amplifier of Fig. 11-20a is

$$v_{out} = A(v_1 - v_2)$$

where A is the voltage gain of the difference amplifier. By using the ideal-transistor approximation we can show that

$$A \cong \frac{R_L}{r'_e} \qquad (11\text{-}5)$$

For instance, if $R_L = 10$ kilohms and $r'_e = 50$ ohms, we have a voltage gain of 200. Thus, large voltage gains are possible with the difference amplifier. Since it is direct-coupled, there is no lower-frequency limit.

Let us obtain a qualitative understanding of how the difference amplifier of Fig. 10-20a works. The circuit acts like a bridge circuit. Voltages

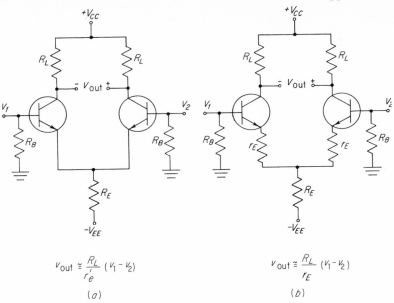

$$v_{\text{out}} \cong \frac{R_L}{r'_e}\,(v_1 - v_2)$$

$$(a)$$

$$v_{\text{out}} \cong \frac{R_L}{r_E}\,(v_1 - v_2)$$

$$(b)$$

Fig. 11-20   Difference amplifiers.

v_1 and v_2 control the currents produced by each transistor. Thus, if v_1 and v_2 are exactly equal, the bridge will be balanced, and there will be a zero output. On the other hand, when v_1 and v_2 are unequal, the bridge is unbalanced, and there will be an output voltage equal to the voltage gain times the algebraic difference of v_1 and v_2.

The difference amplifier of Fig. 11-20a can be stabilized against changes in r'_e by swamping the emitter diode, as shown in Fig. 11-20b. As indicated, the output voltage becomes

$$v_{\text{out}} \cong \frac{R_L}{r_E}\,(v_1 - v_2) \qquad \text{for } r_E \gg r'_e \qquad (11\text{-}6)$$

Thus, in Fig. 11-20b, if $R_L = 10$ kilohms and $r_E = 500$ ohms, the voltage gain will be about 20.

There is no need to actually use two inputs. One of the inputs can be zero, as shown in Fig. 11-21a and b. The formulas for the voltage gain and input resistance are given in Fig. 11-21.

Another important form of the difference amplifier is the circuit of Fig. 11-22a. Note that the output is referenced with respect to ground. As indicated, the output of this circuit is

$$v_{\text{out}} = \frac{R_L}{2r'_e}\,(v_1 - v_2)$$

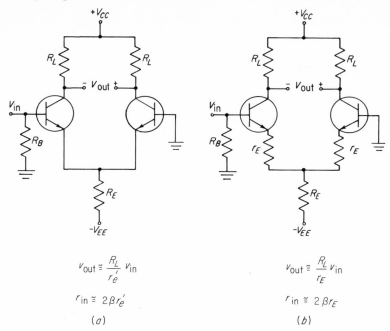

$$v_{out} \cong \frac{R_L}{r_e'} v_{in}$$

$$r_{in} \cong 2\beta r_e'$$

(a)

$$v_{out} \cong \frac{R_L}{r_E} v_{in}$$

$$r_{in} \cong 2\beta r_E$$

(b)

Fig. 11-21 Difference amplifiers with single input.

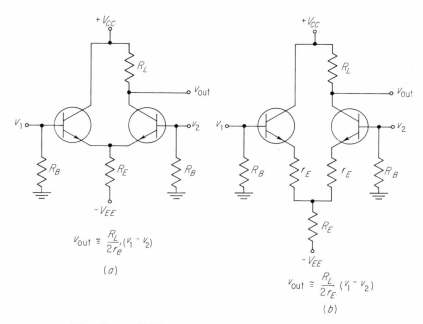

$$v_{out} \cong \frac{R_L}{2r_e'}(v_1 - v_2)$$

(a)

$$v_{out} \cong \frac{R_L}{2r_E}(v_1 - v_2)$$

(b)

Fig. 11-22 Difference amplifiers with single output.

We can swamp the emitter diodes if desired; we then have the circuit of Fig. 11-22b.

We have briefly examined some of the more widely used forms of the difference amplifier. One major advantage of these circuits is that they are direct-coupled circuits capable of much higher voltage gains than the previously discussed direct-coupled amplifiers.

EXAMPLE 11-9

Sketch the output waveform for the difference amplifier of Fig. 11-23a. Get an approximate answer using a β of 100 and an $r_e' = 50$ mv/I_E.

SOLUTION

First, note the use of a small potentiometer in the collector circuit. Such an adjustment is normally added to a difference amplifier to allow us to remove any unbalance caused by differences in transistors, load resistors, and so on. We adjust this potentiometer to produce a zero output when the input is at zero.

Next, note that the d-c current flowing in the 10-kilohm emitter resistor is about 3 ma. The reason for this is simply that with both

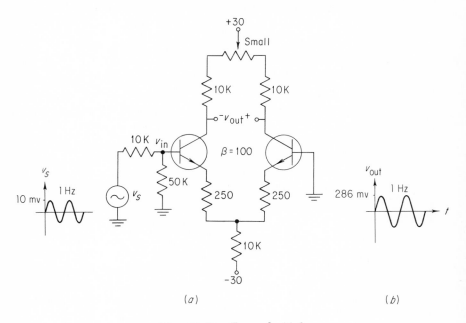

(a) (b)

Fig. 11-23   Example 11-9.

transistors using emitter bias, almost all the emitter supply voltage must appear across the 10-kilohm emitter resistor.

Since there are two transistors sharing the 3 ma, there is about 1.5 ma in each transistor. This produces about 15 volts from each collector to ground.

We can now calculate the value of r'_e. Using 50 mv/I_E, we get

$$r'_e = \frac{50\ \text{mv}}{1.5\ \text{ma}} \cong 33\ \text{ohms}$$

This 33 ohms is quite a bit smaller than the 250 ohms in each emitter circuit, so that we can say the emitter diodes are reasonably well swamped out.

The voltage gain from input to output is simply

$$A \cong \frac{R_L}{r_E} = \frac{10,000}{250} = 40$$

and the input resistance looking into the base of the left transistor is

$$r_{\text{in(base)}} \cong 2\beta r_E = 2(100)(250) = 50\ \text{kilohms}$$

This 50 kilohms of resistance is in parallel with the 50-kilohm base return resistor, so that the input resistance of the circuit is 25 kilohms.

The source has a 10-kilohm resistance; therefore the actual input voltage is

$$v_{\text{in}} = \frac{r_{\text{in}}}{r_s + r_{\text{in}}}\, v_s = \frac{25,000}{35,000}\, 10(10^{-3}) = 7.15\ \text{mv peak}$$

This input voltage is amplified by a factor of 40 to produce an output voltage of

$$v_{\text{out}} = 40(7.15\ \text{mv}) = 286\ \text{mv peak}$$

The output wave is sketched in Fig. 11-23b.

The obvious advantage of this amplifier over an RC-coupled amplifier is that it has amplified an extremely low frequency (1 Hz).

SUMMARY

RC coupling is the most widely used method of cascading transistor stages. The output from a resistively loaded stage is coupled through a capacitor into the input of another transistor stage. The load seen by a collector in a cascade of RC stages is its own load resistance shunted by the input resistance of the next stage.

Two-stage feedback is often used to stabilize the overall voltage gain of a two-stage cascade. To a first approximation, the voltage gain equals the ratio of the feedback resistor to the emitter resistance receiving the feedback signal.

Sometimes inductors are used in the place of the collector load resistors. The advantage is that the only load seen by the collector is the input resistance of the next stage, which means that all the signal power is delivered to the next stage. The disadvantage is that the lower-frequency response is degraded by the inductors.

We can use transformers as coupling elements between stages. They are especially useful when load is so small that it would reduce both gain and signal-handling capability. By means of a transformer, the load seen by the collector can be increased to the point where we get good voltage gain and signal-handling capability.

Tuned tanks give a response that is centered on the resonant frequency of the tuned circuits. In this way, we can amplify a desired band of frequencies.

When we need extremely low-frequency response, we can use direct coupling. There are a number of ways to direct-couple stages. The difference amplifier is quite important in direct-coupled amplifiers because it can provide large voltage gains down to zero frequency.

GLOSSARY

bandwidth　　In a tuned amplifier, this refers to the band of frequencies between the lower and upper 3-db points.

cascade　　An arrangement using the output of one stage as the input to another.

difference amplifier　　A circuit that amplifies the algebraic difference of two input signals.

direct coupling　　A circuit in which the d-c voltages of one stage are coupled into another stage. Such circuits have no capacitors.

error voltage　　In feedback systems where part of the output is fed back to the input, the error voltage is the difference between the input signal and the feedback signal.

r-f chokes　　Inductors that look like open circuits at radio frequency.

REVIEW QUESTIONS

1. In an *RC*-coupled amplifier, the a-c load resistance seen by a collector consists of what resistances?

2. In a well-designed two-stage feedback amplifier, what is the approximate relation between the input signal v_{in} and the feedback signal v_F?
3. Define the error voltage as used in this chapter.
4. What is the approximate voltage gain of the two-stage feedback amplifier discussed in this chapter?
5. For a cascade of inductively coupled stages operating at higher frequencies, what is the effective a-c load resistance seen by a collector?
6. When a load resistance is extremely small, transformer coupling is sometimes used. What are the two advantages of a transformer in this situation?
7. Why are tuned tanks sometimes used in the collector of a transistor amplifier?
8. Why are direct-coupled amplifiers necessary in some situations?
9. What is a difference amplifier? Draw the schematics of some of the difference amplifiers discussed in this chapter.

PROBLEMS

11-1 Suppose that the β of the transistors in Fig. 11-1 is 200 instead of 100. What is the approximate voltage gain of the two-stage cascade? Use 50 mv/I_E.

11-2 In Fig. 11-2, suppose that the r_E of the first stage is 300 ohms instead of 500 ohms. What is the overall voltage gain? ($\beta = 100$.)

11-3 Work out the voltage gain of the circuit in Fig. 11-3 for transistors with a β of 200 and r'_e of 50 mv/I_E.

11-4 The two-stage feedback amplifier of Fig. 11-4 has an r_F of 10 kilohms and an r_E of 82 ohms. What is the approximate voltage gain of the two-stage feedback amplifier?

11-5 Suppose that 100-mh chokes are used in Fig. 11-6. At what frequency will these chokes have a reactance of 10 kilohms? Should the amplifier be operated at this frequency if maximum voltage gain is desired? Why?

11-6 In Fig. 11-8, a 500-ohm load is used instead of a 100-ohm load. What is the voltage gain and maximum unclipped signal output for this 500-ohm load?

11-7 Suppose that the transistors of Fig. 11-11 have $r'_e = 25$ mv/I_E. If the input signal is 1 mv rms, what is the output signal?

11-8 In Fig. 11-14, $L = 200$ μh, and $C = 500$ pf. What is the resonant frequency of each tuned circuit? Suppose that the r_L seen by each collector at resonance is 12 kilohms. What is the Q and the bandwidth of each tuned tank?

11-9   The value of V_{EE} is -25 volts in Fig. 11-20a. The value of R_E is 10 kilohms. What is the d-c emitter current in each transistor?

11-10   In Fig. 11-20a, r'_e is 25 ohms and R_L is 5 kilohms. What is the approximate value of voltage gain?

11-11   In Fig. 11-20b, the value of R_L is 7.5 kilohms and r_E is 680 ohms. The emitter diode is swamped. What is the voltage gain?

11-12   The value of R_E in Fig. 11-21a is 10 kilohms. The emitter supply $V_{EE} = 20$ volts. If the input signal is a 2-mv-peak sine wave, what is the output voltage (use $r'_e = 25$ mv/I_E)? Use an R_L of 5000.

11-13   In Fig. 11-21b, v_{in} is a 10-mv-rms signal. The emitter diodes are swamped. With an R_L of 6.8 kilohms and an r_E of 390 ohms, what is the approximate value of v_{out}?

11-14   What is the voltage gain of the circuit in Fig. 11-22a when $R_L = 7.5$ kilohms, $R_E = 10$ kilohms, $V_{EE} = 25$ volts, and $r'_e = 35$ mv/I_E?

12

Temperature
Effects

We mentioned in Chap. 1 that the number of carriers in a semiconductor will increase as the temperature increases. Because of this, virtually every transistor characteristic is temperature-dependent. In some circuits, the changes caused by temperature variations are so serious that the transistor cannot function normally.

In this chapter, we discuss four important transistor quantities that are temperature-dependent. These are the a-c resistance r'_e, the β, the base-emitter voltage V_{BE}, and the collector leakage current.

12-1 Changes in Emitter-junction Resistance

In our approximation of r'_e we have used

$$\frac{25 \text{ mv}}{I_E} < r'_e < \frac{50 \text{ mv}}{I_E}$$

The lower extreme in this inequality applies to abrupt p-n junctions operating at room temperature (around 25°C). The upper extreme more closely applies to diffused p-n junctions. In either case, when the temperature of the junction changes, the value of r'_e will change from its room-temperature value.

By applying calculus to the general diode equation, it is possible to find out how much r'_e changes with temperature. The result of such a derivation is the following: r'_e increases about 1 percent for each 3°C rise in ambient temperature.[1] (The ambient temperature is the temperature of the surrounding air.)

For instance, suppose that a transistor circuit is operating in an ambient temperature of 20°C and that r'_e is 25 ohms. If the ambient temperature were to rise to 50°C, the r'_e would rise about 10 percent to a new value of 27.5 ohms. On the other hand, if the ambient temperature were to drop from 20 to −40°C (a change of 60°C), the r'_e would decrease about 20 percent (1 percent for each 3°C change) to a new value of 20 ohms.

Recall that a CB or CE transistor stage without feedback has a voltage gain of approximately

$$\frac{v_{out}}{v_{in}} \cong \frac{r_L}{r'_e}$$

By inspection of this equation, it is clear that the voltage gain will drop about 10 percent for each 30°C rise, and vice versa. If such changes are objectionable, we can swamp out the emitter diode, as discussed in earlier chapters.

Example 12-1

The transistor in Fig. 12-1a has an r'_e of 50 ohms for an ambient temperature of 25°C. Find the approximate voltage gain at 25 and 85°C.

Solution

At 25°C, the voltage gain is approximately

$$\frac{v_{out}}{v_{in}} \cong \frac{r_L}{r'_e} = \frac{10,000\|10,000}{50} = 100$$

When the ambient temperature rises to 85°C (a 60°C rise), the r'_e will increase about 20 percent to a new value of 60 ohms. The voltage gain at 85°C is approximately

$$\frac{v_{out}}{v_{in}} \cong \frac{r_L}{r'_e} = \frac{10,000\|10,000}{60} = 83.5$$

---

[1] We are assuming that the power dissipation at the emitter junction remains the same so that the junction temperature rises by the same number of degrees as the ambient temperature.

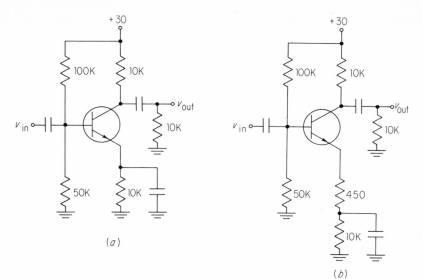

Fig. 12-1   Examples 12-1 and 12-2.

EXAMPLE 12-2

Suppose that we swamp the emitter diode of the transistor in the preceding example as shown in Fig. 12-1b. Find the approximate voltage gain at 25 and 85°C.

SOLUTION

At 25°C, the circuit of Fig. 12-1b has an approximate voltage gain of

$$\frac{v_{\text{out}}}{v_{\text{in}}} \simeq \frac{r_L}{r_E + r'_e} = \frac{10,000\|10,000}{450 + 50} = 10$$

At 85°C, the voltage gain is

$$\frac{v_{\text{out}}}{v_{\text{in}}} \simeq \frac{r_L}{r_E + r'_e} = \frac{10,000\|10,000}{450 + 60} = 9.8$$

Thus, we see that by swamping the emitter diode, we have stabilized the gain. The original circuit (Fig. 12-1a) showed a change in gain of about 16 percent over the temperature range, whereas the new circuit (Fig. 12-1b) changes only 2 percent over the same temperature range. Of course, we give up voltage gain when we swamp the emitter diode; however, there are many situations where it is preferable to have a stable voltage gain despite the reduction in gain.

12-2   Changes in β

Both the d-c and the a-c β change with changes in temperature. No general formula can be given for β changes because they depend a great deal upon the techniques used in the manufacture of the transistor. Usually, as the temperature increases, both the d-c and a-c β will increase, but there are exceptions. In some transistor structures, the a-c β can actually decrease as the temperature increases.

About all we can say in general about the β changes is that they can be quite large. For instance, in some transistors, the a-c β can change by a factor of 4 as the temperature changes -65 to $150°C$.

Specific information on the changes in the d-c and a-c β is sometimes given on the data sheet for the particular transistor. The usual approach in design is to allow for the worst-case β to be encountered.

The changes in the d-c β affect the d-c operating point of the transistor. In Chap. 9, we discussed the sensitivity of the d-c operating point to changes in β. We saw that base-biased circuits were relatively sensitive to changes in β, whereas the emitter-biased circuits showed almost no dependence upon the changes in β. Thus, in any circuit that is to operate over a large change in temperature, emitter bias is far preferable to base bias.

The changes in the a-c β primarily affect the a-c input resistance looking into the base of a CE or CC circuit. Recall the following formulas for a-c input resistance:

$$r_{\text{in(base)}} \cong \beta r'_e \qquad \text{for a CE circuit with no feedback}$$
$$r_{\text{in(base)}} \cong \beta r_E \qquad \text{for a CE circuit with emitter feedback}$$
$$r_{\text{in(base)}} \cong \beta r_L \qquad \text{for a CC circuit (emitter follower)}$$

All these input resistances are directly proportional to the a-c β. Thus, the input resistance is a function of temperature. The usual design approach is to use the worst-case β (the lowest) that can occur over the expected temperature range. The reason for using the lowest β as the worst case is that the input resistance will produce maximum loading on the source when the β is at its lowest value.

12-3   Changes in V_{BE}

In our past work, we have approximated the d-c voltage V_{BE} across the base-emitter diode by allowing 0.3 volt for germanium and 0.7 volt for silicon. These are room-temperature values. When the emitter-junction temperature changes, the V_{BE} drop will change. By applying calculus to the general diode equation, the following approximations can be derived:

1. For germanium transistors, V_{BE} *decreases* about 1 mv for each 1°C *rise*.
2. For silicon transistors, V_{BE} *decreases* about 2.5 mv for each 1°C *rise*.

For instance, if the junction temperature rises 50°C, the V_{BE} drop in a germanium transistor will decrease about 50 mv to a new value of 0.25 volt.

Whether or not the changes in V_{BE} are important will depend upon the particular biasing arrangement. For instance, in Fig. 12-2a, the d-c base current is

$$I_B \cong \frac{20 - 0.7}{10^6} \cong 20 \ \mu\text{a}$$

We neglected the 0.7-volt drop because it is much smaller than the 20 volts driving the base circuit. Also note that even if the temperature changes, the value of V_{BE} is still negligible. In other words, in Fig. 12-2a, the small value of V_{BE} is swamped out by the much larger value of 20 volts.

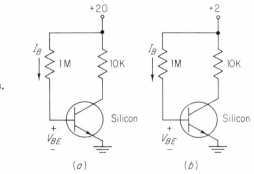

Fig. 12-2 Effect of V_{BE} changes.

The circuit of Fig. 12-2b is different. The supply voltage is only 2 volts; therefore, V_{BE} is no longer negligible. At room temperature, the base current is

$$I_B \cong \frac{2 - 0.7}{10^6} = 1.3 \ \mu\text{a}$$

Since V_{BE} is no longer negligible, changes in V_{BE} can be important in setting the base current. For instance, if the temperature rises 60°C, the change in V_{BE} will be

$$\Delta V_{BE} = -60(2.5)(10^{-3}) = -0.15 \text{ volt}$$

The base current at the elevated temperature will be

$$I_B \cong \frac{2 - 0.55}{10^6} = 1.45 \ \mu\text{a}$$

This change in base current will change the d-c operating point of the transistor and can lead to clipping if a large signal is involved.

It should be apparent that the shift in operating point caused by changes in V_{BE} can be minimized by making the supply voltages much larger than the V_{BE}. In other words, we must make sure that V_{BE} is swamped out.

EXAMPLE 12-3

The transistor shown in Fig. 12-3 has a V_{BE} drop of 0.7 volt for a junction temperature of 20°C. Find the collector-ground voltage at 20 and 70°C.

SOLUTION

The circuit of Fig. 12-3 is a single-supply emitter-biased arrangement. The voltage from base to ground is

$$V_B \cong \frac{10,000}{20,000 + 10,000} \ 4.5 = 1.5 \text{ volts}$$

About 0.7 volt is dropped across the base-emitter diode at 20°C so that the voltage actually appearing across the 10-kilohm emitter resistor is

$$V_E \cong 1.5 - 0.7 = 0.8 \text{ volt}$$

and the d-c emitter current is

$$I_E \cong \frac{0.8}{10^4} = 0.08 \text{ ma}$$

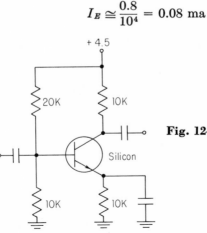

Fig. 12-3   Example 12-3.

The d-c voltage from collector to ground is

$$V_C = V_{CC} - I_C R_L \cong 4.5 - 0.08(10^{-3})(10^4) = 3.7 \text{ volts}$$

When the temperature increases to 70°C, the change in V_{BE} is

$$\Delta V_{BE} = -50(2.5)(10^{-3}) = -0.125 \text{ volt}$$

The d-c collector current becomes

$$I_C = \frac{1.5 - 0.575}{10^4} = 0.0925 \text{ ma}$$

and the collector-ground voltage becomes

$$V_C = 4.5 - 0.0925(10^{-3})(10^4) = 3.58 \text{ volts}$$

12-4   Leakage Current in a Grounded-base Circuit

In a grounded-base circuit like that shown in Fig. 12-4a, the emitter diode is forward-biased and the collector diode is back-biased. Because

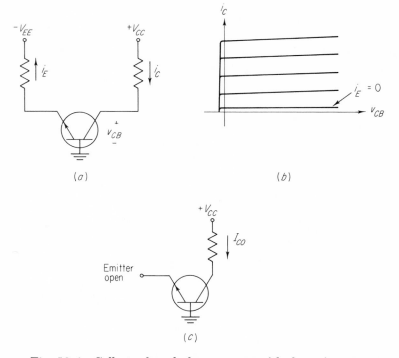

(a)   (b)

(c)

Fig. 12-4   Collector-base leakage current with the emitter open.

there are thermally produced minority carriers in the collector, there exists a leakage component of collector current in addition to the collector current produced by normal transistor action. For instance, in Fig. 12-4a, we know that as the emitter current i_E is changed, the collector current i_C will change. Typical characteristic curves for these changes are shown in Fig. 12-4b. Note that there is some collector current even when $i_E = 0$. In the ideal-transistor approximation, we neglected this small amount of collector current. Now we are going to take it into account.

The condition $i_E = 0$ can be represented by the equivalent circuit of Fig. 12-4c, where the emitter lead has been opened. Under this condition, there can be no emitter current. However, there is still a small amount of collector current because of the reverse current in the collector diode. This reverse current is symbolized by I_{CBO}, where the subscripts CBO stand for *collector* to *base* with the emitter *open*. Very often, I_{CBO} is simply written as I_{CO}.

In a grounded-base circuit the total collector current is actually the sum of two components. First, there is the component produced by normal transistor action, that is, the collector current controlled by the emitter current. Second, there is I_{CO}, which is the result of thermally produced minority carriers. To utilize our earlier work in transistors, we can represent the effect of reverse or leakage current by using an ideal transistor in shunt with a current source of I_{CO}, as shown in Fig. 12-5. Note that

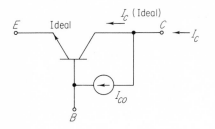

Fig. 12-5 Equivalent circuit for I_{CO} leakage current.

the leakage component I_{CO} is in the same direction as the ideal component of collector current. Therefore, the total collector current is

$$I_C = I_{C(\text{ideal})} + I_{CO}$$

Since I_{CO} is the result of thermally produced carriers, we can expect I_{CO} to increase with temperature. The amount of increase in I_{CO} with temperature can be found by using the following approximate rules:

1. *For germanium, I_{CO} doubles for every 10°C rise in temperature.*
2. *For silicon, I_{CO} doubles for every 6°C rise in temperature.*

For instance, suppose that I_{co} is 1 μa at 25°C. For a silicon transistor, I_{co} will be 2 μa at 31°C, 4 μa at 37°C, 8 μa at 43°C, etc.

It is worth mentioning again that at room temperature the leakage currents in silicon transistors are generally much smaller than the leakage currents in germanium transistors. In earlier times, the germanium transistors were widely used because the silicon units were much more expensive. This is no longer the case. Silicon units are now comparably priced with germanium units. Because of this, silicon transistors are gaining wide acceptance. Other things being equal, the silicon transistor is far preferable to the germanium transistor because of its much lower leakage current.

The leakage current I_{co} is undesirable. The reason for this is simply that as the temperature increases, the leakage current increases and causes a shift in the d-c operating point of the transistor. For instance, in Fig. 12-6a, the d-c emitter current is

$$I_E \cong \frac{20}{20(10^3)} = 1 \text{ ma}$$

If there were no leakage current, the collector current I_C would approximately equal the emitter current of 1 ma. The collector-base voltage would then be

$$V_C = 20 - 10^{-3}(10^4) = 10 \text{ volts}$$

We have shown the ideal d-c operating point in Fig. 12-6b.

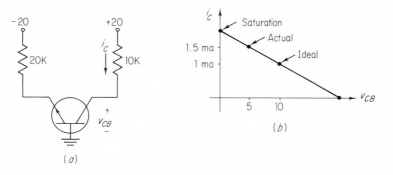

Fig. 12-6 The effect of leakage current.

Now, let us take the leakage current I_{co} into account. Suppose that $I_{co} = 0.5$ ma at an elevated temperature. The actual collector current is the sum of the ideal current plus the leakage current. Hence,

$$I_C = I_{C(\text{ideal})} + I_{co} = 1 \text{ ma} + 0.5 \text{ ma} = 1.5 \text{ ma}$$

and the collector-base voltage is

$$V_C = 20 - 1.5(10^{-3})(10^4) = 5 \text{ volts}$$

The actual operating point is shown in Fig. 12-6b. Thus, the operating point has shifted because of the leakage current.

In fact, if the temperature were to increase, I_{CO} would increase, and the operating point would shift upward along the d-c line. It is clear that if the temperature increases enough, the d-c operating point can shift all the way to the saturation point, which would lead to clipping of an a-c signal.

The general rule for avoiding a significant shift in the d-c operating point of a grounded-base circuit is simply this: the leakage current I_{CO} must be much smaller than the ideal collector current at the highest temperature to be encountered.

EXAMPLE 12-4

The transistor of Fig. 12-7a is made of germanium and has an I_{CO} of 1 μa at 20°C. Calculate the value of V_{CB} at 20 and 80°C.

SOLUTION

The d-c emitter current is

$$I_E \cong \frac{10}{100(10^3)} = 0.1 \text{ ma}$$

At 20°C, the collector current is the sum of 0.1 ma and 1 μa. We can neglect the 1 μa since it is much smaller than 0.1 ma. The collector-base voltage is

$$V_{CB} = 10 - 0.1(10^{-3})(50)(10^3) = 5 \text{ volts}$$

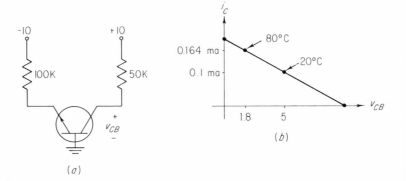

(a)

(b)

Fig. 12-7   Examples 12-4 and 12-5.

At 80°C, the temperature has risen by 60°C. Since I_{CO} doubles for every 10°C rise, I_{CO} will double six times, so that

$$I_{CO} = 10^{-6}(2^6) = 64 \ \mu a = 0.064 \ ma$$

The total collector current is the sum of the ideal component and the leakage component. Therefore,

$$I_C = 0.1 + 0.064 \ ma = 0.164 \ ma$$

and the collector voltage is

$$V_{CB} = 10 - 0.164(10^{-3})(50)(10^3) = 1.8 \ volts$$

Note that there has been a significant shift in the d-c operating point as shown in Fig. 12-7b. If the temperature should increase further, the transistor would soon saturate.

EXAMPLE 12-5

The germanium transistor of the preceding example is replaced by a silicon transistor of similar characteristics except that $I_{CO} = 1$ na $(10^{-9}$ amp) at 20°C. Find the value of V_{CB} in Fig. 12-7a for temperatures of 20 and 80°C.

SOLUTION

At 20°C, 1 na is negligible compared to the ideal collector current of 0.1 ma. Hence, $V_{CB} = 5$ volts.

The leakage current in silicon transistors doubles for every 6°C rise. When the temperature changes from 20 to 80°C, the leakage current will have doubled 10 times. That is, at 80°C,

$$I_{CO} = 10^{-9}(2^{10}) = 1.02 \ \mu a$$

Note that even at 80°C this leakage current is still negligible compared to the ideal collector current of 0.1 ma. Therefore, $V_{CB} = 5$ volts as before.

12-5   Leakage Current in a Grounded-emitter Circuit

Consider the grounded-emitter circuit of Fig. 12-8a. When we vary the value of base supply voltage V_{BB}, the size of the base current will vary, which in turn changes the collector current. As we have seen before, the transistor action of this circuit can be summarized by the typical characteristic of Fig. 12-8b. Note carefully that there is some collector current even when the base current is zero (bottom curve).

The condition of zero base current is depicted by Fig. 12-8c, where we have shown the base lead open. With zero base current, there is a leakage component of collector current labeled I_{CEO}. The subscripts CEO stand for the *collector* to *emitter* with the base *open*.

Here is an interesting phenomenon. The current I_{CEO} is much larger than I_{CO}. In fact, $I_{CEO} \cong \beta I_{CO}$. The reason for this can be seen by considering Fig. 12-8d, where we have shown the real transistor as an ideal

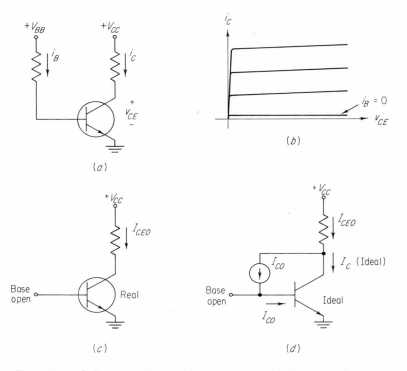

Fig. 12-8 Collector-emitter leakage current with the base open.

transistor shunted by a current source I_{CO}. Since the base lead is open, all the I_{CO} current must flow into the base of the ideal transistor. This produces a collector current of βI_{CO}. By inspection of the circuit, I_{CEO} is

$$I_{CEO} = \beta I_{CO} + I_{CO} = (\beta + 1)I_{CO}$$

or

$$I_{CEO} \cong \beta I_{CO} \qquad \text{for } \beta \gg 1 \qquad (12\text{-}1)$$

Note that for the circuit of Fig. 12-8a, I_{CEO} is in the same direction as the normal collector current. The total collector current in the circuit is

$$I_C = \beta I_B + I_{CEO}$$

The first component βI_B is the ordinary component of collector current that we have discussed in earlier chapters; it is the component of collector current that we want and need for normal transistor action. The second component I_{CEO} is the leakage component of collector current; it is undesirable because it will disturb the d-c operating point of a transistor circuit. Since I_{CEO} is temperature-dependent, it can cause serious shifts in the d-c operating point as the temperature increases. This, of course, must be avoided. More is said about d-c operating-point shift in the next section.

EXAMPLE 12-6

The silicon transistor shown in Fig. 12-9 has an $I_{CO} = 1$ na at 20°C. Find the value of V_{CE} at 20 and 80°C. ($\beta = 100$)

SOLUTION

At 20°C, the value of I_{CEO} is

$$I_{CEO} \cong \beta I_{CO} = 100(10^{-9}) = 0.1 \ \mu a$$

The approximate value of base current is

$$I_B \cong \frac{V_{CC}}{R_B} = \frac{20}{2(10^6)} = 10 \ \mu a$$

The total collector current at 20°C is

$$I_C = \beta I_B + I_{CEO} = 100(10)(10^{-6}) + 0.1(10^{-6}) \cong 1 \ ma$$

and the collector-emitter voltage is

$$V_{CE} = 20 - 0.001(10,000) = 10 \ volts$$

At 80°C, the value of I_{CO} has doubled 10 times so that

$$I_{CO} = 10^{-9}(2^{10}) = 1.02 \ \mu a$$

Fig. 12-9 Example 12-6.

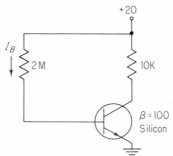

Assuming that the β is still 100, the value of I_{CEO} is

$$I_{CEO} \cong \beta I_{CO} = 100(1.02)(10^{-6}) \cong 0.1 \text{ ma}$$

The normal component of collector current βI_B is still 1 ma. To this we add 0.1 ma of leakage current to obtain a total collector current of 1.1 ma. Thus, at 80°C, the collector-emitter voltage becomes

$$V_{CE} = 20 - (0.0011)(10{,}000) = 9 \text{ volts}$$

Note that there has been a slight shift in the d-c operating point as the temperature changed from 20 to 80°C. As the temperature increases further, the shift will become more pronounced until eventually the transistor saturates.

12-6   The Stability Factor

Leakage current is undesirable; it causes the d-c operating point to shift as temperature increases. Ideally, we would like to have zero leakage current. More realistically, we would like to have the leakage component much smaller than the normal component of collector current. In this section, we reexamine the six biasing arrangements studied in Chap. 9. Our aim is to find out how much the d-c operating point shifts in each of these biasing arrangements.

For any of the six common bias circuits, the total collector current is the sum of the ideal component and the leakage component. That is,

$$I_C = I_{C(\text{ideal})} + I_{\text{leakage}}$$

The size of the leakage current will depend upon the bias arrangement used and the value of the resistors in the circuit.

In dealing with the leakage current, it is common practice to speak of the *stability factor*. We will define the stability factor S by

$$I_{\text{leakage}} = SI_{CO}$$

In other words, S is a constant of proportionality between I_{CO} and I_{leakage}.[1] The stability factor tells us how good a particular biasing arrangement is as far as leakage current is concerned: the smaller the S, the better the bias arrangement.

By means of calculus, we can find the stability factor for each of the six common bias circuits discussed in Chap. 9. The results of this analysis are summarized by Figs. 12-10 and 12-11. For each circuit, the formula

---

[1] This is approximately the same as $\partial I_C / \partial I_{CO}$ and is more easily understood by the reader who does not have a knowledge of calculus.

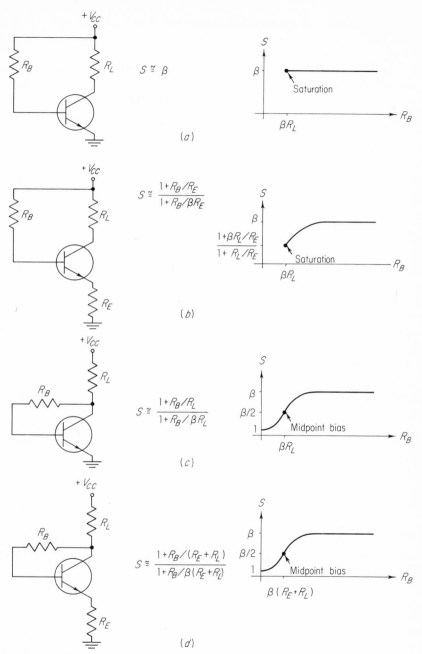

Fig. 12-10 The stability factor of base-bias circuits.

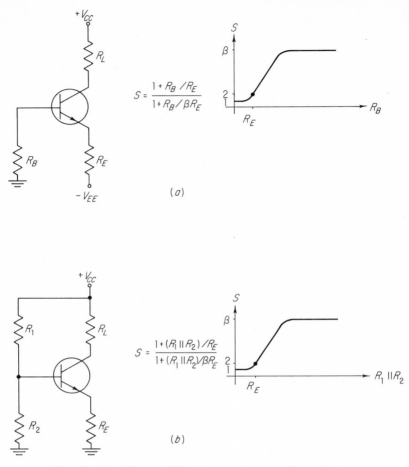

Fig. 12-11   The stability factor of emitter-bias circuits.

for S is shown. Also, a sketch of S vs. R_B (or $R_1\|R_2$) is given. In all six circuits, *note that the value of S lies between unity and β.* These two extremes are the lowest and highest values of S. *Since the leakage current in any circuit equals SI_{co}, the better bias arrangements are those with low values of S.*

Generally speaking, the simple base-biased circuit of Fig. 12-10a is the worst way to bias a transistor since it always has an S equal to β. This means that the leakage current in this circuit always equals βI_{co}.

The remaining base-biased circuits of Fig. 12-10 can be designed to have a value of S that is less than β; however, very low values of S can be had only by almost saturating the transistor (this is analogous to obtaining low values of K by almost saturating the transistor, as discussed in Chap. 9).

Generally speaking, the emitter-biased circuits of Fig. 12-11 are the circuits in which we can get a very low value of S without saturating the transistor. With these circuits, we can easily set the current at the middle of the d-c load line and still have a very low value of S. For instance, in Fig. 12-12, we have a two-supply emitter-biased circuit. There is about

Fig. 12-12 Stability of a typical emitter-bias circuit.

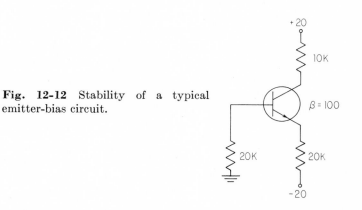

1 ma of current in the collector, and this produces a collector-ground voltage of about 10 volts. Thus, the operating point is in the middle of the d-c load line. Since $R_B = R_E$, the stability factor of this circuit is

$$S = \frac{1 + R_B/R_E}{1 + R_B/\beta R_E} = \frac{1 + 1}{1 + 1/\beta} \cong 2$$

This means that the leakage current in the collector is only 2 times the I_{CO} of the transistor.

In summary, leakage current is no longer the serious problem it was when germanium transistors were widely used almost to the exclusion of silicon transistors. However, even with the low-I_{CO} silicon transistors, leakage current may sometimes cause a problem. As a simple guide in determining whether leakage current is a problem, the following can be used:

1. Since S can be no greater than β, first check to see whether

$$\beta I_{CO} \ll I_{C(\text{ideal})}$$

at the highest junction temperature to be encountered. If this condition is satisfied, the d-c operating point is stable, and there is no need to find the S of the circuit.

2. If the foregoing inequality is not satisfied, it is necessary to find the S of the circuit. After S is known, check to see whether

$$SI_{CO} \ll I_{C(\text{ideal})}$$

at the highest junction temperature to be encountered. If this condition is satisfied, the d-c operating point is stable. If not, there is a leakage-current problem, and it is necessary to reduce the S of the circuit by redesigning, or to reduce the I_{CO} by selecting a better transistor.

EXAMPLE 12-7

The germanium transistor of Fig. 12-13 has a β of 100 at all temperatures. The transistor has an $I_{CO} = 5 \ \mu a$ at 20°C. Determine whether or not the leakage current causes a significant shift in the d-c operating point over the temperature range of 20 to 50°C.

SOLUTION

The circuit of Fig. 12-13 is a standard single-supply emitter-bias arrangement. With approximately 10 volts developed from base to ground, there is an ideal emitter current of about 2 ma. Therefore, the ideal or normal component of collector current is about 2 ma.

The leakage component is to be added to the 2 ma of ideal collector current. To find the leakage current, we must first find the I_{CO} at 50°C. At 50°C, I_{CO} will have doubled three times for the germanium transistor. Therefore, at 50°C,

$$I_{CO} = 5(10^{-6})(2^3) = 0.04 \ \text{ma}$$

To determine whether leakage current is a problem, let us first make a quick check to see whether βI_{CO} is much smaller than 2 ma (the ideal collector current).

$$\beta I_{CO} = 100(0.04)(10^{-3}) = 4 \ \text{ma}$$

This indicates that we must actually find the stability factor S for the circuit of Fig. 12-13. (Note that had βI_{CO} been much smaller than 2 ma, we could have concluded immediately that there was no problem at all.)

The stability factor S for the circuit of Fig. 12-13 is

$$S = \frac{1 + (R_1 \| R_2)/R_E}{1 + (R_1 \| R_2)/\beta R_E} = \frac{1 + 3.33(10^3)/5(10^3)}{1 + 3.33(10^3)/100(5)(10^3)} \cong 1.65$$

Therefore, the leakage current in the collector is

$$I_{\text{leakage}} = SI_{CO} = 1.65(0.04 \ \text{ma}) = 0.066 \ \text{ma}$$

Clearly, 0.066 ma is much less than the 2 ma of ideal collector current.

We conclude that the leakage current is small enough at 50°C not to cause a significant shift in the d-c operating point.

Note that if the same transistor had been used in a simple base-biased circuit, the stability factor would equal 100 instead of 1.65. The leakage current would then cause a large enough shift in the operating point to saturate the transistor.

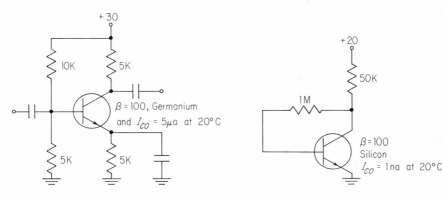

Fig. 12-13   Example 12-7.   **Fig. 12-14**   Example 12-8.

EXAMPLE 12-8

Determine whether or not the leakage current in the circuit of Fig. 12-14 will be a problem at 50°C.

SOLUTION

First, we need the approximate value of ideal collector current. Using the methods of Chap. 9, we get

$$I_C \cong \frac{V_{CC}}{R_L + R_B/\beta} = \frac{20}{5(10^4) + 10^6/100} = 0.333 \text{ ma}$$

In order not to be a problem, the leakage current must be much smaller than 0.333 ma at the highest temperature. At 50°C,

$$I_{CO} = 10^{-9}(2^5) = 32 \text{ na}$$

First, let us use the quick check of $\beta I_{CO} \ll I_{C(\text{ideal})}$.

$$\beta I_{CO} = 100(32 \text{ na}) = 3.2 \text{ } \mu\text{a}$$

Since 3.2 µa is much smaller than the ideal collector current of 0.333 ma, we conclude that the leakage current is negligible. There is no point in even calculating the S value since SI_{CO} will be smaller than 3.2 µa.

SUMMARY

The characteristics of a transistor change when the temperature changes. This means that the d-c and a-c operation of a transistor circuit depend to some extent upon the ambient temperature.

The r_e' of a transistor increases about 1 percent for each 3°C rise in ambient temperature. This will change the voltage gain of a transistor circuit unless the emitter diode is swamped.

Both the d-c and a-c β change when the temperature changes. Usually, both of these will increase with temperature, but sometimes the a-c β shows a decrease with rising temperature.

The d-c voltage drop V_{BE} is affected by temperature change. In a germanium transistor circuit, V_{BE} decreases about 1 mv for each 1°C rise. In a silicon transistor circuit, V_{BE} decreases about 2.5 mv for each 1°C rise. To minimize the effects of a changing V_{BE} drop, we can use a base or emitter supply voltage that is much larger than V_{BE}.

In any biasing arrangement, the d-c collector current is the sum of the ideal collector current and a leakage component. The leakage component equals SI_{CO}, where S is the stability factor of the circuit. As a rule, we must keep the leakage current at the highest junction temperature much smaller than the ideal collector current to avoid a shift in the d-c operating point.

Silicon transistors are preferable to comparable germanium transistors because the I_{CO} currents in silicon are much smaller than in germanium.

GLOSSARY

ambient temperature   The surrounding temperature. The temperature of the environment in which the transistor circuit is operating.

I_{CEO} The reverse current that flows from the collector to the emitter when the base lead is open.

I_{CO} Also designated I_{CBO}. This is the reverse current that flows from the collector to the base when the emitter lead is open.

leakage current   This is the undesired component of collector current that flows in addition to the normal or ideal component. The leakage current in any biasing arrangement equals SI_{CO}.

stability factor (S) This is the ratio of the leakage current in a given bias arrangement to the I_{CO} of the transistor. The value of S is between 1 and β for any bias circuit.

REVIEW QUESTIONS

1. What is the percent change in r'_e for a 30°C rise in temperature?
2. When the temperature increases, what usually happens to the d-c and a-c β?
3. In a germanium transistor circuit, how much does V_{BE} change for each centigrade degree rise in temperature? How much is the change for a silicon transistor circuit?
4. Why is it possible to have some collector current even when there is no emitter current?
5. What does I_{CBO} stand for? And I_{CO}?
6. The I_{CO} of a germanium transistor doubles when the temperature rises how many degrees centigrade? What is the answer for a silicon transistor?
7. In general, which transistors have lower values of I_{CO}, silicon or germanium?
8. What does I_{CEO} stand for?
9. What is the stability factor S?
10. Which biasing arrangements usually have the lowest values of S?
11. What is the smallest possible value of S? The largest?

PROBLEMS

12-1 The value of r'_e is 40 ohms at 25°C. What is the value of r'_e if the temperature rises to 65°C?

12-2 The transistor in Fig. 12-15 has an r'_e of 50 mv/I_E when the temperature is 25°C. What is the approximate voltage gain of the circuit when the temperature rises to 65°C?

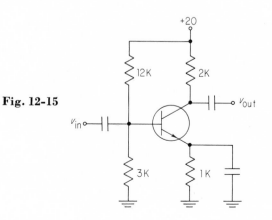

Fig. 12-15

12-3 Suppose that instead of bypassing all the 1-kilohm emitter resistor in Prob. 12-2, we bypass only 900 ohms, that is, use an r_E of 100 ohms. Find the voltage gain at 25 and 65°C using

$$\frac{v_{\text{out}}}{v_{\text{in}}} \cong \frac{r_L}{r_E + r_e'}$$

12-4 The β of the transistor in Fig. 12-15 equals 75 at 25°C and 125 at 65°C. Find the a-c input resistance at each temperature. Use $r_e' = 50$ mv/I_E. (Include the change in r_e'.)

12-5 In Fig. 12-16, suppose that the β of the transistor equals 50 at 25°C and 100 at 75°C. What is the value of v_{out} for each of these temperatures? Neglect r_e'.

12-6 Suppose that a silicon transistor has a V_{BE} of 0.6 volt at 25°C. What value does V_{BE} have at 75°C?

12-7 Suppose a germanium transistor has a V_{BE} drop of 0.25 volt at 25°C. What value does V_{BE} have at −25°C?

12-8 The silicon transistor of Fig. 12-17 has a V_{BE} drop of 0.7 volt at 25°C. Find the collector current at 25 and 75°C (take V_{BE} into account).

12-9 Suppose a germanium transistor is used instead of a silicon transistor in Fig. 12-17. Compute the collector current at 25 and at 75°C. Use a V_{BE} drop of 0.3 volt at 25°C.

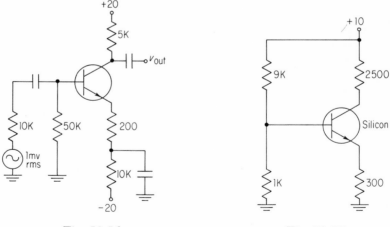

Fig. 12-16   Fig. 12-17

12-10 Find the stability factor S for the circuit of Fig. 12-15. If the I_{CO} of the transistor is 1 μa, what is the leakage component of collector current? (Use a β of 100.)

12-11 In Fig. 12-15, if the I_{co} of the transistor is 1 μa at 25°C, what would the leakage current be at 55°C if the transistor is made of germanium? Use a β of 100.

12-12 In Fig. 12-16, the transistor is made of silicon and has an I_{co} of 3 na at 25°C. Will leakage current be a problem in this circuit if the temperature rises to 75°C? ($\beta = 100$.)

12-13 What is the stability factor S for the circuit of Fig. 12-16? Use a β of 100.

12-14 Suppose $R_B = 1$ megohm, $R_L = 10$ kilohms, $R_E = 1$ kilohm, and $\beta = 50$. What is the stability factor S for the circuit of Fig. 12-10b?

12-15 The circuit of Fig. 12-10c has an R_L of 5 kilohms, an R_B of 500 kilohms, and a β of 75. The transistor is made of silicon and has an I_{co} of 10 na at 25°C. Find the leakage component of collector current at 25 and 75°C. Assume the β remains fixed with temperature change.

13 | Frequency Response

In earlier chapters we treated all coupling and bypass capacitors as a-c shorts. Obviously, this is incorrect when the frequency of operation is so low that the capacitive reactances become comparable to the resistances in the circuit. In other words, coupling and bypass capacitors impose a lower-frequency limit on any amplifier in which they are used.

We have also treated all internal transistor capacitances and stray wiring capacitances as negligibly small. When the frequency is high enough, however, this is no longer valid, because these capacitances provide shunt paths for the a-c currents. In effect, the transistor and stray capacitances impose an upper-frequency limit on the operation of amplifiers.

In this chapter we discuss the frequency response of single stages and cascaded stages. We are especially interested in the upper and lower cutoff frequencies of typical RC-coupled amplifiers.

13-1 Response of an RC-coupled Amplifier

The RC-coupled amplifier is the most common type of amplifier. It uses resistors to develop the a-c signal and capacitors to couple and bypass the a-c signal. A typical response for a fixed input voltage is shown in Fig. 13-1. For very low or very high frequencies, the output voltage drops off. Toward the middle of the frequency range, however, the output voltage is fixed and equals a constant value K; it is in this middle range of frequencies that most RC amplifiers are normally operated.

The *cutoff frequencies* of an amplifier are those frequencies where the output voltage equals 0.707 of its mid-frequency value. For instance, in Fig. 13-1 the output voltage equals K in the mid-frequency range; if we increase or decrease the frequency of operation, we reach a frequency where the output voltage has dropped to $0.707K$. (In terms of decibels, this is equivalent to saying that the output voltage has dropped 3 db.)

Fig. 13-1 Typical response of an RC-coupled amplifier.

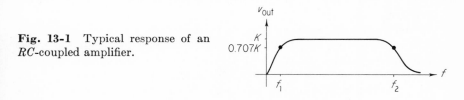

There are two cutoff frequencies f_1 and f_2 in Fig. 13-1. The lower cutoff frequency f_1 is caused by the coupling and bypass capacitors; the upper cutoff frequency is caused by the internal transistor capacitances and the stray wiring capacitances.

The *passband* of an amplifier refers to the range of frequencies between f_1 and f_2. Most RC-coupled amplifiers are normally operated at frequencies well in the passband, and up to now we have analyzed the a-c operation of transistor circuits by assuming frequencies of operation well in the passband. Throughout the remainder of this chapter, however, we will discuss the cutoff frequencies of various transistor amplifiers.

13-2   Lower Cutoff Frequency of a Typical CB Stage

In this section, we find the formulas for the lower-frequency limit of a typical CB stage. The analysis used here will be used again in the discussion of CE stages.

In the typical CB circuit of Fig. 13-2a, we know that the approximate voltage gain from the source to the load is

$$\frac{v_{out}}{v_s} \cong \frac{r_L}{r_s + r_e'}$$

We derived this formula by treating the capacitors as a-c shorts. For normal amplifier operation, this is precisely how the capacitors are supposed to act; that is, they should be short circuits to a-c-current but open circuits to d-c current. In this way, the biasing of the transistor is not disturbed by the source resistance r_s or the load resistance R, and yet the a-c signal is coupled into and out of the transistor.

As the frequency of the input signal becomes lower and lower, the reactances of the capacitors will increase, because

$$X_C = \frac{1}{2\pi f C}$$

When the reactance becomes comparable in size to the resistances in the circuit, we can expect to drop some of the a-c signal across the capacitors. In other words, the voltage gain will drop off from its normal value of $r_L/(r_s + r'_e)$.

To determine the lower-frequency limit, we draw the a-c equivalent circuit as shown in Fig. 13-2b. The input resistance r_{in} represents the biasing resistor R_E in parallel with the input resistance looking into the emitter of the transistor. As an approximation, we can say that $r_{in} \cong r'_e$.

Examine the input side of Fig. 13-2b. When the capacitor looks like

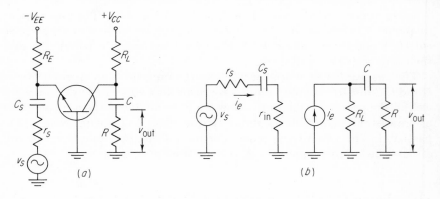

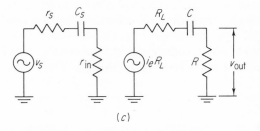

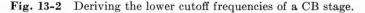

Fig. 13-2   Deriving the lower cutoff frequencies of a CB stage.

an a-c short, the emitter current is simply

$$i_e = \frac{v_s}{r_s + r_{in}} \tag{13-1}$$

However, as the frequency decreases, the capacitive reactance increases to the point where the emitter current becomes less than the value given by Eq. (13-1). Recall from basic electricity theory that in a series RC circuit, the current is down by a factor of 0.707 (3 db) when the capacitive reactance equals the total resistance in the circuit. In other words, in Fig. 13-2b, the emitter current is down 3 db when

$$\frac{1}{2\pi f C_s} = r_s + r_{in}$$

or

$$f = \frac{1}{2\pi (r_s + r_{in}) C_s} \tag{13-2}$$

At this frequency the a-c emitter current is 0.707 of its value at higher frequencies. Since the emitter current is down 3 db at this frequency, the voltage gain from source to load is also down by a factor of 0.707, or 3 db.

Equation (13-2) is the formula for the lower cutoff frequency produced by the input coupling capacitor. The output coupling capacitor also limits the lower-frequency response. By applying Thévenin's theorem, we can redraw the output circuit as shown in Fig. 13-2c. The output circuit is a series RC circuit; therefore, we again use the argument that the current is down by a factor of 0.707 when the capacitive reactance equals the total series resistance. That is,

$$\frac{1}{2\pi f C} = R_L + R$$

or

$$f = \frac{1}{2\pi (R_L + R) C} \tag{13-3}$$

We can use Eqs. (13-2) and (13-3) to find the input and output cutoff frequencies. Usually, these frequencies are different. In this case, the *higher* of the two frequencies is more critical. For example, suppose that a circuit like that of Fig. 13-2a has an input cutoff frequency of 10 Hz and an output cutoff frequency of 90 Hz. The 90 Hz is the more critical value because the amplifier response has already dropped off at 90 Hz.

If the input and output cutoff frequencies happen to be *identical*, the amplifier response will be down 6 db at this cutoff frequency (3 db for each capacitor). The actual cutoff frequency of the amplifier itself (where its output voltage is down 3 db) will be higher than the frequency found by Eqs. (13-2) and (13-3). A useful approximation for this overall cutoff frequency is

$$f_1 \cong 1.5f \tag{13-4}$$

where f is the cutoff frequency of the input and output capacitors and f_1 is the cutoff frequency of the amplifier. As an example, suppose we calculate an input cutoff frequency of 50 Hz and an output cutoff frequency of 50 Hz. At 50 Hz, the amplifier output voltage is down 6 db. The approximate 3-db cutoff frequency of the amplifier is 1.5(50 Hz), which equals 75 Hz.

EXAMPLE 13-1

Find the lower cutoff frequency of the CB amplifier shown in Fig. 13-3.

SOLUTION

First, we find the cutoff frequency produced by the input coupling capacitor. Using Eq. (13-2),

$$f = \frac{1}{2\pi(r_s + r_{\text{in}})C_s} \cong \frac{1}{2\pi(500 + 25)(10^{-6})} \cong 300 \text{ Hz}$$

Note that for r_{in} we used the theoretical value of r_e' because the 20-kilohm biasing resistor is negligible.

Next, we find the cutoff frequency produced by the output coupling capacitor. With Eq. (13-3), we get

$$f = \frac{1}{2\pi(R_L + R)C} = \frac{1}{2\pi(10^4 + 10^4)(10^{-6})} \cong 8 \text{ Hz}$$

The input capacitor in conjunction with the source resistance and the input resistance of the stage produces a cutoff frequency of 300 Hz. On

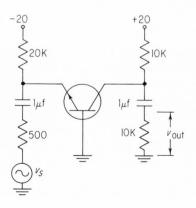

Fig. 13-3   Example 13-1.

the output side, the cutoff frequency is much lower and occurs at 8 Hz. As far as the overall amplifier response is concerned, the higher frequency of 300 Hz is the more critical value, and to a good approximation we can say that the lower cutoff frequency of the entire stage is about 300 Hz.

13-3 Upper Cutoff Frequency of a CB Stage

Consider the circuit of Fig. 13-4a. When the frequency is too low, we know that the coupling capacitors produce a lower-frequency cutoff. When we raise the frequency of operation, these coupling capacitors act like a-c shorts, and then the mid-frequency value of voltage gain is approximately

$$\frac{v_{\text{out}}}{v_s} \cong \frac{r_L}{r_s + r_e'}$$

If we continue raising the frequency of operation, we will find an upper-frequency limit where the voltage gain drops off. There are two major causes for this drop-off, and we will discuss both.

Recall that the a-c α of a transistor is defined as

$$\alpha = \frac{i_c}{i_e}$$

In the ideal-transistor approximation, $i_c = i_e$, so that $\alpha = 1$. In a real transistor, the a-c collector current is slightly less than the a-c emitter current. In fact, we have already indicated that most transistors have a-c α's between 0.95 and 0.999.

When the frequency of operation is high enough, however, the α of

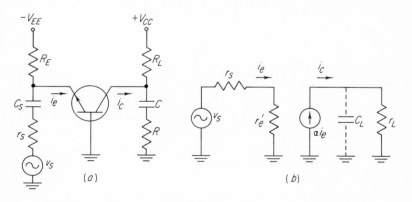

Fig. 13-4 Deriving the upper cutoff frequency of a CB stage.

the transistor begins to decrease. This drop-off in α is related to transit-time effects of the carriers as they move from the emitter to the collector.

The α cutoff frequency f_α is that frequency where the α has dropped to 0.707 of its low-frequency value. For instance, if a transistor has an α with a low-frequency value of 0.98 and an $f_\alpha = 1$ MHz, then at 1 MHz the α will equal

$$\alpha = 0.707(0.98) = 0.693$$

This means that at 1 MHz the collector current is only 0.693 times the input emitter current.

Thus, the f_α of a transistor represents one of the limitations on the upper-frequency response of a CB circuit. When possible, we select a transistor whose f_α is much higher than the highest frequency at which we want to operate.

The second major limitation on the high-frequency response of the CB circuit of Fig. 13-4a is the capacitance from the collector to ground. Even though no capacitance is shown, there is always some stray wiring capacitance that appears from collector to ground. In addition, the back-biased collector diode has capacitance, as discussed in Sec. 4-5. Both of these capacitive effects are represented by C_L in the a-c equivalent circuit of Fig. 13-4b. The coupling capacitors are shown as short circuits because we are now analyzing higher-frequency operation.

When we increase the frequency sufficiently, the reactance of C_L eventually becomes low enough to shunt some of the a-c collector current. This means that there is less current in r_L, so that the output voltage is less. The cutoff frequency occurs when the reactance of C_L equals the value of r_L. That is,

$$\frac{1}{2\pi f C_L} = r_L$$

Solving for f gives us the cutoff frequency.

$$f = \frac{1}{2\pi r_L C_L} \tag{13-5}$$

There are other high-frequency effects, but the two we have discussed are the major limitations on the high-frequency response of a CB circuit like that of Fig. 13-4a. Normally, to maintain a flat frequency response up to the cutoff point, the source resistance r_s is deliberately made much larger than the r'_e of the transistor. In other words, the emitter diode is swamped; this avoids certain inductive effects that occur in a CB circuit.

The f_α and the frequency given by Eq. (13-5) are usually different. In this case, the *lower* of the two frequencies is more critical. For instance, suppose that a CB circuit like that of Fig. 13-4a has an f_α of 10 MHz and that the cutoff frequency given by Eq. (13-5) is 2 MHz. The 2 MHz is the more critical value because the response has already dropped off at 2 MHz. The cutoff frequency of the overall amplifier (the 3-db frequency) is approximately equal to 2 MHz.

If the two frequencies happen to be exactly equal, the amplifier response will be down 6 db at this cutoff frequency. The actual cutoff frequency of the amplifier is lower than this cutoff frequency and is approximately equal to

$$f_2 \cong 0.65 f_\alpha$$

As an example, suppose that the f_α is 10 MHz and that the cutoff frequency caused by C_L is also 10 MHz. The output of the amplifier will be down 6 db at 10 MHz. The approximate 3-db cutoff frequency of the amplifier will be at 0.65(10 MHz), which equals 6.5 MHz.

EXAMPLE 13-2

The transistor in Fig. 13-5 has a collector capacitance C_c of 30 pf and an f_α of 5 MHz. The stray wiring capacitance from collector to ground is 20 pf. Find the approximate value of the upper cutoff frequency.

SOLUTION

The f_α represents one of the upper-frequency limits. Since it equals 5 MHz, we know that the a-c emitter current is down 3 db at 5 MHz.

Next, we determine the cutoff frequency produced by the capacitance from collector to ground. This capacitance C_L is the sum of the collector capacitance and the stray wiring capacitance.

$$C_L = C_c + C_{\text{stray}} = (30 + 20)(10^{-12}) = 50 \text{ pf}$$

Using Eq. (13-5), we get

$$f = \frac{1}{2\pi(5000)(50)(10^{-12})} = 635 \text{ kHz}$$

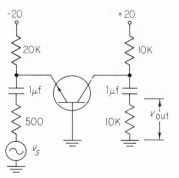

Fig. 13-5 Examples 13-2 and 13-3.

The frequency limitation of 635 kHz is the more critical value. At this frequency, the output voltage is down 3 db from the mid-frequency value. At this frequency, there is no problem at all with the α cutoff of the transistor.

EXAMPLE 13-3

The transistor of Fig. 13-5 has an f_α of 300 kHz and a collector capacitance C_c of 2 pf. The stray capacitance from collector to ground is 3 pf. Find the approximate lower and upper cutoff frequencies of the amplifier.

SOLUTION

In Example 13-1, we analyzed the circuit to determine the lower cutoff frequency. We found that the input coupling capacitor produces a cutoff frequency of 300 Hz, while the output coupling capacitor caused a cutoff of 8 Hz. Thus, the lower cutoff frequency of the amplifier is approximately 300 Hz.

The upper cutoff frequency of the CB circuit is determined by the cutoff frequency produced by C_L or by the f_α of the transistor, whichever is lower. Using Eq. (13-5), we get

$$f = \frac{1}{2\pi(5000)(5)(10^{-12})} = 6.35 \text{ MHz}$$

Since we are given that $f_\alpha = 300$ kHz, it is clear that in this case the f_α is lower than the cutoff frequency produced by C_L. Thus, the upper cutoff frequency is 300 kHz.

13-4   Lower Cutoff Frequency of a CE Amplifier

In a CE amplifier like that of Fig. 13-6a, the coupling capacitors again produce a lower cutoff frequency. For the moment, let us assume that the bypass capacitor C_E is extremely large so that the emitter is held at a-c ground. In this case, we can draw the a-c equivalent circuit as in Fig. 13-6b. On the input side, it is clear that the series RC circuit is similar to that analyzed for the CB amplifier. Again, we note that when the reactance of the input capacitor equals the total series resistance, the input current will be down 3 db. We can find the cutoff frequency produced by the input capacitor as follows.

$$\frac{1}{2\pi f C_s} = r_s + r_{\text{in}}$$

or

$$f = \frac{1}{2\pi(r_s + r_{\text{in}})C_s} \tag{13-6}$$

Equation (13-6) tells us how to find the cutoff frequency produced by the input coupling capacitor. To find the cutoff frequency produced by the output coupling capacitor, we can use Thévenin's theorem to redraw the output circuit, as shown in Fig. 13-6c. In the output circuit, we again have a series RC circuit. This means that cutoff occurs when

$$\frac{1}{2\pi f C} = R_L + R$$

or

$$f = \frac{1}{2\pi(R_L + R)C} \tag{13-7}$$

By using Eqs. (13-6) and (13-7), we can find the cutoff frequencies produced by the coupling capacitors. Again, note that the higher of these

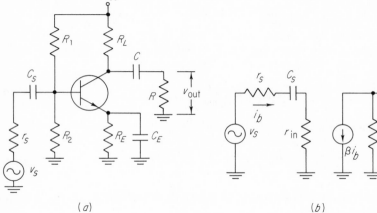

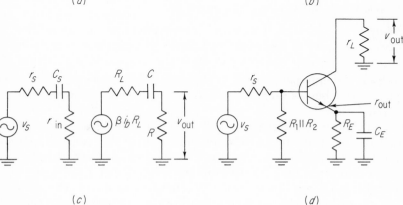

Fig. 13-6 Deriving the lower cutoff frequencies of a CE stage.

two frequencies is the more important as far as the overall low-frequency response is concerned.

The bypass capacitor C_E also causes a lower-frequency cutoff to occur. The reason for this is as follows. The bypass capacitor is supposed to keep the emitter at a-c ground. At low enough frequencies, however, this capacitor no longer looks like an a-c short to the signal. Because of this, degeneration takes place at the emitter, with a resulting loss in voltage gain.

To find the cutoff frequency caused by the bypass capacitor, consider Fig. 13-6d, where we have shown the essential parts of the a-c equivalent circuit. Looking back into the emitter of the transistor, there is a resistance labeled r_{out}. As far as the bypass capacitor is concerned, it sees r_{out} in parallel with R_E. To hold the emitter at a-c ground, the reactance of C_E must be much smaller than r_{out} in parallel with R_E. But when the frequency is so low that the reactance of C_E equals $r_{\text{out}} \| R_E$, the voltage gain will be down by 3 db. In other words, cutoff occurs when

$$\frac{1}{2\pi f C_E} = r_{\text{out}} \| R_E$$

or

$$f = \frac{1}{2\pi (r_{\text{out}} \| R_E) C_E} \tag{13-8}$$

It can be shown that the resistance r_{out} is

$$r_{\text{out}} \cong r_e' + \frac{r_s \| R_1 \| R_2}{\beta} \tag{13-9}$$

when the emitter is bypassed to ground. When some of the emitter resistance is left unbypassed, r_{out} becomes

$$r_{\text{out}} = r_E + r_e' + \frac{r_s \| R_1 \| R_2}{\beta}$$

where r_E is the unbypassed part of the emitter resistance. Also, when two-supply emitter bias is used, R_B takes the place of $R_1 \| R_2$ in the last two equations.

In analyzing a CE circuit to find its lower cutoff frequency, we use Eqs. (13-6) to (13-8) to find the individual cutoff frequencies produced by the different capacitors. As usual, the largest of these frequencies is the most important because the amplifier voltage gain first begins dropping at this frequency. Since these cutoff frequencies are usually different, we can approximate the cutoff frequency of the overall stage by using the largest of these frequencies.

EXAMPLE 13-4

Find the approximate value of the lower cutoff frequency in Fig. 13-7.

SOLUTION

First, we find the cutoff frequency produced by the input coupling capacitor. This cutoff frequency is given by Eq. (13-6).

$$f = \frac{1}{2\pi(r_s + r_{in})C_s}$$

The value of r_s and C_s are given, but we need to estimate the value of r_{in}. Recall that for a CE stage of this type,

$$r_{in} \cong R_B \| \beta r'_e$$

There is about 1 ma of d-c emitter current, so that r'_e is between 25 and 50 ohms. Arbitrarily, let us use the upper limit of 50 ohms. With a β of 100, $\beta r'_e = 5000$ ohms. Thus, the input resistance of the stage is

$$r_{in} \cong R_B \| \beta r'_e = 30,000 \| 5000 \cong 4300$$

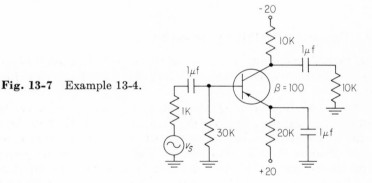

Fig. 13-7 Example 13-4.

Now, we can find the cutoff frequency produced by the input coupling capacitor.

$$f = \frac{1}{2\pi(1000 + 4300)(10^{-6})} = 30 \text{ Hz}$$

By using Eq. (13-7), we can find the cutoff frequency produced by the output coupling capacitor.

$$f = \frac{1}{2\pi(R_L + R)C} = \frac{1}{2\pi(10,000 + 10,000)(10^{-6})} \cong 8 \text{ Hz}$$

Also, we can find the cutoff frequency produced by the bypass capacitor. To do this, we need the value of r_{out}. With Eq. (13-9), we calculate

$$r_{out} = r'_e + \frac{r_s\|R_1\|R_2}{\beta} = 50 + \frac{1000\|30{,}000}{100} \cong 60$$

Now, we use Eq. (13-8) to find the cutoff frequency.

$$f = \frac{1}{2\pi(r_{out}\|R_E)C_E} = \frac{1}{2\pi(60\|20{,}000)(10^{-6})} = 2650 \text{ Hz}$$

Of the three frequencies, 30, 8, and 2650 Hz, the most important is 2650 Hz, because the amplifier response first falls off at this frequency. Therefore, the approximate lower cutoff frequency of the amplifier in Fig. 13-7 is 2650 Hz.

The low-frequency response of the amplifier in Fig. 13-7 is quite poor. One way to lower this cutoff frequency is to use a larger bypass capacitor. For example, if we increase C_E from 1 to 10 μf, the cutoff frequency will change from 2650 to 265 Hz. Another approach to reducing the cutoff frequency is to leave some of the emitter resistance unbypassed. This is equivalent to increasing the size of r_{out}, which in turn reduces the cutoff frequency.

13-5   Transistor Cutoff Frequencies

In the preceding section, we discussed the α cutoff frequency of a transistor, which is the frequency where the α drops to 0.707 of its low-frequency value.

The β cutoff frequency, symbolized by f_β, is another important transistor cutoff frequency. The f_β is the frequency where the β of the transistor drops to 0.707 of its low-frequency value. To bring the idea out more clearly, consider the CE connection of Fig. 13-8. A voltage source with a large source resistance drives the transistor so that the input a-c base current remains fixed at all frequencies. Here is what we find when we increase the frequency. As we approach higher frequencies, the a-c collector current begins to decrease. Since the a-c base current is fixed, this is equivalent to saying that the β is decreasing. Eventually, we find a frequency at which the β has decreased to 0.707 of its low-frequency value; this frequency is called the β cutoff frequency f_β.

The f_T of a transistor is still another important high-frequency characteristic of a transistor. In Fig. 13-8, if the frequency of operation is increased above the f_β of the transistor, the β will continue to decrease. *Eventually, we find a frequency where the $\beta = 1$; this frequency is called the f_T of the transistor.*

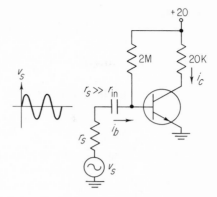

Fig. 13-8 The f_β and f_T of a transistor.

The f_T of a transistor is much higher than the f_β. The relation between these two frequencies is

$$f_\beta = \frac{f_T}{\beta} \tag{13-10}$$

where β is the low-frequency value of β. As an example, suppose that a data sheet gives an f_T of 100 MHz and a low-frequency β of 50. The β cutoff frequency would then be

$$f_\beta = \frac{100 \text{ MHz}}{50} = 2 \text{ MHz}$$

The f_α and the f_T of a transistor are also related. As a rough approximation, they are often treated as equal, that is,

$$f_T \cong f_\alpha \tag{13-11}$$

Actually, the f_T is less than the f_α. For simple junction transistors, a better approximation is

$$f_T \cong \frac{f_\alpha}{1.2} \tag{13-12}$$

The various cutoff frequencies are important in the high-frequency analysis of transistor circuits. The f_α is one of the limitations of the CB amplifier. The f_β and the f_T are important in the analysis of a CE amplifier, which will be discussed in a later section.

EXAMPLE 13-5

We have two transistors. The first has an f_T of 200 MHz and a low-frequency β of 150. The second has an f_T of 100 MHz and a low-frequency β of 20. Calculate the f_β for each transistor. Which transistor has the higher f_β?

SOLUTION

The first transistor has a β cutoff frequency of

$$f_\beta = \frac{f_T}{\beta} = \frac{200(10^6)}{150} = 1.33 \text{ MHz}$$

The second has an f_β of

$$f_\beta = \frac{100(10^6)}{20} = 5 \text{ MHz}$$

Clearly, the second transistor has the higher β cutoff frequency.

EXAMPLE 13-6

A simple junction transistor has an f_α of 50 MHz and a low-frequency β of 75. Estimate the f_β of the transistor.

SOLUTION

As a rough approximation, we can treat f_α and f_T as equal, so that

$$f_\beta = \frac{f_T}{\beta} \cong \frac{f_\alpha}{\beta} = \frac{50 \text{ MHz}}{75} = 667 \text{ kHz}$$

We can improve this estimate by using Eq. (13-12) to get a more accurate value of f_T.

$$f_T \cong \frac{f_\alpha}{1.2} = \frac{50 \text{ MHz}}{1.2} = 41.6 \text{ MHz}$$

And now we can find f_β.

$$f_\beta \cong \frac{41.6 \text{ MHz}}{75} = 555 \text{ kHz}$$

13-6   Base Spreading Resistance

Another quantity that is important in the high-frequency analysis of a CE stage is the base spreading resistance r_b'. We discussed this in Chap. 5. Recall that r_b' is the bulk, or ohmic, resistance of that part of the base in which base current flows. The r_b' of a transistor depends upon the dimensions of the base as well as upon the d-c operating point of the transistor. There is no simple rule of thumb for the value of r_b'. Usually, the value of r_b' is in the range of 5 to 500 ohms. For many transistors, r_b' is between 50 and 150 ohms.

We can improve the ideal-transistor approximation by taking r_b' into account. This resistance is in series with the base lead, so that we can add it to base, as shown in the a-c equivalent circuit of Fig. 13-9. A derivation similar to that given in Sec. 6-7 shows that the voltage gain is

$$\frac{v_{\text{out}}}{v_{\text{in}}} = \frac{r_L}{r'_e + r'_b/\beta} \tag{13-13}$$

Also, the input resistance is

$$r_{\text{in}} = r'_b + \beta r'_e \tag{13-14}$$

In the ideal-transistor approximation, we have neglected the effect of r'_b on the input resistance and the voltage gain. This is usually a reasonable approximation. For instance, suppose a transistor has a β of 100. For a d-c emitter current of 1 ma, r'_e is about 25 to 50 ohms. The base spreading resistance is typically 50 to 150 ohms. If we use an r'_e of 25 and an r'_b of 150, we would calculate an input resistance of

$$r_{\text{in}} = r'_b + \beta r'_e = 150 + 100(25) = 2650 \text{ ohms}$$

By neglecting r'_b, as we do in the ideal-transistor approximation, we get

$$r_{\text{in}} \cong \beta r'_e = 100(25) = 2500$$

Similarly, in the voltage-gain formula, Eq. (13-13), we usually find that r'_e is much greater than r'_b/β, so that the effects of r'_b are negligible.

Fig. 13-9 Base spreading resistance.

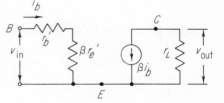

Occasionally, we cannot neglect r'_b. This is especially true at very high d-c emitter currents, where the value of r'_e becomes quite small. In this case, Eqs. (13-13) and (13-14) are useful in getting a more accurate prediction of voltage gain and input resistance. (Also, h parameters, which are discussed in the next chapter, can be used.)

The base spreading resistance r'_b is not too important at lower frequencies; however, when we increase the frequency of operation, we find that the internal transistor capacitances begin to shunt the $\beta r'_e$ of Fig. 13-9. When this happens, the r'_b does become quite important in determining the upper-frequency limitations of a transistor. This is discussed in the next section.

EXAMPLE 13-7

The transistor of Fig. 13-10 has an r_b' of 100 ohms, a β of 50, and an r_e' of 25 mv/I_E. Find the approximate voltage gain and input resistance (including the bias resistances) in the passband of the amplifier.

SOLUTION

In the passband, or mid-frequency range of the amplifier, all capacitive effects are negligible. Hence, we have straightforward calculations involving Eqs. (13-13) and (13-14). We first need the value of r_e'.

$$r_e' = \frac{25 \text{ mv}}{I_E} \cong \frac{25 \text{ mv}}{5 \text{ ma}} = 5 \text{ ohms}$$

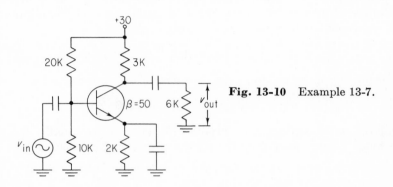

Fig. 13-10   Example 13-7.

Now, we can find the voltage gain.

$$\frac{v_{\text{out}}}{v_{\text{in}}} \cong \frac{r_L}{r_e' + r_b'/\beta} = \frac{3000\|6000}{5 + {}^{100}\!/_{50}} = \frac{2000}{7} = 286$$

The input resistance looking into the base without accounting for the biasing resistors is

$$r_{\text{in}} = r_b' + \beta r_e' = 100 + 50(5) = 350$$

The biasing resistors, 20 and 10 kilohms, appear in parallel with 350 ohms. Since the biasing resistors are large enough to neglect, the input resistance of the stage is approximately 350 ohms.

13-7   Upper-frequency Limit of a CE Stage

In Sec. 13-3 we discussed the upper cutoff frequency of a CB stage. We saw that the high-frequency response of such a circuit is limited by the f_α or by the cutoff produced by the output capacitance.

The CE circuit also has high-frequency limitations, one of which is the cutoff produced by the capacitance from collector to ground. In Fig. 13-11 we have shown the a-c equivalent circuit of a CE stage. The capacitance C_L includes the stray-wiring capacitance and the collector-diode capacitance C_c. That is,

$$C_L = C_{\text{stray}} + C_c$$

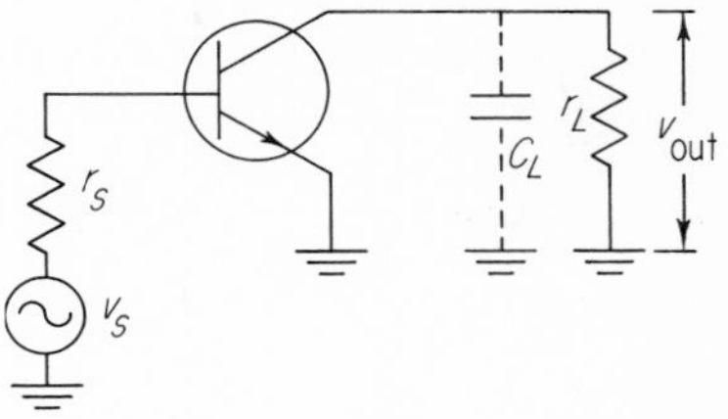

Fig. 13-11 Deriving the output cutoff frequency.

A cutoff frequency occurs when the reactance of C_L equals the value of r_L, because under this condition the current in r_L is down 3 db. We can write

$$\frac{1}{2\pi f C_L} = r_L$$

or

$$f = \frac{1}{2\pi r_L C_L} \tag{13-15}$$

The frequency given by this equation is one of the major limitations on a CE amplifier. We will call this frequency the *output cutoff frequency*.

The decrease in β mentioned in a previous section is another major limitation on the high-frequency response of a CE circuit. An a-c equivalent circuit often used to account for this decrease in β is the circuit shown in Fig. 13-12a. There is an emitter capacitance C_e across the emitter-base junction and a collector capacitance C_c across the collector-base junction. β_0 is the low-frequency value of β. Note that the current through the $\beta_0 r'_e$ resistor is labeled i'_b. At lower frequencies, all the input base current i_b passes through r'_b and through $\beta_0 r'_e$. In effect, $i'_b = i_b$ at lower frequencies. However, as the frequency increases, the reactances decrease until some of the input base current i_b is diverted from the $\beta_0 r'_e$ resistor. In other words, when the frequency is increased enough, the value of i'_b begins to drop off; therefore, the $\beta_0 i'_b$ current source begins to decrease in value, resulting in less collector current.

When a high-impedance source drives the transistor, the value of i_b remains fixed as the frequency increases. If we place an a-c short across the output terminals, as in Fig. 13-12b, and measure i_c, we find that i_c begins to drop off as we approach higher frequencies. The reason for this is simply that the internal capacitances shunt input base current

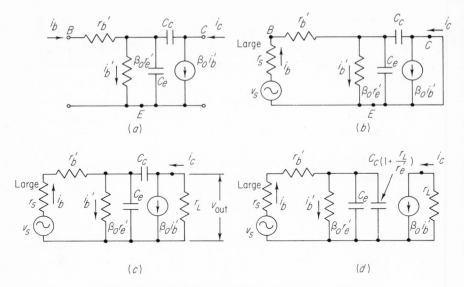

Fig. 13-12 High-frequency equivalent circuits.

away from the $\beta_0 r'_e$ resistor. The actual current through $\beta_0 r'_e$ then drops off, and this causes the output current $\beta_0 i'_b$ to drop off. The β cutoff frequency discussed earlier is the frequency where the collector current in Fig. 13-12b drops to 0.707 of its low-frequency value.

If we connect an a-c load r_L across the output terminals (Fig. 13-12c) instead of a short, we will get an output voltage. As a rough approximation, we can say that the output voltage will be down 3 db from its low-frequency value when the frequency equals the f_β of the transistor.

The use of f_β as the upper cutoff frequency for the output voltage of a CE stage is only a rough approximation, because the presence of a load resistor r_L instead of a short introduces a complicating effect known as the *Miller capacitance*. When a capacitor like C_c spans from the output back to the input, as in Fig. 13-12c, the effective capacitance seen by the source is $C_c(1 + A)$, where A equals r_L/r'_e. This Miller capacitance is normally shown by redrawing the circuit as in Fig. 13-12d. Note that as far as the input base current is concerned, C_c appears larger by a factor of $1 + r_L/r'_e$. This means that the shunting effect of this capacitor can be significant at frequencies that are lower than f_β.

To summarize our results up to this point, we can say that when a CE stage is driven by a large source impedance, the voltage gain will drop off at a frequency that is less than the f_β of the transistor.

When the source impedance is not large enough to hold i_b fixed at all frequencies, the analysis of a CE stage becomes quite complicated. We will merely indicate that the following approximation can be used to estimate the upper cutoff frequency caused by internal transistor capacitances.

$$f_c \cong f_\beta \left(1 + \frac{\beta_0 r'_e}{r_s + r'_b}\right) \frac{1}{1 + 2\pi f r r_L C_c} \tag{13-16}$$

For convenience, we will call this the *internal cutoff frequency*.

In estimating the cutoff frequency of a CE stage we must calculate the output cutoff frequency by using Eq. (13-15) and the internal cutoff frequency by using Eq. (13-16). The lower of these two frequencies is the more critical value; it is the frequency where the output voltage of the CE amplifier is down about 3 db from its low-frequency value.

When troubleshooting or making an initial analysis of a CE stage, we often do not have the values of r'_b, β_0, f_T, etc. In this case, we can crudely estimate the internal cutoff frequency of Eq. (13-16) by the f_β of the transistor.

EXAMPLE 13-8

The transistor of Fig. 13-13 has an f_T of 100 MHz and a low-frequency β of 100. The stray-wiring capacitance plus the collector capacitance equals 20 pf. Estimate the upper cutoff frequency of the amplifier by using the f_β of the transistor or the output cutoff frequency (Eq. 13-15), whichever is smaller.

SOLUTION

The β cutoff frequency is

$$f_\beta = \frac{100 \text{ MHz}}{100} = 1 \text{ MHz}$$

Using Eq. (13-15), we calculate an output cutoff frequency of

$$f = \frac{1}{2\pi r_L C_L} = \frac{1}{2\pi (2000)(20)(10^{-12})} = 4 \text{ MHz}$$

Fig. 13-13   Examples 13-8 and 13-9.

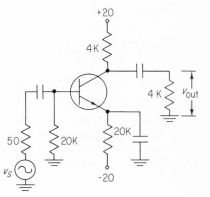

We therefore can estimate the upper cutoff frequency of the amplifier by using the lower value, which is 1 MHz.

EXAMPLE 13-9

In addition to the values given in the preceding example, the transistor has an r_b' of 100 ohms, an r_e' of 25 ohms, and a C_c of 5 pf. Find the cutoff frequency of the amplifier by using the internal cutoff frequency or the output cutoff frequency, whichever is smaller.

SOLUTION

We find the internal cutoff frequency by using Eq. (13-16).

$$f_c = 10^6 \left(1 + \frac{100(25)}{50 + 100}\right) \frac{1}{1 + 2\pi(10^8)(2)(10^3)(5)(10^{-12})}$$
$$= 2.43 \text{ MHz}$$

The stray and collector capacitances produce an output cutoff frequency of 4 MHz, as shown in the preceding example; therefore, as an estimate, we can say that the cutoff frequency of the amplifier is the lower value, 2.43 MHz.

13-8   Response of Cascaded States

When several amplifier stages are cascaded together, the overall voltage gain is the product of the individual stage gains. In addition, the cutoff frequency of the cascade must be less than the cutoff frequency of the individual stages. For instance, if we cascade three identical stages together, each of which has an upper cutoff frequency of 1 MHz, the overall amplifier has a cutoff frequency much lower than 1 MHz.

There are some useful approximations for estimating the overall cutoff frequency of several identical stages in cascade. The lower cutoff frequency f_1 can be found by using

$$f_1 \cong 1.1 f_c \sqrt{n} \qquad\qquad (13\text{-}17)$$

where f_1 is the lower cutoff frequency of the cascade
    f_c is the lower cutoff frequency of one stage
    n is the number of stages

For nonidentical stages, the exact formula for the cutoff frequency is complicated. We will only observe that if the cutoff frequencies of the individual stages are reasonably close together, Eq. (13-17) still applies as an approximation if we use the average of the individual cutoff frequencies. On the other hand, if one of the stages has a much higher cutoff

frequency than the others, this stage predominates, and the overall cascade has a lower cutoff frequency approximately equal to the cutoff
frequency of the dominant stage.

Similarly, there is a useful approximation for the upper cutoff frequency
of a cascade of identical stages. It is

$$f_2 \cong \frac{f_c}{1.1 \sqrt{n}} \tag{13-18}$$

where f_2 is the upper cutoff frequency of the cascade
   f_c is the upper cutoff frequency of one stage
   n is the number of stages

Again note that we can use this formula even when the stages are not
identical. As long as the individual stages have cutoff frequencies that
are close to each other, we can use the average value for f_c in Eq. (13-18).
If one of the stages has a much lower cutoff frequency than the others,
it predominates in the cascade, and the overall amplifier has an upper
cutoff frequency approximately equal to that of the critical stage.

EXAMPLE 13-10

Suppose that five identical stages are cascaded. Each has a lower
cutoff frequency of 100 Hz and an upper cutoff frequency of 10 MHz.
Find the lower and upper cutoff frequencies of the overall amplifier.

SOLUTION

The lower cutoff frequency is

$$f_1 \cong 1.1 f_c \sqrt{n} = 1.1(100) \sqrt{5} \cong 250 \text{ Hz}$$

and the upper cutoff frequency is

$$f_2 \cong \frac{f_c}{1.1 \sqrt{n}} = \frac{10(10^6)}{1.1 \sqrt{5}} \cong 4 \text{ MHz}$$

Thus, we see that the passband of a single stage extends from 100 Hz
to 10 MHz, whereas a cascade of five such stages has a passband of 250 Hz
to 4 MHz.

SUMMARY

The cutoff frequencies of an amplifier are those frequencies where the output voltage drops to 0.707 of its mid-frequency value. This is equivalent
to saying that the output voltage is down 3 db at the cutoff frequencies.

For a simple CB amplifier, the input and output coupling capacitors determine the lower-frequency limit of the amplifier. Each of these capacitors produces a cutoff frequency, and the larger of these two frequencies is the more critical value.

The f_α and the output cutoff frequency are the two major limitations on the high-frequency response of a CB amplifier. The f_α is the frequency where the α has dropped to 0.707 of its low-frequency value. The output cutoff frequency is the frequency where the reactance of the collector-ground capacitance equals the a-c load resistance seen by the collector. The approximate cutoff frequency of a CB amplifier is the f_α or the output cutoff frequency, whichever is smaller.

The coupling capacitors in a CE amplifier produce lower cutoff frequencies. In addition, the emitter bypass capacitor (when used) produces a lower cutoff frequency. Of the three cutoff frequencies (input capacitor, output capacitor, and bypass capacitor), the largest is the most critical and can be used as an estimate of the lower cutoff frequency of a CE amplifier.

The β cutoff frequency f_β is the frequency where the β of a transistor drops to 0.707 of its low-frequency value. The f_T is the frequency where the β has dropped to unity.

The internal cutoff frequency and the output cutoff frequency are the two major limitations on the high-frequency voltage gain of a CE amplifier. The internal cutoff frequency can be crudely estimated by using the f_β. We can get a more accurate value for this internal cutoff frequency by using Eq. (13-16). The output cutoff frequency is that frequency where the reactance of the collector-ground capacitance equals the a-c load resistance seen by the collector. The approximate upper cutoff frequency of a CE amplifier is the internal cutoff frequency or the output cutoff frequency, whichever is smaller.

GLOSSARY

α cutoff frequency (f_α)   The frequency at which the α of a transistor equals 0.707 of its low-frequency value.

base spreading resistance (r_b')   The resistance of that part of the base region through which base current flows.

β cutoff frequency (f_β)   The frequency at which the β of a transistor equals 0.707 of its low-frequency value.

f_T   The frequency where the β of the transistor equals unity. The f_T is sometimes called the gain-bandwidth product of the transistor.

internal cutoff frequency   A term used in this chapter to describe the cutoff frequency produced by the internal transistor capacitances, including the Miller effect.

output cutoff frequency The cutoff produced by the collector-ground capacitance in conjunction with the a-c load resistance r_L seen by the collector.

passband In an amplifier, this is the range of frequencies between the lower and upper cutoff frequencies.

REVIEW QUESTIONS

1. How are the cutoff frequencies of an amplifier defined?
2. What is the passband of an amplifier?
3. In a CB amplifier, the input and output coupling capacitors each produce a cutoff frequency. Which of these frequencies is the more critical as far as the overall amplifier response is concerned?
4. What are the two major limitations on the high-frequency response of a CB amplifier?
5. Define the α cutoff frequency f_α of a transistor.
6. Does the emitter bypass capacitor in a CE circuit produce a low or a high cutoff frequency?
7. Define the f_β and the f_T of a transistor.
8. Is the f_T of a junction transistor much greater than, much less than, or approximately equal to the f_α?
9. Define the base spreading resistance r_b'. What is a typical range in value for r_b'?
10. What are the two major limitations on the high-frequency response of a CE circuit? Which of these is the more critical cutoff frequency?
11. If four identical stages are cascaded, is the lower cutoff frequency of the cascade higher or lower than the lower cutoff frequency of one stage? What about the upper cutoff frequency of the overall amplifier?

PROBLEMS

13-1 Find the cutoff frequencies produced by the input and output coupling capacitors in Fig. 13-14a. Which of these sets the lower frequency limit on the CB amplifier?

13-2 What are the cutoff frequencies produced by the coupling capacitors in Fig. 13-14b? To make these frequencies exactly equal, what size should the output coupling capacitor be changed to?

13-3 If the 50-ohm source resistance in Fig. 13-14b is changed to a 500-ohm resistor, what new value can be used for the input coupling capacitor to maintain the same cutoff frequency (approximately)?

13-4 The transistor in Fig. 13-14a has an f_α of 10 MHz. The collector diode capacitance is 20 pf, and the stray wiring capacitance from collector

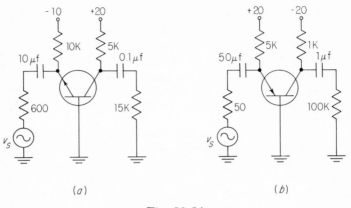

Fig. 13-14

to ground is 45 pf. Find the approximate value of the upper cutoff frequency of the amplifier.

13-5   The transistor in Fig. 13-14a has an f_α of 300 MHz. The collector capacitance and the stray wiring capacitance total 10 pf. What is the approximate upper cutoff frequency of the amplifier?

13-6   The transistor of Fig. 13-15a has a β of 75 and an r_e' of 25 mv/I_E. Find the cutoff frequency produced by the emitter bypass capacitor.

13-7   The transistor of Fig. 13-15b has a β of 50 and an r_e' of 35 mv/I_E. What is the cutoff frequency produced by the emitter bypass capacitor?

13-8   In Fig. 13-15a, the transistor has an r_b' of 100 ohms and an r_e' of 25 mv/I_E. The β is 100. Find the voltage gain from base to collector and the voltage gain from the source to the collector. Use Eq. (13-13).

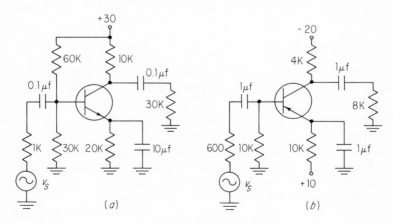

Fig. 13-15

13-9 The transistor of Fig. 13-15b has an r_b' of 250 ohms and an r_e' of 25 mv/I_E. If the β is 50, what is the voltage gain from the source to the output? Use Eq. (13-13).

13-10 The f_β of a transistor is 3 MHz and the β is 75. What is the f_T of the transistor?

13-11 A junction transistor has an f_α of 500 MHz. What is the approximate value of f_T? If the β spread is from 50 to 150, what is the spread in the f_β?

13-12 The transistor in Fig. 13-15a has an f_T of 250 MHz and a low-frequency β of 75. The stray wiring capacitance plus the collector diode capacitance is 15 pf. Estimate the upper cutoff frequency by using the f_β or the output cutoff frequency, whichever is lower.

13-13 In Fig. 13-16a, the transistor has the following characteristics: $C_c = 3$ pf, $f_T = 300$ MHz, $\beta_0 = 75$, $r_e' = 25$, and $r_b' = 50$. The stray wiring capacitance from collector to ground is 7 pf. Calculate the output cutoff frequency and the internal cutoff frequency.

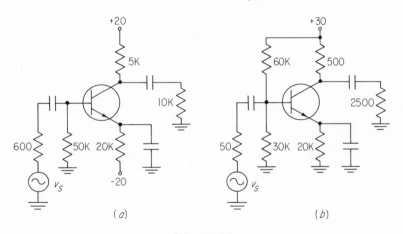

Fig. 13-16

13-14 The transistor in Fig. 13-16b has the following parameters: $r_b' = 75$ ohms, $C_c = 5$ pf, $\beta_0 = 100$, $r_e' = 50$ ohms, and $f_T = 200$ MHz. The stray wiring capacitance from collector to ground is 10 pf. Calculate the internal and output cutoff frequencies of the amplifier.

13-15 Using the data given in Prob. 13-14, calculate the internal cutoff frequency if the source resistance is changed from 50 ohms to 5 kilohms.

14 | h Parameters

The ideal-transistor approximation is adequate for most preliminary analysis and design. When more accurate predictions of transistor behavior are needed, we must take into account the second-order effects that are neglected in the ideal-transistor approximation.

One of the methods that takes all transistor characteristics into account is the h-parameter approach. This method of analysis is complicated and somewhat impractical; nevertheless, we must have a basic knowledge of h parameters because many transistor data sheets describe the transistor in terms of its h parameters. Further, there are times when we need as accurate a prediction as possible for the behavior of a transistor circuit. The h-parameter approach, in theory at least, can give us exact answers.

14-1   Concept of the h Parameters

Suppose we have a linear circuit, as shown in Fig. 14-1. (A linear circuit is one in which the resistances, inductances, and capacitances remain fixed when the voltage across them changes.) This circuit has an input voltage and current labeled v_1 and i_1. The circuit also has an output voltage and current labeled v_2 and i_2. The upper terminals are arbitrarily shown as *positive* with respect to the lower terminals. Also, we have shown the currents flowing *into* the box.

The actual voltages and currents can have different polarities and directions; however, we need to agree on a convention at the outset of our discussion. Therefore, we adopt the convention shown in Fig. 14-1. We assume that currents flow *into* the box and that voltages are *positive* from the upper to the lower terminals. When we analyze circuits in which the voltages are of opposite polarity or where the currents flow out of the box, we simply treat these voltages and currents as negative quantities.

In Fig. 14-1, we certainly expect the voltages and currents to be related to each other. For instance, if we were to change the value of v_1, we would not be surprised if i_1, i_2, and v_2 were to change. In other words, we expect the two currents and two voltages of Fig. 14-1 to be mathematically related.

Fig. 14-1 Developing the concept of *h* parameters.

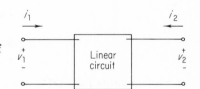

One of the theorems proved in advanced circuit theory is that the voltages and currents of Fig. 14-1 can be related by the following set of equations.

$$v_1 = h_{11}i_1 + h_{12}v_2 \qquad (14\text{-}1)$$
$$i_2 = h_{21}i_1 + h_{22}v_2 \qquad (14\text{-}2)$$

In these equations, the *h*'s are fixed coefficients, or constants, for any given circuit. For instance, we might have a particular circuit whose voltages and currents are related by

$$v_1 = 10i_1 + 5v_2$$
$$i_2 = 2i_1 + 3v_2$$

In this case, we would say that the circuit has *h* parameters given by $h_{11} = 10$, $h_{12} = 5$, $h_{21} = 2$, and $h_{22} = 3$.

If we change the circuit, the set of *h* parameters would change. In other words, for each distinct circuit there is a set of *h* parameters associated with that circuit. Once these *h* parameters are known, we can use Eqs. (14-1) and (14-2) to find the voltages and currents in the circuit.

How do we find the *h* parameters of a given circuit? To answer this, consider Fig. 14-2. A linear circuit is driven by an input voltage of v_1. This input voltage sets up an input current of i_1, whose size depends upon what is inside the box. Notice that we are using a zero-resistance load on the output side, that is, a short circuit. With a short on the output

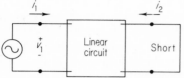

Fig. 14-2 Finding the forward parameters, h_{11} and h_{21}.

terminals, we can definitely say that the output voltage v_2 must be zero. Since $v_2 = 0$ when the output is shorted, Eqs. (14-1) and (14-2) simplify to

$$v_1 = h_{11}i_1 + h_{12}(0)$$
$$i_2 = h_{21}i_1 + h_{22}(0)$$

or

$$v_1 = h_{11}i_1$$
$$i_2 = h_{21}i_1$$

Now we can solve for each h value to get

$$h_{11} = \frac{v_1}{i_1} \qquad \text{for } v_2 = 0 \qquad \text{output shorted} \qquad (14\text{-}3)$$

and

$$h_{21} = \frac{i_2}{i_1} \qquad \text{for } v_2 = 0 \qquad \text{output shorted} \qquad (14\text{-}4)$$

It is important to realize the physical meaning of these equations. Eq. (14-3) tells us that h_{11} is the ratio of v_1 to i_1 with the output terminals shorted. The ratio of a voltage to a current is an impedance. Because of this, we interpret h_{11} as the input impedance with the output shorted.

Equation (14-4) tells us that h_{21} is the ratio of i_2 to i_1 with the output terminals shorted. Since the ratio of the output current to the input current is involved, we can interpret h_{21} as the current gain of the circuit with the output shorted.

In general, if we are given the schematic of a circuit, we can find h_{11} and h_{21} by calculating the input impedance and the current gain of the circuit under the condition that the output terminals are shorted together.

A method for finding h_{12} and h_{22} is the following. Consider Fig. 14-3. Note that we are now driving the output terminals with a voltage v_2. This sets up a current of i_2. Especially note that the input terminals are open. We have deliberately left the input terminals open so that we can unequivocally state that $i_1 = 0$. In other words, with the input terminals open, there can be no current on the input side. With $i_1 = 0$, the general *h*-parameter equations reduce to

$$v_1 = h_{11}(0) + h_{12}v_2$$
$$i_2 = h_{21}(0) + h_{22}v_2$$

or

$$v_1 = h_{12}v_2$$
$$i_2 = h_{22}v_2$$

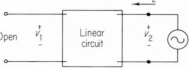

Fig. 14-3 Finding the reverse parameters, h_{12} and h_{22}.

We can solve these equations for each *h* value to get

$$h_{12} = \frac{v_1}{v_2} \qquad \text{for } i_1 = 0 \qquad \text{input open} \qquad (14\text{-}5)$$

and

$$h_{22} = \frac{i_2}{v_2} \qquad \text{for } i_1 = 0 \qquad \text{input open} \qquad (14\text{-}6)$$

Equation (14-5) tells us that h_{12} is the ratio of v_1 to v_2 with the input terminals open. We already know that the ratio of two voltages is called a voltage gain. Since the generator of Fig. 14-3 is driving the output terminals, we can say that h_{12} is the reverse voltage gain with the input open.

Equation (14-6) says that h_{22} is the ratio of i_2 to v_2 with the input terminals open. Current-voltage ratios represent admittances, that is, the reciprocal of impedances. Thus, h_{22} is the admittance looking into the output terminals when the input terminals are open.

Let us summarize the physical meaning of the *h* parameters:

h_{11} is the input impedance with the output shorted
h_{21} is the forward current gain with the output shorted
h_{12} is the reverse voltage gain with the input open
h_{22} is the output admittance with the input open

One more item. Note that h_{11} has the dimensions of ohms because it is an impedance and h_{22} has the dimensions of mhos because it is an admittance. The two remaining parameters, h_{12} and h_{21}, do not have dimensions; they are pure numbers.

EXAMPLE 14-1

Find the h parameters of the circuit in Fig. 14-4a.

SOLUTION

The circuit inside the box is a simple voltage divider consisting of a 20-ohm resistor in series with a 10-ohm resistor. To find the h parameters, we proceed as follows. First, visualize that the output terminals are shorted, as shown in Fig. 14-4b. Obviously, the input impedance of this circuit is simply 20 ohms because the 10-ohm resistor is shorted out. Thus, we have found that $h_{11} = 20$ ohms.

Next, we find the forward current gain h_{21}. With a short across the output, as in Fig. 14-4b, it should be clear that any current i_1 flowing into the box will flow through the 20-ohm resistor and then through the shorted output as shown. (Obviously, there is no current in the 10-ohm resistor because there is zero voltage across it.) Remember that i_2 is the output current flowing *into* the box. Since the current in Fig. 14-4b is actually flowing out of the box, i_2 is negative. In other words,

$$i_2 = -i_1$$

As a result,

$$h_{21} = \frac{i_2}{i_1} = \frac{-i_1}{i_1} = -1$$

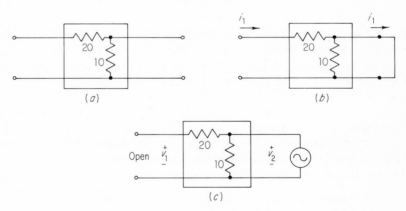

Fig. 14-4   Example 14-1.

To find the reverse parameters, we proceed as follows. First, we visualize the circuit as in Fig. 14-4c. Any voltage v_2 applied to the output terminals will appear across the 10-ohm resistor. With the input terminals open, there can be no current through the 20-ohm resistor, and therefore there can be no voltage drop across this resistor. As a result, all the voltage across the 10-ohm resistor appears across the input terminals. In other words,

$$v_1 = v_2$$

Because of this,

$$h_{12} = \frac{v_1}{v_2} = \frac{v_2}{v_2} = 1$$

Finally, notice in Fig. 14-4c that the impedance looking into the output terminals with the input open is simply 10 ohms. Therefore, to find h_{22} we take the reciprocal to get

$$h_{22} = \frac{1}{10} = 0.1 \text{ mhos}$$

To summarize, we say that the circuit of Fig. 14-4a has the following *h* parameters: $h_{11} = 20$ ohms, $h_{21} = -1$, $h_{12} = 1$, and $h_{22} = 0.1$ mhos.

Very often, a set of *h* parameters is displayed in matrix form. This is nothing more than showing the *h* parameters in a 2 by 2 display in the same relative positions that they have in Eqs. (14-1) and (14-2). In other words, for convenience we can show a set of *h* parameters as follows:

$$\begin{bmatrix} h_{11} & h_{12} \\ h_{21} & h_{22} \end{bmatrix} = \begin{bmatrix} 20 & 1 \\ -1 & 0.1 \end{bmatrix}$$

The position of the *h*'s should be memorized. In the first row, we have h_{11} and h_{12}. In the second row, there is h_{21} and h_{22}. The dimensions are usually not written, since it is understood that h_{11} is always in ohms, h_{12} and h_{21} are dimensionless, and h_{22} is in mhos.

EXAMPLE 14-2

Find the *h* parameters of the circuit in Fig. 14-5a.

SOLUTION

First, we visualize a short across the output terminals as depicted in Fig. 14-5b. Under this condition, the input impedance is

$$h_{11} = 2 + 2\|2 = 3 \text{ ohms}$$

Next, realize that the input current i_1 will divide equally at the junction of the 2-ohm resistors, so that the output current will be $i_1/2$, as shown in Fig. 14-5b. Therefore,

$$i_2 = -\frac{i_1}{2} = -0.5i_1$$

and

$$h_{21} = \frac{i_2}{i_1} = -0.5$$

To find the reverse parameters, we visualize the circuit as in Fig. 14-5c. Note that with the input terminals open, any voltage v_2 applied to the output will be divided by a factor of 2, so that

$$v_1 = \frac{v_2}{2} = 0.5v_2$$

and

$$h_{12} = \frac{v_1}{v_2} = 0.5$$

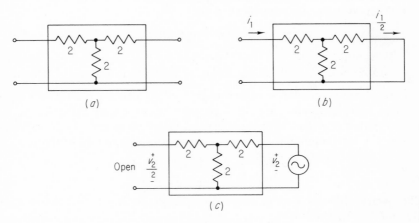

Fig. 14-5   Example 14-2.

Also, in Fig. 14-5c the impedance looking into the output terminals is 4 ohms. Therefore,

$$h_{22} = \frac{1}{4} = 0.25 \text{ mho}$$

We can summarize the set of h parameters for the original circuit of Fig. 14-5a by the following matrix:

$$\begin{bmatrix} 3 & 0.5 \\ -0.5 & 0.25 \end{bmatrix}$$

14-2   Input Impedance of a Network

We know that any linear circuit with input and output terminals has a set of h parameters. What we want to do in this section is to find a formula for the input impedance in terms of the h parameters.

Consider Fig. 14-6, where we have shown a linear circuit *with a load resistance of* r_L across its output terminals. On the input side the voltage source v_1 drives the circuit and sets up an input current of i_1.

How can we find a formula for z_{in}, the input impedance of the circuit, in terms of the *h* parameters? First, realize that the input impedance is the ratio of the input voltage to the input current. That is,

$$z_{in} = \frac{v_1}{i_1} \qquad (14\text{-}7)$$

Recall from Eq. (14-1) that the input voltage in terms of *h* parameters is

$$v_1 = h_{11}i_1 + h_{12}v_2$$

We can substitute this expression for v_1 into Eq. (14-7) to get

$$z_{in} = \frac{v_1}{i_1} = \frac{h_{11}i_1 + h_{12}v_2}{i_1}$$

or

$$z_{in} = h_{11} + \frac{h_{12}v_2}{i_1} \qquad (14\text{-}8)$$

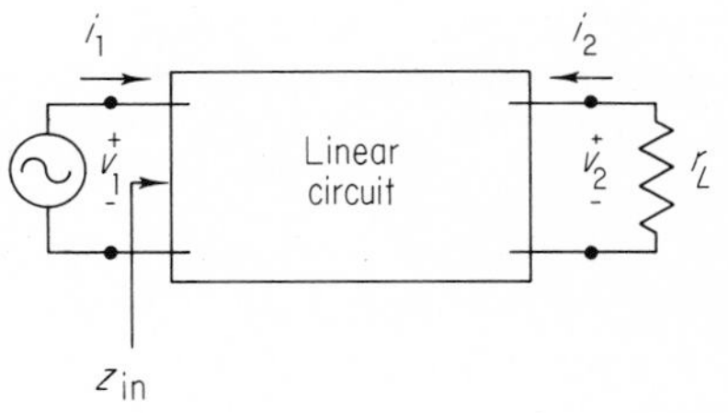

Fig. 14-6 Finding the input resistance in terms of *h* parameters.

This is not the final expression we want; it still contains v_2 and i_1. These quantities can be eliminated as follows. From Eq. (14-2) we know that the output current i_2 is

$$i_2 = h_{21}i_1 + h_{22}v_2 \qquad (14\text{-}9)$$

Further, in Fig. 14-6 we can see that

$$i_2 = -\frac{v_2}{r_L} \qquad (14\text{-}10)$$

(The minus sign is used because the actual load current is opposite to the direction of i_2.)

Now we can substitute Eq. (14-10) into (14-9) to get

$$-\frac{v_2}{r_L} = h_{21}i_1 + h_{22}v_2$$

or

$$-h_{21}i_1 = h_{22}v_2 + \frac{v_2}{r_L} = v_2\left(h_{22} + \frac{1}{r_L}\right)$$

or

$$\frac{v_2}{i_1} = -\frac{h_{21}}{h_{22} + 1/r_L} \tag{14-11}$$

Finally, we can substitute this expression into Eq. (14-8) to get

$$z_{in} = h_{11} - \frac{h_{12}h_{21}}{h_{22} + 1/r_L} \tag{14-12}$$

This result is very important. It tells us exactly how to find the input impedance of a circuit given the h parameters of the circuit and the value of load connected to the output terminals.

EXAMPLE 14-3

Find the input impedance of the circuit shown in Fig. 14-7.

SOLUTION

By inspection, we can see that the input impedance equals 20 ohms plus two 10-ohm resistances in parallel.

$$z_{in} = 20 + 10\|10 = 25 \text{ ohms}$$

Alternatively, we can get this same result by using Eq. (14-12). Recall that the h parameters of the circuit inside the box were found in Example 14-1. These parameters are

$$\begin{bmatrix} h_{11} & h_{12} \\ h_{21} & h_{22} \end{bmatrix} = \begin{bmatrix} 20 & 1 \\ -1 & 0.1 \end{bmatrix}$$

Since the circuit is loaded by 10 ohms, we use Eq. (14-12) as follows.

$$z_{in} = h_{11} - \frac{h_{12}h_{21}}{h_{22} + 1/r_L} = 20 - \frac{1(-1)}{0.1 + \frac{1}{10}} = 20 + 5 = 25 \text{ ohms}$$

By using two different approaches, we have found that the input impedance in Fig. 14-7 is 25 ohms. Ordinarily, with a simple circuit like

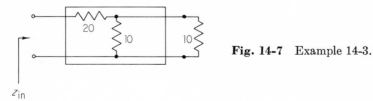

Fig. 14-7   Example 14-3.

that of Fig. 14-7, we would not use the complicated *h*-parameter approach because the answer can be found directly by inspection. However, there are more complicated circuits in which the input impedance cannot be found by inspection. In these circuits, Eq. (14-12) will be useful.

EXAMPLE 14-4

Find the input impedance of the circuit in Fig. 14-8 for the following values of r_L:

(*a*) $r_L = 0$.
(*b*) $r_L = \infty$.
(*c*) $r_L = 30$ ohms.

SOLUTION

The *h* parameters for the circuit inside the box are the same as those of the preceding example. We need only substitute the different values of r_L into Eq. (14-12) to get the input impedance.

(*a*) When $r_L = 0$,

$$z_{\text{in}} = 20 - \frac{-1}{0.1 + 1/0} = 20 - \frac{-1}{\infty} = 20 \text{ ohms}$$

Note that the input impedance equals h_{11}. The second term $h_{12}h_{21}/(h_{22} + 1/r_L)$ dropped out because $r_L = 0$. This always must happen when $r_L = 0$, because we know that the input impedance with the output terminals shorted equals h_{11}.

(*b*) When $r_L = \infty$,

$$z_{\text{in}} = 20 - \frac{-1}{0.1 + 1/\infty} = 20 - \frac{-1}{0.1} = 30 \text{ ohms}$$

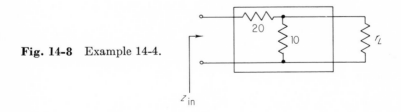

Fig. 14-8   Example 14-4.

Z_{in}

This same answer is apparent by inspection of Fig. 14-8. It is obvious that when $r_L = \infty$ (an open circuit), the input impedance is simply 20 ohms plus 10 ohms.

(c) When $r_L = 30$ ohms,

$$z_{in} = 20 - \frac{-1}{0.1 + \frac{1}{30}} = 20 + 7.5 = 27.5 \text{ ohms}$$

Again, this same result can be obtained by inspection of Fig. 14-8. It is clear that when $r_L = 30$ ohms, the input impedance must be 20 ohms plus the parallel combination of 10 ohms and 30 ohms. That is,

$$z_{in} = 20 + 10\|30 = 27.5 \text{ ohms}$$

14-3 Voltage Gain Using h Parameters

Another useful formula involving the h parameters is the formula for the voltage gain of a linear circuit that is loaded by a resistance of r_L.

Refer again to Fig. 14-6. The voltage gain of this circuit is simply

$$A = \frac{v_2}{v_1}$$

The input voltage v_1 must equal the input current i_1 times the input impedance z_{in}. That is,

$$v_1 = i_1 z_{in}$$

Hence, we can express the voltage gain as

$$A = \frac{v_2}{i_1 z_{in}} \tag{14-13}$$

In the preceding section, we found an expression for v_2/i_1 in terms of the h parameters (Eq. 14-11). If we substitute this expression for v_2/i_1 into Eq. (14-13), we get

$$A = \frac{-h_{21}}{z_{in}(h_{22} + 1/r_L)} \tag{14-14}$$

This equation is quite useful; it tells us exactly how to find the voltage gain of a circuit given its h parameters and the value of load resistance. Thus, given a circuit, we first find the input impedance z_{in} by using Eq. (14-12). Then, we can find the voltage gain by using Eq. (14-14).

EXAMPLE 14-5

Find the voltage gain v_2/v_1 for the circuit of Fig. 14-9.

SOLUTION

The h parameters of the circuit inside the box were found in Example 14-1.

They are:

$$\begin{bmatrix} h_{11} & h_{12} \\ h_{21} & h_{22} \end{bmatrix} = \begin{bmatrix} 20 & 1 \\ -1 & 0.1 \end{bmatrix}$$

In Example 14-3 we found the input impedance of the circuit to be 25 ohms. (This should also be apparent by inspection of Fig. 14-9.) To find the voltage gain, we use Eq. (14-14).

$$A = \frac{-h_{21}}{z_{\text{in}}(h_{22} + 1/r_L)} = \frac{-(-1)}{25(0.1 + \frac{1}{10})} = \frac{1}{25(0.2)} = \frac{1}{5}$$

Thus, the output voltage is one-fifth of the input voltage. This should be apparent by inspection of Fig. 14-9. The two 10-ohm resistors have

Fig. 14-9 Example 14-5.

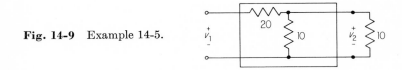

a net resistance of 5 ohms. Therefore, we have a voltage divider consisting of a 20-ohm resistor in series with a 5-ohm resistor, which implies that the output voltage will be one-fifth of the input voltage.

Again, note that for a simple circuit like that of Fig. 14-9, we would not ordinarily use *h* parameters to find the voltage gain because we can get the answer more easily by a direct analysis of the circuit. Up to now, we have used the *h*-parameter approach merely to illustrate the use of Eqs. (14-12) and (14-14). In succeeding sections, however, we will use these equations to find the input impedance and voltage gain of transistor circuits.

14-4 The *h* Parameters of a Transistor

We have seen that any linear circuit has a set of *h* parameters associated with it. When the linear circuit is terminated by a load of r_L, we can find the input impedance and voltage gain by using Eqs. (14-12) and (14-14).

In a class A transistor amplifier, the transistor is biased to some convenient d-c operating point. We can then inject an a-c signal into the transistor to get an amplified output signal. If *small* a-c signals are involved, the transistor is a linear device because the output a-c signal is directly proportional to the input a-c signal. Under this condition, the *a-c operation* of the transistor can be described by the *h* parameters. In other words, for *small* a-c signals, each transistor has a set of *h* parameters associated with it. These *h* parameters and the a-c load r_L seen by the transistor can be used to find the input impedance and the voltage gain.

The set of *h* parameters will, of course, depend upon which transistor connection is used, that is, CB, CE, or CC. For instance, suppose that the CB circuit of Fig. 14-10*a* has an $h_{11} = 25$ ohms. If we use the same transistor in a CE circuit (Fig. 14-10*b*), we will find that the new value

(*a*)   (*b*)

Fig. 14-10   CB and CE connections.

of h_{11} is quite different. Typically, the value of h_{11} might be around 2500 ohms. Similarly, we will find that the remaining *h* parameters (h_{12}, h_{21}, and h_{22}) also depend upon which connection is used.

To distinguish the *h* parameters of a transistor for its three possible connections, we use the following notation. For CB connection, we can add the subscript *b* to each of the *h* parameters. Thus, to indicate a set of CB *h* parameters we write h_{11b}, h_{12b}, h_{21b}, h_{22b}.

For CE connections of a transistor, we add a subscript *e* to get h_{11e}, h_{12e}, h_{21e}, h_{22e}.

For CC connections of a transistor, we add a subscript *c* to get h_{11c}, h_{12c}, h_{21c}, h_{22c}.

The foregoing is one of the notational systems used for distinguishing the three different transistor connections. Another notational system is the following. Recall the meaning of the *h* parameters:

h_{11} = *i*nput impedance with output shorted
h_{21} = *f*orward current gain with output shorted
h_{12} = *r*everse voltage gain with input open
h_{22} = *o*utput admittance with input open

Note that the first letter on the right-hand side of each equation is italicized. These letters are *i*, *f*, *r*, and *o*. In order to simplify the notation of the *h* parameters the numerical subscripts can be replaced by the corresponding first letters. That is, we can replace numbers by letters according to this code:

Replace	By
11	i
21	f
12	r
22	o

Thus, the *h* parameters become:

$$\begin{bmatrix} h_{11} & h_{12} \\ h_{21} & h_{22} \end{bmatrix} = \begin{bmatrix} h_i & h_r \\ h_f & h_o \end{bmatrix}$$

Finally, to distinguish the different connections CB, CE, or CC, we add *b*, *e*, or *c* to the matrix just given.

Thus, for CB connections of a transistor, we have

$$\begin{bmatrix} h_{11b} & h_{12b} \\ h_{21b} & h_{22b} \end{bmatrix} = \begin{bmatrix} h_{ib} & h_{rb} \\ h_{fb} & h_{ob} \end{bmatrix}$$

For CE connections of a transistor, we use

$$\begin{bmatrix} h_{11e} & h_{12e} \\ h_{21e} & h_{22e} \end{bmatrix} = \begin{bmatrix} h_{ie} & h_{re} \\ h_{fe} & h_{oe} \end{bmatrix}$$

For CC connections of a transistor, we use

$$\begin{bmatrix} h_{11c} & h_{12c} \\ h_{21c} & h_{22c} \end{bmatrix} = \begin{bmatrix} h_{ic} & h_{rc} \\ h_{fc} & h_{oc} \end{bmatrix}$$

The first system of notation (matrices on the left) is easier to remember; however, the second system of notation (matrices on the right) is much more widely used and should be memorized because many transistor data sheets use this notation.

EXAMPLE 14-6

A transistor data sheet gives the following *h* parameters of a transistor used in a CB connection with $V_{CB} = 10$ volts and $I_C = 1$ ma:

$$h_{ib} = 25 \text{ ohms} \qquad h_{rb} = 5(10^{-4}) \qquad h_{fb} = -0.98 \qquad \text{and} \qquad h_{ob} = 10^{-7}$$

If this transistor is used in a CB amplifier, what are the a-c input impedance and the voltage gain for a load $r_L = 10$ kilohms?

SOLUTION

The a-c input impedance is found by using Eq. (14-12).

$$z_{in} = h_{11} - \frac{h_{12}h_{21}}{h_{22} + 1/r_L}$$

By substituting the given set of h parameters and the value of r_L, we get

$$z_{in} = 25 - \frac{5(10^{-4})(-0.98)}{10^{-7} + 1/10^4} = 25 + 4.9 = 29.9 \text{ ohms}$$

Also, we know that the voltage gain is given by Eq. (14-14).

$$A = \frac{-h_{21}}{z_{in}(h_{22} + 1/r_L)} = \frac{0.98}{29.9(10^{-7} + 1/10^4)} = 328$$

EXAMPLE 14-7

A transistor used in a CE connection has the following set of h parameters when the d-c operating point is $V_{CE} = 10$ volts and $I_C = 1$ ma:

$h_{ie} = 1250$ ohms, $h_{re} = 7.5(10^{-4})$ $h_{fe} = 50$ and $h_{oe} = 0.5(10^{-4})$

Find the input impedance and voltage gain when the transistor is used in a CE connection with an r_L of 10 kilohms.

SOLUTION

$$z_{in} = h_{11} - \frac{h_{12}h_{21}}{h_{22} + 1/r_L} = 1250 - \frac{7.5(10^{-4})(50)}{0.5(10^{-4}) + 1/10^4}$$
$$= 1250 - 250 = 1000 \text{ ohms}$$

The voltage gain is

$$A = \frac{-h_{21}}{z_{in}(h_{22} + 1/r_L)} = \frac{-50}{10^3[0.5(10^{-4}) + 10^{-4}]} = -333$$

The minus sign merely indicates that there is a 180° phase shift between the input and the output. The magnitude of the voltage gain is 333. In other words, the output signal is 333 times greater than the input, and it is 180° out of phase with the input.

14-5   The h Parameters of the Ideal CB Transistor

In this section, we want to find the h parameters of an ideal transistor when used in the CB connection. Consider the a-c equivalent circuit of the ideal CB transistor (Fig. 14-11a). First, we find the forward parameters by shorting the output terminals, as shown in Fig. 14-11b. It is apparent that the input impedance under this condition is simply

$$h_{ib} = r'_e$$

The magnitude of the a-c output current is simply i_e, the same as the input current. Therefore, the magnitude of the current gain is unity. We need to add a minus sign, however, because the output current flows out of the box. Thus,

$$h_{fb} = -1$$

Next, we find the reverse parameters by opening the input terminals, as shown in Fig. 14-11c. With the input terminals open, there can be no

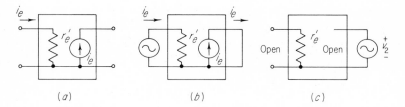

(a)   (b)   (c)

Fig. 14-11   Finding the *h* parameters of the ideal CB transistor.

a-c emitter current i_e; therefore, the a-c current source has a value of zero and appears as an open circuit. Under this condition, the reverse voltage gain must be zero, since no matter what voltage we apply to the output terminals, the input voltage must remain at zero. Thus,

$$h_{rb} = 0$$

Finally, note that the impedance looking into the output terminals of Fig. 14-11c is infinite. As a result, the admittance is zero. That is,

$$h_{ob} = 0$$

To summarize, the *h* parameters of an ideal transistor used in a CB connection are

$$\begin{bmatrix} h_{ib} & h_{rb} \\ h_{fb} & h_{ob} \end{bmatrix} = \begin{bmatrix} r'_e & 0 \\ -1 & 0 \end{bmatrix}$$

With these parameters, we can find the a-c input impedance and voltage gain of an ideal CB transistor amplifier in terms of *h* parameters.

Recall that the a-c input impedance and the voltage gain of a CB amplifier using the ideal transistor approximation are simply

$$z_{\text{in}} = r'_e$$

and

$$A = \frac{r_L}{r'_e}$$

Since $h_{ib} = r'_e$, we can rewrite the a-c input impedance and the voltage gain as

$$z_{\text{in}} = h_{ib} \tag{14-15}$$

and

$$A = \frac{r_L}{h_{ib}} \tag{14-16}$$

Equations (14-15) and (14-16) can be used when the value of h_{ib} is given on the transistor data sheet. These equations give fairly accurate answers even though they are for the ideal CB transistor.

Of course, if we want exact answers, we would use Eqs. (14-12) and (14-14). Written in terms of CB parameters, these equations become

$$z_{\text{in}} = h_{ib} - \frac{h_{rb}h_{fb}}{h_{ob} + 1/r_L} \tag{14-17}$$

and

$$A = \frac{-h_{fb}}{z_{\text{in}}(h_{ob} + 1/r_L)} \tag{14-18}$$

EXAMPLE 14-8

Find the a-c input impedance and the voltage gain for the circuit of Fig. 14-12 using the ideal-transistor approach.

SOLUTION

There is about 1 ma of d-c emitter current, so that r'_e is the range of 25 to 50 ohms. The a-c load r_L seen by the collector is 7.5 kilohms. Therefore, the voltage gain is

$$A = \frac{r_L}{r'_e} = \frac{7500}{25} = 300$$

When r'_e is 50 ohms, A would be 150. Therefore, we expect a voltage gain A in the range of

$$150 < A < 300$$

Of course, the a-c input impedance is simply

$$z_{\text{in}} = r'_e = 25 \text{ to } 50 \text{ ohms}$$

EXAMPLE 14-9

The data sheet of the transistor used in Fig. 14-12 indicates that $h_{ib} = 30$ ohms when $I_E = 1$ ma. Find the input impedance and voltage gain for the amplifier of Fig. 14-12 by using Eqs. (14-15) and (14-16).

Fig. 14-12   Examples 14-8 to 14-10.

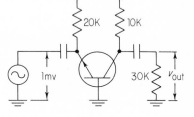

SOLUTION

Using Eq. (14-15), we get

$$z_{in} = h_{ib} = 30 \text{ ohms}$$

With Eq. (14-16), we find that

$$A = \frac{r_L}{h_{ib}} = \frac{7500}{30} = 250$$

EXAMPLE 14-10

Suppose that the transistor of Fig. 14-12 has the following set of *h* parameters: $h_{ib} = 30$, $h_{fb} = -0.98$, $h_{rb} = 5(10^{-4})$, and $h_{ob} = 10^{-6}$. Find the a-c input impedance and the voltage gain.

SOLUTION

Using the exact equations, we get

$$z_{in} = h_{ib} - \frac{h_{rb}h_{fb}}{h_{ob} + 1/r_L} = 30 - \frac{5(10^{-4})(-0.98)}{10^{-6} + 1/7.5(10^3)} = 30 + 3.6 = 33.6 \text{ ohms}$$

(Note the small effect that the correction term of 3.6 ohms has upon the input impedance. This is typical for a CB circuit.)

The voltage gain is

$$A = \frac{-h_{fb}}{z_{in}(h_{ob} + 1/r_L)} = \frac{0.98}{33.6(10^{-6} + 1/7500)} = 218$$

In Examples 14-8 to 14-10 we have an opportunity to compare the various approaches in finding a-c input impedance and voltage gain. In

Example 14-8 we used the ideal-transistor approach and found

$$25 < z_{\text{in}} < 50 \qquad \text{and} \qquad 150 < A < 300$$

Note that we bracketed the value of z_{in} and A without using any information from the transistor data sheet.

In Example 14-9 we used the fact that the h_{ib} of the transistor is 30 ohms. We found that

$$z_{\text{in}} = 30 \qquad \text{and} \qquad A = 250$$

Note that these results are still approximations because h_{rb} and h_{ob} are not taken into account.

Finally, in Example 14-10, we get exact answers by using Eqs. (14-17) and (14-18). We found that

$$z_{\text{in}} = 33.6 \qquad \text{and} \qquad A = 218$$

14-6 The h Parameters of the Ideal CE Transistor

When the ideal transistor is used in a CE connection, the a-c equivalent circuit becomes that shown in Fig. 14-13a. What are the h parameters of this a-c equivalent circuit?

First, we short the output terminals, as in Fig. 14-13b. The input impedance under this shorted condition is obviously

$$h_{ie} = \beta r_e'$$

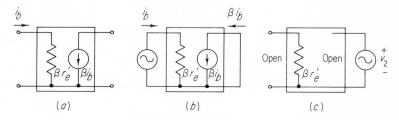

(a) $\qquad\qquad$ (b) $\qquad\qquad$ (c)

Fig. 14-13 Finding the h parameters of the ideal CE transistor.

(In fact, the input impedance is $\beta r_e'$ whether the output terminals are shorted or not.) Also, the forward current gain is

$$h_{fe} = \frac{i_2}{i_1} = \frac{\beta i_b}{i_b}$$

or

$$\boldsymbol{h_{fe} = \beta}$$

To find the remaining parameters, we visualize the circuit as shown in Fig. 14-13c, where the input terminals are open and the output terminals are driven by a voltage source of v_2. Since the input terminals are open, there can be no a-c base current; that is, $i_b = 0$. With $i_b = 0$, the collector current source has a zero value and therefore looks like an open circuit. Under this condition, it is apparent that there is no feedback into the base circuit. In other words,

$$h_{re} = \frac{v_1}{v_2} = \frac{0}{v_2}$$

or

$$h_{re} = 0$$

It is also clear that looking into the output terminals the impedance is infinite; therefore, the output admittance is zero.

$$h_{oe} = 0$$

To summarize, the *h* parameters of an ideal transistor used in a CE connection are

$$\begin{bmatrix} h_{ie} & h_{re} \\ h_{fe} & h_{oe} \end{bmatrix} = \begin{bmatrix} \beta r'_e & 0 \\ \beta & 0 \end{bmatrix}$$

Especially remember that $h_{fe} = \beta$. On data sheets for transistors, we are usually given the transistor characteristics in terms of the *h* parameters. Thus, if a data sheet indicates that $h_{fe} = 75$, we immediately know that the a-c β of the transistor is 75. Furthermore, the d-c β is normally specified on a data sheet by using h_{FE} (capital subscripts).

Let us now find the a-c input impedance and the voltage gain for a CE amplifier using the ideal-transistor approximation and the *h* parameters. Recall that the input impedance is

$$z_{\text{in}} = \beta r'_e$$

and that the voltage gain is

$$A = \frac{r_L}{r'_e}$$

Since $\beta r'_e = h_{ie}$, the input impedance becomes

$$z_{\text{in}} = h_{ie} \tag{14-19}$$

and the voltage gain becomes

$$A = \frac{r_L}{r'_e} = \frac{r_L}{h_{ie}/\beta} = \beta \frac{r_L}{h_{ie}}$$

Since $\beta = h_{fe}$, we can rewrite this as

$$A = h_{fe} \frac{r_L}{h_{ie}} \tag{14-20}$$

A useful equivalent formula for the voltage gain of a CE circuit is obtained by realizing that $r'_e = h_{ib}$, so that

$$A = \frac{r_L}{r'_e} = \frac{r_L}{h_{ib}} \tag{14-21}$$

These formulas for a-c input impedance and voltage gain in terms of h parameters will give fairly accurate results; however, they are approximations based upon the use of an ideal transistor.

If the exact formulas for input impedance and voltage gain are needed, we must use Eqs. (14-12) and (14-14). Written in terms of CE parameters, these equations become

$$z_{in} = h_{ie} - \frac{h_{re}h_{fe}}{h_{oe} + 1/r_L} \tag{14-22}$$

and

$$A = \frac{-h_{fe}}{z_{in}(h_{oe} + 1/r_L)} \tag{14-23}$$

EXAMPLE 14-11

The transistor in Fig. 14-14 has an $h_{fe} = 50$ and $h_{ie} = 1500$.

(a) Find the voltage gain of the circuit.

(b) Find the a-c input impedance of the stage including the bias resistors.

SOLUTION

(a) Since we have an incomplete set of h parameters, we must use the approximate formula based on the ideal transistor. With Eq. (14-20), we find that

$$A = h_{fe}\frac{r_L}{h_{ie}} = 50\,\frac{7500}{1500} = 250$$

(b) We can find the a-c input impedance looking into the base by using Eq. (14-19).

$$z_{in} = h_{ie} = 1500 \text{ ohms}$$

This is not the total impedance of the stage. We also have the biasing resistors which appear in parallel with 1500 ohms. The a-c input impedance of the entire stage is

$$R_1\|R_2\|h_{ie} = 80(10^3)\|40(10^3)\|1.5(10^3) \cong 1420 \text{ ohms}$$

Thus, the voltage gain is 250, and the input impedance of the stage is 1420 ohms. Remember that these are still approximate results. If exact answers are desired, all four h parameters must be known, as the next example illustrates.

EXAMPLE 14-12

The transistor of Fig. 14-14 has the following complete set of h parameters: $h_{ie} = 1500$, $h_{fe} = 50$, $h_{re} = 4(10^{-4})$, and $h_{oe} = 5(10^{-5})$. Find the voltage gain and the a-c input impedance of the stage.

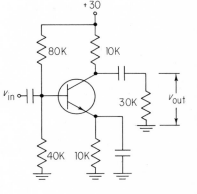

Fig. 14-14   Examples 14-11 and 14-12.

SOLUTION

First, we find the input impedance looking into the base by using Eq. (14-22).

$$z_{in} = h_{ie} - \frac{h_{re}h_{fe}}{h_{oe} + 1/r_L} = 1500 - \frac{4(10^{-4})(50)}{5(10^{-5}) + 1/7.5(10^3)} = 1390 \text{ ohms}$$

This is the input impedance looking into the base. The input impedance of the stage includes the bias resistors in parallel with this 1390 ohms and is

$$R_1 \| R_2 \| z_{in} = 80(10^3) \| 40(10^3) \| 1.39(10^3) = 1320 \text{ ohms}$$

Next, we can find the voltage gain by using Eq. (14-23).

$$A = \frac{-h_{fe}}{z_{in}(h_{oe} + 1/r_L)} = \frac{-50}{1390[5(10^{-5}) + 1/7500]} = -196$$

The minus sign, as usual, indicates phase inversion of the signal. The magnitude of the voltage gain is 196.

14-7   Conversion of *h* Parameters

Transistor data sheets most often specify the transistor in terms of its h parameters. Sometimes only a partial set of h parameters is given, such as h_{fe} and h_{ie}. When a complete set of h parameters is given, this set is usually for the CB connection of a transistor, that is, h_{ib}, h_{fb}, h_{rb}, and h_{ob}.

If we want to use the transistor in a CE connection, we need to convert this set of CB parameters into a set of CE parameters.

The derivation of the conversion formulas from CB to CE is complicated and beyond the scope of this book. Therefore, we will simply list these conversion formulas for future reference.

To convert from CB to CE parameters, the following formulas can be used:

$$D = (1 + h_{fb})(1 - h_{rb}) + h_{ib}h_{ob} \cong 1 + h_{fb}$$

$$h_{ie} = \frac{h_{ib}}{D}$$

$$h_{fe} = \frac{-(h_{fb} + h_{ib}h_{ob} - h_{fb}h_{rb})}{D} \cong \frac{-h_{fb}}{D}$$

$$h_{re} = \frac{h_{ib}h_{ob} - h_{rb}(1 + h_{fb})}{D} \cong \frac{h_{ib}h_{ob}}{D} - h_{rb}$$

$$h_{oe} = \frac{h_{ob}}{D}$$

We must use these rather formidable-looking equations when we are given a complete set of CB parameters and need a set of CE parameters. First, we calculate the value of D, and then we can proceed to calculate h_{ie}, h_{fe}, h_{re}, and h_{oe}. If approximate values are acceptable, we can use

$$D \cong 1 + h_{fb}$$

This simplifies the work to some extent, but it still is tedious to convert a set of CB parameters to a corresponding set of CE parameters.

The two most important conversion formulas are those involving h_{ie} and h_{fe}. If approximate conversion formulas are acceptable, then we can use

$$h_{ie} \cong \frac{h_{ib}}{1 + h_{fb}} \tag{14-24}$$

and

$$h_{fe} = \frac{-h_{fb}}{1 + h_{fb}} \tag{14-25}$$

As a numerical example, suppose that a data sheet specifies $h_{ib} = 50$ and $h_{fb} = -0.99$. Then we would calculate h_{ie} and h_{fe} as follows:

$$h_{ie} \cong \frac{50}{1 - 0.99} = \frac{50}{0.01} = 5000$$

and

$$h_{fe} \cong \frac{-(-0.99)}{1 - 0.99} = 99$$

If we wish to use h parameters for a CC circuit, we need the set of CC parameters, that is, h_{ic}, h_{fc}, h_{rc}, and h_{oc}. Again, if the data sheet gives a complete set of CB parameters, we must convert these into CC parameters. The following formulas can be used for this purpose.

$$D = (1 + h_{fb})(1 - h_{rb}) + h_{ib}h_{ob} \cong 1 + h_{fb}$$

$$h_{ic} = \frac{h_{ib}}{D}$$

$$h_{fc} = -\frac{1}{D}$$

$$h_{rc} = \frac{1 + h_{fb}}{D}$$

$$h_{oc} = \frac{h_{ob}}{D}$$

As already indicated, the task of converting from one parameter set to another is a tedious one. However, when analyzing a CE or CC circuit with h parameters, we must use the appropriate set of parameters. Complete sets of h parameters are usually given for the CB connection. (Occasionally, we may get a complete set of CE parameters.) Thus, we often need to use the foregoing conversion formulas to get the CE or CC parameters if we want to use the h-parameter approach.

EXAMPLE 14-13

A data sheet indicates that the h parameters of a transistor biased to $V_{CB} = 10$ volts and $I_C = 1$ ma are

$$h_{ib} = 25 \qquad h_{rb} = 3(10^{-4})$$
$$h_{fb} = -0.99 \qquad h_{ob} = 5(10^{-7})$$

Find the CE parameters using the approximate conversion formulas.

SOLUTION

$$D \cong 1 + h_{fb} = 1 - 0.99 = 0.01$$

$$h_{ie} = \frac{h_{ib}}{D} = \frac{25}{0.01} = 2500$$

$$h_{fe} = \frac{-h_{fb}}{D} = \frac{0.99}{0.01} = 99$$

$$h_{re} \cong \frac{h_{ib}h_{ob}}{D} - h_{rb} = \frac{25(5)(10^{-7})}{0.01} - 3(10^{-4}) = 9.5(10^{-4})$$

$$h_{oe} \cong \frac{h_{ob}}{D} = \frac{5(10^{-7})}{0.01} = 5(10^{-5})$$

14-8 Practical Observations on the h Parameters

The search for exact answers in transistor work is a frustrating one. It is true that the h-parameter approach does give us exact answers if we have a complete and *exact* set of h parameters for the particular transistor used in a circuit. However, it is quite difficult in practice to get the exact values of the h parameters for a particular transistor.

The data sheet for a transistor type is only a guide. Very often we find that only one or two of the h parameters are given. Sometimes the data sheet for a transistor type does give a complete set of h parameters at one d-c operating point. If we use a different operating point, the given set of h parameters is only an approximate guide. Another important fact about the h parameters is that for any one transistor type, the h parameters typically vary over a 2:1 range, or more. Data sheets usually indicate this range of variation by listing the minimum and maximum values of the h parameters.

Thus, even though we have exact formulas for predicting the a-c operation of CB, CE, and CC transistor circuits, we seldom know the exact values of h's to use in these formulas. It is possible, of course, to individually measure the h parameters of each transistor that we use. In most transistor work, however, this is hardly feasible.

In short, while the h-parameter formulas are exact, we seldom know the exact h parameters of a given transistor. Normally, we must use a typical set of h parameters to get an approximate prediction of how a transistor will operate in a circuit. As practical matter, much transistor circuit analysis and design must be done by approximation. Because of this, we find that the ideal-transistor approximation developed throughout the earlier chapters is quite useful for preliminary analysis and design. To improve circuit performance, we can swamp the emitter diode or use some other form of negative feedback, in which case the exact transistor characteristics are not too critical. When we really need as accurate a prediction as possible for transistor circuit operation, we can use the h-parameter approach.

SUMMARY

Any linear circuit with input and output terminals has a set of h parameters associated with it. The input impedance of a linear circuit terminated by a load of r_L is

$$z_{\text{in}} = h_{11} - \frac{h_{12}h_{21}}{h_{22} + 1/r_L}$$

and the voltage gain is

$$A = \frac{-h_{21}}{z_{\text{in}}(h_{22} + 1/r_L)}$$

The voltage gain of CB or CE circuits using the ideal-transistor approximation is r_L/r_e'. In terms of h parameters, this voltage gain is r_L/h_{ib}. This is still an approximate voltage gain, but it does give reasonably accurate answers.

Exact values of voltage gain and input impedance can be found by using Eqs. (14-12) and (14-14) with the appropriate set of *h* parameters.

The h_{fe} of a transistor is the same as the a-c β. The h_{FE} is the same as the d-c β.

Data sheets often give the *h* parameters for the transistor used in a CB connection. If we want CE or CC parameters, we must use the conversion formulas given in Sec. 14-7. Of special importance are the conversion formulas for h_{ie} and h_{fe}. These are approximately given by

$$h_{ie} \cong \frac{h_{ib}}{1 + h_{fb}}$$

and

$$h_{fe} \cong \frac{-h_{fb}}{1 + h_{fb}}$$

The ideal-transistor approximation and the various formulas developed throughout the earlier chapters are adequate for much transistor circuit analysis and design. When more accurate answers are needed, we can use the *h*-parameter approach.

GLOSSARY

admittance   The ratio of a current to a voltage. The reciprocal of impedance.

class A amplifier   An amplifier in which the transistor conducts current through the entire cycle of the a-c signal without saturating.

forward parameters   Those parameters which we find by driving the input terminals while the output terminals are shorted, that is, h_{11} and h_{21}.

matrix   A rectangular array of numbers.

reverse parameters   Those parameters which we obtain by driving the output terminals while the input terminals are open, that is, h_{12} and h_{22}.

REVIEW QUESTIONS

1. What is the physical meaning of the *h* parameters in terms of impedance, gain, etc.?
2. What are the dimensions of the four *h* parameters?

3. What is the general formula for the input impedance of a circuit in terms of its h parameters and the load?

4. What is the general formula for the voltage gain of a circuit in terms of its h parameters and the load on its output terminals?

5. What are the notations for h parameters of a transistor when used in the CB connection? In the CE connection? In the CC connection?

6. What is the h_{ib} of an ideal transistor? What is the h_{fe} of an ideal transistor? And the h_{ie}?

7. On a transistor data sheet, a complete set of h parameters is usually given for which transistor connection?

8. Even though the h-parameter formulas are exact, what are some of the practical shortcomings of this approach?

PROBLEMS

14-1 Find the h parameters for the circuit of Fig. 14-15a.

14-2 What are the h parameters of the circuit in Fig. 14-15b?

14-3 Find the h parameters of the ideal transformer of Fig. 14-15c.

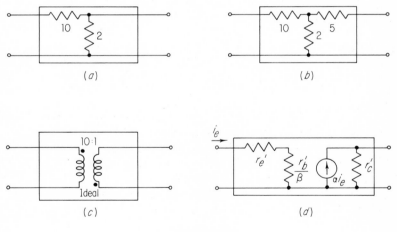

Fig. 14-15

14-4 The circuit of Fig. 14-15d is an accurate a-c equivalent circuit of a transistor used in the CB connection. The r_b' is the base spreading resistance and the r_c' is the reverse collector resistance. Find the h parameters of the circuit.

14-5   The *h* parameters of a circuit are $h_{11} = 20$, $h_{12} = 2$, $h_{21} = -4$, and $h_{22} = 10$. If the circuit is terminated by a load $r_L = 40$, what is the input impedance of the circuit?

14-6   The circuit of Fig. 14-16a is the a-c equivalent circuit of a pentode vacuum tube. Find the *h* parameters of this circuit.

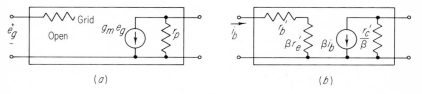

(a)   (b)

Fig. 14-16

14-7   The circuit of Fig. 14-16b is an accurate a-c equivalent circuit for a CE connection of a transistor. What are the *h* parameters of this circuit? What is the voltage gain of the circuit when it is loaded by r_L? What is the input impedance?

14-8   A transistor has the following *h* parameters: $h_{ib} = 100$, $h_{fb} = -0.98$, $h_{rb} = 2(10^{-4})$, and $h_{ob} = 2(10^{-7})$. If this transistor is loaded by an r_L of 10 kilohms in a CB connection, what is the input impedance? What is the voltage gain?

14-9   A transistor used in a CE connection has the following set of *h* parameters: $h_{ie} = 1000$, $h_{fe} = 80$, $h_{re} = 5(10^{-4})$, and $h_{oe} = 2(10^{-5})$. What is the input impedance when the transistor is loaded by r_L of 2.5 kilohms? And the voltage gain?

14-10   A transistor data sheet indicates that the h_{ib} is 50 ohms at 1 ma. What is the approximate voltage gain if this transistor is used in a CB circuit with an r_L of 8200 ohms? What is the approximate voltage gain if it is used in a CE connection with the same value of r_L?

14-11   If the h_{ib} of a transistor is 50 ohms and the h_{fb} is -0.975, what is the approximate value of h_{ie} and h_{fe}? What is the value of β and the approximate value of r'_e?

14-12   The data sheet of a transistor gives the following set of *h* parameters for $I_E = 1$ ma and $V_{CB} = 10$ volts:

$$h_{ib} = 55 \qquad h_{fb} = -0.985 \qquad h_{rb} = 4(10^{-4}) \qquad \text{and} \qquad h_{ob} = 5(10^{-7})$$

What are the approximate CE parameters of this transistor?

14-13   Find the approximate CC parameters for the transistor of Prob. 14-12.

14-14 The transistor of Fig. 14-17 is at a d-c operating point of about $I_E = 1$ ma and $V_{CE} = 10$ volts. The h parameters for this condition are $h_{ib} = 35$ ohms and $h_{fe} = 150$. Find the approximate value of voltage gain and input impedance (including the bias resistors).

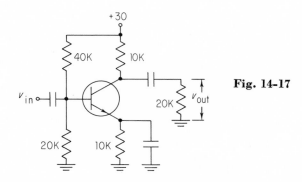

Fig. 14-17

14-15 The transistor of Fig. 14-17 has the following set of h parameters at its d-c operating point: $h_{ib} = 30$, $h_{fb} = -0.995$, $h_{rb} = 10^{-4}$, and $h_{ob} = 0.1(10^{-6})$. Find the voltage gain and the input impedance (including bias resistors).

14-16 Show that $h_{fb} = -\alpha$.

References
for Further
Reading

Corning, J. J.: "Transistor Circuit Analysis and Design," Prentice-Hall, Inc., Englewood Cliffs, N.J., 1965.

Cutler, P.: "Semiconductor Circuit Analysis," McGraw-Hill Book Company, New York, 1964.

Fitchen, F. C.: "Transistor Circuit Analysis and Design," D. Van Nostrand Company, Inc., Princeton, N.J., 1960.

Hunter, L. P.: "Handbook of Semiconductor Electronics," 2d ed., McGraw-Hill Book Company, New York, 1962.

Kiver, M. S.: "Transistors," 3d ed., McGraw-Hill Book Company, New York, 1962.

Leach, D. P.: "Transistor Circuit Measurements," McGraw-Hill Book Company, New York, 1968.

Pierce, J. F.: "Transistor Circuit Theory and Design," Charles E. Merrill Books, Inc., Columbus, Ohio, 1963.

Risenbatt, M. P., and R. L. Riddle: "Transistor Physics and Circuits," Prentice-Hall, Inc., Englewood Cliffs, N.J., 1965.

Shea, R. F.: "Transistor Circuit Engineering," John Wiley & Sons, Inc., New York, 1957.

Smith, R. J.: "Circuits, Devices, and Systems," John Wiley & Sons, Inc., New York, 1966.

Surina, T., and C. Herrick: "Semiconductor Electronics," Holt, Rinehart and Winston, Inc., New York, 1964.

Texas Instruments, Inc.: "Transistor Circuit Design," McGraw-Hill Book Company, New York, 1963.

Answers to
Odd-numbered
Problems

CHAPTER 2

2-1 250 ma   **2-3** 1.25 volts

CHAPTER 3

3-1 1 ma   **3-3** A sine wave, positively clipped at the 0-volt level, with a negative peak of 14 volts.   **3-5** The waveform is positively clipped at the +10-volt level.   **3-7** 0.93 ma, 49.4 ma   **3-9** The positive peak voltage is 29.3 volts, and the negative peak is 18 volts.   **3-11** The waveform is positively clipped at the 10.7-volt level and negatively clipped at the 20.7-volt level. **3-13** 70 ohms, 43.3 ma   **3-15** (*a*) The waveform is positively clipped at 0 volts, and the negative peak voltage is 24 volts.   (*b*) The waveform is positively clipped at 0 volts and has a negative peak voltage of 29.9 volts.   **3-17** 1 ma, 9 ma   **3-19** 0.98 watt, 0.7 watt

CHAPTER 4

4-1 2 amp   **4-3** The current waveform is a d-c component of 0.2 ma and an a-c component of 0.5 μa peak. The voltage waveform has a d-c component of

6 volts and an a-c component of 15 mv peak.   **4-5** The waveform has a d-c component of about 0.6 volt and an a-c component of 2 mv peak.   **4-7** 50 ohms   **4-9** 3.75 ohms   **4-11** 37 ohms, approximately (33.3 ohms for r_j and 3.75 ohms for r_B)   **4-13** 2 ma, 0.08 ma   **4-15** It changes from 0.04 to 0.02 ma.   **4-17** (*a*) 1 ma in each diode   (*b*) 62.5 μv

CHAPTER 5

5-1 0.98, 0.97   **5-3** 0.5 ma, 2.5 volts   **5-5** 80 kilohms   **5-7** 0.5 volt **5-9** 2.5 kilohms   **5-11** The waveform has a d-c component of 7.5 volts and an a-c component of 0.3 volt peak.   **5-13** (*a*) 5 volts (*b*) Approximately 10 mv rms   **5-15** 7.5 mv rms   **5-17** 0, 12.5 mv rms

CHAPTER 6

6-1 75   **6-3** 16 μa   **6-5** 0.465 ma, 17.7 volts   **6-7** 6.67 kilohms **6-9** 15 volts, 7.5 volts   **6-11** 0.96 ma   **6-13** (*a*) 0.5 ma (*b*) −20 volts **6-15** 13.3 kilohms   **6-17** A sine wave with a peak value between 112 and 224 mv.   **6-19** The collector voltage changes from 12.5 to 18.8 volts, and the output voltage changes from 1.13 to 0.562 volt.   **6-21** 462 mv, 93 mv

CHAPTER 7

7-1 50 kilohms   **7-3** Approximately 3 mv peak   **7-5** 50 ohms   **7-7** 70.7 and 141   **7-9** $\beta\beta^2 = \beta^3$

CHAPTER 8

8-1 (*a*) Cutoff is 30 volts; saturation is 30 ma; the Q point is 1 ma, 29 volts. (*b*) Cutoff is 30 volts; saturation is 3 ma; the Q point is 1 ma, 20 volts.   (*c*) Cutoff is 30 volts; saturation is 1.5 ma; the Q point is 1 ma, 10 volts.   **8-3** (*a*) Cutoff is 30 volts; saturation is 1.5 ma; the Q point is 0.5 ma, 20 volts.   (*b*) Cutoff is 30 volts; saturation is 1.5 ma; the Q point is 1 ma, 10 volts.   **8-5** Negative, 0.5 volt peak   **8-7** 33.3 kilohms   **8-9** D-c load line: cutoff is 30 volts, saturation is 2 ma, and the Q point is 1.5 ma, 7.5 volts. A-c load line: passes through the Q point and a cutoff point of 22.5 volts.   **8-11** (*a*) D-c load line: cutoff is 30 volts, saturation is 3 ma, Q point is 1.5 ma, 15 volts. A-c load line: passes through the Q point and a cutoff of 27 volts.   (*b*) D-c load line stays the same as before; the Q point changes to 0.75 ma, 22.5 volts; the a-c load line passes through the new Q point and a new cutoff of 28.5 volts.   **8-13** 1.8 megohms **8-15** 10 volts on positive swing, 20 volts on negative swing.

CHAPTER 9

9-1 2.45% **9-3** 8.33 μa, 0.833 ma, 16.7 volts **9-5** 0.4 ma, 4 volts **9-7** 0.93, 6.2% **9-9** 0.4 ma, 4 volts, 4 μa **9-11** (a) 0.37 ma (b) 1.76 ma (c) 0.815 (d) 1.2 volts **9-13** (a) 15 volts (b) 7.5 volts (c) 7.5 volts **9-15** (a) 0.4 ma (b) 0.286 ma (c) 2.5 megohms **9-17** 0.0244 **9-19** (a) 0.5 ma (b) 25 volts (c) 15 volts **9-21** $R_1 = 500$ kilohms, $R_2 = 214$ kilohms **9-23** -10 volts **9-25** -10 volts, -25 volts **9-27** About -16 volts

CHAPTER 10

10-1 114, 570 mv **10-3** 26.7 to 53.4, 9.9 to 13.4 kilohms **10-5** 0 to 200 mv rms **10-7** 667 ohms **10-9** 9.83, 13.4 **10-11** 18.2 kilohms **10-13** About 21 and 1 kilohm **10-15** 17.4 to 25.5 kilohms **10-17** About 125 and 250 mv **10-19** (a) 3 mv rms (b) 1.44 to 1.92 mv **10-21** 71 mv rms **10-23** 4.55 mv rms

CHAPTER 11

11-1 8700 **11-3** 765 **11-5** 15.9 kHz; no, because the a-c load seen by each collector is not maximum at this frequency. **11-7** 2 volts rms **11-9** About 1.25 ma **11-11** 11 **11-13** 174 mv rms

CHAPTER 12

12-1 45.3 ohms **12-3** 17.8, 17.5 **12-5** 11.4 mv rms, 14.7 mv rms **12-7** 0.3 volt **12-9** 2.33 ma and 2.5 ma **12-11** 27 μa **12-13** About 6 **12-15** 0.43 μa at 25°C; about 150 μa at 75°C (using interpolation)

CHAPTER 13

13-1 25.4 and 79.5 Hz; the output coupling capacitor **13-3** About 5 μf **13-5** 4.24 MHz **13-7** 3.38 kHz **13-9** 61 **13-11** 416 MHz; between 2.78 and 8.33 MHz **13-13** 4.77 MHz, 782 kHz **13-15** 1.1 MHz

CHAPTER 14

14-1 $h_{11} = 10$, $h_{21} = -1$, $h_{12} = 1$, $h_{22} = 0.5$ **14-3** $h_{11} = 0$, $h_{21} = 10$, $h_{12} = -10$, $h_{22} = 0$ **14-5** 20.8 ohms **14-7** $h_{11} = r_b' + \beta r_e'$, $h_{21} = \beta$, $h_{12} = 0$, $h_{22} = \beta/r_c'$ **14-9** 905 ohms, 210 **14-11** 2000 ohms, 39; $\beta = 39$ and $r_e' = 50$ ohms **14-13** $h_{ic} = 3660$, $h_{fc} = -66.7$, $h_{rc} = 1$, $h_{oc} = 3.33(10^{-5})$ **14-15** 216, 3.85 kilohms

Index

Base bias

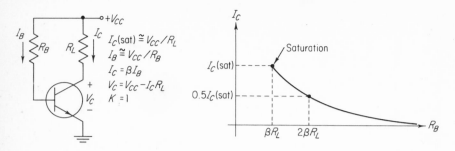

$$I_C(\text{sat}) \cong V_{CC}/R_L$$
$$I_B \cong V_{CC}/R_B$$
$$I_C = \beta I_B$$
$$V_C = V_{CC} - I_C R_L$$
$$K = 1$$

Base bias with emitter feedback

$$I_C(\text{sat}) \cong V_{CC}/(R_E + R_L)$$
$$I_C \cong V_{CC}/(R_E + R_B/\beta)$$
$$V_C = V_{CC} - I_C R_L$$
$$V_E = I_E R_E \cong I_C R_E$$
$$V_{CE} = V_C - V_E$$
$$K = 1/(1 + \beta R_E/R_B)$$

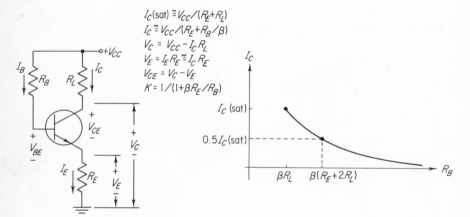

Base bias with collector feedback

$$I_C(\text{sat}) \cong V_{CC}/R_L$$
$$I_C \cong V_{CC}/(R_L + R_B/\beta)$$
$$V_C = V_{CC} - I_C R_L$$
$$K = 1/(1 + \beta R_L/R_B)$$

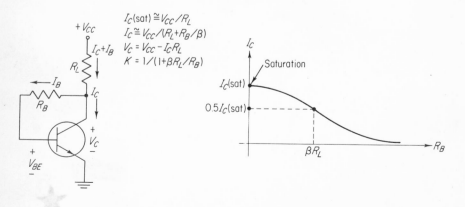